D0203999

# HISTORICAL DICTIONARY OF RECONSTRUCTION

# Historical Dictionary of Reconstruction

Hans L. Trefousse

025576

GREENWOOD PRESS

New York • Westport, Connecticut • London

*For Roger and Kathy*

**Library of Congress Cataloging-in-Publication Data**

Trefousse, Hans Louis.
    Historical dictionary of reconstruction / Hans L. Trefousse.
      p.    cm.
    Includes bibliographical references and index.
    ISBN 0-313-25862-7 (alk. paper)
    1. Reconstruction—Dictionaries.  2. United States—Politics and
government—1865-1877—Dictionaries.  I. Title.
E668.T66      1991
973.8'03—dc20     91-10419

British Library Cataloguing in Publication Data is available.

Library of Congress Catalog Card Number: 91-10419
ISBN: 0-313-25862-7

First published in 1991

Greenwood Press, 88 Post Road West, Westport, CT 06881
An imprint of Greenwood Publishing Group, Inc.

Printed in the United States of America

The paper used in this book complies with the
Permanent Paper Standard issued by the National
Information Standards Organization (Z39.48-1984).

10  9  8  7  6  5  4  3  2  1

# CONTENTS

# PREFACE

During the past thirty to forty years, the historiography of Reconstruction has undergone so complete a change that a single reference volume containing the latest concepts ought to be of great help to scholars as well as the general public. Until World War II, and sometimes even afterwards, still following the guidelines set by William A. Dunning and his students, Reconstruction was usually pictured in books as well as in motion pictures as a time of horror for suffering Southerners, ground down by vindictive radicals seeking economic advantages while speaking of Negro rights. Corruption, misrule by carpetbaggers and scalawags, and general profligacy in government were said to have led to the "nadir of national disgrace." President Andrew Johnson, it was said, merely tried to follow in Abraham Lincoln's footsteps, holding out the hand of reconciliation to a gallant fallen foe perfectly willing to resume federal relations under the Constitution. According to prevailing notions, however, he was hounded by an unrelenting Congress that frustrated his plans and finally impeached him. Even the Ku Klux Klan found defenders who justified its terrorist activities with racist explanations of the importance of preserving white supremacy.

During World War II, another conflict with a racist enemy, an entirely changed point of view began to take hold. The radicals were no longer seen as cynical exploiters of the South, vengefully seeking to exact punishment and using the freedmen as an excuse for economic gains, but as reformers trying to integrate the blacks into American society. Corruption was shown to have been nationwide, rather than confined to the South, and many carpetbaggers and scalawags were conceded to have been able politicians. Favorable biographies appeared about the major figures involved—Charles Sumner, Thaddeus Stevens, Benjamin F. Wade, Edwin M. Stanton, and George W. Julian, to mention but a few—and new histories of Reconstruction in individual states as well as in the nation superseded their Dunningite predecessors. As the radicals began to rise in popular estimation, the reputation of their opponents—President Andrew Johnson, conservatives, and Southern "redeemers"—started to decline. The racist bias of earlier writers disappeared, and a great deal of literature concerning the freedmen and black issues took its place. Although many unresolved issues still remain, the field has benefited by this reassessment.

This dictionary is an attempt to present these findings in convenient form. It contains entries dealing with the major personalities of Reconstruction, the principal issues during that period, and the ideas current at the time. Those states involved in the process, including the border commonwealths, have also been included, as well as the most important decisions of the Supreme Court.

It is evident that in a dictionary of this kind the length of the various entries must vary. Depending on their importance, the concepts or personalities included have been given more or less space. At the end of each article, there is a listing of the latest available literature, principally monographs and biographies rather than articles, in order to facilitate further research. Cross-references, marked (q.v.), indicate that the term immediately preceding is a separate entry in this dictionary.

The selection of items can create great difficulty. By and large, the importance of individuals in reference to Reconstruction rather than their general significance has determined their inclusion, so that any number of distinguished people and memorable facts concerning the nineteenth century but not primarily Reconstruction do not appear. Likewise, the question of the time limit of Reconstruction is problematic. The most exhaustive book on the subject, Eric Foner's authoritative *Reconstruction, 1863–1877*, takes those years for its perimeter. The dictionary focuses on matters pertaining to the integration of the freedmen and the restoration of the states, thus starting in 1862 and at times extending to 1896. In these earlier and later periods, however, only concepts, ideas, and personalities affecting the Reconstruction process have been detailed, not those with no connection to it.

This book would have been impossible without the able assistance of David Osborn, whose tireless research contributed greatly to its completion. I should also like to thank Cynthia Harris, executive editor of Greenwood Press, who first suggested the preparation of the dictionary. Finally, my gratitude is due to my wife, Dr. Rashelle F. Trefousse, whose constant support has been most encouraging.

# CHRONOLOGY

**1862**  *February 11*: Charles Sumner introduces resolutions declaring that the seceded states had committed "suicide"

*March 2*: Andrew Johnson is appointed Military Governor of Tennessee (followed by the appointment of military governors for Louisiana, North Carolina, and Arkansas)

*April 16*: emancipation of the slaves in the District of Columbia

*July 22*: discussion of Emancipation Proclamation in cabinet

*September 22*: Lincoln issues Preliminary Emancipation Proclamation

*December 3*: election of two congressmen in Louisiana (admitted to the House of Representatives in February 1863)

**1863**  *January 1*: Lincoln promulgates Emancipation Proclamation

*April 20*: admission of West Virginia

*June 20*: adoption of Constitution providing for gradual emancipation in West Virginia

*December 8*: Lincoln issues his Amnesty Proclamation and announces the Ten Percent Plan of Reconstruction

**1864**  *March 4*: inauguration of free state government of Louisiana

*April 18*: inauguration of Union Governor of Arkansas

*July 2*: passage of Wade-Davis Bill

*July 8*: pocket-veto proclamation of Wade-Davis Bill

*August 5*: publication of Wade-Davis Manifesto

*October 29*: constitution of Maryland abolishing slavery in force

*November 8*: reelection of Abraham Lincoln

**1865**    *January 11*: emancipation in Missouri

*January 31*: passage of Thirteenth Amendment

*February 22*: emancipation in Tennessee

*March 3*: establishment of Freedmen's Bureau

*March 11*: Lincoln's last speech advocating limited black suffrage in Louisiana

*April 14*: Lincoln's assassination

*April 15*: inauguration of Andrew Johnson

*May 9*: Johnson recognizes Pierpont government in Virginia

*May 29*: Johnson's Proclamation of Amnesty and inauguration of Presidential Reconstruction starting with North Carolina

*July to December*: reorganization of Southern states (except Texas) in accordance with Johnson's plan

*July 7* execution of Lincoln assassins

*December 4*: Congress convenes and refuses to recognize Southern members-elect

*December 13*: Congress establishes Joint Committee on Reconstruction

**1866**    *February 19*: veto of Freedmen's Bureau Bill

*April 9*: passage of Civil Rights Bill over Johnson's veto

*May 1*: Memphis riot

*June 16*: passage of Fourteenth Amendment

*July 16*: passage of second Freedman's Bureau Bill over President's veto

*July 24*: Tennessee readmitted

*July 30*: New Orleans riot

*August 14*: Philadelphia National Union Convention meets

*August 28–September 15*: "swing around the circle"

*September 3*: Southern Loyalist Convention assembles in Philadelphia

*October–November*: Johnson defeated in congressional elections

*December 17*: *ex parte Milligan* decided

**1867**    *January 14*: *Test Oath* cases decided

*March 2*: passage of first Reconstruction, Tenure of Office, and Army Appropriation Acts (first two over Johnson's veto)

*March 22*: second Reconstruction Act passes over Johnson's veto

*April 15*: decision in *Mississippi* v. *Johnson*

*July 19*: passage of third Reconstruction Act

*August 12*: Johnson suspends Edwin M. Stanton and appoints U. S. Grant Secretary of War *ad interim*

*October 18*: Alaska becomes part of the United States

*October to November*: Democratic victories in various Northern states

*December 7*: failure of first attempt to impeach Johnson

**1868**   *January 13*: Senate refuses to concur in suspension of Stanton

*January 14*: Johnson breaks with Grant

*February 10*: decision in *Georgia* v. *Stanton*

*February 21*: Johnson again dismisses Stanton

*February 24*: impeachment of Johnson

*March 27*: Congress deprives Supreme Court of jurisdiction in *McCardle* case

*March 11*: fourth Reconstruction Act

*May 16, 26*: acquittal of Johnson

*May 20*: nomination of U. S. Grant

*June 22–25*: admission of Arkansas, North Carolina, South Carolina, Georgia, Florida, Alabama, and Louisiana

*July 20*: ratification of Fourteenth Amendment

*November 3*: U. S. Grant elected President

**1869**   *February 25*: passage of Fifteenth Amendment

*April 12*: decision in *Texas* v. *White*

*August 5*: conservative victory in Tennessee

*October 16*: decision in *ex parte Yerger*

**1870**   *January 26*: readmission of Virginia

*February 23*: readmission of Mississippi

*February 25*: adoption of Fifteenth Amendment

*March 30*: readmission of Texas

*May 31*: passage of First Enforcement Act

*July 15*: final readmission of Georgia

*July to August*: Kirk-Holden War

*August 4*: conservative victory in North Carolina

**1871**   *February 28*: passage of second Enforcement Act

*March 22*: impeachment of W. W. Holden

*April 20*: passage of third Enforcement (Ku Klux) Act

*May 8*: ratification of Treaty of Washington

**1872**   *May 3*: Cincinnati Liberal Republic Convention nominates Horace Greeley

*June 5–6*: Republican National Convention at Philadelphia and nomination of U. S. Grant

*July 9–10*: Democratic National Convention at Baltimore endorses Greeley

*August 25*: decision of Geneva Tribunal

*September 4*: New York *Sun* exposes Crédit Mobilier scandal

*November 5*: reelection of U. S. Grant

**1873**   *April 14*: decision in *Slaughterhouse* cases

*September 18*: failure of Jay Cooke and beginning of Panic of 1873

**1874**     *January 15*: Democratic governor inaugurated in Texas

        *April to May*: Brooks-Baxter War

        *October 13*: Democrats take over government of Arkansas

        *October to November*: Democrats win control of House of Representatives

        *November 24*: inauguration of conservative governor in Alabama

**1875**     *March 1*: passage of Civil Rights Act

        *May 10*: Whiskey Ring indictments

        *October to November*: terrorist methods procure a conservative victory in Mississippi

**1876**     *January 4*: inauguration of conservative government in Mississippi

        *March 2*: impeachment of William W. Belknap

        *March 27, 28*: decision in *U.S.* v. *Cruikshank* and *U.S.* v. *Reese*

        *June 16*: Cincinnati Republican National Convention nominates Rutherford B. Hayes

        *June 27–29*: Democratic National Convention at St. Louis and nomination of Samuel J. Tilden

        *November 7*: disputed election

        *December to March 1877*: deadlock in Congress and Compromise of 1877

**1877**     *January 2*: establishment of conservative rule in Florida

        *January 20*: establishment of Electoral Commission

        *February 9–28*: Electoral Commission awards victory to Hayes

        *February 26*: Wormley Conference

        *March 2*: Hayes declared elected

        *March 5*: inauguration of Hayes

        *April 3*: withdrawal of federal troops from South Carolina statehouse and abandonment of Republican administration

        *April 20*: withdrawal of federal troops from Louisiana statehouse and abandonment of Republican administration

**1883**     *October 15*: *Civil Rights* cases decided

**1896**     *May 18*: decision in *Plessy* v. *Ferguson*

# A

ALABAMA, one of the states subject to Reconstruction. With the surrender of the Southern forces, the Confederate state government ceased to exist, and on June 21, 1865, President Andrew Johnson (q.v.) appointed Lewis E. Parsons Provisional Governor. In accordance with the Presidential Plan of Reconstruction (q.v.), Parsons was to initiate a state government by calling on the existing electorate to choose delegates for a constitutional convention to propose amendments to the state constitution. The voting provisions excluded all blacks as well as those former Confederates exempted from the President's Proclamation of Amnesty of May 29, 1865.

Parsons carried out the President's wishes. Chosen at an election late in August, the convention met on September 12, abolished slavery, declared the secession ordinanace "null and void," and repudiated the rebel debt. It also provided for elections for a legislature, Governor, and members of Congress.

The elections were held and the legislature convened on November 20. It ratified the Thirteenth Amendment and passed a black code that was less onerous than that of neighboring states but still left freedmen in a distinctly inferior position. It also elected George S. Houston and Governor Parsons as U.S. Senators, although neither they nor the delegation to the House of Representatives was seated.

Less affected than other areas by wartime devastation, Alabama gradually experienced an economic recovery. The former plantation system was transformed into an economy marked by sharecropping, and the extensive coal deposits around Birmingham eventually gave rise to sustained industrial development.

Largely because of the unwillingness of Southerners to grant equal rights to freedmen, in March 1867 Congress passed the Reconstruction Acts (q.v.), which placed Alabama once more under military rule. Together with Georgia (q.v.) and Florida (q.v.), it constituted the Third Military District commanded by General John Pope (q.v.) (later George Gordon Meade [q.v.] ). The law called for a new convention elected by universal male suffrage, including blacks but excluding a number of former Confederates. Meeting in November 1867, this convention drew up a radical constitution safeguarding racial equality, which it submitted to the voters in February 1868. However, when the conservatives, in order to defeat the constitution, registered but abstained from voting, it failed to obtain the necessary majority. To remedy this difficulty, Congress passed a supplementary Reconstruction Act providing for the adoption of constitutions by a majority of ballots actually cast. Nevertheless, Alabama was readmitted in July 1868 without holding new elections.

The new government, consisting largely of scalawags (q.v.), carpetbaggers (q.v.), and a decided minority of blacks—including the highly competent James T. Rapier (q.v.)—ratified the Fourteenth Amendment (q.v.), set up a public school system, and sought to protect the freedmen. Hampered by Republican factionalism, corruption, and the hostility of most whites, however, the Reconstructionists were unable to deal effectively with the Ku Klux Klan (q.v.) and other terrorist bands organized to subvert the government. Further weakened by the Grant administration's failure to support it adequately, the Republican regime was unable to prevent the conservatives, who had already elected a governor in 1870, from recapturing the state in 1874. The period of "Redemption" (q.v.) followed.

*See also* Congressional Reconstruction; Presidential Reconstruction; "Redemption."

Walter L. Fleming, *Civil War and Reconstruction in Alabama* (New York, 1905); Peter Kolchin, *First Freedom: The Responses of Alabama's Blacks to Emancipation and Reconstruction* (Westport, Conn., 1972); James T. Schweninger, *James T. Rapier and Reconstruction* (Chicago, 1978); Sarah Woolfolk Wiggins, *The Scalawag in Alabama Politics, 1865–1881* (University, Ala., 1977).

**ALABAMA CLAIMS.** *See* WASHINGTON, TREATY OF.

**ALASKA.** *See* FOREIGN AFFAIRS.

**ALCORN, JAMES LUSK** (1816–1894), Reconstruction Senator and Governor of Mississippi (q.v.), was born at Golconda, Illinois, and spent his early years in neighboring Salem, Kentucky. A lawyer and member of the Kentucky (q.v.) legislature, in 1844 he removed to Coahoma County, Mississippi, in the Mississippi-Yazoo Delta, which became his permanent home. Prospering as a lawyer and planter, in 1845 he was elected to the lower house of the state legislature and in 1847 to the Senate, to which he was returned until he became a member of the House once more in 1856. He was a Unionist Whig, bitterly opposed Jefferson Davis, and took a strong stand in favor of a centralized levee system for his home region.

Although in 1850 Alcorn represented the Unionists in the Southern convention at Nashville and in 1861 in the secession convention at Jackson, he voted for the secession ordinance. After serving briefly as a brigadier general in the state forces, he returned home, where he spent most of the remainder of the war. In 1863 he was reelected to the legislature, and in 1865 he proposed the abolition of slavery as a bargaining chip for the defeated state.

During the period of Presidential Reconstruction (q.v.), Alcorn, serving again in the legislature, was elected a U.S. Senator but failed to be seated. Seeking to build up a moderate Whig-Republican organization in the state, he gradually shifted his political allegiance, counseled cooperation with the freedmen, and became the state's leading scalawag (q.v.).

In 1869, when Mississippi adopted a new constitution in accordance with the Reconstruction Acts (q.v.), Alcorn was elected Governor. His administration was characterized by efforts to bridge the gap between the races, the establishment of a public school system, and the appointment of an able judiciary. In 1871 he resigned to take a seat in the Senate but soon fell out with his colleague, Adelbert Ames (q.v.). The feud led to the gubernatorial campaign of 1873 in which the two Senators opposed each other, Ames relying on the blacks and carpetbaggers (q.v.) and Alcorn on the moderate whites and scalawags. Ames won; yet Alcorn continued to oppose him. In fact, during the period of violence sweeping the state in 1875, he took a prominent part in the Friar's Point riot in which, after a debate with a black adherent of Ames, he was one of the leaders of a group of whites who skirmished with the freedmen.

At the end of his term, Alcorn retired to his home. Notwithstanding his former advice to Southerners to collaborate with the blacks, he participated in the constitutional convention of 1890 that effectively disfranchised them. A persistent Whig, he was the most prominent scalawag in Mississippi.

*See also* Ames, Adelbert; Mississippi; Scalawags.

Lillian Pereyra, *James Lusk Alcorn, Persistent Whig* (Baton Rouge, 1966).


**AMES, ADELBERT** (1835–1933), Reconstruction Governor and Senator from Mississippi (q.v.), was born at Rockland, Maine, the son of a sea captain. A West Pointer, he earned a Congressional Medal of Honor for gallantry at the first battle of Bull Run and distinguished himself at Antietam, Fredericksburg, Gettysburg, Fort Fisher, and other engagements. After serving with the occupation forces in South Carolina, Ames, now a brevet major general, was detailed to Mississippi. On June 15, 1868, he was appointed Military Governor of the state, and in 1870, when Mississippi was readmitted to the Union, the legislature elected him to the U.S. Senate. His term of office was marked by a feud with his colleague, James L. Alcorn (q.v.), who, representing the moderate whites and scalawags (q.v.), entered the Senate in 1871. The controversy led to the gubernatorial campaign of 1873, in which the two Senators opposed each other. With the support of his fellow carpetbaggers (q.v.) and the blacks, Ames won and resigned his seat to return to Jackson.

As Governor, Ames sought to give Mississippi an economical administration and to safeguard the freedmen's rights. In spite of his honesty and ability, however, he was unable effectively to counter the violence inaugurated by the Democrats in 1875 to overthrow Republican rule. Failing to secure the Grant administration's support, Ames could not avert the Democrats' capture of the legislature. The result was that early in 1876 he had to face trumped-up charges of impeachment that were withdrawn only in return for his resignation, after which he left the state for good.

Ames, who was married to Blanche Butler, the daughter of General Benjamin F. Butler (q.v.), spent the remaining years of his long life in the North, principally in Minnesota, New York, New Jersey, and Massachusetts. During the Spanish-American War, he entered the army again and saw action in Cuba. His honorable record goes far toward dispelling the traditionally unfavorable view of the carpetbaggers.

*See also* Alcorn, James Lusk; Carpetbaggers; Mississippi.

Blanche Ames Ames, *Adelbert Ames, 1835–1933; General, Senator, Governor* (New York, 1964); Blanche Butler Ames, comp., *Chronicles from the Nineteenth Century: Family Letters of Blanche Butler and Adelbert Ames* (2 vols., Clinton, Mass., 1957); Richard Nelson Current, *Those Terrible Carpetbaggers: A Reinterpretation* (New York, 1988).

**AMNESTY.** Several proclamations of amnesty were issued during the Civil War and Reconstruction. The first of these was Abraham Lincoln's (q.v.) Proclamation of Amnesty and Reconstruction of December 8, 1863, offering a full pardon to all insurgents willing to take an oath to support the Constitution as well as all acts and proclamations in respect to slaves as long as not modified or held void by act of Congress or the Supreme Court. As soon as 10 percent of the voters of 1860 had taken the oath, they were authorized to reestablish a state government, "republican in form," that would be recognized by the United States. Six classes, including high Confederate officials and military officers, members of the armed forces who had resigned their commissions to join the Confederacy, members of Congress or the federal judiciary who had left their seats to aid the rebellion, and those who had mistreated black prisoners of war, were exempt from this offer.

The next important Proclamation of Amnesty was issued by Andrew Johnson (q.v.) on May 29, 1865. Again offering amnesty to all insurgents willing to take the oath of allegiance, it exempted fourteen classes from its provisions, including those singled out by Lincoln, those who had broken their former amnesty oath, commerce raiders, graduates of West Point or Annapolis, and all whose taxable property was worth more than $20,000. Nevertheless, special applications for pardons could be made by the exempted classes and the President liberally granted them. This proclamation omitted the 10 percent requirement, but it was coupled with a companion order appointing a Provisional Governor for North Carolina (q.v.), and later for other states, who was authorized to initiate the reestablishment of loyal governments based on the prewar electorate. These two proclamations ushered in the process of postwar Presidential Reconstruction (q.v.) and led to the struggle between President and Congress.

On September 7, 1867, Johnson issued a second Proclamation of Amnesty extending full pardon to all willing to take the oath with the exception of some three hundred high-ranking Confederate civil and military officers, persons who had mistreated prisoners of war, and those in confinement for specific offenses or implicated in the assassination of President Lincoln. A third proclamation followed on July 4, 1868, for all but those still under indictment, such as Jefferson Davis (q.v.), and a fourth was promulgated on Christmas 1868 finally granting universal amnesty.

Congress also passed various measures of amnesty and pardon. In the second Confiscation Act of July 16, 1862, it specifically authorized the President to issue such proclamations; in the Fourteenth Amendment (q.v.), it provided for a removal of Confederate disabilities by a two-thirds vote, and in 1872, in accordance with this provision, it passed a special Amnesty Act. The measure pardoned all except members of the Thirty-sixth and Thirty-seventh Congress and ranking civil and military officers of the United States. An 1876 bill to remove even these restrictions failed, and it was not until 1896 that the last disabilities were removed.

*See also* North Carolina Proclamation; Presidential Reconstruction.

Jonathan Truman Dorris, *Pardon and Amnesty Under Lincoln and Johnson* (Chapel Hill, N.C., 1953).

**ARKANSAS,** one of the states affected by Abraham Lincoln's Ten Percent Plan (q.v.). As early as July 19, 1862, after the capture of Helena, the President appointed John S. Phelps, a Union general from Missouri, Military Governor, but the general was unable to promote the restoration of a loyal government and in March 1863 lost his commission.

In December 1863, Lincoln published his Proclamation of Amnesty. As soon as 10 percent of the voters of 1860 had taken the prescribed oath, they were authorized to form a new government. In Arkansas, this process began in March 1864, when Isaac Murphy, the only member of the secession convention who had refused to vote for separation, was elected Provisional Governor. A loyal state government was set up, slavery abolished, and Murphy elected governor. Although he gave the state an honest administration, in 1866 he was unable to prevent the capture of the legislature by the conservatives. All he could do in protest was to veto the obnoxious legislation they passed.

In 1867, in accordance with the Reconstruction Acts (q.v.), Arkansas was once more placed under military rule. In the following year, a newly elected constitutional convention, including a small minority of blacks, met and drafted a constitution providing for universal manhood suffrage with some Confederate disfranchisement and considerable centralization of power in the hands of the Governor. After the constitution was ratified in a disputed election, in June 1868, the state was readmitted. Powell Clayton (q.v.), a Union general who had settled in Arkansas, was elected chief executive and soon became enmeshed in questionable railroad deals. In addition, to combat the Ku Klux Klan (q.v.), he placed parts of the state under martial law. His opponents in the House impeached him, but the Senate dropped the charges, and when in 1871 he was elected to the federal Senate, he refused to take his seat so that he would not have to give up his office to his antagonist, Lieutenant Governor J. M. Johnson. Only after highly dubious arrangements had been made for the transfer of power to O. A. Hadley, a political ally, did Clayton accept an election to the U.S. Senate.

The Republican party (q.v.) in the state soon broke up into several factions, divided by differences about the repeal of the disfranchising clauses in the constitution. The regular Republicans, called "minstrels," who were dominated by Clayton, supported Grant in 1872 and nominated the scalawag (q.v.) Elisha Baxter for Governor. A second group, the "brindletails," endorsed the carpetbagger (q.v.) Joseph Brooks, and the liberals, who backed Horace Greeley (q.v.), supported Dr. Andrew Hunter. The Democratic conservatives sought to exploit this split to their advantage, and with their backing, Brooks maintained that he had won. The Baxter forces, however, also claimed victory, and the dispute kept the Republicans divided for the next two years.

In the aftermath of the election of 1872, Baxter was inaugurated governor, though his title was disputed. In March 1873 the legislature passed a franchise amendment repealing the disqualifying clauses of the 1868 constitution, a development that greatly strengthened the Democrats. Attacked by Brooks, who sought quo warranto proceedings against him, Baxter increasingly sought Democratic support, a policy that alienated him from his former sponsors. His appointment of conservatives to militia positions as well as his refusal to support Clayton's railroad schemes led the Senator to favor Brooks, who now secured a court decision declaring him to be Governor. The Brooks-Baxter War (q.v.) of 1874 was the result, with the two claimants contending for office with armed retainers. Although the Grant administration first favored Brooks, it finally declared for Baxter, who thereupon secured control, and the legislature, which the Democrats had recaptured in 1873, called elections for a new constitutional convention. The convention met, wrote a new constitution greatly reducing the power of the Governor, and in effect marked the end of congressional Reconstruction (q.v.).

Under the new constitution, the Democrats elected the former Confederate Augustus H. Garland Governor. Although the President now again sought to sustain Brooks, Garland's control was confirmed when a congressional committee chaired by Luke Poland of Vermont reported in favor of nonintervention. The usual process of "Redemption" (q.v.) ensued.

*See also* Brooks-Baxter War; Congressional Reconstruction; Presidential Reconstruction.

George Thompson, *Arkansas and Reconstruction* (Port Washington, N.Y., 1976); Thomas W. Staples, *Reconstruction in Arkansas* (New York, 1923); David Y. Thomas, *Arkansas in War and Reconstruction, 1861–1874* (Little Rock, 1926).

**ARMY, U.S.,** played an important role during Reconstruction. Charged with the occupation and maintenance of order in the South, the army faced a difficult task, particularly because of the conflicting policies of the President and Congress during Andrew Johnson's (q.v.) administration. At first, the military assumed total control of the defunct Confederate states. Then it lent military support to Johnson's efforts to restore the seceded states as quickly as possible. Finally, with the inauguration of congressional Reconstruction (q.v.), it was given the mission of administering the five military districts established by the Reconstruction Acts (q.v.) and of supervising the restoration of an acceptable civil government. This assignment was beset by problems; the commanding generals had to administer justice, set election rules, and enforce unpopular congressional mandates, and policies varied according to the political preconceptions of individual commanders.

Although in protecting the freedmen the army achieved only limited success, partially due to lack of personnel, it performed about as well as could be expected. At times, it became enmeshed in political controversies both in Washington and in the South, particularly when General U.S. Grant (q.v.) collaborated with Secretary of War Edwin M. Stanton (q.v.) to frustrate some of Johnson's purposes, and when General Philip Sheridan (q.v.) ejected five Democratic members of the Louisiana legislature. By and large, however, the army succeeded in keeping a semblance of order despite great complications.

*See also* Congressional Reconstruction; Grant, Ulysses Simpson; Stanton, Edwin McMasters.

James E. Sefton, *The United States Army and Reconstruction, 1865–1877* (Baton Rouge, 1967); Harold M. Hyman, "Johnson, Stanton, and Grant: A Reconsideration of the Army's Role in the Events Leading to the Impeachment," *American Historical Review*, 66 (1960); 85–100.


**ASHLEY, JAMES MITCHELL** (1824–1896), a radical Republican congressman, was born in Allegheny, Pennsylvania. The son of a Campbellite minister who settled in Portsmouth, Ohio, he accompanied his father on trips to neighboring Kentucky, where he became imbued with an intense dislike of slavery, an attitude confirmed by his experiences as a boatman on various Southern rivers. After engaging in various trades, journalism, and the law in Portsmouth, Ashley opened a drugstore in Toledo, which became his home. An antislavery Jacksonian Democrat, he took part in the founding of the Republican party (q.v.) in his district and in 1858 was elected to Congress. Reelected in 1860, 1862, 1864, and 1866, he was a firm supporter of Salmon P. Chase (q.v.)

After the Republicans gained control of the House, in 1861 Ashley became chairman of the Committee on Territories. As early as March, 1862, he introduced a bill for the reconstruction of the seceded states by congressional action reducing them to territorial status. When in December 1863 President Abraham Lincoln (q.v.) promulgated his Ten Percent Plan (q.v.), Ashley sought to offer a companion bill in the House providing for similar procedures but mandating black suffrage (q.v.). Subsequently, he supported the Wade-Davis Bill (q.v.); in December 1864, however, he again attempted to adjust differences between the executive and Congress concerning Reconstruction by sponsoring a measure recognizing Lincoln's free state government in Louisiana while retaining the outlines of the Wade-Davis Bill elsewhere.

His collaboration with the President reached a climax in the winter of 1864–1865 in their joint success in passing the Thirteenth Amendment (q.v.). After his great accomplishment in participating in the abolition of slavery in the District of Columbia and the territories, he turned to the problem of amending the Constitution to end the "peculiar institution" throughout the country. Having lost the measure for this purpose in June 1864, he switched his vote at the last moment in order to be able to move for a later reconsideration. In December he renewed his effort and, with the active help of Abraham Lincoln, saw to it that the amendment received the necessary two-thirds majority on January 31, 1865.

When Andrew Johnson (q.v.) became President, Ashley soon fell out with him because of differences about black suffrage (q.v.). By the beginning of 1867, Ashley had become one of the principal advocates of the impeachment of the President, and on January 7 he announced that Johnson ought to be impeached of high crimes and misdemeanors and introduced a resolution calling on the judiciary committee to initiate hearings on the subject. Ashley saw to it that the investigation was continued by the Fortieth Congress; because of his efforts to obtain information about Johnson's alleged complicity in the assassination of Lincoln from the convicted perjurer Charles A. Dunham alias Sanford Conover, however, he soon lost credibility. He had long believed that all the Vice Presidents who succeeded to the presidency had been implicated in the deaths of their predecessors and harbored similar unfounded suspicions about Andrew Johnson.

When the President was impeached, Ashley did not play a major role in the proceedings. Deeply disappointed at Johnson's acquittal, he sought reelection in 1868 but was defeated. President U. S. Grant (q.v.) appointed him Governor of Montana but soon recalled him, and he spent the rest of his life in railroading and law in Ohio and Michigan. In 1890 and 1892 he once again ran unsuccessfully for Congress. Untiring in his efforts to free the slaves, and particularly in seeing to the passage of the Thirteenth Amendment, he was undoubtedly a radical of considerable importance.

*See also* Impeachment of Andrew Johnson; Thirteenth Amendment.

Robert Horowitz, *The Great Impeacher* (New York, 1979).

# B

BABCOCK, ORVILLE ELIAS, aide-de-camp and secretary to General U. S. Grant (q.v.), was born at Franklin, Vermont, in 1834. An engineer trained at West Point, during the Civil War Babcock joined the staff of General Grant, who, taken by his genial personality, regarded him highly and entrusted him with important missions. Eventually, Babcock became one of the General's closest friends.

After the war, as aide-de-camp and secretary to the President, Babcock gained notoriety for his involvement in various scandals. Persistent rumors linked him to the gold conspirators of 1869; that same year, ostensibly on behalf of the State Department to investigate conditions in the Dominican Republic but in reality on behalf of Grant to look into the feasibility of annexation, he went to Santo Domingo. While there, he signed protocols with President Buenaventura Baez either to buy the entire republic or to lease Samana Bay, where he himself had acquired some property. In return, the United States was not only to provide funds but also to assist Baez against his enemies. Upon his return, Babcock encountered considerable hostility to this project. Nevertheless, he was sent back to conclude formal treaties, for the acceptance of which he lobbied extensively if unsuccessfully in Washington.

By 1875 it had become evident that Babcock had been deeply implicated in the Whiskey Ring (q.v.). Keeping the main perpetrators in St. Louis informed of the planned moves against them, he himself was finally unable to escape indictment. Following Grant's deposition in his favor, he was acquitted but had to leave the White House. The President appointed him inspector of lighthouses, and in pursuit of his duties, he drowned in Florida in 1884.

*See also* Foreign Affairs; Grant, Ulysses Simpson; Whiskey Ring.

Allan Nevins, *Hamilton Fish: The Inner History of the Grant Administration* (New

York, 1936); William B. Hesseltine, *Ulysses S. Grant: Politician* (New York, 1935); William S. McFeely, *Grant: A Biography* (New York, 1981).

**BANKS, NATHANIEL PRENTISS,** congressman, Governor of Massachusetts, and Civil War general, was born in Waltham, Massachusetts, in 1816. After working in a cotton mill and dabbling in the law and journalism, he turned to politics. A Democratic member of the lower house of the state legislature from 1849 to 1853, he was a prominent supporter of the Democratic-Free Soil coalition in the Bay State and in 1852, 1854, and 1856 was elected to Congress. He opposed the Kansas-Nebraska Act, joined the Know-Nothings and then the Republicans, and in 1855 became the first Republican Speaker of the House. In 1858 he was elected Governor and served until 1860, when he accepted the presidency of the Illinois Central Railroad. Appointed a major general of volunteers in 1861, he was defeated in the Shenandoah Valley, at Cedar Mountain, and in the Red River Campaign but captured Port Hudson and played an important role in the reconstruction of Louisiana (q.v.), where he took command in December 1862. Attempting to conciliate the conservatives, he failed to cooperate fully with local Unionists, set up a contract labor system for the blacks, and insisted on holding elections for state officers before the summoning of a constitutional convention. Michael Hahn (q.v.) was elected Governor; the subsequent convention abolished slavery, and Banks saw to it that the new Free State government was ratified by the voters. He then traveled to Washington to work for its acceptance by Congress as well but because of his split with the radicals failed in this endeavor. He went back to New Orleans only to fall out with Andrew Johnson (q.v.) and returned to Massachusetts, where he was reelected to his old seat in Congress.

During his postwar service in the House of Representatives, Banks became chairman of the Committee on Foreign Affairs and was an active proponent of expansionist policies. He favored the annexation of Alaska as well as that of various Caribbean islands and sought to bring about the acquisition of British North America. As a moderate, he opposed the first Reconstruction Act (q.v.) and in 1872 joined the Liberal Republicans (q.v.). Defeated for reelection that year, in 1874 he was returned as an independent to the Massachusetts Senate. In 1876 he regained his congressional seat as a Democrat but rejoined the Republican party two years later. From 1879 to 1888 he served as U.S. marshal for Massachusetts. After a tenth term in Congress from 1889 to 1891, he retired to Waltham, where he died in 1894.

*See also* Foreign Affairs; Hahn, Michael; Louisiana.

Fred Harvey Harrington, *Fighting Politician: Major General N. P. Banks* (Philadelphia, 1948); Peyton McCrary, *Abraham Lincoln and Reconstruction: The Louisiana Experiment* (Princeton, N.J.: 1978); LaWanda Cox, *Lincoln and Black Freedom: A Study in Presidential Leadership* (Columbia, S.C., 1981).

**BEECHER, HENRY WARD,** Congressional minister, publicist, and orator, was born in 1813 in Litchfield, Connecticut, the eighth child of the Rev. Lyman Beecher, the famous Calvinist divine. Educated at Amherst College and Lane

Theological Seminary, he entered the ministry and was ordained by the New School Presbyterians. As a clergyman at Lawrenceburg and Indianapolis, Indiana, he gained fame because of his popular sermons and in 1847 was called to the newly founded Congregational Plymouth Church in Brooklyn. There he rapidly established a reputation as a most effective preacher whose success in attracting congregants and a public hearing was phenomenal. In time, he drifted away from Calvinist orthodoxy and preached a more liberal, romantic Christianity, well attuned to the needs of his urban middle-class parishoners.

After first steering clear of the slavery controversy, Beecher, who also favored temperance and women's suffrage, by 1848 embraced the cause of emancipation. He vigorously opposed the Fugitive Slave Law of 1850 and the Kansas-Nebraska Act and gained fame by auctioning off a slave girl in his church and buying her freedom. His support for the Free State settlers of Kansas was so strong that the Sharp's rifles sent there were called "Beecher's Bibles," and when the Civil War broke out, the minister became an enthusiastic adherent of the Union cause. Exhorting the government to emancipate the slaves, he faulted Abraham Lincoln (q.v.) for moving too slowly and, in 1863, while in Great Britain, delivered a series of speeches in favor of the North. Thus it was not surprising that it was Beecher who was selected to deliver an oration at the raising of the Stars and Stripes at Fort Sumter on April 14, 1865.

Beecher, who sympathized with the Reconstruction policies of Andrew Johnson (q.v.), spoke and wrote in favor of the administration, although he advised the President to sign the Civil Rights and Reconstruction Acts (q.v.). Expressing his favorable sentiments in a letter to the 1866 Johnson Soldiers and Sailors Convention at Cleveland, he was severely criticized for his stand by members of his congregation, including his fellow editor of the radical New York *Independent*, Theodore Tilton. In the final days of the election of 1866, he at last supported the Republican ticket, however, and in 1868 endorsed the candidacy of Ulysses S. Grant (q.v.).

In 1870 Beecher became the editor of the newly founded *Christian Union*. He wrote frequently for various newspapers, published the *Life of Christ* as well as essays and novels, and was increasingly critical of corruption in government. Although not supporting the Liberal Republicans (Liberal Republican Movement, q.v.) in 1872, he was characteristic of the "best men" who sought all manner of reforms, particularly of the civil service, and in 1884 came out for Grover Cleveland against James G. Blaine (q.v.). His later years were clouded by Tilton's charges that he had committed adultery with his coeditor's wife, an accusation that led to a trial lasting some six months and ending in a split jury with the majority upholding the minister. His influence undiminished, he continued to preach, lecture, and write in favor of liberal Christianity. He died in Brooklyn in 1887.

*See also* Johnson, Andrew.

Clifford E. Clark, Jr., *Henry Ward Beecher: Spokesman for a Middle-Class America* (Urbana, Ill., 1978); Paxton Hibben, *Henry Ward Beecher: An American Portrait* (New York, 1927).

**BELKNAP, WILLIAM WORTH** (1829–1890), Civil War general and U. S. Grant's Secretary of War, was born in Newburg, New York, in 1829. The son of an army officer, he was educated at Princeton and Georgetown, where he studied law. Admitted to the bar in Keokuk, Iowa, in 1851, he pursued his profession and served as a Democratic member of the state legislature. During the Civil War, rising swiftly from the rank of major to that of brevet major general, he saw action at Shiloh, Corinth, Vicksburg, and in Georgia.

After serving as collector of internal revenue in Iowa, in 1869 he was appointed Secretary of War in the cabinet of President U. S. Grant (q.v.). While enjoying the confidence both of the President and General William T. Sherman (q.v.), he disappointed both in the performance of his duties. Although he attempted to back up General Philip Sheridan (q.v.) in his effort to uphold the Republican legislature of Louisiana (q.v.), he failed to come to the aid of James W. Smith, the first black cadet at West Point, who had been subject to merciless harassment and was dismissed after an unusual examination.

In 1876 Belknap became involved in a scheme of bribery by accepting annual payments from the occupant of a trading post at Fort Sill in the Indian Territory in return for permission to retain his position. This practice began when the Secretary's wife made an arrangement with the incumbent's rival; after her death the payments continued both to her husband and her sister, a woman of expensive tastes, who married Belknap soon afterward. When a committee of the Democratically controlled House of Representatives revealed the scandal, the Secretary quickly tendered his resignation, which Grant accepted. Although this hasty action did not shield Belknap from impeachment in the House, it contributed to his acquittal, since the Senate, largely because of doubts about the appropriateness of the impeachment process in the case of an official no longer in office, failed to muster the necessary two-thirds vote to convict. Nevertheless, the affair materially contributed to the failure of the Grant administration and the subsequent end of Reconstruction.

After the impeachment, Belknap practiced law in Washington, where he died in 1890.

*See also* Grant, Ulysses Simpson.

William S. McFeely, *Grant: A Biography* (New York, 1981); Allan Nevins, *Hamilton Fish: The Inner History of the Grant Administration* (New York, 1936); Claude G. Bowers, *The Tragic Era: The Revolution after Lincoln* (New York, 1929).


**BINGHAM, JOHN ARMOR** (1815–1900), moderate Republican congressman, was born in Mercer, Pennsylvania. After an education at Franklin College, he settled at Cadiz, Ohio, where he established a flourishing law practice. An antislavery Whig, he entered politics during the 1840 campaign, was elected district attorney of Tuscarawas County in 1846, and served in Congress as a Republican from 1855 to 1863 and again from 1865 to 1873. Abraham Lincoln (q.v.) appointed him judge advocate, and he played an important part in the trial of the President's assassins.

In the Reconstruction Congresses, Bingham, a member of the Joint Committee on Reconstruction (q.v.), was a leader of the moderates in the House. Always insisting upon safeguarding constitutional forms, he opposed the Civil Rights Act of 1866 (q.v.), which he thought unconstitutional, though he later incorporated some of its provisions in the Fourteenth Amendment (q.v.), in the framing of which he distinguished himself as the author of the equal protection of the laws clause. He also paved the way for the Senate's substitution of milder disfranchisement provisions. Favoring the admission of Tennessee (q.v.) in 1866, he contended that the state governments in the South were still legal. For this and other reasons, he caused the Reconstruction Bill of 1867 to be committed to the Reconstruction Committee and eventually saw to it that the state governments retained at least nominal authority. In addition, he opposed the wholesale disfranchisement of former Confederates.

In 1867 Bingham resisted all steps looking toward the impeachment of President Andrew Johnson (q.v.), but when the President openly challenged Congress by dismissing Secretary of War Edwin M. Stanton (q.v.) and appointing Lorenzo B. Thomas in his stead, he not only changed his mind but became one of the managers of the impeachment of the President. As one of the managers of the case against Judge West W. Humphries in 1861, who was found guilty of treason, he had experience in official prosecutions and delivered a ringing closing speech.

After Johnson's acquittal, Bingham successfully opposed restrictive fundamental conditions for the readmission of the Southern states and favored the more conservative version of the Fifteenth Amendment (q.v.) which omitted all officeholding provisions. After his defeat for reelection, President U. S. Grant (q.v.) appointed him minister to Japan, a position he held until 1885. He died at Cadiz in 1900.

*See also* Fourteenth Amendment; Impeachment of Andrew Johnson; Reconstruction Act.

Erving E. Beauregard, *Bingham of the Hills: Politician and Diplomat Extraordinary* (New York, 1989); Michael Les Benedict, *A Compromise of Principle: Congressional Republicans and Reconstruction, 1863–1869* (New York, 1974); Joseph R. James, *The Framing of the Fourteenth Amendment* (Urbana, Ill., 1956); Chicago *Tribune*, March 20, 1900.

**BLACK CODES,** a series of laws in the former Confederate states designed to regulate the behavior and legal status of the freedmen and women. Passed in 1865 and 1866, these enactments were justified by their proponents on the grounds that the old regulations governing the relations between whites and blacks had lapsed and that some substitute would have to be found; yet they were often so harsh as to constitute a thinly veiled effort to remand the blacks to a condition as close to slavery as possible.

Although the black codes gave freedmen the right to sue and be sued, regularized marriages, and declared the offspring of such unions legitimate, they generally attempted to confine the black population to the position of agricultural laborers or servants, while severely restricting freedom of movement and association through stringent vagrancy and other laws.

The first of these enactments was passed in Mississippi (q.v.). It prohibited blacks (q.v.) from leasing or renting land except in incorporated towns, from carrying arms without police permission, and from selling or receiving spirituous liquors. Obliged to sign written contracts for all long-term labor, blacks could be forcibly brought back if they broke them. If they were found to be without visible support or generally not behaving according to white standards of propriety, they were to be considered vagrants and could be hired out if unable to pay their fines. All orphans and others under age eighteen whose parents did not provide for them were also to be hired out under an apprentice system that gave preference to the former owner, who had the right to inflict physical chastisement if necessary. In addition, blacks could be fined for vagrancy if they failed to pay the taxes levied for the support of black schools.

South Carolina (q.v.) copied many features of these codes and added innovations of its own, such as the prohibition of blacks from engaging in trades other than agricultural labor or service except upon the procurement of an annual license. Louisiana (q.v.) passed similarly harsh codes and added fines for disobedience; Florida (q.v.) made disrespectful behavior evidence of vagrancy, and Virginia (q.v.) declared combining for higher wages evidence of larceny. Other states had less onerous laws, North Carolina (q.v.) confining itself to regularizing marriage and legal relations while declaring a black's rape of a white woman a capital offense.

The effect of these enactments upon the North was startling. Generally condemned as clear signs that Southerners were not willing to abide by the results of the war, they led to a hardening of attitudes, particularly in Congress. The Civil Rights Act of 1866 (q.v.) and the subsequent Fourteenth Amendment (q.v.) were in part designed to nullify these codes, although some had already been repealed. Army commanders, particularly General Daniel E. Sickles (q.v.) in South Carolina and General Alfred H. Terry in Virginia, at times interfered to prevent the rankest forms of discrimination, and Governor Robert M. Patton of Alabama (q.v.) vetoed some of the bills, but the black codes' role in demonstrating Southern opposition to full emancipation cannot be exaggerated.

*See also* Blacks; Presidential Reconstruction.

Theodore Bantner Wilson, *The Black Codes of the South* (University, Ala., 1965); Rembert W. Patrick, *The Reconstruction of the Nation* (New York, 1967); Robert Cruden, *The Negro in Reconstruction* (Englewood Cliffs, N.J., 1969); Eric Foner, *Reconstruction: America's Unfinished Revolution, 1863–1877* (New York, 1988); Edward McPherson, *The Political History of the United States of America During the Period of Reconstruction* (Washington, 1871).

**BLACK FRIDAY,** the collapse of a scheme to corner the New York gold market, which the Grant administration broke on September 24, 1869. Hatched by Jay Gould (q.v.) in collaboration with James Fisk, Jr., the operation involved the cooperation of Abel Corbin, the President's brother-in-law, at whose house

Gould met U. S. Grant (q.v.) in June 1869. Invited to travel on one of Gould's and Fisk's steamships, Grant was royally entertained at dinner and told that if the government withheld its gold sales, the price of the metal would go up and benefit the farmers by enabling them to sell their produce abroad. Grant seemed convinced, and Gould and Fisk proceeded to bid up the gold market from 133 to 143 within a few weeks; just before the break, it reached more than 160 and a panic resulted, particularly among the short sellers upon whose needs the speculators had counted.

By September 20 Grant, now in Washington, Pennsylvania, had become suspicious, and, in a letter to his sister, his wife asked her to stop speculating. Back in the capital, on the 23rd, he ordered Secretary of the Treasury George S. Boutwell (q.v.) to sell gold if its price kept rising, and on Friday, September 24, the corner was broken. Gould, who had an inkling of this change of policy, managed to unload his holdings at the last minute without informing his partner. The sudden plunge in the market price of the metal by more than 20 points ruined many dealers, and the entire affair cast the administration in an unfavorable light, not only because of the involvement of the President's family but also because of the failure to interfere earlier.

*See also* Boutwell, George Sewall; Corruption; Grant, Ulysses Simpson.

William S. McFeely, *Grant: A Biography* (New York, 1981); Allen Nevins, *Hamilton Fish: The Inner History of the Grant Administration* (New York, 1936); Claude Bowers, *The Tragic Era: The Revolution After Lincoln* (New York, 1929).

**BLACKS,** largely freedmen whose place in American society constituted one of the principal issues of Reconstruction. Emancipated by the Emancipation Proclamation (q.v.), various separate state enactments, and the Thirteenth Amendment (q.v.), the freedmen faced a difficult future. Without land, capital, and education, their place in society would have to be determined by the policies adopted by the government. Various attempts at a contract labor system, such as that set up by General Nathaniel P. Banks (q.v.) in Louisiana (q.v.), formed one way of easing the transition between slavery and freedom; individual land-holdings, such as on the Sea Islands (q.v.), was another method. Nevertheless, at the end of the war the problem of the integration of the blacks had not been solved.

What Abraham Lincoln (q.v.) would have done had he lived remains problematical. It is certain that his approach would have been pragmatic. At first, he attempted to carry out a plan of colonization, probably chiefly to assuage the conservatives, and shipped a number of volunteers to the Ile à Vache off Haiti. Then, when the experiment failed, he brought them back. His record of favoring emancipation and accepting blacks for military service marked him as a progressive leader, so it was in character for him to exert constant pressure on areas exempt from the Proclamation to initiate emancipation on their own and to exert all of his power to force the Thirteenth Amendment through the House. In the end, he went so far as to advocate publicly the enfranchisement of capable blacks, only to be assassinated three days later.

Andrew Johnson (q.v.) was no friend of the blacks. A former slaveholder himself, he firmly believed in white supremacy, and under his plan of Reconstruction blacks not only did not obtain the vote but were left to the mercy of their former masters. Black codes (q.v.) reduced them to a condition not far removed from slavery, and race riots, particularly in Memphis and New Orleans, left many killed or injured.

The question of black suffrage (q.v.) was one of the most controversial of the entire Reconstruction process. The more advanced radicals (Radical Republicans, q.v.) in Congress demanded it, but opponents argued that the freedmen were hardly prepared for it and that the federal government had no constitutional right to interfere with the franchise. Nevertheless, it was certain that the Republican party could not hope for success in the South without black support, and thus sentiment for enfranchisement grew. Although between 1865 and 1868 various Northern states rejected the reform, the Fourteenth Amendment (q.v.) sought to encourage it by threatening to diminish the representation in Congress of states denying the vote to any male citizen over age twenty-one.

If the blacks suffered politically under the Johnson governments, they experienced economic difficulty as well. Largely agricultural laborers, they generally became sharecroppers caught in a never-ending circle of indebtedness to the landowner. Proposals to give them land (forty acres and a mule) found little support in Congress.

Otherwise, Congress attempted to assist the freedmen. In 1864 it established the Freedmen's Bureau (q.v.), which it continued to support in 1866. That year it also passed a Civil Rights Act (q.v.) with provisions for black citizenship, and in 1867 it accepted three Reconstruction Acts (q.v.) mandating black suffrage (q.v.) and the acceptance of the Fourteenth Amendment. By 1868 all but three Southern states had complied with these conditions, and the blacks had become full citizens.

The period that followed has often been miscalled "black Reconstruction." In view of the fact that blacks always remained a minority in the South as a whole and that they did not fully control a single state legislature, the appellation is misleading. It is true that because of the disfranchisement of about 150,000 whites, black majorities existed for a time in South Carolina (q.v.), Mississippi (q.v.), and Louisiana (q.v.), at least among the voters, but only in the legislature of South Carolina was this even partially reflected, and even there, control was always in the hands of scalawags (q.v.) and carpetbaggers (q.v.). Moreover, the Reconstruction legislatures were unable to do very much for black constituents, who remained poor and victims of discrimination. Yet they obtained the franchise and the right to hold office as well as access to various welfare institutions on a segregated basis. In 1869 the passage of the Fifteenth Amendment (q.v.) gave blacks the right to vote not only in the South but also in the North, and three Enforcement Acts (q.v.) in 1870 and 1871 sought to safeguard newly won black rights.

Because of the lack of black economic power, terror, especially by the Ku

Klux Klan (q.v.); the abandonment of the cause in the North; and political changes due to the Panic of 1873, the Republican governments in the South were gradually overthrown and replaced by "Redeemer" ("Redemption," q.v.) regimes. This process was completed by Rutherford B. Hayes' (q.v.) withdrawal of federal troops from Southern statehouses following the disputed election of 1876. Gradually, but surely, the blacks were once more relegated to the position of second-class citizens. Not even the Civil Rights Act of 1875 (q.v.) guaranteeing integration in various public facilities could arrest this process, and the law was held to be unconstitutional in 1883. In addition, the courts were lax in their enforcement of the post–Civil War amendments, and by the 1890s, partially in response to Populist agitation, the blacks were totally excluded from politics and subjected to almost complete segregation. The Supreme Court finally sanctioned this development in *Plessy* v. *Ferguson* (q.v.), 1896. Not until after World War II would the civil rights struggle resume in earnest.

*See also* Black Codes; Black Suffrage; Congressional Reconstruction; Presidential Reconstruction; "Redemption."

Eric Foner, *Reconstruction: America's Unfinished Revolution, 1863–1877* (New York, 1988); Robert Cruden, *The Negro in Reconstruction* (Englewood Cliffs, N.J., 1969); Leon Litwak, *Been in the Storm So Long: The Aftermath of Slavery* (New York, 1979); Herman Belz, *Emancipation and Equal Rights: Politics and Constitutionalism in the Civil War Era* (New York, 1978); LaWanda Cox, *Lincoln and Black Freedom: A Study in Presidential Leadership* (Columbia, S.C., 1981); W.E.B. Du Bois, *Black Reconstruction* (New York, 1935).

**BLACK SUFFRAGE,** an issue of great significance during Reconstruction. Radicals and abolitionists demanded the enfranchisement of blacks early during the war, but popular prejudice against nonwhite voting was so great that it was politically impossible for the Republican party to endorse it fully at that time. Not only the Southern but also all except a few Northern states, mostly in New England, restricted the right to vote to the dominant race.

Neither of the Reconstruction proposals promulgated during the war, Lincoln's Ten Percent Plan (q.v.) and the Wade-Davis Bill (q.v.), included black suffrage, although a preliminary Senate version of the latter had done so. Abraham Lincoln (q.v.), however, suggested privately to Michael Hahn (q.v.), the first Free State Governor of Louisiana (q.v.), that voting rights be extended at least to well-educated blacks, those with property, and those who had served in the armed services, but his plea was unheeded. In Congress, a radical group led by Charles Sumner (q.v.) held up the readmission of Louisiana because of this omission, and in his last public speech, Lincoln publicly advocated his program of limited enfranchisement for Louisiana. After hearing this appeal, John Wilkes Booth made up his mind to carry out his assassination plot and three days later shot the President.

Andrew Johnson (q.v.) did not favor federal action in support of universal suffrage. In fact, his opposition to black voting rights became one of the main differences between him and an ever-increasing majority of the Republican party, which by 1866 realized that it could not control the Southern states without the help of the freedmen. To be sure, Johnson, like Lincoln, had privately urged Governor William L. Sharkey (q.v.) of Mississippi to extend the suffrage to qualified blacks, but he had done so merely to blunt the radical opposition. None of the states organized under his plan extended the franchise to nonwhites, so Congress in 1866, passing the Fourteenth Amendment (q.v.), threatened a reduction of representation for states disfranchising males over twenty-one years of age. The Republicans voting for this and other measures to aid the freedmen were partially motivated by idealism and partially by political considerations, although they did not yet dare to mandate black voting in the South.

In the elections of 1866, the issue of black suffrage was used by the Democrats to frighten voters while Republicans tended to play it down. After the latters' victory, however, they became bolder, and in 1867 Congress passed the Reconstruction Acts (q.v.), imposing black enfranchisement upon the South and inaugurating the freedmen's participation in politics.

In the North, in the meantime, various state proposals for votes for blacks were uniformly rejected, by Connecticut, Wisconsin, and Minnesota in 1865; Ohio, Kansas, and Minnesota again in 1867; and Michigan and Missouri in 1868. Only in Minnesota and Iowa was the reform finally accepted in 1868, while it had long been voted down in various territories and the District of Columbia, where Congress overode the result of a popular referendum. As late as 1869, however, New York still defeated the reform.

After the election of Ulysses S. Grant (q.v.), the Republican party at last felt strong enough to advocate a constitutional amendment mandating black voting. The Fifteenth Amendment (q.v.), passed in 1869, attested to this resolve, although in its final version it failed to mention the right to hold office or to include safeguards against circumventions. Some viewed the constitutional change as a last fulfillment of an ideological commitment, while others considered it a political device to boster the Republican party (q.v.) in the North.

After the coming of the "Redeemers" ("Redemption," q.v.), black voting in the South gradually diminished. It was not substantially ended, however, until the 1890s, when various Southern states, partially in response to the Populist challenge, found ways of excluding blacks from the suffrage. Poll taxes, understanding-of-the-Constitution, and grandfather clauses were widely used, and it was not until the later twentieth century that the promise of the Fifteenth Amendment was fulfilled.

*See also* Blacks; Congressional Reconstruction; Fifteenth Amendment; Presidential Reconstruction; "Redemption."

William Gillette, *The Right to Vote: Politics and the Passage of the Fifteenth Amendment* (Baltimore, 1965); LaWanda Cox and John H. Cox, "Negro Suffrage and Republican Politics: The Problem of Motivation in Reconstruction Historiography," *Journal of Southern History*, 33 (1967): 303–30; C. Vann Woodward, *The Strange Career of Jim Crow* (3d ed., New York, 1974); Eric Foner, *Reconstruction: America's Unfinished Revolution, 1863–1877* (New York, 1988).

**BLAINE, JAMES GILLESPIE** (1830–1893), Republican political leader, presidential candidate, and Secretary of State, was born in West Brownsville, Pennsylvania. Educated at Washington College, he taught school at the Western Military Institute at Georgetown, Kentucky, and, while studying law, at the Pennsylvania Institute for the Blind at Philadelphia. In 1854 he moved to Augusta, Maine, the home of his wife, to become the editor of the *Kennebec Journal*. For a short time, he was also connected with the Portland *Advertiser*.

Blaine's real interest, however, was politics. A convinced Whig who detested slavery, he was active in the founding of the Republican party (q.v.) in Maine, became a delegate to its first national convention in 1856, and ever after considered loyalty to the party the greatest of virtues. Elected to the lower house of the state legislature in 1858, he served as Speaker of the House from 1861 to 1862 and headed the State Republican Committee from 1859 to 1881. A strong supporter of Abraham Lincoln (q.v.), in 1862 he was elected to the national House of Representatives where he remained until 1876. In 1869 he was chosen Speaker of the House, a position he retained until the Democrats returned to power in 1875.

Like Lincoln, Blaine favored antislavery policies and the uplifting of the blacks (q.v.) but shunned extreme measures. A moderate, he supported the party in its struggle with President Andrew Johnson (q.v.) and endorsed most congressional Reconstruction measures. Yet he believed the Reconstruction Act (q.v.) ought to provide for the restoration of the states complying with it and introduced an amendment for that purpose.

A genial colleague and captivating public speaker, he enjoyed great popularity. Yet in 1866 he so insulted Roscoe Conkling (q.v.) by referring to the New Yorker's "turkey gobbler strut" that a lifelong enmity resulted. The two bitter antagonists each had his following within the Republican party, the Stalwarts supporting Conkling and the Half-Breeds sympathizing with Blaine.

In 1876, in support of his amendment to an amnesty bill excluding Jefferson Davis (q.v.), Blaine, successfully waving the "bloody shirt" (q.v.), delivered a slashing speech attacking the Confederate leader. It seemed to make the "Plumed Knight," as he was called, the logical successor to the President; yet revelations of favors he had bestowed upon land-grant railroads, in particular the Little Rock and Ft. Smith, allegedly in return for preferred treatment, frustrated his ambition. Although he attempted to refute the charges by reading excerpts from the so-called Mulligan letters in the House, and although this dramatic reply appeared to be successful, it did not dispel the ugly rumors ever after connected with his name. He failed to win the nomination but was elected to the Senate, where he remained until 1881. When in 1880 he sought the nomination, he defeated the bid of U. S. Grant (q.v.) for a third term, but Conkling made his own success impossible, so the prize went to James A. Garfield (q.v.), who in 1881 appointed him Secretary of State.

Blaine was widely considered the leading figure of the new administration.

He frustrated the Stalwarts' hopes for patronage and carried out a "spirited" foreign policy of involvement in Latin American affairs and resistance to British pretensions. The President's assassination interrupted the Secretary's career, and he resigned in December 1881.

In 1884 Blaine, who had used the interval to write the first volume of his *Twenty Years of Congress*, finally obtained his party's nomination for the presidency. But Republican reformers, repelled by his dubious reputation, bolted and supported his Democratic opponent, Grover Cleveland, who narrowly defeated him. The vanquished candidate then completed the second volume of his *Twenty Years of Congress*, traveled to Europe, and seemed hesitant to run again in 1888, when Benjamin Harrison won the nomination and election. Blaine's reward was a renewed appointment to the State Department, which he used to carry out his dream of founding an inter-American organization, to add a reciprocity clause to the McKinley tariff of 1890, and to defend American claims to control pelagic sealing. Three days before the 1892 Republican convention he handed in his resignation and died in January 1893.

Blaine was a good example of the Gilded Age politicians who succeeded the Civil War and Reconstruction Republican leaders. Still using "bloody shirt" (q.v.) oratory to win political victories, he was probably more interested in the economic and party-political issues of the postwar period than in the problems of Reconstruction.

*See also* Bloody Shirt; Conkling, Roscoe.

David Saville Muzzey, *James Gillespie Blaine: A Political Idol of Other Days* (New York, 1935); Charles Edward Russell, *Blaine of Maine: His Life and Times* (New York, 1931).

**BLAIR, FRANCIS PRESTON, JR.** (1821–1875), statesman, general, Unionist, was born at Lexington, Kentucky, the son of Francis P. Blair, the famous Jacksonian Democrat. Educated at Yale, the University of North Carolina, Princeton, and Transylvania University, he settled in St. Louis to practice law. During the Mexican War, he took part in Stephen Kearney's campaign in New Mexico and served briefly as Attorney General of the territory. Elected to the state legislature in 1852, he became one of the founders of the free soil movement and later the Republican party (q.v.) in Missouri (q.v.). In spite of his strong opposition to slavery, he was convinced of the inferiority of the black race, which he believed ought to be colonized in Latin America.

In his racial and political views, he reflected the ideas of his family, particularly those of his father and his brother Montgomery. Together, the Blairs exercised a strong influence on succeeding administrations as well as on Congress, to which Frank was elected in 1856. He immediately stood out as a critic of slavery and a strong Unionist, so in 1860 he campaigned enthusiastically for Abraham Lincoln (q.v.). After Fort Sumter, he was instrumental in holding St. Louis for the Union. Although he favored the appointment of General John C. Frémont to command the Western Department, after the general's arrival at St. Louis, he became highly critical of the Pathfinder. The two men differed in ideology; Blair was conservative and Frémont radical, and Blair also became convinced that the general was incompetent. He so informed his brother Montgomery, then Lincoln's Postmaster General, an action for which Frémont put him under arrest. In the long run, the President finally recalled the flamboyant commander.

Resigning his seat in Congress in order to enter the army, Blair distinguished himself in the Yazoo expedition, at Chattanooga, Atlanta, and in the march through Georgia, where he commanded the Seventeenth Army Corps. Though briefly returning to Congress in 1863, he was present at the Confederates' surrender to General William T. Sherman (q.v.) in North Carolina.

After the war, the Blairs became strong supporters of President Andrew Johnson (q.v.) and his conservative Reconstruction policy. Convinced of the necessity for white supremacy, the family sought to use its considerable influence with the President in favor of colonization, continued opposition to black suffrage (q.v.), and a speedy restoration of Southern leaders to citizenship. Frank, whom Johnson appointed a railroad commissioner, actively fought against the radical constitution of Missouri, which he attempted to defy by refusing to take the required test oath for voting, and became one of the mainstays of the opposition Conservative Union party. Like his father and brother, he had hopes for the emergence of a new alignment of conservative Republicans and Democrats in 1866 and heartily supported the Philadelphia National Union Convention (q.v.). Rejoining the Democrats, in 1868 he became their candidate for Vice President.

The 1868 campaign was seen by the Blairs as a splendid opportunity to reverse the hated Reconstruction policy of Congress. However, his injudicious letter to the Missouri politician James O. Broadhead, in which Frank advocated presidential resistance to the Reconstruction Acts (q.v.) whether or not the Republican controlled Senate concurred, stamped him a revolutionary extremist, and it contributed to his defeat and that of his running mate, Horatio Seymour (q.v.).

Yet after the election of U. S. Grant (q.v.), neither Frank nor his family gave up their struggle against Congressional Reconstruction (q.v.). Actively engaged in the reorganization of parties in Missouri, Frank, who was elected to another term in the state legislature, became a leader of the new Liberal Republican (q.v.) organization. Elevated to the Senate in 1870, he took a prominent part in the 1872 Cincinnati Convention, which nominated Horace Greeley (q.v.) for the presidency.

The defeat of the Liberal Republican ticket ended Blair's political career. Weakened by a stroke, he died in St. Louis in 1875.

*See also* Liberal Republican Movement; Missouri; Seymour, Horatio.

William Ernest Smith, *The Francis Preston Blair Family in Politics* (2 vols., New York, 1933); Elbert B. Smith, *Francis Preston Blair* (New York, 1980); William E. Parrish, *Missouri Under Radical Rule, 1865–1870* (Columbia, Mo., 1965).

**BLAIR, FRANCIS PRESTON, SR.** *See* BLAIR, FRANCIS PRESTON, JR.

**BLAIR, MONTGOMERY.** *See* BLAIR, FRANCIS PRESTON, JR.

**BLOODY SHIRT,** "waving the bloody shirt," an expression referring to the invocation of wartime hatreds to gain votes for the Republican party. General Benjamin F. Butler (q.v.) actually displayed a bloodied shirt of a Unionist murdered by the Ku Klux Klan (q.v.) to the Senate, and public orators made use of the device in various election campaigns. The best-known examples are speeches by Oliver P. Morton (q.v.) in 1866 calling the Democratic party (q.v.) "a common sewer and loathsome receptacle into which is emptied every element of treason North and South," by James G. Blaine (q.v.) in 1876 in support of an amendment excluding Jefferson Davis (q.v.) from an amnesty bill, and by Robert G. Ingersoll during the campaign of 1876 claiming that "every enemy this government has had for twenty years has been and is a Democrat." With the passing of wartime passions, the practice waned.

　*See also* Blaine, James Gillespie; Morton, Oliver Perry.

　Paul H. Buck, *The Road to Reunion, 1865–1900* (New York, 1937); Kenneth M. Stampp, *The Era of Reconstruction, 1865–1877* (New York, 1965); Stanley F. Horn, *Invisible Empire: The Story of the Ku Klux Klan, 1866–1871* (Boston, 1939).

**BOUTWELL, GEORGE SEWALL** (1818–1905), Governor of Massachusetts, radical congressman and Senator, and Secretary of the Treasury, was born in Brookline, Massachusetts. Taken to Lunenburg by his farmer father at the age of two, he was educated in the local schools, clerked in a store, and in 1835 settled in nearby Groton. He was an active Democrat who in 1841 was elected to the lower house of the state legislature. Reelected frequently until 1850, he established an enviable reputation for leadership, which in 1851 and 1852 resulted in his election as Governor by a combination of Democrats and Free Soilers. From 1855 to 1861 he served as secretary of the Massachusetts Board of Education.

　One of the founders of the state Republican party (q.v.), he was a member of the national convention that nominated Abraham Lincoln (q.v.) as well as the 1861 Peace Convention in Washington. In 1862, when he was admitted to the bar, Lincoln appointed him the first commissioner of internal revenue.

　From 1863 to 1869 Boutwell was a member of the House of Representatives. A radical Republican, he served on the Joint Committee of Fifteen on Reconstruction (q.v.), helped draft the Fourteenth Amendment (q.v.) and particularly the Fifteenth Amendment (q.v.) and submitted the report in support of the first attempt to impeach President Andrew Johnson (q.v.) in December 1867. Two months later, he became one of the managers of the impeachment trial.

　In 1869 President U. S. Grant (q.v.) appointed Boutwell Secretary of the Treasury, a position the radical statesman used chiefly to reduce the national debt. He broke the gold conspiracy somewhat belatedly on Black Friday (q.v.)

in September 1869 and in 1870 recommended the passage of the Funding Bill of that year. Elected Senator in 1873, he remained true to his radical convictions and conducted an investigation into the fraudulent Mississippi (q.v.) election of 1875. Failing to secure reelection in 1877, he was appointed a commissioner to revise the statutes of the United States and then returned to Boston to practice law.

Although no longer in Congress, Boutwell continued to be an active Republican until he broke with his party on the issue of imperialism and assumed the presidency of the Anti-Imperialist League. He represented the government before a board of international arbitrators attempting to settle claims of citizens of France and of the United States while appearing as counsel for Hawaii in opposition to abrogate the reciprocity treaty with that country. In addition, he was active as an author, particularly in writing his memoirs, *Reminiscences of Fifty Years in Public Affairs*. He died at Groton in 1905.

A thoroughgoing radical whose devotion to freedmen's rights was sincere, Boutwell at times seemed too extreme to be effective. Nevertheless, his efforts in behalf of Reconstruction and especially the Fifteenth Amendment were impressive.

*See also* Black Friday; Fifteenth Amendment; Fourteenth Amendment; Grant, Ulysses Simpson; Johnson, Andrew.

George S. Boutwell, *Reminiscences of Fifty Years in Public Affairs* (New York, 1902); Hans L. Trefousse, *The Radical Republicans: Lincoln's Vanguard for Racial Justice* (New York, 1969); Michael Les Benedict, *A Compromise of Principle: Congressional Republicans and Reconstruction, 1863–1869* (New York, 1974).

**BRISTOW, BENJAMIN HELM** (1832–1896), Kentucky Unionist, Secretary of the Treasury, and reformer, was born in Elkton, Kentucky, the son of a prominent local lawyer and congressman. Educated at Jefferson (now Washington and Jefferson) College in Washington, Pennsylvania, he early imbibed strong nationalistic antislavery opinions. A convinced Whig, he practiced law, first with his father at Elkton and then on his own at Hopkinsville, and in 1860 supported the Constitutional Union ticket. Joining the Hopkinsville Guards, he recruited Union forces and took part in the capture of Ft. Donelson as well as the Battle of Shiloh, where he was wounded. From 1863 to 1865 he served in the state Senate, in which he stood out as the leader of the unconditional Unionists.

When the war was over, Bristow was appointed Assistant and then U.S. Attorney for Kentucky and moved to Louisville. Distinguishing himself by prosecuting marauding Regulators and members of the Ku Klux Klan (q.v.), he fearlessly enforced the Civil Rights Act of 1866 (q.v.) and sought justice for the blacks.

President Ulysses S. Grant (q.v.) appointed Bristow Solicitor General (1870), a position in which he established an enviable record as a government attorney who successfully upheld the constitutionality of the Civil Rights Act (q.v.) and the Confiscation and Force Acts. Resigning in 1872, he became general counsel of the Texas and Pacific Railroad and later president of the Texas and Pacific Construction Company but soon returned to private practice in Louisville. Although he was rumored to be in line for Attorney General, in 1874 the President appointed him Secretary of the Treasury to take the place of the severely compromised William A. Richardson.

Bristow's tenure of office marked him as a reformer of the first rank. Fearlessly striking at corrupt officials, he cleaned out his department and established civil service rules for his subordinates. At the same time, he successfully negotiated the conversion of government bonds from 6 to 5 percent and joined Hamilton Fish (q.v.) in seeking to end military intervention in Louisiana (q.v.). In 1875 he moved against the powerful Whiskey Ring (q.v.), which he managed to destroy. In the process, however, he became estranged from the President, particularly as his investigations led to the indictment of Grant's private secretary, Orville E. Babcock (q.v.). He also learned of the corrupt dealings of Secretary of War William W. Belknap (q.v.) and brought them to the President's attention, but Grant became convinced that the Secretary was using the office to advance his own ambitions for the presidency.

In 1876, because of his record as a reformer, Bristow became an active candidate for the nomination. Although he received a large vote on the first ballot at the Cincinnati Convention, he finally lost to Rutherford B. Hayes (q.v.). Resigning from the cabinet in June 1876, he loyally supported the ticket but failed to be appointed either to the cabinet or to the Supreme Court. He resumed the practice of law, first in Kentucky and then in New York; frequently advised several Presidents; and in 1884, like other reform Republicans, supported Grover Cleveland against James G. Blaine (q.v.), with whom he had broken in 1876. Rejoining the Republican party (q.v.) in 1888, he was one of the counsel for the appellants in the famous income tax case of 1895. He died in New York one year later.

*See also* Corruption; Grant, Ulysses Simpson; Whiskey Ring.

Ross A. Webb, *Benjamin Helm Bristow: Border State Politician* (Lexington, Ky., 1969).


**BROOKS-BAXTER WAR,** a conflict in Arkansas (q.v.) between the carpetbagger (q.v.) Joseph Brooks and the scalawag (q.v.) Elisha Baxter, two rival claimants for the office of governor. In the elections of 1872, Baxter, backed by the "Minstrel" faction of radical Republicans, claimed victory, but Brooks, a member of the opposing "Brindletails," who had run on a reform Republican ticket backed by the Democratic-Conservatives, disputed the result. Despite Brooks' efforts to obtain a court ruling in his favor, Baxter was inaugurated. A franchise-law election in March 1873 repealed the disabilities under which the former Confederates had been laboring, and Baxter, refusing to countenance some of Senator Powell Clayton's (q.v.) railroad schemes, drew closer to his former opponents. At the same time, Brooks became more and more beholden to the radical Republicans and, in April 1874, finally found a judge who ruled in his favor. The two contestants now confronted each other with two rival sets of officials and two groups of clashing armed retainers. Although Baxter had lost the backing of his former patron, Senator Clayton, the Grant administration, after first favoring his opponent, in May 1874 upheld Baxter. The "war" ended, elections for a new constitutional convention were called, and the "Redeemers" ("Redemption," q.v.) recaptured the state. Notwithstanding a last-minute effort of the administration to interfere, now in favor of Brooks, Congress refused to countenance federal action, and the new administration of Augustus H. Garland was left unmolested.

*See also* Arkansas; Clayton, Powell.

J. M. Harrell, *The Brooks-Baxter War: A History of the Reconstruction Period in Arkansas* (St. Louis, 1893); William Gillette, *Retreat from Reconstruction, 1869–1879* (Baton Rouge, 1979); George Thompson, *Arkansas and Reconstruction* (Port Washington, N.Y., 1976).

**BROWN, BENJAMIN GRATZ** (1826–1885), Missouri Senator and Governor, was born in Lexington, Kentucky, the son of Mason Brown, a lawyer and later judge, and Judith Bledsoe Brown, whose aunt married Benjamin Gratz, of the famous Philadelphia family. Brought up in Frankfort, Brown was educated at Transylvania and Yale Universities as well as at the Louisville Law School. In 1849 he moved to St. Louis to join his cousin Francis P. Blair (q.v.) in a law firm. Although of Whig background, he joined the Benton Democratic party and engaged in journalism, becoming the editor-in-chief of the *Missouri Democrat* in 1854. Elected to the state legislature in 1852, 1854, and 1856, he furthered the political fortunes of Thomas Hart Benton and gained the support of the important German-American element in Missouri (q.v.). He was defeated in 1858 but soon recovered as one of the founders of the Free Soil and Republican parties (q.v.) in the state.

A convinced Unionist, Brown took a determined stand against secession. Breaking with Blair, during the Civil War he favored the radicals who advocated speedy emancipation. In 1863 he was elected to the U.S. Senate, where he opposed the renomination of Abraham Lincoln (q.v.), favored the enfranchisement of freedmen as well as women, but opposed the Wade-Davis Bill (q.v.) on the grounds that Reconstruction was too important a subject to be considered in haste.

In Missouri, still adamantly calling for black and female suffrage, Brown opposed the radical Drake constitution, which omitted these features. "Freedom and Franchise" was his slogan; yet he gradually turned more conservative and opposed the stringent test oath that kept former secessionists and their sympathizers from voting. After his retirement from the Senate in 1867, he became one of the leaders of the Liberal Republican movement (q.v.). Elected governor in 1870, he effected a reconciliation with Blair, who was sent to the Senate. In 1872, at the Liberal Republican convention in Cincinnati, he had hopes of obtaining the presidential nomination, but when he saw that this ambition could not be realized, he appeared in person to secure the victory of Horace Greeley (q.v.). He himself was nominated for Vice President. His actions greatly annoyed leading Liberals such as Carl Schurz (q.v.), and the ticket was defeated in the ensuing election.

After this debacle, Brown retired to Ironton to engage in business and the law. He rejoined the Democratic party, moved to Kirkwood near St. Louis, and died there in 1885.

*See also* Blair, Francis Preston, Jr.; Liberal Republican Movement; Missouri.

Norma Peterson, *Freedom and Franchise: The Political Career of B. Gratz Brown* (Columbia, Mo., 1965).


**BROWN, JOSEPH EMERSON** (1821–1894), Governor of Georgia (q.v.), scalawag, and Democratic Senator, was born at Long Creek, Pickens District, South Carolina. When still a small boy, he was taken to Union County in northern Georgia, where he worked on the family farm and in 1840 went to South Carolina to attend Calhoun Academy in the Anderson District. He returned to Georgia in 1844 to take charge of an academy at Canton, read law, and was admitted to the bar in 1845. The completion of his legal education at Yale gave him a good grounding in his profession, which he then practiced successfully at Canton. He defeated Benjamin H. Hill in a race for the state senate in 1849, became a Democratic presidential elector in 1852, and was elected judge of the Blue Ridge Circuit in 1855. Two years later, as a result of a deadlock between other contenders, he won the governorship, a position to which he was reelected until the end of the Civil War.

As Governor, Brown furthered public education and the state-owned Western and Atlantic Railroad. A determined secessionist, he called the secession convention, seized Fort Pulaski before Georgia had even seceded, and proceeded to arm the state. Nevertheless, he was such a staunch advocate of states rights that he continually quarreled with Jefferson Davis (q.v.), generally about conscription and the Georgia state troops.

After the war, Brown sought to reassemble the state legislature but was arrested by the federal authorities. Quickly released by Andrew Johnson (q.v.), he established close relations with the President, whose policies he wholeheartedly supported. However, believing that submission to the victor was the best policy for Georgia, he advised the acceptance of not only the Fourteenth Amendment (q.v.) but later of the Reconstruction Acts (q.v.) as well.

This action signaled Brown's transition into the Republican party (q.v.). Advising compliance with congressional demands but trying to keep them to a minimum, he exercised a moderating influence on the constitutional convention of 1868 and used his influence to help elect Rufus B. Bullock (q.v.) Governor. Yet in spite of the latter's support, he failed to win a seat in the U.S. Senate. The Governor then appointed him Chief Justice of the Supreme Court, a position that was congenial to him.

Contrary to the expectations of many Republicans whom he addressed amid much applause at the National Convention of 1868, Brown never became a radical. Opposing further Republican measures, he broke with Bullock and in 1872 supported the Liberal Republican ticket (Liberal Republican Movement, q.v.). Rejoining the Democratic party, he went to Florida in 1876–1877 to argue the Democratic case before the local canvassing board. Although he lost the case and Rutherford B. Hayes (q.v.) was elected, his reward was an appointment to the Senate after Senator John B. Gordon resigned in 1880. Reelected later that year and in 1884, he served in the upper house until 1891 as a typical representative of the New South.

Brown's identification with the New South was marked by his interest in various industrial and business enterprises. Settled in Atlanta, he continued to practice law but also invested in mining, banking, and agriculture. He even resigned from the court in 1880 to accept the presidency of the Western and Atlantic Railroad. Known for his business acumen, he amassed a fortune, although his reputation was clouded by the employment of convict labor. He died in 1894 in Atlanta.

*See also* Georgia; Scalawags.

Derrell C. Roberts, *Joseph E. Brown and the Politics of Reconstruction* (University, Ala., 1973); Joseph H. Parks, *Joseph E. Brown of Georgia* (Baton Rouge, 1977).

**BROWNING, ORVILLE HICKMAN** (1806–1881), conservative Republican Senator and Secretary of the Interior, was born near Cynthiana, Kentucky. After attending nearby Augusta College and reading law with local attorneys, he was admitted to the bar in 1831 and settled in Quincy, Illinois, to pursue his profession. An active Whig, in 1836 he was elected to the state Senate, where he formed a friendship with Abraham Lincoln (q.v.), then a member of the lower house, with whom he cooperated in moving the state capital from Vandalia to Springfield, although opposing the simultaneous scheme of aid to internal improvements. Refusing to run again at the expiration of his term in 1840, he was nevertheless elected to the lower house two years later and in 1843 unsuccessfully challenged Stephen A. Douglas in a bid for the national House of Representatives. Further attempts to obtain a seat in Congress in 1850 and 1852 ended in failure.

Browning was firmly opposed to the extension of slavery into the territories and cooperated in the founding of the Republican party (q.v.) in Illinois. But, believing in the inferiority and colonization of blacks (q.v.), he represented the conservative wing of the new organization, for which he framed platform planks designed to attract former Whigs. In keeping with his conservative convictions, in 1860 he favored the nomination of Edward Bates.

After the death of Senator Douglas, Governor Richard Yates appointed Browning to Douglas' seat in the U.S. Senate. There he at first supported Lincoln's policies, but dissatisfaction with the second Confiscation Act and the Emancipation Proclamation (q.v.) drove the two men apart. His bitter opposition to the radical Republicans' (q.v.) racial and constitutional policies caused him to become their determined antagonist and to refuse to support the Union party ticket in 1864. At the end of his term in 1863, he established a Washington law firm in partnership with fellow conservatives such as Thomas Ewing, Sr., and Edgar Cowan and engaged in extensive lobbying.

After the assassination of Lincoln, Browning drew close to the new President. Fully in accord with Andrew Johnson's (q.v.) Reconstruction policy of considering the seceded states still part of the Union and totally hostile to Congressional Reconstruction (q.v.), by the summer of 1866 he had become one of the President's confidential advisers. Together with Cowan, James R. Doolittle (q.v.), Alexander W. Randall, and other conservatives, he participated in Johnson's call for the National Union Convention (q.v.) in Philadelphia, took an active part in its proceedings, and afterward joined the cabinet as Secretary of the Interior. During the impeachment, he briefly occupied the vacant office of Attorney General as well and loyally supported the President. In 1868 his opposition to congressional policies led him to endorse the Democratic candidate for President, Horatio Seymour (q.v.).

At the close of his term, Browning returned to Quincy, where he was elected a delegate to the Illinois constitutional convention of 1869–1870. Still a confirmed conservative, he opposed black suffrage (q.v.) and furthered minority representation in voting. His diary furnishes a valuable source for his years in politics. Toward the end of his life, he was active as a railroad attorney and represented the Chicago, Burlington, and Quincy Railroad in the *Granger* cases. He died in Quincy in 1881.

*See also* Johnson, Andrew; National Union Convention.

Maurice Baxter, *Orville H. Browning: Lincoln's Friend and Critic* (Bloomington, Ind., 1957); *The Diary of Orville Hickman Browning*, in Theodore C. Pease and J. G. Randall, eds., *Illinois Historical Collections*, 20, 22 (Springfield, Ill., 1927–1933).


**BROWNLOW, WILLIAM GANNAWAY** (1805–1877), Methodist preacher, journalist, Unionist Governor, and Senator from Tennessee, was born near Wytheville, Virginia. Orphaned at an early age, he was reared by an uncle, then engaged in carpentry at Abingdon, and at a Methodist camp meeting decided to enter the ministry. Studying by himself, in 1826 he was accepted as a circuit rider in the Holston Conference of the Methodist Church and four years later given elder's orders.

Brownlow's preaching was so marked by his characteristic style of vituperation and denunciation of opponents, chiefly Presbyterians and Baptists, that in 1833 he was convicted of libel at Franklin, North Carolina, and as early as 1834 published the first of a series of contentious books, *Helps to the Study of Presbyterianism*, an attack on the competing denomination with an appended autobiography.

In 1836 Brownlow married Eliza O'Brien of Carter County, Tennessee, whose father gave him employment in his ironworks. But then he discovered his second vocation, journalism, and in 1839 published his first newspaper, the *Tennessee Whig*, in Elizabethtown.

From the very beginning, the Parson's vituperative articles caught the attention of friends and opponents alike. A convinced Whig, he praised his idol, Henry Clay, while engaging in furious rows with Democrats, Presbyterians, and Baptists. One of his antagonists was Andrew Johnson (q.v.), then at the beginning of his political career, whom he attacked unmercifully.

Brownlow soon moved his paper to Jonesboro, where he continued to engage in perpetual controversy. In 1843 he ran for Congress against Johnson, who, after a campaign marked by unparalleled slander, defeated him. In 1849 he took his newspaper, renamed *Brownlow's Knoxville Whig and Independent Journal*, to Knoxville, where he resided until his death. A spokesman for the Whig party, he endorsed the Know-Nothings after its demise and continued thundering against Democrats and abolitionists. In 1858 he even traveled to Philadelphia to engage in a spirited debate on slavery with the abolitionist clergyman Abraham Pryne.

But Brownlow loved the Union, and when the secession crisis threw Tennessee into turmoil, he became one of the leaders of the Unionists. Ever more aggressive, his newspaper continued its attacks on the Confederates even after the state seceded. Not until October 1861 did he suspend the *Whig* and flee into the mountains; he returned only after a promise of protection and a pass through the lines by the Confederate authorities. Nevertheless, he was arrested following the Unionists' burning of bridges in East Tennessee and was briefly confined to the Knoxville jail until in March 1863 he was permitted to pass through the lines.

Upon his arrival in Nashville, the Parson was welcomed by his old antagonist and recent ally, Andrew Johnson. Giving full expression to his loyalist and anti-Confederate opinions on a speaking tour throughout the North and in his autobiographical *Parson Brownlow's Book*, he became a celebrity and was widely hailed as a hero. When in 1863 Knoxville fell to the federal forces, he returned to resume the publication of his newspaper, now called *Brownlow's Knoxville Whig and Rebel Ventilator*, espoused emancipation though still favoring colonization, and in 1865 was elected Governor of the state under its new constitution.

As Governor of Tennessee (q.v.), Brownlow was responsible for the franchise law that deprived former Confederates of the right to vote. In 1866, favoring Congress in its struggle with the President, he broke once again with his old foe and, by forcibly retaining some legislators in the capitol to obtain a quorum, saw to it that the state ratified the Fourteenth Amendment (q.v.). Reelected in 1867, he strengthened the franchise law, raised a state militia to enforce it, fought the Ku Klux Klan (q.v.), and finally came out in favor of black suffrage (q.v.). In 1869 he went to the U.S. Senate and supported his successor, DeWitt C. Senter (q.v.), the speaker of the state Senate, for Governor, although Senter was ready to repeal the franchise law. The Parson, ill and barely able to speak, served out his term to return to Knoxville in 1875, where he died two years later.

An outspoken, quarrelsome editor and politician, Brownlow was personally honest but unable to prevent widespread corruption, particularly in connection with the railroads, while he was Governor. His steadfastness in defense of the Union was his greatest contribution.

*See also* Johnson, Andrew; Senter, DeWitt Clinton; Tennessee.

E. Merton Coulter, *William G. Brownlow, Fighting Parson of the Southern Highlands* (Chapel Hill, N.C., 1937); Steve Humphrey, *"That D—d Brownlow"* (Boone, N.C., 1978).

**BRUCE, BLANCHE KELSO** (1841–1898), Senator from Mississippi (q.v.), was born a slave in Prince Edward County, Virginia. Brought up as his master's son's companion, the light-skinned Bruce received a good education at the plantation and never experienced the harsher aspects of slavery. His master took him to Mississippi and then to Missouri, but he left the plantation during the Civil War and moved to Lawrence, Kansas, where he established a school for blacks. In 1864 he settled in Hannibal, Missouri, to found a similar institution, while working as a printer's devil at the same time.

After the war, Bruce attended Oberlin College but soon returned to Missouri to work on a Mississippi steamboat. With opportunity beckoning in the heavily black state of Mississippi, he decided to try his fortune there. Soon becoming politically active, he was appointed a voter registrar in Tallahatchie County and, when in 1870 the new legislature convened, was selected as sergeant-at-arms of the Senate. Two years later, Governor James L. Alcorn (q.v.) appointed him tax assessor of Bolivar County. Making this Delta county his home, he established a powerful political organization there and in the following election was returned to his former office as well as to that of sheriff. In addition, he was appointed superintendent of education. A man of excellent manners, he distinguished himself by his honest, efficient, and nonvindictive performance of his duties and gained the respect of all factions, black and white alike. His business acumen led him to acquire land and a plantation in the county, and eventually he amassed a considerable fortune.

In 1872 Bruce was one of the Mississippi delegates to the Republican national convention—in fact, he was a member of every one from 1868 to 1896. After turning down an offer to become Lieutenant Governor tendered to him by Senator Adelbert Ames (q.v.), in 1874 he was elected to the U.S. Senate. When his colleague, Senator James Lusk Alcorn (q.v.), now the head of the opposing Republican faction, refused to escort him to the chair to take the oath of office, Roscoe Conkling (q.v.) performed this service instead and became a lifelong friend.

During his term of office, Bruce again distinguished himself by honest, efficient service. A member of the standing committees on pensions, manufactures, and education and labor, as well as of the select ones on Mississippi River improvements and on the Freedman's Bank, he spoke forcefully for the interests of his race, opposed restrictions on Chinese immigration, and pleaded for better treatment of the Indians. In addition, he cooperated with other Senators from the valley in an unsuccessful effort to obtain the passage of a bill safeguarding the Mississippi against floods.

Bruce's belief in black assimilation into American life never wavered. A determined opponent of emigration and colonization, he refused to countenance the 1879 Kansas and Liberia schemes. He also pleaded strongly though unsuccessfully for the right of Louisiana's black Senator-elect, Pinckney P.B.S. Pinchback (q.v.), to take his seat and sought to have Congress investigate the scandalous Mississippi elections of 1875, which were marked by force and violence and resulted in the overthrow of the radical regime in the state. Together with John R. Lynch (q.v.) and James Hill, he established black control over the Republican party in Mississippi, yet maintained good relations with his colleague the "Redeemer" ("Redemption," q.v.) Lucius Q. Lamar (q.v.) while favoring the removal of disabilities from former Confederates.

Having married a light-skinned, polished, Cleveland dentist's daughter, Bruce moved freely in white society, and after the expiration of his term of office he remained in Washington. President James A. Garfield appointed him register of the treasury; Benjamin Harrison, recorder of deeds; and William McKinley, register of the treasury again. He died at Washington in 1898.

Always a strong assimilationist, Bruce earned the enmity of a number of blacks. Yet his refined manners, probity, and impeccable honesty in an age of widespread corruption gained him the respect of many others, both black and white. As the only black Senator to serve a full term before the 1960s, he established a record of which he could be proud.

*See also* Alcorn, James Lusk; Ames, Adelbert; Conkling, Roscoe; Lynch, John Roy; Mississippi.

William C. Harris, "Blanche K. Bruce of Mississippi: Conservative Assimilationist," in Howard N. Rabinowitz, ed., *Southern Black Leaders in the Reconstruction Era* (Urbana, Ill., 1982).


**BULLOCK, RUFUS BROWN** (1834–1907), Reconstruction Governor of Georgia (q.v.). Born in Bethlehem, New York, Bullock was educated at Albion Academy, from which he graduated at the age of sixteen. He mastered the House system of telegraphy, a skill that enabled him to become a trusted employee at the Adams Express Co. In 1859 his employer sent him to Augusta, Georgia, where he organized the Southern Express Company and made the city his home.

Opposed to secession, he nevertheless went with his adopted state and served in the Confederate army. After the war, he organized the first National Bank of Augusta and assumed the presidency of the Macon and Atlanta Railroad.

Bullock favored the acceptance of Congressional Reconstruction (q.v.). Joining the radical Republicans (q.v.), he played an important role in the constitutional convention of 1867, and in 1868, with the aid of Joseph E. Brown (q.v.), became Governor of Georgia. But he was faced with a hostile legislature, which, defying his wishes, ousted its black members. Thereupon he advised Congress to reestablish military rule, a policy that caused moderate Republicans, including Brown, to break with him. His proposal was not accepted until December 1869, when Congress required Georgia to fulfill certain conditions before readmission. These included the restoration of blacks (q.v.) to their offices, the ratification of the Fifteenth Amendment (q.v.), and the strict enforcement of the test oath for members of the legislature. The result was a purge of the body and the establishment of a pro-Bullock majority that ratified the amendment. To perpetuate his regime, the Governor tried to have the legislature elected in 1868 remain in office for two more years, but Congress refused. When in 1871 the Democrats had reestablished control, Bullock resigned to escape impeachment and fled from the state.

Because of charges of corruption against the Governor, particularly in connection with mismanagement of state-owned railroads and his collaboration with the dubious financier Hannibal I. Kimball, an investigating committee of the legislature thoroughly examined Bullock's tenure of office and concluded that gross corruption had permeated the administration. Bullock, who had moved to Albion, New York, was arrested there in 1876 and brought back to Atlanta. Acquitted after his ensuing trial, he reestablished himself in Georgia. Serving as president of the chamber of commerce as well as one of the directors of the Atlanta Piedmont Exhibition of 1887, he seemed to have overcome the prejudices against him; yet a few years later he had to leave once again under dubious circumstances and returned to Albion, where he died in 1907.

An affable, able entrepreneur, Bullock was never fully able to refute the charges of corruption brought against him. His dubious methods of attempting to prolong his regime also seriously stained his reputation.

See also Brown, Joseph Emerson; Congressional Reconstruction; Georgia.

Alan Conway, *The Reconstruction of Georgia* (Minneapolis, 1966); C. Mildred Thompson, *Reconstruction in Georgia: Economic, Social, Political, 1865–1872* (New York, 1915); Elizabeth Studley Nathans, *Losing the Peace: Georgia Republicans and Reconstruction, 1865–1871* (Minneapolis, 1966).

**BUTLER, BENJAMIN FRANKLIN** (1818–1893), Civil War general, congressman, and Governor of Massachusetts, was born at Deerfield, New Hampshire, the son of a seaman who died five months after Butler's birth. After a term at Phillips Exeter, he attended the local high school at Lowell, Massachusetts, where his mother had opened a boarding house for the factory girls, as well as Waterville College in Maine. Admitted to the bar in 1840, he soon established a flourishing practice at Lowell and Boston. Joining the Democratic party as a convinced Jacksonian, in 1853 he was elected to the lower house at the state legislature and in 1859 to the state Senate. As a member of the 1860 Democratic convention at Charleston, he voted more than fifty times for Jefferson Davis (q.v.), and his party nominated him for Governor on the Breckinridge Democratic ticket.

In April 1861 Butler, a brigadier general, led his troops to the relief of beleaguered Washington and secured Baltimore. Promoted to major general, he took command at Fortress Monroe, where he made a name for himself by declaring runaway slaves who had been employed by the Confederate army "contraband of war." He lost the engagement at Big Bethel but retrieved his reputation by assisting in the capture of the forts at Cape Hatteras. In 1862 he accompanied David G. Farragut to seize New Orleans, which he then ruled with an iron hand. He saw to it that elections were held for Congress, raised one of the first black regiments, and, severely punishing those who resisted federal rule, executed a gambler who had torn down the American flag. Rumors of corruption and his frequent clashes with foreign consuls brought about his recall, even though he had gained great popularity in the North because of his order to treat any "female" who misbehaved toward his troops as "a woman of the town plying her avocation."

In November 1863 Butler, now turned radical, was placed in command of the Department of Virginia and North Carolina. Leading the Army of the James against Richmond in 1864, he found himself "bottled up" at Bermuda Hundred and in January 1865 was recalled after his failure to take Fort Fisher.

When Andrew Johnson (q.v.) became President, Butler was mentioned as a possible member of the cabinet, but he soon broke with the President. Elected to Congress as a radical Republican (q.v.), he stood out as one of the most contentious members who was one of the earliest advocates of the impeachment of Johnson (q.v.) and served as one of the managers during the trial. In U.S. Grant's (q.v.) first Congress he took over the House Committee on Reconstruction, a position he used to work for the imposition of new conditions on the remaining unreconstructed states, the remanding of Georgia (q.v.) to military rule, and the passage of the 1871 Ku Klux and 1875 Civil Rights Acts (q.v.). In addition, he built up a powerful machine that steadfastly supported President Grant. Defeated in 1874, he returned to Congress in 1877, this time from the Middlesex District.

As early as 1871, Butler sought the governorship. He tried again in 1873, but his soft-money views and unpopularity with the Brahmin establishment defeated his quest for the nomination. In 1878 and 1879 he made the race, now as an independent Democrat, only to be beaten again. In 1882 Butler, having finally returned to the Democratic party of his youth, at last achieved success and was elected Governor of Massachusetts. Defeated the following year, in 1884 he vainly sought the presidential nomination of the Democratic party (q.v.). Failing to obtain it, he made an independent race as the candidate of the Anti-Monopolists. His remaining years were spent in the pursuit of his profession and the composition of his memoirs, *Butler's Book*, which was published in 1892. One year later he died at Lowell.

A flamboyant, controversial politician, Butler was never able to live down his reputation as a spoilsman and corruptionist. Nevertheless, he greatly furthered the cause of blacks, workers, and women, rallied the pro-Southern New England Democrats to the Union cause and, despite fierce opposition, favored a great many progressive measures.

*See also* Grant, Ulysses Simpson; Johnson, Andrew; Radical Republicans.

Hans L. Trefousse, *Ben Butler: The South Called Him Beast!* (New York, 1957); Richard W. West, Jr., *Lincoln's Scapegoat General: A Life of Benjamin F. Butler, 1818–1893* (Boston, 1965).

# C

---

**CAMERON, SIMON** (1799–1889), Secretary of War, Pennsylvania Senator, and political leader, was born at Maytown, Pennsylvania, the son of a Scottish tailor and tavern keeper and his Pennsylvania German wife. Privately educated at the home of a Sunbury doctor and influenced by the latter's brother-in-law, Lorenzo da Ponte, Cameron became a printer and newspaperman in Harrisburg and soon made a fortune in canal and railroad construction as well as in banking and other business enterprises.

Long politically active in the state Democratic-Republican party, and always in favor of protective tariffs, in 1829 Cameron was appointed Adjutant General of Pennsylvania. In 1832 he unified the Pennsylvania delegation to the Democratic national convention in support of the vice presidential candidacy of Martin Van Buren and in the next year materially facilitated James Buchanan's election to the Senate. President Van Buren appointed him a commissioner to adjust certain Winnebago Indian claims, a position that gained him notoriety because of a dispute about his use of notes from his own bank to buy Indian drafts. Then, when Buchanan became Secretary of State, Cameron secured his own election as his successor by refusing to support the regular Democratic nominee and welcoming the support of some Whigs and nativists. His rise as Pennsylvania's most astute political boss had begun.

In the Senate, Cameron, as a bolter, did not enjoy good relations with either President James K. Polk or his former friend Buchanan. In addition, he severely criticized the administration's course on the tariff. Defeated for reelection in 1848, he tried again for the Senate in 1855 with Know-Nothing help and clashed with Andrew Curtin, whose bitter opponent he was to become for the rest of his career. Although unsuccessful in his quest, in 1857, having become a Republican, he was finally returned to the Senate with the help of a few Democratic votes.

Cameron's power in the state made him a presidential contender at the 1860 convention. After a bargain with the representatives of Abraham Lincoln (q.v.), he withdrew, confidently expecting a cabinet position in return. Yet Lincoln, pressed by Cameron's opponents, hesitated, and only after considerable soul searching appointed Cameron Secretary of War. It was a position in which Cameron was soon overwhelmed by scandals and inefficient management. In the first draft of his report to Congress in December 1861, he advocated the arming of blacks, a proposition he had not cleared with the President who ordered him to omit it. Shortly afterward Lincoln dismissed him and appointed him minister to Russia, and in April 1862 the House passed a resolution of censure concerning the administration of the department. Lincoln promptly assumed the blame for any of the Secretary's shortcomings, and after the war the censure was revoked.

Cameron did not stay long in Russia. Returning to attempt to regain his Senate seat, he failed in 1863 but, in spite of the popularity of his opponent, Governor Curtin, reestablished his influence in Pennsylvania and his good relations with Lincoln. In 1864, on behalf of the President, he sounded out General Benjamin F. Butler (q.v.) about a possible vice presidential candidacy and at the Baltimore convention acted as instructed by switching to Andrew Johnson (q.v.) for Vice President. After first attempting to maintain good relations with President Johnson, he broke with him and supported radical policies. In 1867, at last succeeding in completely defeating Curtin, he returned to the Senate, favored the impeachment of Johnson (q.v.), and during the administration of U.S. Grant (q.v.) became one of the President's principal supporters. After the deposition of Charles Sumner (q.v.), he assumed the chairmanship of the Senate Foreign Relations Committee.

Cameron's political machine, which included his lieutenants Matthew Quay, Robert W. Mackey, and his son, J. Donald, so dominated the state that he was easily reelected in 1873. Such was his power that in 1876 he was able to place his son into the cabinet as Secretary of War and that in 1877, when he resigned because of his disappointment with the policies of Rutherford B. Hayes (q.v.), his son became his successor. He died at Donegal Springs shortly after reaching his ninetieth birthday.

One of the most successful machine politicians in the United States, Cameron was a perspicacious political leader whose efforts on behalf of protection and the Republican party were widely appreciated.

*See also* Grant, Ulysses Simpson; Hayes, Rutherford B.

Erwin Stanley Bradley, *Simon Cameron, Lincoln's Secretary of War: A Political Biography* (Philadelphia, 1965).

**CAMILLA RIOT,** a melee in Camilla, Georgia (q.v.), on September 19, 1868, in which several blacks (q.v.) were killed. A group of black Republicans, led by a presidential elector, John Murphy, and a congressional candidate, W. P.

Pierce, had called a meeting in the small southwestern Georgia town. Several hundred blacks, some armed, marched toward Camilla, and were intercepted at the entrance to the town by the local sheriff, Munford Poore, who demanded that they disarm before proceeding further. When they refused, he summoned a posse, and a drunken onlooker fired a gun. In the resulting affray, in which the posse pursued them into the woods, nine blacks were killed and twenty-five to thirty wounded, while only a few whites suffered minor injuries. Governor Rufus B. Bullock (q.v.) charged that the incident justified his call for renewed federal intervention and asked the legislature to apply for military aid. That body, controlled by the Democrats, appointed an investigating committee instead that, whitewashing the rioters, blamed the Republicans. The riot, taking place at the same time as the expulsion of black legislators, served to strengthen the demand for further intervention in Georgia.

*See also* Bullock, Rufus Brown; Georgia.

Theodore B. FitzSimmons, Jr., "The Camilla Riot," *Georgia Historical Quarterly*, 35 (1951): 116–25; Alan Conway, *The Reconstruction of Georgia* (Minneapolis, 1965); C. Mildred Thompson, *Reconstruction in Georgia: Economic, Social, Political, 1865–1872* (New York, 1915).

**CARPETBAGGERS,** Northerners active as Republican officials in the South during Reconstruction. Long pilloried by traditional writers as largely penniless opportunists waxing rich on Southern misery by setting white against black and engaging in an orgy of corruption, many carpetbaggers were actually fairly well-educated migrants, often former federal soldiers, who moved to the South not to go into politics but either as members of the army or to seek economic opportunity. If corruption was common in the South at the time, it was equally prevalent in the North, particularly during the administration of U. S. Grant (q.v.), and Northern newcomers to Dixie seem to have been no more guilty of malfeasance in office than their Southern and Democratic counterparts. Well-known carpetbaggers such as Adelbert Ames (q.v.), Daniel H. Chamberlain (q.v.), Powell Clayton (q.v.), Albert T. Morgan (q.v.), Harrison Reed (q.v.), Albion W. Tourgée (q.v.), and Willard Warner were able men, and Chamberlain and Tourgée were exceptionally well educated.

In view of the ignorance of many of the freedmen, it is not surprising that many carpetbaggers, elected in the black belt, emerged as leaders of the black community. Some genuinely sympathized with their constituents; others were less committed, and some even became racists in the end. It is true that they organized the freedmen for political purposes and that there were unscrupulous adventurers among them. In general, however, the record of the Northern newcomers has been grossly distorted. Many of them arrived long before the start of Congressional Reconstruction (q.v.), and their services in writing constitutions, establishing public schools, and inaugurating welfare institutions cannot be denied.

*See also* Congressional Reconstruction; Scalawags.

Richard Nelson Current, *Those Terrible Carpetbaggers: A Reinterpretation* (New York,

1988); Eric Foner, *Reconstruction: America's Unfinished Revolution, 1863–1877* (New York, 1988); John Hope Franklin, *Reconstruction after the Civil War* (Chicago, 1961).

**CHAMBERLAIN, DANIEL HENRY** (1835–1907), Reconstruction Attorney General and Governor of South Carolina (q.v.), was born at West Brookfield, Massachusetts, the son of farmers. Educated at Phillips Academy at Andover, Worcester High School, and Yale, he studied law at Harvard but left during his second year to serve as an officer in the Fifth Massachusetts Calvary, a black unit. Visiting South Carolina (q.v.) in 1866 to investigate the drowning of a Yale classmate, he settled in the Sea Islands (q.v.) to plant cotton.

Chamberlain, who had always sympathized with abolition, favored Congressional Reconstruction (q.v.) and in 1867 was elected to the state constitutional convention. He took so prominent a part in its deliberations that in 1868 he became Attorney General in the administration of Governor Robert K. Scott. As the state's chief law officer, he served on various commissions that were accused of dubious financial transactions, and although he never broke any laws, his reputation suffered.

In 1872, after losing the Republican nomination for Governor to the corruptionist Franklin J. Moses, he began to practice law at Columbia, only to be elected Governor two years later. Attempting to root out corruption and extravagance, he succeeded in winning the approbation of a number of South Carolina conservatives who were especially pleased by his refusal to sign the commissions of two radical judges elected by the legislature contrary to his wishes.

Because of his good record as Governor, Chamberlain hoped that in 1876 the conservatives would endorse him. This expectation proved vain, however. The conservatives, resenting his courageous castigation of the Hamburg Massacre (q.v.) as "a barbarity which could only move a civilized person to shame and disgust," nominated General Wade Hampton (q.v.) to oppose him. In the ensuing campaign the conservatives resorted to intimidation by Red Shirts and outright fraud, particularly in Edgefield and Laurens. When the outcome was found to hinge on the returns from those two counties, the board of canvassers rejected them, but the state supreme court upheld the dubious votes. As a consequence, two rival legislatures, one Republican and the other Democratic, assembled, and both Chamberlain and Hampton were inaugurated, with the Republicans in possession of the statehouse. Although Chamberlain had supported Rutherford B. Hayes (q.v.) at the Cincinnati Convention, and the President's own election hinged on Republican victories in the disputed states, he decided to withdraw the federal troops from the statehouse, and the Chamberlain régime fell.

After his abandonment by the federal government, Chamberlain moved to New York to practice law. Becoming ever more conservative with time, he supported the Mugwumps and finally reestablished good relations with his erstwhile Southern opponents. In 1886 he was appointed visiting professor of law at Cornell and, contributing to learned publications, spent many years in the pursuit of scholarly activities. By the end of the 1890s he retired, returned briefly to his birthplace, traveled widely, and died at Charlottesville, Virginia, in 1907.

Chamberlain was a cultivated, well-intentioned administrator whose manners and interests belied the conventional image of a carpetbagger (q.v.). Not entirely free of suspicions of sharp business practices during his term as Attorney General, he nevertheless tried to give the state a good government as chief executive.

*See also* Carpetbaggers; South Carolina.

Richard Nelson Current, *Those Terrible Carpetbaggers: A Reinterpretation* (New York, 1988); Walter Allen, *Governor Chamberlain's Administration in South Carolina: A Chapter of Reconstruction in the Southern States* (New York, 1888).

**CHANDLER, ZACHARIAH** (1813–1879), radical Republican Senator from Michigan and Secretary of the Interior, was born in Bedford, New Hampshire, to a family of farmers. Educated at local schools and academies at Pembroke and Derry, in 1833 he moved to Detroit to enter the general retail business with his brother-in-law. Three years later, he went into the drygoods trade for himself and eventually acquired a fortune in business, land speculation, and plank roads.

A Whig by conviction, Chandler campaigned for Zachary Taylor in 1848. In 1851 he was elected Mayor of Detroit but defeated for Governor the following year. One of the founders of the Republican party in Michigan, he attended the national conventions at Pittsburgh and Philadelphia and in 1857 was elected a U.S. Senator.

During Chandler's long tenure in the Senate (1857–1875, 1879), he stood out as a radical of radicals (Radical Republicans, q.v.), incessantly demanding forceful measures to counter secessionists, prosecute the war, and reconstruct the nation. Equally devoted to high tariffs, a hard currency, and internal improvements, he also favored a strong anti-British policy and the annexation of Canada. In 1861 he gained notoriety by writing to Governor Austin Blair that "without a little bloodletting this Union would not be worth a rush," and after the outbreak of war he consistently harassed the administration to carry out his policies. Immediate military moves against the enemy, the removal of George B. McClellan, and the stern suppression of dissent—all of these demands frequently brought him into conflict with the administration, although Abraham Lincoln (q.v.) finally implemented many of them. As chairman of the Senate Committee on Commerce, he also endorsed many of Salmon P. Chase's (q.v.) financial policies. It was Chandler who in 1864 arranged for the simultaneous withdrawal of John C. Frémont from the presidential race and the dismissal of Montgomery Blair from the cabinet, and throughout its existence, he served on the Joint Committee on the Conduct of the War.

Chandler continued to advocate radical policies after the war. One of the fiercest critics of Andrew Johnson (q.v.), he demanded that the President be impeached, insurgents punished, and freedmen aided. When U. S. Grant (q.v.) became President, Chandler's influence grew. As one of the stalwart supporters of the administration, he relied upon his powerful political machine in Michigan to further the President's policies, including the annexation of the Dominican Republic, and when in 1874 he was defeated in his fourth contest for the Senate,

Grant appointed him Secretary of the Interior. His performance in this office surprised his critics; he was efficient and attempted to root out corruption.

In 1876 Chandler, who had favored the nomination of James G. Blaine (q.v.) became the national chairman of the Republican party (q.v.), despite his opposition to the actual nominee, Rutherford B. Hayes (q.v.). It was he who on election day released the statement that "Hayes has 185 electoral votes and is elected," and then he used all his skill and money to make good his claim. The electoral commission (q.v.) that he had opposed certified the Republicans' victory, but he was soon to be disappointed. Totally opposed to Hayes' Southern policy, he broke completely with the President.

In the meantime, he continued his efforts on behalf of the party. In 1878, as state chairman of the Michigan Republicans, he led them to victory, and when in 1879 his successor in the Senate, Isaac Christiancy, resigned to accept a diplomatic mission, Chandler was promptly reelected to his old seat. Immediately resuming his attacks on the Democrats and the South he castigated Jefferson Davis (q.v.) as a "double-dyed traitor to his government." He resumed his electioneering in 1879 and died at Chicago in the midst of a campaign tour.

*See also* Grant, Ulysses Simpson; Hayes, Rutherford B.; Radical Republicans.

Mary Carl George, *Zachariah Chandler: A Political Biography* (East Lansing, Mich., 1969); Wilmer C. Harris, *The Public Life of Zachariah Chandler, 1851–1875* (Lansing, Mich., 1917); Detroit *Post and Tribune, Zachariah Chandler: An Outline Sketch of His Life* (Detroit, 1880); Hans L. Trefousse, *The Radical Republicans: Lincoln's Vanguard for Racial Justice* (New York, 1969).

**CHASE, SALMON PORTLAND** (1808–1873), Ohio antislavery leader, Secretary of the Treasury, and Chief Justice of the United States, was born at Cornish, New Hampshire, the son of a farmer and entrepreneur in nearby Keene. After attending district schools at Keene and Windsor, Vermont, Chase moved to Worthington, Ohio, to live with his uncle Philander Chase, the Episcopal bishop of the state. When the bishop assumed the presidency of Cincinnati College, the nephew enrolled there. In 1823 he returned to New England, where in preparation for Dartmouth College he attended Royalton Academy. After graduating from Dartmouth in 1826, he moved to Washington to open a school. Soon he became friendly with Attorney General William Wirt under whose guidance he pursued the study of law.

In 1831 Chase settled in Cincinnati to establish a law practice that soon involved him in fugitive slave cases. In time, he left the Whigs to play an active part in the new Liberty and Free Soil parties, which attracted him because of their antislavery position. By 1849 he had become prominent enough to be elected U.S. Senator by a Free Soil–Democratic coalition. Ably representing the antislavery forces in the Senate, he was the author of the "Appeal of the Independent Democrats" against the Kansas-Nebraska Act. One of the founders of the state Republican party (q.v.), in 1855 and 1857 he was elected Governor of Ohio. But he was always ambitious for higher honors and in 1856 and 1860 sought the nomination for the presidency, an attempt that failed because of opposition in the Ohio delegation.

In 1861 Abraham Lincoln (q.v.) appointed Chase, just reelected to the Senate, Secretary of the Treasury. An able administrator, the Ohioan furthered the emission of greenbacks and the establishment of a national banking system, while maintaining the government's credit through frequent loans arranged by the banking house of Jay Cooke & Co. Using his position to strengthen antislavery forces and to speed the enrollment of blacks in the army, Chase favored generals who sympathized with his views and strongly opposed George B. McClellan. Because his radical policies also made him a candidate for the 1864 presidential nomination, relations between him and Lincoln became more and more strained. Although he had been forced to withdraw his candidacy, in June 1864, following a disagreement about patronage in New York, Chase, who had done so several times before, offered to resign again. This time, much to the Secretary's consternation, the President accepted the offer.

In spite of these differences with Chase, after Justice Roger B. Taney's death, in December 1864 Lincoln appointed the Ohioan Chief Justice of the United States. In this position, he steered the court on a moderate course. While striking down military tribunals when the civil courts were open (*ex parte Milligan*, q.v.), declaring test oaths for lawyers and clergymen unconstitutional (*ex parte Garland* and *Cummings* v. *Missouri*, q.v.), and upholding habeas corpus restrictions (*ex parte Yerger*, q.v.), he refused to interfere with the Reconstruction Acts (q.v.) (*Mississippi* v. *Johnson*, q.v., *Georgia* v. *Stanton*, q.v., and *ex parte McCardle*, q.v.). Finally, in *Texas* v. *White* (q.v.), he wrote the majority opinion upholding the "forfeiture of rights" theory, according to which the Constitution provided for "an indestructible Union, composed of indestructible States," but in the absence of legal state government the United States could assume the power necessary to restore it.

Chase's tolerant attitude toward Congressional Reconstruction (q.v.) began to sour during the impeachment trial of Andrew Johnson (q.v.). As the presiding officer at the trial, he angered many Republicans by ruling in favor of the contention of the defense that the Senate, sitting as a High Court, ought to follow all the rules of a judicial proceeding. His shift became even more marked when in the summer of 1868 he actively sought the Democratic nomination for President. Hampered by his insistence on the maintenance of freedmen's rights, he did not succeed, but four years later, some of his friends still vainly hoped to obtain the Liberal Republican (Liberal Republican Movement, q.v.) nomination for him.

Although the Chief Justice was thus drawing close to the opposition, he never abandoned his quest for racial justice. He not only insisted on it in 1868 but in 1873 in the *Slaughterhouse* cases (q.v.) joined the minority in asserting that the Fourteenth Amendment (q.v.) applied to all citizens, state or federal. Yet in the *Legal Tender* cases (q.v.), he decided that his own sanction of greenbacks had merely been an emergency measure and that the paper currency was not legal tender in contracts made before the passage of the Legal Tender Act (*Hepburn* v. *Griswold*). When the decision was overturned in *Knox* v. *Lee*, he voted with the minority.

Chase's family life was beset by tragedy. Three times widowed and stricken by the loss of four children, he bestowed his affection on his two remaining daughters. The elder, Kate Sprague, the unhappily married wife of a wealthy Rhode Island Senator, was one of Washington's best-known hostesses who sought to aid him in his pursuit of the presidency. The younger, Nettie Hoyt, married a New Yorker, at whose home Chase died in 1873.

One of the most influential antislavery statesmen of the time, Chase contributed greatly to the cause of emancipation and equal rights for blacks (q.v.). His record as Secretary of the Treasury was distinguished, and his years as Chief Justice revealed him as a jurist of no mean ability. Although his effectiveness was marred by his inordinate ambition and his inability to hide his aloof manner, he was nevertheless a man of great dignity and one of the most outstanding radical leaders of the period.

*See also* Radical Republicans; Supreme Court.

Frederick J. Blue, *Salmon P. Chase: A Life in Politics* (Kent, Ohio, 1987); David Donald, ed., *Inside Lincoln's Cabinet: The Civil War Diaries of Salmon P. Chase* (New York, 1954); Harold M. Hyman, *A More Perfect Union: The Impact of the Civil War and Reconstruction on the Constitution* (New York, 1973); Stanley I. Kutler, *Judicial Power and Reconstruction* (Chicago, 1968); Charles Fairman, *History of the Supreme Court of the United States*, vol. 6, *Reconstruction and Reunion, 1864–1888* (New York, 1971).

**CIVIL RIGHTS ACT OF 1866,** the first attempt to enforce the equal rights of freedmen by federal legislation. Passed by the Senate on February 2 and the House on March 13, 1866, the bill declared all persons born in the United States, excepting Indians not taxed, citizens of the United States. Whenever any state or territory deprived any citizen of his civil rights, it empowered federal courts, aided by federal officers, to enforce its stipulations.

The measure, framed by Senator Lyman Trumbull (q.v.), was intended as a companion piece to the Freedmen's Bureau Bill (q.v.) of February 1866. Based on the enforcement clause of the Thirteenth Amendment (q.v.), it was designed to guarantee freedmen's rights against state interference of the type exemplified by the Black Codes (q.v.) enacted by many Southern states organized in accordance with Andrew Johnson's Presidential Plan of Reconstruction (Presidential Reconstruction, q.v.). Although it sought to maintain the federal system by holding out to the states the possibility of ending federal interference if they complied with its injunctions, it met with the determined opposition of the President. Objecting to its alleged violation of the reserved rights of the states and its supposed preferential treatment of blacks, he vetoed it on March 27.

The veto was not sustained. On April 6 the Senate, and three days later the House, overrode it, so the bill became law. It was the first major legislation ever to be passed over an executive veto, and it exacerbated the growing rift between the President and Congress. The precursor of the Fourteenth Amendment (q.v.), which largely superseded it, the act was nevertheless still invoked by the Supreme Court during the civil rights revolution of the twentieth century to extend the prohibition of racial discrimination to sale and rental of private as well as public property.

*See also* Fourteenth Amendment; Presidential Reconstruction; Thirteenth Amendment; Trumbull, Lyman.

Harold M. Hyman, *A More Perfect Union: The Impact of the Civil War and Reconstruction on the Constitution* (New York, 1973); Patrick W. Riddleberger, *1866: The Critical Year Revisited* (Carbondale, Ill., 1979); Michael Les Benedict, *A Compromise of Principle: Congressional Republicans and Reconstruction, 1863–1869* (New York, 1974); Herman Belz, *A New Birth of Freedom: The Republican Party and Freedmen's Rights, 1861 to 1866* (Westport, Conn., 1976); Charles Fairman, *Reconstruction and Reunion, 1864–1888*, Vol. 6 of the Oliver Wendell Holmes Devise: *History of the Supreme Court of the United States* (New York, 1971).

**CIVIL RIGHTS ACT OF 1875,** the last nineteenth-century legislation seeking to enforce the civil rights of blacks (q.v.) by federal statute. The special concern of Charles Sumner (q.v.), who during the Grant administration repeatedly introduced it in the Senate, the measure met with repeated failure. After Sumner's death, it was finally guided through the Senate by Frederick T. Frelinghuysen and through the House by Benjamin F. Butler (q.v.) and, after much parliamentary maneuvering during the lame-duck session following the Republican defeat in the fall of 1874, became law in February 1875.

Mandating equal accommodations for both races in inns, public conveyances, and theaters, as well as prohibiting discrimination in jury selection, the bill conferred jurisdiction over both criminal and civil cases arising under it to federal courts and made all such cases, regardless of the sum involved, reviewable by the Supreme Court. In its original version, it also included schools and cemeteries, but because of widespread opposition, these clauses were omitted in the end. The bill was fiercely resisted step by step by the Democratic minority, even though the Republicans fought back by adding to it a preamble taken directly from the Liberal and Democratic platform of 1872. In the elections of 1874, bitter resentment of the proposed measure resulted in Republican losses, particularly in the Southern and border states, while weakening the party elsewhere. In 1883, in the so-called *Civil Rights* cases (q.v.), the Supreme Court held most of its provisions unconstitutional, and it was not until the 1960s that a similar, more inclusive measure could finally become law.

*See also* Civil Rights Cases; Sumner, Charles.

Harold M. Hyman, *A More Perfect Union: The Impact of the Civil War and Reconstruction on the Constitution* (New York, 1973); William Gillette, *Retreat from Reconstruction, 1869–1879* (Baton Rouge, 1979); David H. Donald, *Charles Sumner and the Rights of Man* (New York, 1970).

**CIVIL RIGHTS CASES,** five cases arising under the Civil Rights Act of 1875 (q.v.) in which the Supreme Court declared the equal-accommodations portions of the statute unconstitutional. Although the government argued that under the

Thirteenth and Fourteenth Amendments (q.v.) private cases of discrimination could be outlawed by federal legislation, Justice Joseph P. Bradley, speaking for the majority, held that the Fourteenth Amendment restricted merely state and not private actions and denied that discrimination—in these instances in inns, theaters, and trains—was the result of slavery; therefore, the Thirteenth Amendment was also not applicable. In addition, he ruled that the Fourteenth Amendment gave Congress no power to prevent but merely to correct abuses after they had occurred.

Justice John Marshall Harlan wrote a lone, classic dissent. Insisting that there were burdens and disabilities that constituted "badges of slavery and servitude" and that the Thirteenth Amendment conferred upon Congress the power to eradicate them by appropriate legislation, he believed that the denial of civil rights fit this description. In any case, he pointed out that inns, public conveyances, and places of amusement were affected with the public interest and therefore liable to government regulation. Contradicting the majority's interpretation of the Fourteenth Amendment, he declared that it guaranteed equal rights to all citizens, particularly civil rights, and differed with the view that Congress had no power to act to prevent violations of the law. "The supreme law of the land has decreed," he wrote, "that no authority shall be exercised in this country on the basis of discrimination, in respect to civil rights, against freedmen and citizens because of their race, color, or previous condition of servitude." He ended with a ringing reaffirmation of the egalitarian spirit of the post–Civil War constitutional changes.

The majority decision, marking the virtual end of Reconstruction, practically nullified the two amendments' purpose of safeguarding black rights. Not until the civil rights revolution of the twentieth century did Justice Harlan's minority view finally prevail.

*See also* Fourteenth Amendment; Supreme Court; Thirteenth Amendment.

109 U.S. 3 (1883); Loren P. Beth, *The Development of the American Constitution, 1877–1917* (New York, 1971); Harold M. Hyman and William M. Wiecek, *Equal Justice Under Law: Constitutional Development, 1835–1875* (New York, 1982).

**CIVIL SERVICE REFORM,** a movement to end the patronage practices of both political parties by instituting a civil service system based on merit. As early as April 10, 1864, Charles Sumner (q.v.) introduced a bill calling for competitive examinations for government positions to be administered by a civil service commission. The idea was later taken up by Thomas A. Jenckes, a Republican from Rhode Island who, beginning in December 1865, consistently sponsored similar bills in the House of Representatives. In 1869 Jenckes was joined by Carl Schurz (q.v.), Lyman Trumbull (q.v.), and Henry Wilson (q.v.) in the Senate, and in March 1871 Trumbull succeeded in attaching to an appropriations bill a rider to establish a civil service commission.

In accordance with this congressional mandate, President Ulysses S. Grant (q.v.), who repeatedly endorsed the reform, appointed the commission with the reformer George William Curtis (q.v.) as chairman. The commission issued a report recommending the classification of government positions and competitive examinations to obtain them, but Congress failed to sustain these recommendations. Because the Grant administration was largely dependent on powerful political machines such as those of Roscoe Conkling (q.v.), Benjamin F. Butler (q.v.), Simon Cameron (q.v.), and Oliver P. Morton (q.v.), civil service reform found little support from the President's backers. As a result, in 1872 the Liberal Republicans (Liberal Republican Movement, q.v.), espousing the cause, made it one of their chief demands. Their defeat did little to further the reform; in 1873 George William Curtis resigned and was succeeded by Dorman B. Eaton, but in 1875 Congress cut off appropriations, and the commission expired.

Yet civil service reform was not dead. After the debacle of 1872, many of the reformers, most conspicuously Carl Schurz, who had left the Republican party rejoined it. Actively campaigning for Rutherford B. Hayes (q.v.) in 1876, he was rewarded with the post of Secretary of the Interior and, with the President's full support, introduced stringent civil service standards in his department. In 1877 the New York Civil Service Reform Association was founded, and when it was revived some three years later, it served as a model for similar organizations elsewhere, including a National Civil Service Reform League headed by Curtis.

The election of 1880 brought James A. Garfield (q.v.) to power. The new President was somewhat lukewarm toward the movement, but his assassination by a disgruntled officeseeker gave the cause a great boost. Garfield's successor, Chester A. Arthur, the former Collector of the Port of New York who had been a Stalwart spoilsman and was dismissed by Hayes, now became a convert to civil service reform, and after the Republican defeat of 1882, Congress finally passed the Pendleton Bill. Providing for the establishment of a new civil service commission to set rules for competitive examinations for positions to be classified, the measure met many of the objectives of the reformers and was promptly signed into law by the President. Starting with about fourteen thousand positions, the system of classification was gradually expanded by succeeding administrations until it became the standard practice of the government.

Chiefly advocated by a group of gentlemanly, generally Northeastern reformers sometimes known as "the best men," civil service reform often appealed to the "outs" who hoped to be "ins." Its undemocratic features—few people possessed a college education that could give them an advantage in passing examinations—alienated many, particularly the freedmen, and although the reformers thought their cause was as important as abolitionism had been, its end results fell short of their expectations.

*See also* Liberal Republicans; Schurz, Carl; Trumbull, Lyman.

Ari Hoogenboom, *Outlawing the Spoils: A History of the Civil Service Reform Movement, 1865–1883* (Urbana, Ill., 1961); John G. Sproat, *"The Best Men": Liberal Reformers in the Gilded Age* (London, 1968); Hans L. Trefousse, *Carl Schurz: A Biography* (Knoxville, 1982).

**CLAYTON, POWELL** (1833–1914), Carpetbag Governor and Senator from Arkansas (q.v.), was born at Bethel, Pennsylvania, where he went to the local schools. After attending Partridge Military Academy in Bristol and completing his education in civil engineering in Wilmington, in 1855 he moved to Leavenworth, Kansas, and within a short time was elected civil engineer and surveyor.

When war broke out, Clayton entered the army and distinguished himself in the defense of Pine Bluff, Arkansas, a feat that led to his promotion to brigadier general. After the war, Clayton settled in Arkansas, became a planter, and married a local belle.

Although he had been a Democrat before the war, in 1867 Clayton entered Republican politics and in 1868 was elected Governor under the new constitution, which conferred considerable powers upon the executive. Making full use of these prerogatives, he stimulated the construction of new railroads as well as the establishment of an educational system and by forceful means employed the militia to break the power of the Ku Klux Klan (q.v.)

In the meantime, a split was developing in the Republican party of the state. The scalawags (q.v.) and moderates, under the leadership of Lieutenant Governor James M. Johnson, were willing to combine with some Democrats against Clayton, and when the Governor went to New York to arrange for the funding of state bonds, his enemies planned to supplant him. Charging that he had absconded with the public money, they sought to install Johnson, only to be outmaneuvered by Clayton, who arrived at the capitol before his rival could take possession. He himself now offered to cooperate with the Democrats by repealing the disfranchisement clauses of the constitution and obtained enough support to win election to the U.S. Senate. Refusing to accept the office as long as Johnson was his successor, he easily overcame an effort to impeach him. In the end, the Lieutenant Governor was induced to step down and accept appointment as Secretary of State, whereupon Clayton was elected once again to the Senate (1871).

Clayton's opponents would not give up. At the very beginning of his Senate term, they secured an indictment charging him with fraudulently certifying the election of a member of Congress but were unable to sustain the accusations. After a thorough congressional investigation, additional efforts to have him declared unfit for his seat were also defeated, and he remained the most powerful Republican in the state. His firm support of President U. S. Grant (q.v.) and his success in carrying the state for the President in 1872 secured him unlimited access to the federal patronage.

In the state elections that year, Clayton's opponents, the Brindletails, nominated the carpetbagger Joseph Brooks while the Senator backed the scalawag Elisha Baxter. He so manipulated the results that Baxter was declared the winner, but Brooks challenged his adversary's claims to office. As time went on, Clayton gradually lost faith in Baxter, who was allying himself more and more with the Democrats. Consequently, when Brooks sued for a quo warranto to oust his rival, the Senator changed sides and supported the claimant. The disorders that resulted were known as the Brooks-Baxter War (q.v.), in which, after a great deal of maneuvering, Baxter emerged as the winner, and Clayton had to admit defeat.

After the conclusion of his term, Clayton retired to Eureka Springs, where he engaged in traction and railroad enterprises. Continuing as the Arkansas member of the Republican National Committee and enjoying the support of the freedmen, he still dominated the state Republican party (q.v.) and in 1897 was appointed envoy to Mexico. Retiring in 1905, he moved to Washington, where he wrote his memoirs and vigorously defended his record during Reconstruction.

A powerfully built, fearless, and energetic public official, Clayton successfully withstood all attempts to brand him as corrupt. A carpetbagger only if the term is applied to all Northerners who came South after the Civil War, he deserves to be remembered for his efforts on behalf of the freedmen and the development of his adopted state.

*See also* Arkansas; Brooks-Baxter War; Carpetbaggers.

Richard N. Current, *Those Terrible Carpetbaggers: A Reinterpretation* (New York, 1988); George Thompson, *Arkansas and Reconstruction* (Port Washington, N.Y., 1976); Thomas S. Staples, *Reconstruction in Arkansas* (New York, 1923).

**COLFAX, SCHUYLER** (1823–1885), representative from Indiana, Speaker of the House of Representatives, and Vice President of the United States, was born in New York City, the posthumous son of a bank employee. When he was eleven, his mother married George W. Matthews who in 1836 took the family to New Carlisle, Indiana, where he opened a store. When in 1851 the Matthews moved to South Bend, Colfax became his stepfather's assistant as deputy Whig auditor of the county. He acquired experience in journalism by writing articles for the New York *Tribune* and by serving as senate reporter for the *Indiana State Journal* in 1842–1843. In 1843 he accepted the editorship of the South Bend *Free Press*, which he bought two years later and renamed it the *St. Joseph Valley Register*. Remaining in charge of the paper for nine years, he turned it into a mouthpiece for antislavery and Whig-Republicanism in Northern Indiana.

In 1850 Colfax was elected to the state constitutional convention, which met that year. Although he was not yet in favor of universal suffrage, he strongly opposed a proposal to ban the migration of blacks (q.v.) into the state. In 1851 he ran unsuccessfully for Congress and in 1854 became one of the founders of the People's party, the forerunner of the Republicans in Indiana. After briefly joining the Know-Nothings, in 1854 he was elected to the House of Representatives and retained his seat until 1869.

In Congress, Colfax collaborated with other Republicans in resisting Southern pretensions. Moving ever closer to the radicals, during the war he denounced the Copperhead Alexander Long, who had advocated disunion. As chairman of the committee on the post office and post roads, he favored improved communications and transcontinental railroads. His reward came in 1863 when he was elected Speaker of the House, a position in which his parliamentary skill soon brought him general recognition.

During Reconstruction, Colfax, now thoroughly radical, closely cooperated with the advocates of black suffrage (q.v.) and soon entered into opposition to Andrew Johnson (q.v.). In 1868 he became U. S. Grant's (q.v.) running mate and was elected Vice President. Loyally supporting the administration, he was offered the position of Secretary of State, which he refused, and was mentioned as a possible successor to the President. He used his casting vote to support Charles Sumner's (q.v.) Civil Rights Bill but in 1872 failed to win renomination. Shortly afterward, he was found to have been involved in the Crédit Mobilier scandal, although he always denied any impropriety. His political career over, he retired to South Bend and busied himself in delivering public lectures. He died on a speaking tour at Mankato, Minnesota.

Colfax, who was a teetotaler, had a winning personality, which won him the nickname "Smiler." Not particularly identified with any particular measure during his years in Congress, he was mainly known for his parliamentary abilities. He was married twice, his second wife being the niece of Senator Benjamin F. Wade (q.v.). Besmirched by the Crédit Mobilier affair, he was unable to refute successfully the general impression of his complicity.

*See also* Grant, Ulysses Simpson.

Willard H. Smith, *Schuyler Colfax: The Changing Fortunes of a Political Idol* (Indianapolis, 1952).


**COLFAX RIOT,** a massacre of blacks on Easter Sunday, April 13, 1873, at Colfax, Louisiana. During the rivalry between the Fusion and Republican claimants to the government of the state after the election of 1872, the parish judge and sheriff appointed by Fusionist Henry Clay Warmoth (q.v.) in Grant Parish on the Red River were replaced by the radical Governor William Pitt Kellogg (q.v.). To sustain the Republicans, armed blacks, taking over the courthouse at Colfax, the parish seat, alarmed their opponents, whereupon the displaced sheriff summoned a posse of some two hundred whites and demanded the blacks' surrender. Meeting with a refusal, he attacked his adversaries with a cannon and set fire to the courthouse, and the posse shot the fleeing blacks. Those who were taken prisoner were later murdered in cold blood. The total casualties amounted to two whites and fifty-nine blacks.

The extent and ferocity of the riot embittered Northern opinion. But although the perpetrators were indicted under the provisions of the Enforcement Act of 1870 (q.v.), the Supreme Court held the indictment invalid on the grounds that the Fourteenth Amendment (q.v.) prohibited only state, not private, actions, thus rendering the amendment practically useless in the enforcement of civil rights for blacks (*U.S.* v. *Cruikshank*, 1876, q.v.).

*See also* Kellogg, William Pitt; Louisiana; McEnery, John.

Joe Gray Taylor, *Louisiana Reconstructed, 1863–1877* (Baton Rouge, 1974); Ella Lonn, *Reconstruction in Louisiana after 1868* (New York, 1918); William Gillette, *Retreat from Reconstruction, 1869–1879* (Baton Rouge, 1979); *U.S.* v. *Cruikshank et al.*, 92 U.S. 542.

**COMPROMISE OF 1877,** an informal arrangement between Southern Democrats, often former Whigs, and the representatives of Rutherford B. Hayes (q.v.). Under its terms, no further obstacles would be put in the way of Hayes' assumption of the presidency in return for certain political and economic concessions to the Southerners. Some of these stipulations consisted of promises to assist in the construction of the Texas and Pacific Railroad as well as other economic benefits for the South; others, repeated at a meeting in the Wormley's Hotel in Washington on February 26, 1877, involved the withdrawal of federal troops from the remaining Republican Southern statehouses and the appointment of a Southerner to the cabinet. Although the economic promises were either carried out only imperfectly or not at all, the political arrangements resulted in Hayes' inauguration as President, the appointment of David M. Key of Tennessee as Postmaster General, and the end of Reconstruction in Louisiana (q.v.) and South Carolina (q.v.). In these states, Francis T. Nicholls (q.v.) and Wade Hampton (q.v.) were recognized as Governors instead of Steven P. Packard (q.v.) and Daniel H. Chamberlain (q.v.), although certain Democratic commitments to allow the Republicans to organize the House came to naught. Thus the compromise effectively put an end to federal interference in the South and ushered in the period of "Redemption" (q.v.).

*See also* Chamberlain, Daniel; Hampton, Wade; Hayes, Rutherford B.; Nicholls, Francis Tillou; "Redemption."

C. Vann Woodward, *Reunion and Reaction: The Compromise of 1877 and the End of Reconstruction* (Boston, 1951); Keith I. Polakoff, *The Politics of Inertia: The Election of 1876 and the End of Reconstruction* (Baton Rouge, 1973).

**CONGRESSIONAL RECONSTRUCTION,** the second phase of Reconstruction embodying the congressional program of black suffrage (q.v.) combined with the disfranchisement of former Confederates. Following the elections of 1866, the Republican leadership in Congress, frustrated by Andrew Johnson's (q.v.) continued opposition to the ratification of the Fourteenth Amendment (q.v.), took matters into its own hands. It rapidly enacted a series of laws to control the President. Among them were the Tenure of Office Act (q.v.), the bill calling for the immediate assembly of the Fortieth Congress after the expiration of the Thirty-ninth, and the command of the army provisions of the Military Appropriations Act of 1867. In addition, it framed the Reconstruction Acts (q.v.), which remanded ten states to military rule and required them to ratify new constitutions based on black suffrage as well as the Fourteenth Amendment. Passed over the President's veto or his objections, these measures ushered in a period sometimes misnamed "radical" Reconstruction in the affected states.

By the middle of 1868, all but three states had complied with the requirements of the Reconstruction Acts. The Fourteenth Amendment was ratified and the states in question readmitted. In Virginia (q.v.), Texas (q.v.) and Mississippi (q.v.), as well as in Georgia (q.v.), which was returned to military rule after its legislature expelled black members, the process was not completed until after the ratification of the Fifteenth Amendment (q.v.) in 1870. Republican regimes, sustained by carpetbaggers (q.v.), scalawags (q.v.), and freedmen, were established in all the states involved. Resentment by conservative whites, however, coupled with charges of corruption and the failure of continued federal support, led to their overthrow between 1869 and 1877. The accusations of mammoth corruption, wastefulness, and incapacity brought against them by traditional historians have been generally discounted as exaggerated by their successors.

During this entire period, the power of the executive branch tended to be diminished. Andrew Johnson's strenuous opposition to the congressional program led to his impeachment, and although his acquittal was a sign that the radical Republicans (q.v.) were not as strong as had been assumed, he was left powerless during the remainder of his term. During the administration of U. S. Grant (q.v.), the President tended to sympathize with congressional measures but in the long run was unable or unwilling to sustain the Southern regimes. It was not until the beginning of the twentieth century that the executive branch recovered some of the powers it had lost.

The Supreme Court (q.v.) did little to stop congressional pretensions. True, in *ex parte Milligan* (q.v.) and the *test oath* cases it had declared military tribunals to be unconstitutional when the civil courts were open and had outlawed test oaths. But in *Mississippi* v. *Johnson* (q.v.) and *Georgia* v. *Stanton* (q.v.) it refused to assume jurisdiction when asked to enjoin the administration from enforcing the Reconstruction Acts, and in *ex parte McCardle* (q.v.) it allowed itself to be deprived of jurisdiction while the case was pending. Although it did not hesitate to interfere when it believed such action warranted (*ex parte Yerger*, q.v.), by implication it upheld the right of Congress to set terms for Reconstruction in *Texas* v. *White* (q.v.).

With the Compromise of 1877 (q.v.), Congressional Reconstruction came to an end. Never as radical as has been charged, it nevertheless represented a real effort to enforce equal rights by federal legislation.

*See also* Grant, Ulysses Simpson; Johnson, Andrew; Presidential Reconstruction; Reconstruction Acts.

Eric Foner, *Reconstruction, 1863–1877* (New York, 1988); Michael Les Benedict, *A Compromise of Principle: Congressional Republicans and Reconstruction, 1863–1869* (New York, 1974); Rembert W. Patrick, *The Reconstruction of the Nation* (New York, 1967); Kenneth M. Stampp, *The Era of Reconstruction, 1865–1877* (New York, 1965); John Hope Franklin, *Reconstruction after the Civil War* (Chicago, 1961).

**CONKLING, ROSCOE** (1829–1888), New York political leader, was born in Albany, the son of a federal judge. Taken by his family to Auburn at the age of ten, he attended Mt. Washington Collegiate Institute in New York City and Auburn Academy. In 1846 he moved to Utica, read law in the firm of Spencer & Kennan, and after admission to the bar in 1850 established a flourishing law practice in the central New York city. He married Julia Catherine Seymour, the sister of Democratic Governor Horatio Seymour.

Despite his marriage into a Democratic family, Conkling was a convinced

Whig. Appointed district attorney in 1850, he lost the position in the ensuing election. But his speaking ability combined with handsome features and a splendid physique made him a popular candidate for office, and after his transition into the new Republican party (q.v.), in 1858 he was elected mayor and shortly afterward, congressman, a position he held for a total of four terms.

During the war, Conkling was noted as a moderate Republican. Afterward, as one of the members of the Joint Committee of Fifteen on Reconstruction (q.v.), he took a hand in the shaping of the Fourteenth Amendment (q.v.) and became an active opponent of President Andrew Johnson (q.v.). During arguments concerning the proposed abolition of the position of provost marshal, which he favored, he clashed with James G. Blaine (q.v.), who sneeringly referred to his "turkey-gobbler strut," an insult he never forgave. The altercation was to lead to the serious split among Conkling's supporters, the Stalwarts, and Blaine's adherents, the Half-Breeds, a division that weakened the Republican party for years to come.

In 1867 Conkling was elected to the Senate and during the presidency of U. S. Grant (q.v.) built up a powerful machine in the Empire State that was largely based on the patronage of the New York Custom House. One of the mainstays of the administration, the organization, defeating its local rival Reuben E. Fenton, was able to dictate policies in the state as well as in the nation. So impressed was the President with Conkling that in 1873 he offered him the position of Chief Justice of the United States, which the Senator declined.

In 1876 Conkling was an active candidate for the presidency and, when Rutherford B. Hayes (q.v.) obtained the prize instead, took little part in the campaign. One of the authors of the bill creating the Electoral Commission (q.v.) to settle the disputed count of 1876, he continued to doubt the legitimacy of Hayes' title. His dislike of the President was fueled by the administration's civil service policies, particularly by its attempts to displace his supporters, New York Collector Chester A. Arthur and naval officer Alonzo B. Cornell. By appealing to senatorial courtesy to defeat the confirmation of their successors, in 1877 he managed to save them, but in the next year Hayes dismissed them again, and this time he prevailed.

In spite of this setback, Conkling continued to dominate New York politics. He himself was reelected in 1879; Cornell became Governor, and in 1881 another supporter, Thomas C. Platt, was elevated to the Senate. As the chief backer of a third term for General Grant, he nominated the ex-President in a flamboyant speech at the Chicago National Convention, only to see James A. Garfield (q.v.) obtain the prize instead. Conkling's support enabled Garfield to carry New York and win. But then the Senator, piqued by Garfield's alleged failure to honor patronage commitments to New York Stalwarts, fell out with the President. The appointment of one of Conkling's adversaries as Collector of New York caused the Senator and his colleague to resign their seats in the hope of vindication by reelection, but they failed.

Resuming private practice in New York City, Conkling never reentered active politics. He turned down the offer of a seat on the Supreme Court and in 1884, declaring that he did not engage in criminal practice, refused to support Blaine. Following exposure during the blizzard of 1888, he died in New York.

A powerful political leader, Conkling failed to make his mark as a sponsor of significant legislation. Perhaps his most important legacy was his argument in *San Mateo County* v. *Southern Pacific Railroad* (1882), which maintained that the Fourteenth Amendment's due process clause was designed not only to protect the freedmen but also corporations.

*See also* Fourteenth Amendment; Grant, Ulysses Simpson; Hayes, Rutherford B.

David M. Jordan, *Roscoe Conkling of New York: Voice in the Senate* (Ithaca, N.Y., 1972); Donald Barr Chidsey, *The Gentleman from New York: A Life of Roscoe Conkling* (New Haven, 1935).

**CORRUPTION,** a widespread problem during the post–Civil War period, was formerly generally blamed on the Reconstruction governments. While undoubtedly common in the South, it was at least as prevalent in the North, where it was totally unconnected with black suffrage (q.v.). Democrats as well as Republicans benefited, and scandals were nationwide. The 1860s and 1870s witnessed the emergence of the Tweed Ring in New York, the attempt by Jay Gould (q.v.) and James Fisk to corner the gold market, and the revelations connected with the Crédit Mobilier involving the bribery of congressmen with stock of the construction company for the Union Pacific Railroad. It was also the period of the other scandals of the Grant administration, the Whiskey Ring (q.v.), the Sanborn contracts, and the impeachment of Secretary of War William W. Belknap (q.v.). None of these had anything to do with the Reconstruction of the Southern states.

That there were glaring instances of wrongdoing in the South is undeniable. The legislature of Florida (q.v.) incurred enormous printing costs; the Louisiana (q.v.) Lottery was a means of general corruption; the Georgia (q.v.) legislature brought an unfinished opera house for a large sum; in Arkansas (q.v.) a bridge worth $500 was bought for $9,000, and in South Carolina (q.v.) not only did the legislature engage in land frauds, but it voted $1,000 to the Speaker of the House after he had lost $1,000 in a horse race. In addition, railroad speculations affected many states and involved several public figures in frauds.

If the expenses of various states sharply increased during Reconstruction, it must be remembered that some of these debts were the result of the default of railroads, the bonds of which were held by individual governments. Moreover, the end of slavery sharply increased the cost of social services. Before the war, public education for whites had been minimal and nonexistent for blacks; its introduction for both races cost money. Hospitals, alms houses, and similar institutions were established where there had been none before, so the charges of extravagance must be viewed in the light of special circumstances.

Reconstruction certainly was not free from corruption; but the exclusive emphasis upon it without considering the larger picture can no longer be sustained.

*See also* Gould, Jay; Littlefield, Milton Smith; Swepson, George; Tweed, William Magear, Whiskey Ring.

John Hope Franklin, *Reconstruction after the Civil War* (Chicago, 1961); Kenneth M. Stampp, *The Era of Reconstruction, 1865–1877* (New York, 1965); J. G. Randall and David Donald, *The Civil War and Reconstruction* (Lexington, Mass., 1969); James M. McPherson, *Ordeal by Fire: The Civil War and Reconstruction* (New York, 1982).

**COUSHATTA MASSACRE,** a terrorist attack on white and black Republicans in Red River Parish, Louisiana (q.v.), in August 1874. Local conservatives, resenting the influence of carpetbag state Senator Marshall Twitchell and his relatives, reacted violently to a series of racial incidents that led them to believe the blacks were ready to revolt. Calling for help from their fellow members of the White League (q.v.) in the vicinity, they assembled hundreds of armed men in Coushatta to induce Republican officeholders to resign. They arrested several of them, allegedly for their own protection; proceeded to try them; and prevailed on them to leave the state. On August 31 the "prisoners" were escorted out of town under guard, but a mob intercepted them and killed six Republicans. A few days later, two blacks who also had been arrested, were lynched as well.

Directed chiefly at the power of Senator Twitchell, the massacre resulted in the murder of his brother and other relatives. Although the Senator himself was reelected, in 1876 he and his brother-in-law were waylaid as they were crossing the river in a skiff. Struck in the leg by a bullet, Twitchell jumped into the water, only to be shot through both arms, while his relative was killed. His arms had to be amputated, but he lived for another thirty years and was appointed consul at Kingston, Ontario.

The Coushatta massacre received a lot of publicity in the North and showed how vulnerable Republican officeholders were in the rural South in the face of terrorist tactics used by their opponents to make an end of Reconstruction.

*See also* Louisiana; White League.

George C. Rable, *But There Was No Peace: The Role of Violence in the Politics of Reconstruction* (Athens, Ga., 1984); Joe Gray Taylor, *Louisiana Reconstructed, 1863–1877* (Baton Rouge, 1974).

**CRÉDIT MOBILIER SCANDAL.** *See* CORRUPTION.

**CUMMINGS v. MISSOURI** (1867), one of the *test oath* cases involving a provision of the constitution of Missouri (q.v.) requiring clergymen, lawyers, candidates for office, and voters to take an ironclad oath (q.v.) that they had never supported the Confederacy. Father John Cummings, a Roman Catholic priest and teacher, refused to comply and was sentenced to pay $500 and to be jailed until the fine was paid. Upheld on appeal by the Supreme Court of Missouri, the case was taken to the Supreme Court of the United States by his attorneys, Montgomery Blair, Reverdy Johnson (q.v.), and David Dudley Field. A majority of five to four made up of all the prewar justices as well as Stephen J. Field, in an opinion written by the latter, decided that the clause in question was void because it constituted an ex post facto law and a bill of attainder, both prohibited by the Constitution. On the same day, January 14, 1867, in the companion case of *ex parte Garland* (q.v.), the justices struck down federal test oaths for lawyers, thus declaring post–Civil War test oaths unconstitutional.

*See also Garland, Ex Parte*; Supreme Court.

*Cummings* v. *Missouri* (4 Wallace 277); Harold M. Hyman and William W. Wiecek, *Equal Justice Under Law: Constitutional Development, 1835–1875* (New York, 1982); Charles Fairman, *Reconstruction and Reunion*, Vol. 6 of the Oliver Wendell Holmes Devise: *History of the Supreme Court of the United States, 1864–88*.


**CURTIS, GEORGE WILLIAM** (1824–1892), editor, author, and reformer, was born in Providence, Rhode Island, the son of a banker and of the daughter of a distinguished U.S. Senator. Educated at Jamaica Plains, Massachusetts, and Providence, Curtis moved to New York with his family in 1839. For a short time he worked in a mercantile establishment; then, between 1842 and 1844, he spent a year and a half at Brook Farm, where he was deeply influenced by the transcendentalism of Ralph Waldo Emerson, Margaret Fuller, and Bronson Alcott. In the spring of 1844 young George and his brother Burrill went to live in Concord, Massachusetts, where they performed some farm labor and benefited from a ripening acquaintance with the village's famous residents, particularly Henry David Thoreau, Nathaniel Hawthorne, and Emerson. In 1846 the two brothers left for Europe and the Middle East, not to return for four years.

While traveling abroad, Curtis published several letters about his experiences in the New York *Tribune*. Expanding these in book form upon his return, he wrote *Nile Notes of a Howadji* and *The Howadji in Syria*, two works that went far toward establishing his literary reputation. In 1853 he joined the editorial staff of *Putnam's Monthly*, but the magazine failed three years later, leaving a large debt that he honorably assumed. He had also formed a connection with *Harper's Monthly*, however, for which he wrote the first contribution to the Editor's Easy Chair in 1853 and eventually became one of the editorial writers for *Harper's Weekly*. This position, combined with frequent lectures, enabled him to discharge his debts. His connection with the Easy Chair was to last until his death forty years later.

Curtis's genial personality, good looks, and excellent taste made him a popular lecturer on the lyceum and other circuits. The appearance of *Lotus Eating, Potiphar Papers* (a satire on New York society), and *Prue and I* increased his literary reputation, and he became one of the country's most popular writers and speakers.

During the 1850s Curtis became actively involved in Republican politics. Using his position as an orator and editor forcefully to attack the institution of slavery, in 1856 he strongly supported John C. Frémont for the presidency. As a delegate to the Republican National Convention at Chicago in 1860, he succeeded in having Joshua R. Giddings' proposal to include portions of the Declaration of Independence in the platform adopted. After the outbreak of war he lent his considerable editorial and oratorial influence to the Union cause and in 1864 ran unsuccessfully for Congress in the Staten Island district, where he had made his home. Because of his interest in emancipation and civil rights for the freedmen he proposed the establishment of an agency to help the freed blacks and was gratified to see his suggestion realized in part by the founding of the Freedmen's Bureau (q.v.).

The emancipation of the slaves was not the only cause Curtis espoused. Women's suffrage, the rights of labor, and, above all, civil service reform (q.v.) occupied his attention. Disgusted with the spoils system represented by leaders such as Roscoe Conkling (q.v.), in 1867 he unsuccessfully sought election to the Senate, only to be defeated by the New York politician. One year later, equally without success, he competed for the nomination for Governor of New York against the Conkling candidate. Appointed chairman of the newly established Civil Service Commission by President U. S. Grant (q.v.) in 1871, he occupied the position until its powerlessness caused him to resign in 1873. But he continued his advocacy of the reform, for which he was attacked by Conkling at the 1877 New York State Republican Convention, and served as chairman of the New York Civil Service Association and president of the National Civil Service Reform League, so that the passage of the Pendleton Act in 1883 owed much to his efforts. His disapproval of the candidacy of James G. Blaine (q.v.) led to his break with the Republican party (q.v.) in 1884. He died on Staten Island in 1892.

*See also* Civil Service Reform.

Gordon Milne, *George William Curtis and the Genteel Tradition* (Bloomington, Ind., 1956).

**CUSTER, GEORGE ARMSTRONG** (1839–1876), soldier and Indian fighter, was born in New Rumley, Ohio, and spent much of his youth with his sister's family in Monroe, Michigan. Educated at West Point, he graduated last in his class (1861) but soon earned fame as a cavalry leader in many Civil War engagements. Distinguishing himself particularly at Gettysburg, in the Shenandoah Valley, at Yellow Tavern, and in the Appomattox campaign, in 1863, at the age of twenty-three, he was promoted to the rank of brigadier general. After the war, together with his adored wife Libby, he accompanied General Philip N. Sheridan (q.v.) to Texas, only to be recalled in 1866 when he reverted to his regular army rank of captain.

Always a Democrat, Custer, who opposed black suffrage (q.v.) and favored the policies of Andrew Johnson (q.v.), served as a delegate to the 1866 Philadelphia National Union Convention (q.v.). He also participated prominently in the pro-Johnson Soldiers' and Sailors' Convention at Cleveland.

Appointed lieutenant colonel of the Seventh Cavalry, in 1867 Custer went west to serve in General Winfield Scott Hancock's (q.v.) unsuccessful Indian campaign. After leaving the field without permission, presumably to visit his wife, he was court-martialed and suspended from the service for one year. But

General Sheridan recalled him, and in 1868 he gained new renown by defeating Black Kettle's Cheyennes at the Washita River. Continuing in command of the Seventh cavalry, he saw service at the Yellowstone River and elsewhere in the Dakotas and in 1874 published an account of his experiences entitled *Life on the Plains*. In 1876 he visited Washington to testify in the investigation leading to the impeachment of Secretary of War William W. Belknap (q.v.). When he left the capital without permission, he was arrested on the orders of President Grant but soon freed in order to take part in the campaign against the Sioux.

The expedition against the ably led Indians (q.v.) proved to be his undoing. Underestimating the enemy's strength, he divided his command into three parts in the face of a numerically stronger hostile force and led his command into a trap set for him by Crazy Horse at the battle of Little Big Horn. He was killed with all of his men.

A dashing, impetuous soldier, Custer was a strict disciplinarian who was hated by some of his troops. Yet his bravery, readiness to fight at all times, and his love for his wife made him as popular with great segments of the public as he was disliked by many associates.

*See also* Indians; National Union Convention; Swing Around the Circle.

Jay Monaghan, *Custer: The Life of General George Armstrong Custer* (Boston, 1959); Stephen E. Ambrose, *Crazy Horse and Custer* (Garden City, N.Y., 1975).

# D

DAVIS, DAVID (1815–1886), jurist and political organizer, was born on Sassafras Neck on the Eastern Shore of Maryland. The posthumous son of a physician and a planter's daughter, he was raised by his uncle, an Episcopal rector and the father of Henry Winter Davis (q.v.), and at times by his stepfather, a Baltimore bookseller. He was educated at a boarding school in Ellicott City, the New Ark Academy in Delaware, and at Kenyon College. Upon his graduation, he read law with Henry W. Bishop in Lennox, Massachusetts, where he met his future wife, Sarah Walker, the daughter of a local judge. His education was completed by a brief attendance at the New Haven Law School in 1834.

In 1835 Davis moved to Pekin, Illinois, to start a law practice. The town sent him to the state capital, Vandalia, to lobby for a railroad, and there he met Abraham Lincoln (q.v.), who became his lifelong friend. In 1836 he took over the practice of Jesse Fell in Bloomington, where he then made his permanent residence. After an unsuccessful bid for the state Senate in 1840 he was elected to the lower house four years later and in 1847 served in the state constitutional convention. In 1848 he was elected judge of the eighth circuit of Illinois, an office that enabled him to become intimately acquainted with the leading lawyers of the area, particularly Lincoln.

Always a conservative Whig with a distinct dislike of the abolitionists, Davis nevertheless opposed the expansion of slavery and in 1856 became a Republican. He was vitally interested in the career of his friend Abraham Lincoln and, as principal floor manager at the 1860 Republican convention in Chicago, played a leading role in Lincoln's nomination for the presidency as well as in his subsequent election. In 1862 the President appointed him Associate Justice of the Supreme Court, an office in which he distinguished himself by writing the majority decision in *ex parte Milligan* (q.v.), which held military tribunals unconstitutional when the civil courts were open (1866).

Because of his opposition to universal suffrage in the South and his failure to sympathize fully with the majority's struggle against the policies of President Andrew Johnson (q.v.), following the assassination of Lincoln, Davis became more and more estranged from the Republican party. Although he still dissented in the *test oath* cases of *Cummings* v. *Missouri* (q.v.) and *ex parte Garland* (q.v.), he joined the majority in a narrow interpretation of the Fourteenth Amendment (q.v.) in the *Slaughterhouse* cases (q.v.) of 1873.

Davis' estrangement from the party became complete during the administration of U. S. Grant (q.v.). Emerging as one of the possible nominees of the Liberal Republicans (Liberal Republican Movement, q.v.) after he had already been nominated by the Labor Reform Convention, he was shunted aside at the last moment but supported Horace Greeley (q.v.) in the ensuing election of 1872. Following the disputed election of 1877, Davis was generally considered to be the perfect choice for the independent justice to serve as the fifteenth member of the Electoral Commission (q.v.) but, on the advice of Samuel J. Tilden's (q.v.) nephew, was elected Senator from Illinois. Justice Joseph P. Bradley thereupon took his place on the commission and voted in favor of seating Rutherford B. Hayes (q.v.).

During his service in the Senate—he resigned from the Supreme Court in March 1877—Davis sought to maintain his political independence. Voting with the Democrats to organize the Senate, he nevertheless did not join their caucus and, after the accession of Chester A. Arthur, was elected President *pro tem* of the Senate by a unanimous Republican vote. At the completion of his term, Davis, who had lost his wife, married again. He returned to Bloomington, where he died in 1886.

Although the extremely corpulent Davis was not particularly brilliant, he was a shrewd political organizer. His principal contribution was his astute management of Lincoln's presidential campaign.

*See also* Electoral Commission; Liberal Republicans; *Milligan, Ex Parte*.
Willard L. King, *Lincoln's Manager, David Davis* (Cambridge, Mass., 1960).

**DAVIS, HENRY WINTER** (1817–1865), was born in Annapolis, the son of an Episcopal rector and the cousin of David Davis (q.v.). Educated at a private school in Alexandria, at Kenyon College, and at the University of Virginia, he became a lawyer and settled in Alexandria and then in the District of Columbia, to establish a practice.

From his earliest youth, Davis, strongly influenced by his anti-Jacksonian father, was imbued with a hatred of the Democratic party. He participated actively in Whig politics in Alexandria until, after the death of his wife, he moved to Baltimore in 1849. Quickly reestablishing his legal career as well as his political affiliations, in 1852 he gained national fame as one of the Maryland (q.v.) electors for Winfield Scott for whom he campaigned tirelessly in many parts of the country. The demise of the Whig party led him to join the Know-Nothings in 1855, when he was elected to Congress on the American ticket.

As a representative from a slave state, Davis distinguished himself as a compelling orator who was moderate on the question of slavery and passionately devoted to the Union. Reelected in 1857 and 1859, he was one of the only two Southern members to vote against the Lecompton Constitution of Kansas and created a sensation by his vote for William Pennington, a conservative New Jersey Republican, for Speaker of the House, an action that ended the long struggle for the speakership in 1860. Although he supported the candidacy of John Bell, he welcomed Abraham Lincoln's (q.v.) nomination and election and was considered a leading candidate for a cabinet position in the incoming Republican administration. His Maryland rival Montgomery Blair obtained the prize, however, leaving Davis sorely disappointed. He fearlessly denounced the secessionists and played a major role in saving Maryland for the Union, but his outspoken views led to his defeat for reelection in 1861.

Although temporarily out of office, Davis continued his efforts on behalf of the Union and became one of the principal spokesmen for the radical Unionist faction in Maryland. Won over to the cause of emancipation, he relentlessly labored for the abolition of slavery in the state and finally overcame the opposition of both Democrats and conservative Unionists. When in 1863 he was reelected to Congress, he was made chairman of the Committee on Foreign Relations and of the Select Committee on Rebellious States, which enabled him to challenge Lincoln's Reconstruction program. Dissatisfied with the President's Ten Percent Plan (q.v.), he sought to substitute for it the Wade-Davis Bill (q.v.), a measure requiring an oath of loyalty of 50 percent of the white male citizens registered voters before elections for a new state convention in the seceded states could be held. Only those able to subscribe to an ironclad oath of past loyalty would be enfranchised, and slavery would be abolished. When Lincoln pocketed the measure and published an explanation of his veto, the infuriated Davis, who had long criticized the President for exceeding his constitutional powers, wrote the Wade-Davis Manifesto (q.v.) in which he accused Lincoln of holding the votes of states reorganized under his plan "at the dictation of his personal ambition." Together with other radicals, the Maryland representative also attempted to displace the Emancipator as the head of the Unionist ticket. But the manifesto, issued as it was in the midst of the 1864 presidential campaign, was generally condemned. After George B. McClellan's nomination on a Democratic peace ticket and the capture of Atlanta, the effort to displace Lincoln collapsed, and Davis was eventually induced to lend his support to the Union cause, although he himself was not renominated for his House seat.

During the last session of the Thirty-eighth Congress, Davis succeeded in inducing the House to pass a resolution criticizing the administration's Mexican policy but failed to have his colleagues adopt a modified version of the Wade-Davis Bill, so the Reconstruction problem was unsettled when he left Congress.

After the accession of Andrew Johnson (q.v.), in company with other radicals,

Davis at first sought to win the cooperation of the new President and then sharply turned against him. When in December 1865 the Marylander suddenly died of pneumonia, Congress held an official memorial service for him, a signal honor for a statesman no longer a member of the House.

Davis' powerful oratory, his successful struggle for the Union and emancipation in Maryland, and his contribution to the developing congressional policy of Reconstruction marked him as one of the influential radicals of the time.

*See also* Maryland; Ten Percent Plan; Wade-Davis Bill; Wade-Davis Manifesto.

Gerald S. Henig, *Henry Winter Davis: Antebellum and Civil War Congressman from Maryland* (New York, 1973).


**DAVIS, JEFFERSON** (1808–1889), President of the Confederate States of America, was born in Fairview, Kentucky, the tenth child of a farmer. Taken as a child to Woodville, Mississippi, by his father, he grew up on a cotton plantation. He was educated at the College of St. Thomas Aquinas in Kentucky, at Transylvania University, and at West Point, from which he graduated in 1828. While serving in the army, largely in the Northwest, he met and married the daughter of the commanding officer, Colonel Zachary Taylor. He resigned from the service in 1835 to take up the life of a planter on his plantation in Mississippi, only to lose his wife within a few months. It was not until 1845 that he married again, this time Varina Howell of Vicksburg.

Davis was a convinced Democrat. After an unsuccessful race for the state legislature in 1842, he was elected to Congress three years later but in 1846 resigned to take command of a Mississippi regiment. He distinguished himself at Buena Vista and turned down a proffered general's commission so that Governor Albert Gallatin Brown could appoint him to serve out an unexpired term in the U.S. Senate in 1847. In the next year, he was elected to a full term.

In the Senate, Davis was a strong defender of states rights and opposed the Compromise of 1850. To vindicate his stand, in 1851 he ran for Governor of Mississippi but was defeated by the Unionist Henry S. Foote. In 1853 Franklin Pierce appointed him Secretary of War, an office he held with distinction, and he was reelected to the Senate at the expiration of his term. He again strongly defended Southern rights, supported the Lecompton Constitution and a federal slave code for the territories, but was not a fire-eater.

A natural leader of the South, after the secession of the cotton states, Davis was elected President of the Confederacy. In this position, he exhibited stern devotion to duty and to Southern independence but was not an outstanding executive. Overly loyal to personal friends and unwilling to delegate powers, he became less and less popular. Although he tried to uphold constitutional liberties, he developed more and more into a Southern nationalist, a stance that caused further trouble in the localistic South. Whether anyone else, however, could have led the Confederacy to victory remains problematical.

At the end of the war, Davis, who had a price on his head for alleged complicity in the assassination of Abraham Lincoln (q.v.), was captured by federal troops near Irwinville, Georgia. Incarcerated at Fortress Monroe, he was even manacled for a short time, but his fetters were soon removed.

The disposition of the fallen Confederate leader was a major problem for the administration of Andrew Johnson (q.v.). After ruling out a trial by military commission, the authorities determined to try him for treason in Richmond, but it was difficult to find an impartial jury. In addition, Chief Justice Salmon P. Chase (q.v.) refused to hold court in Virginia, first because martial law still prevailed and then because Congress had not yet firmly established the new judicial districts. In 1867 Davis was finally brought to trial; Horace Greeley (q.v.) and Charles O'Connor put up bail for him, and after further delays, the case was dropped in 1869. But it was not until Johnson's final amnesty (q.v.) in December 1868 that Davis was pardoned, and his citizenship was never restored.

After his release, the former Confederate leader traveled to Canada and Europe and accepted the presidency of the Carolina Life Insurance Co. of Memphis, Tennessee. He then retired to an estate on the Gulf coast left to him by a Mississippi admirer, Belvoir, where he wrote *The Rise and Fall of the Confederate Government*. He died in New Orleans in 1889.

*See also* Amnesty.

Clement Eaton, *Jefferson Davis* (New York, 1977); Hudson Strode, *Jefferson Davis* (3 vols., New York, 1955–1964).

**DELAWARE,** a border state that did not secede or undergo a process of Reconstruction. Although loyal to the Union and containing few slaves, Delaware was distinctly Southern in its racial policies. Refusing to ratify the Thirteenth, Fourteenth, and Fifteenth Amendments (q.v.), it did not free its slaves until compelled to do so by the federal Constitution. Through various devices, such as assessment and innkeepers laws, it continued to restrict black voting and civil rights even after constitutional and congressional enactments sought to secure them, and not until 1875 did it set aside money for black schools. In spite of the extension of the Freedmen's Bureau (q.v.) into the state in 1867, the blacks remained a distinctly disadvantaged class.

Although from time to time special circumstances brought about the election of a Republican congressman, the Governors, Senators, and legislature generally remained safely Democratic throughout the period, so the state supported the policies of Andrew Johnson (q.v.) and opposed Congressional Reconstruction (q.v.). This Democratic dominance was strengthened by the underrepresentation of Newcastle, the only industrialized county. Only after the adoption in 1897 of a new constitution partially rectifying this shortcoming did the Republicans manage to rival the Democrats in importance.

*See also* Thirteenth Amendment.

Harold B. Hancock, "Reconstruction in Delaware," in Richard O. Curry, ed., *Radicalism, Racism, and Party Realignment: The Border States During Reconstruction* (Baltimore, 1969).

**DEMOCRATIC PARTY,** the opposition party during the period of Reconstruction. Hampered by its association with the former Confederates, the Democratic party found it difficult to overcome the wartime prejudices against it. By making attacks on black suffrage (q.v.) and equality its stock in trade, it sought to capitalize on the racist feeling in the North but was unable to win either the presidency or Congress during the immediate postwar years. Nevertheless, it retained a surprising number of supporters, often approaching the victorious Republicans by only a few percentage points of the popular vote.

Divided between "Legitimists" who had wholly supported the war effort and sought the collaboration of conservative Republicans and "Purists" who had often been Peace Democrats and shunned all cooperation with outsiders, the mainstay of the party was the mass of disaffected small farmers and urban workers, often immigrants, in the North, and the former Confederates in the South. Roman Catholics, Lutherans, and Southern Baptists tended to vote Democratic, as did some inflationists. But the party also had a hard money wing, and it continued to insist that it was true to its traditional commitment to states rights, low tariffs, and laissez-faire economics.

When Andrew Johnson (q.v.) broke with the Union party to implement his program of Presidential Reconstruction (q.v.), many Democrats, particularly the Legitimists, hoped to benefit by collaborating with him. A union of sorts was created at the Philadelphia National Union Convention (q.v.) in 1866, but the party's support was always conditional, and the coalition went down to defeat in the fall elections. Moreover, in order to embarrass the Republicans, some Democrats at times voted with their radical opponents as they did in defeating a milder version of the Reconstruction Acts (q.v.), a tactic that set them apart from the administration. Although they succeeded in making some gains in the fall of 1867, they were once more at a disadvantage in trying to defeat the candidacy of the popular U. S. Grant (q.v.) in 1868. After rejecting both Chief Justice Salmon P. Chase (q.v.) and the inflationist George Pendleton, they nominated the hard-money advocate Horatio Seymour (q.v.) and the controversial Francis P. Blair, Jr. (q.v.) and lost the ensuing election.

By 1871 some of the party's spokesmen, particularly the Purist Clement L. Vallandigham, endorsed a "new departure," the acceptance of the wartime amendments and the concentration upon contemporary issues. The emergence of the Liberal Republicans (Liberal Republican Movement, q.v.) appeared to give an impetus to this program, but it was weakened by the Liberals' nomination of Horace Greeley (q.v.). Although the Democrats endorsed the nominee, they could hardly be expected to forget that he had been their lifelong critic and a protectionist, and they were again defeated.

The party's fortunes improved as a consequence of the Panic of 1873. Capturing the House in 1874, it had every expectation of taking the presidency two years later. Its candidate, Samuel J. Tilden (q.v.), did indeed receive more popular votes than his opponent, Rutherford B. Hayes (q.v.), but because twenty electoral votes were in dispute and various deals were made between Southern

Democrats and the Republicans, Hayes was finally awarded the presidency, although the House remained Democratic.

During the entire period under consideration, the Democrats remained what has been called "a respectable minority." Their wartime reputation, however, rendered them comparatively powerless.

*See also* Liberal Republicans; Republican Party.

Joel Silbey, *A Respectable Minority: The Democratic Party in the Civil War Era, 1860–1868*; Leon Friedman, *The Democratic Party, 1860–1884*, in Arthur M. Schlesinger, Jr., ed., History of U.S. Political Parties (4 vols., New York, 1973).

**DOMINICAN REPUBLIC.** See FOREIGN AFFAIRS.

**DOOLITTLE, JAMES ROOD** (1815–1897), conservative U.S. Senator from Wisconsin, was born at Hampton, N.Y. and educated at Hobart College, from which he graduated in 1834. After studying law in Rochester, he moved to Wyoming County to practice his profession. An active Democrat, he served as the county's district attorney between 1847 and 1850 and in 1848, at the New York Democratic convention, introduced the "Corner Stone Resolution" against the extension of slavery, the prelude to his support of the Free Soil party. In 1851 he removed to Racine, Wisconsin, where two years later he became a circuit judge. After joining the Republican party (q.v.), he was elected a U.S. Senator in 1857.

A loyal supporter of the Lincoln administration during the Civil War, after the conflict Doolittle became one of the principal congressional advocates of the policies of Andrew Johnson (q.v.). In 1865 he prevented the Wisconsin Union Convention from adopting a black suffrage (q.v.) plank; in 1866 he took a leading part in the movement for the calling of the National Union Convention (q.v.) at Philadelphia of which he became the permanent president, and in 1867 the Wisconsin legislature called for his resignation because of his support of the President. He refused and during the impeachment trial voted for Johnson's acquittal.

Following the expiration of his second term in the Senate, he joined the Democratic party (q.v.) and was its unsuccessful candidate for Governor in 1871. Thereafter he practiced law in Chicago, taught at the University of Chicago, and was the permanent chairman of the 1872 Democratic convention in Baltimore. He died at Edgewood, Rhode Island in 1897.

*See also* National Union Convention.

Duane Mowry, *An Appreciation of James Rood Doolittle, Proceedings of the State Historical Society of Wisconsin*, 1909, 281–296; *Biographical Directory of the American Congress, 1774–1961* (Washington, D.C., 1961); *George Fort Milton, The Age of Hate: Andrew Johnson and the Radicals* (New York, 1930).

**DOSTIE, ANTHONY PAUL** (1821–1866), Louisiana (q.v.) Unionist, was born in Saratoga, New York, and moved to New Orleans in 1852 to practice dentistry. A convinced Unionist, he had to leave Louisiana after it seceded but returned in the wake of the federal army to take a prominent part in the reconstruction process. Although at first he did not believe the time was ripe for black suffrage (q.v.), he nevertheless promised to back it if the freedmen insisted. As a convinced advocate of the speedy restoration of a loyal government, he lent his support to General Nathaniel P. Banks' (q.v.) plan of electing a new administration under the Constitution of 1852 without its slavery clause and was chosen state auditor under it. After the adoption of a new constitution in 1864, he actively furthered its acceptance. Successful in this endeavor, he was nevertheless defeated in a race for Congress.

One of the most radical of the Louisiana Unionists, Dostie became increasingly identified with the demand for black suffrage. He denounced the conservative regime of Governor J. Madison Wells (q.v.), and when he accused the Governor of wrongdoing, Wells dismissed him. He had to be carried out bodily from his state auditor's office and continued to pursue his radical policies, particularly the demand to reconvene the constitutional convention of 1864, a measure that he urged in a speech considered by many to have been inflammatory. When the recalled convention actually attempted to meet in July 1866, the effort was frustrated by violence. The New Orleans riot (q.v.) ensued, and Dostie was murdered by conservatives.

*See also* Louisiana; New Orleans Riot.

Peyton McCrary, *Abraham Lincoln and Reconstruction: The Louisiana Experiment* (Princeton, N.J., 1978); Joe Gray Taylor, *Louisiana Reconstructed, 1863–1877* (Baton Rouge, 1974); Gerald M. Capers, *Occupied City: New Orleans Under the Federals, 1862–1865* (Lexington, Ky., 1965); Willie Malvin Caskey, *Secession and Restoration of Louisiana* (Baton Rouge, 1938); Emily Hazen Reed, *Life of A. P. Dostie; or, The Conflict in New Orleans* (New York, 1868).

**DOUGLASS, FREDERICK** (1817–1895), abolitionist and black leader, was born Frederick Augustus Washington Bailey in Talbot County, Maryland, the son of a slave mother and a white father. A kindly Baltimore mistress taught him how to read, and he taught himself how to write. Deeply troubled by his status as a slave, he encountered difficulties with his master, Thomas Auld, who sent him to a professional slave breaker. After this experience, he tried unsuccessfully to run away, only to have his master put him to work in a Baltimore shipyard.

In 1838 Douglass finally effected his escape, first to New York and then to New Bedford, Massachusetts, where he adopted his new name while working as a laborer. Coming to the attention of William Lloyd Garrison and the American Anti-Slavery Society, he was called upon to address a meeting at Nantucket and made such an impression upon the abolitionists that they employed him as a lecturer. His effectiveness was such that he soon became famous, particularly after he published his autobiography, *The Narrative of the Life of Frederick Douglass*, in 1845. Afraid of recapture, he sailed to England and spent the next two years lecturing and meeting British fellow abolitionists, two of whom provided the money to purchase his freedom.

After his return to the United States in 1847, Douglass broke with Garrison to cooperate with the political abolitionists. Moving to Rochester, he established his newspaper, *The North Star*, later called *Frederick Douglass' Paper*, and enlisted the political and financial support of Gerrit Smith. In the late 1850s he aided John Brown but refused to take part in the raid upon Harpers Ferry. Continuing his speaking activities, in 1855 he also published an expanded version of his autobiography, *My Bondage and My Freedom*, which, like his predecessor, was a great success.

At the outbreak of the Civil War, Douglass was critical of the Lincoln administration, but upon the promulgation of the Emancipation Proclamation (q.v.), he rallied to the cause and recruited black troops for the Union army. Received by Abraham Lincoln (q.v.) at the White House, he established a satisfactory relationship with the President.

In the postwar years, Douglass continued to champion his race's quest for equality and was particularly active in the cause of black suffrage (q.v.). This attitude brought him in conflict with Andrew Johnson (q.v.), although as late as 1867 the President still offered him the position of commissioner of the Freedmen's Bureau (q.v.), which he turned down. At the 1866 Philadelphia Southern Loyalist Convention (q.v.) he embarrassed the organizers by his prominent appearance but continued loyally to lend his support to the Republican party and the election of Ulysses S. Grant (q.v.). His reward was an appointment as secretary to the Santo Domingo Commission. In 1874 he served briefly as President of the Freedman's Savings Bank (q.v.) in a desperate though vain effort to salvage the institution.

The party offered further rewards to the famous black leader. In 1877 Rutherford B. Hayes (q.v.) appointed him marshal of the District of Columbia; in 1881 James A. Garfield (q.v.) made him recorder of deeds of the District, where he now made his home, and in 1888 Benjamin Harrison sent him to Haiti as minister plenipotentiary. In 1893 he served as Haitian commissioner to the Columbian Exposition at Chicago. He maintained his lecturing activities; published a third version of his autobiography, *The Life and Times of Frederick Douglass*, in 1881; and traveled widely in Europe and the Middle East. He died in Washington in 1895.

Douglass was the most prominent black abolitionist and political leader during much of the nineteenth century. A powerful orator and able writer, he was a passionate advocate of black assimilation and equal rights, a conviction he carried so far as to marry a white woman after his first wife's death. In addition, he was interested in sundry other reforms, especially the struggle for women's rights, and in 1848 attended the Seneca Falls convention. As a role model for his constituency and an example of black achievement, he contributed greatly to the cause he had made his own.

*See also* Blacks; Black Suffrage; Emancipation.

William S. McFeely, *Frederick Douglass* (New York, 1991); Nathan Huggins, *Slave and Citizen: The Life of Frederick Douglass* (Boston, 1980); Benjamin Quarles, *Frederick Douglass* (Washington, D.C., 1948).

**DURANT, THOMAS JEFFERSON** (1817–1882), Louisiana (q.v.) Unionist and legal expert, was born in Philadelphia and moved to New Orleans in the early 1830s. An accomplished attorney, he was active in the Democratic party, particularly in the 1844 campaign that resulted in the election of James K. Polk. In 1846 he was sent to the state Senate and later that year the grateful President appointed him federal attorney for the Eastern District of Louisiana.

In 1860 Durant, a determined foe of secession, supported Stephen A. Douglas. After Louisiana left the Union, he quietly remained in the Confederacy, only to emerge as one of the foremost Unionists when the federal army occupied New Orleans. Establishing close relations with General Benjamin F. Butler (q.v.), he proposed the reorganization of the state under a new constitution and, though a slaveholder, endorsed emancipation. In May 1863 he was elected President of the Union Association, and in the next month General George P. Shepley, the Military Governor, appointed him Attorney General and commissioner of registration. His work in the latter capacity was hampered by a rift with General Nathaniel P. Banks (q.v.), General Butler's successor, who sought to reestablish a state government by elections for executive officers in early 1864. Resigning in protest against these policies, Durant opposed the constitutional convention of 1864 and became one of the principal advocates of black suffrage (q.v.). He traveled to Washington to protest against the administration's endorsement of Banks, influenced the framing of the Wade-Davis Bill (q.v.) and Manifesto (q.v.), and opposed the admission of Louisiana's congressional delegation. After the New Orleans riot (q.v.) he moved to Washington, though maintaining his legal connections in New Orleans. General Philip Sheridan (q.v.) offered him the governorship of Louisiana, which he refused. As an expert on questions affecting the state, he was a frequent practitioner before the Supreme Court and won a significant victory in the *Slaughterhouse* cases (q.v.). Repeatedly mentioned as a possible choice for Associate Justice of the Supreme Court, he was counsel for the United States before the Spanish-American Claims Commission at the time of his death in Washington.

A narrow constitutionalist, Durant was a distinguished member of his profession. His effectiveness in reconstructing Louisiana was hampered by his quarrels with Banks, A. P. Dostie (q.v.), and the Lincoln administration.

*See also* Banks, Nathaniel P.; Louisiana.

Joseph Tregle, Jr., "Thomas J. Durant, Utopian Socialism, and the Failure of Presidential Reconstruction in Louisiana," *Journal of Southern History*, 14 (1979): 485–512; Peyton McCrary, *Abraham Lincoln and Reconstruction: The Louisiana Experiment* (Princeton, N.J., 1978); LaWanda Cox, *Lincoln and Black Freedom: A Study in Presidential Leadership* (Columbia, S.C., 1981); Charles Warren, *The Supreme Court in United States History* (2 vols., Boston, 1922); New Orleans *Daily Picayune*, February 5, 1882.

# E

---

**EDUCATION, BLACK,** an effort to provide education for the freedmen, which began in August 1861 when Mary S. Peake established a school for fellow blacks at Fortress Monroe. In the following year, various Northern philanthropic organizations, particularly the American Missionary Association, sent dedicated teachers to areas occupied by Union troops. Especially in the Sea Islands (q.v.) off Port Royal, South Carolina, a group of Yankee instructors, the Gideonites, as well as some educated blacks, undertook to provide education for the freedmen. Various federal commanders, among them Generals U. S. Grant (q.v.) in the Department of Tennessee, Nathaniel P. Banks (q.v.) in the Department of the Gulf, and Benjamin F. Butler (q.v.) in the Department of North Carolina and Virginia, appointed officers to take care of black education, and the federal government opened schools for blacks (q.v.) in Charleston under the direction of James Redpath of the New York *Tribune*.

After the war, these efforts were partially taken over and generally assisted by the Freedmen's Bureau (q.v.). It provided funds, teachers' houses, and cooperation for the Northern aid societies in establishing and maintaining schools as well as some higher institutions of learning. The Bureau's superintendent of education, John W. Alvord, was greatly encouraged by his superior, General Oliver O. Howard (q.v.), the head of the organization, who considered black education of the utmost importance.

The blacks themselves showed great eagerness for learning. Believing that education was the way to equality and acceptance, they were highly motivated, raised large amounts of money to fund their schools, and greatly impressed Northern schoolmasters. Yet white Southerners were usually hostile to the experiment; they feared racial integration of the schools and detested the Northerners sent among them to teach their former slaves. Nevertheless, after the Civil

War modest advances in state-operated schools were made, particularly following the introduction of Congressional Reconstruction (q.v.), when Southern states established viable public school systems. All of these institutions were segregated, although in Louisiana (q.v.) a brief experiment to integrate schools was made, an effort that resulted in riots and failed after the Compromise of 1877 (q.v.). Public prejudice was too strong, and even the disbursement of the Peabody Fund, a foundation set up to aid Southern education, tended to support segregation.

Federal attempts to further integration also failed. Neither the public schools in Washington nor those under the Freedmen's Bureau were able to overcome the prejudice against mixed education. It is true that Charles Sumner (q.v.) tried for years to pass civil rights bills that included integrated schooling, but when after his death the Civil Rights Bill of 1875 (q.v.) was finally passed, it was shorn of its educational provisions.

In spite of the many obstacles in its way, black education was instrumental in greatly reducing the illiteracy rate among the freedmen. Black schools appeared throughout the South and several black colleges were established, although fully integrated education had to await the coming of the "Second Reconstruction."

*See also* Freedmen's Bureau; Sea Islands.

William Preston Vaughn, *Schools for All: The Blacks and Public Education in the South, 1865–1877* (Lexington, Ky., 1974); Ronald Butchart, *Northern Schools, Southern Blacks, and Reconstruction: Freemen's Education, 1862–1875* (Westport, Conn., 1980); Henry Lee Swint, *Northern Teachers in the South, 1862–1870* (Nashville, 1941); Robert C. Morris, *Reading, 'Riting, and Reconstruction: The Education of Freemen in the South, 1861–1870* (Chicago, 1981).

**ELECTORAL COMMISSION,** a device for the resolution of the disputed election returns of 1876 set up by Congress in January 1877 after two sets of returns from Florida (q.v.), Louisiana (q.v.), South Carolina (q.v.), and a contested election in Oregon had resulted in a deadlock. The Republican presidential candidate, Rutherford B. Hayes (q.v.), had an undisputed total of 165 electoral votes; Samuel J. Tilden, his Democratic opponent, 184. Should all of the 20 doubtful votes be awarded to Hayes, he would become President; if Tilden obtained but 1, the prize would be his. In view of the fact that the Democrats controlled the House and the Republicans the Senate, Congress was unable to resolve the problem, although some Republicans argued that Thomas E. Ferry, the president pro tem of the Senate, whose duty it was to announce the result, should also count the votes. Since Ferry was a Republican, the Democratic House objected. With the country faced with the possibility of an impasse extending beyond March 4, when the new President's term was to begin, it became necessary to find some solution, and Congress established an Electoral Commission consisting of five Senators, three Republicans and two Democrats; five representatives, three Democrats and two Republicans; and two evenly balanced justices of the Supreme Court, who were to elect a fifth colleague, presumably the independent David Davis (q.v.). But at the last minute, the legislature of

Illinois elected Davis a Democratic Senator, and he refused to serve on the commission. Thereupon Joseph P. Bradley of New Jersey, a Republican, was substituted in his stead, and when the commission began to function, it decided all the disputed issues by a strict party vote of eight to seven.

Greatly disturbed by this development, the Democrats were still considering a filibuster to prevent the election of Hayes. But as a result of the Compromise of 1877 (q.v.), involving both economic concessions and political gains such as the appointment of a Southerner to the cabinet as well as the withdrawal of federal troops from the Southern statehouses, a bargain again was sealed at the Wormley Conference (q.v.). The opposition party desisted, and on March 2 Ferry was able to announce the election of Rutherford B. Hayes and William A. Wheeler.

*See also* Compromise of 1877; Hayes, Rutherford B.; Tilden, Samuel Jones; Wormley Conference.

Ari Hoogenboom, *The Presidency of Rutherford B. Hayes* (Lawrence, Kans., 1988); Harry Barnard, *Rutherford B. Hayes and His America* (Indianapolis, 1954); Alexander Clarence Flick, *Samuel Jones Tilden: A Study in Policial Sagacity* (New York, 1939).

**ELLIOTT, ROBERT BROWN** (1842?–1884), black congressman and Republican leader in South Carolina (q.v.). Although Elliott was said to have been a native of Boston and educated at various English schools, it is probable that he was born in Great Britain and then settled in Boston. In 1867 he came to Charleston to assume the associate editorship of the *South Carolina Leader*. Well educated and an excellent speaker, he became a prominent member of the state's Republican party (q.v.), distinguishing himself in the constitutional convention of 1868 by the forceful advocacy of compulsory school attendance, an equal-accommodations act, and universal suffrage unencumbered by poll taxes. As a member of the first legislature elected after the beginning of Congressional Reconstruction (q.v.), he stood out as one of the party's leaders attempting to further the cause of his race by measures such as a public accommodations bill and legislation to outlaw the carrying of concealed weapons. Appointed assistant adjutant general in 1869, he was largely responsible for the organization of the black militia.

In 1870 Elliott was elected to Congress, where he again attracted attention as a fearless defender of black rights. He forcefully pleaded for the passage of the Ku Klux Klan Bill, and, after his reelection in 1872, continued his advocacy of equal rights in a moving speech in favor of Charles Sumner's (q.v.) Civil Rights Bill (q.v.) in 1874. A few months later he delivered a memorial address in Boston about its deceased author, an oration widely praised.

But Elliott never gave up his interest in local South Carolina affairs. Presiding over the Republican convention of 1872, he engineered the nomination for Governor of Franklin J. Moses, Jr., over his rival Daniel H. Chamberlain (q.v.), only to lose a bid for the U.S. Senate soon afterward. In 1874 he resigned his seat in Congress to return to the state legislature, where, after having supported the successful reform candidacy of Chamberlain for Governor, he was elected Speaker of the Assembly. But because he detested Chamberlain's overtures to the conservatives he soon fell out with the Governor again.

In 1876, outraged at the Hamburg Massacre (q.v.), Elliott was the author of the Appeal to the People of the United States protesting against this act of calculated murder. In view of the continued terrorist tactics of the Democrats, Republican unity was essential, so, after first opposing Chamberlain's bid for renomination, Elliott finally joined him to run on the Republican ticket for Attorney General.

The subsequent disputed elections made the outcome in South Carolina vital; Elliott argued the case for the Republicans before the state Supreme Court, but two rival state governments emerged. The Electoral Commission (q.v.) in Washington finally awarded the victory to the Republicans. When President Rutherford B. Hayes (q.v.) withdrew the federal troops, however, Chamberlain's administration was doomed, and Elliott was forced to resign.

In the years that followed, Elliott practiced law in South Carolina and in 1879 was appointed special inspector of customs, first at Charleston and then at New Orleans, where he died in 1884.

Although not free of suspicions of corruption, Elliott was an able political leader whose advocacy of equal rights stamped him as a leading defender of his race.

*See also* Chamberlain, Daniel H.; South Carolina.

Peggy Lamson, *The Glorious Failure: Black Congressman Robert Brown Elliott and the Reconstruction of South Carolina* (New York, 1973).

**EMANCIPATION.** Despite public denials, the abolition of slavery was from the beginning one of the likely outcomes of the Civil War and a concomitant of Reconstruction. Constrained by political and military necessity not to make emancipation one of his war aims, Abraham Lincoln (q.v.), who had always favored freedom, signed a number of laws freeing individual slaves. In August 1861 he gave his assent to the first Confiscation Act liberating bondsmen used in warfare against the United States, a principle established by General Benjamin F. Butler (q.v.) who in May had declared such fugitives "contraband of war"; in April 1862 the President signed the bill for compensated emancipation in the District of Columbia and in July the measure prohibiting slavery in the territories as well as the second Confiscation Act freeing all slaves belonging to insurgents. In addition, he attempted to induce the border states to take measures for emancipation, first privately and then, in March 1862, publicly with a scheme of compensated emancipation.

While favoring freedom, Lincoln nevertheless believed that it was the President, not the commanding generals, who had the right to decide when the time for action had come. For this reason, in September 1861 he revoked General John C. Frémont's edict for emancipation in the Department of Missouri and in May 1862 revoked a similar order by General David Hunter in the Department of the South.

Determined to forestall foreign drives for the recognition of the Confederacy and to satisfy the radicals (Radical Republicans, q.v.) without alienating the border states, in June 1862 the President began to frame the Emancipation Proclamation (q.v.). To spare the border states, it proposed to free all slaves in territories still held by the insurgents but exempting all others. When on July 22, 1862, he submitted the document to the cabinet, Secretary of State William H. Seward (q.v.) advised that it be withheld until Union arms had achieved some successes, a condition that was fulfilled after the Battle of Antietam. Then, on September 22, 1862, Lincoln published the proclamation promising freedom to all slaves in areas still in rebellion by January 1, 1863, one hundred days later. In spite of pressure to reconsider, on the appointed day the President promulgated the proclamation, and slaves in areas still in rebellion were declared to be free.

The Emancipation Proclamation, which became effective as Union armies advanced into the South, left untouched all bondsmen in the border states, in Tennessee (q.v.), and in some occupied portions of Virginia (q.v.) and Louisiana (q.v.). Under considerable pressure from the President, all the exempted states except Kentucky (q.v.) and Delaware (q.v.) enacted emancipation statutes or amendments on their own, starting with West Virginia (q.v.) in 1863, followed by restored Virginia, Louisiana, and Maryland (q.v.) in 1864 and Missouri (q.v.) and Tennessee in 1865. The laggard commonwealths had to await the ratification of the Thirteenth Amendment (q.v.).

Anxious to place emancipation beyond legislative or judicial interference, Lincoln strongly favored a constitutional amendment for the purpose. The Senate passed it in April 1864, and the Union party platform of that year endorsed it. To force it through the House, which had earlier rejected it, the President in the winter of 1864–1865 used all his powers of patronage and persuasion, until on January 31, 1865, the amendment was accepted. On December 18, 1865, Seward, counting the states reconstructed under the presidential plan, certified its ratification.

Because the emancipated slaves possessed neither land nor any other resources, their integration into society proved difficult. Radical efforts to provide them with farms failed, with the result that they tended to become sharecroppers. Thus the legacy of emancipation was an economic and social problem of great magnitude.

*See also* Blacks; Emancipation Proclamation; Thirteenth Amendment.

LaWanda Cox, *Lincoln and Black Freedom: A Study in Presidential Leadership* (Columbia, S.C., 1981); Leon Litwack, *Been in the Storm So Long: The Aftermath of Slavery* (New York, 1979); Hans L. Trefousse, *Lincoln's Decision for Emancipation* (Philadelphia, 1975); Louis S. Gerteis, *From Contraband to Freedman: Federal Policy toward Southern Blacks, 1861–1865* (Westport, Conn., 1973); John Hope Franklin, *The Emancipation Proclamation* (New York, 1963).

**EMANCIPATION PROCLAMATION** (1863), document issued by Abraham Lincoln (q.v.) on January 1, 1863, freeing all slaves in designated areas still in rebellion against the United States.

Always opposed to slavery but unable to move speedily against it because of the necessity of maintaining the loyalty of the border states and the Democratic opposition, Lincoln was continually under pressure from the radical Republicans (q.v.) to begin the process of emancipation (q.v.). In addition, the threat of foreign recognition of the Confederacy also made an antislavery move desirable because Great Britain especially was strongly opposed to the "peculiar institution." Accordingly, in June 1862 the President began the preparation of a proclamation to free the slaves in areas still in rebellion and presented his plan to the cabinet on July 22. On the suggestion of Secretary of State William H. Seward (q.v.) that the measure be withheld pending some federal victory, Lincoln waited until after the Battle of Antietam. Then, on September 22, 1862, he issued the Preliminary Emancipation Proclamation promising to free within one hundred days all slaves in any state or part of a state still in rebellion at that time.

In spite of bitter attacks by conservatives and Democrats, the President refused to modify his proclamation or to withdraw it. Acting under his authority as commander-in-chief of the army and navy in times of actual armed rebellion, on January 1, 1863, "as a fit and necessary war measure," he promulgated his proclamation freeing all slaves in areas designated to be still in rebellion, exempting only Tennessee (q.v.) and parts of Louisiana (q.v.) and Virginia (q.v.). In addition, while enjoining the freedmen to abstain from violence and work for reasonable wages, he authorized their acceptance into the military forces of the United States.

Because of the uncertainty of the permanence of a measure taken by virtue of his authority as commander-in-chief, Lincoln not only pressured the exempted areas and border states to initiate a measure of emancipation of their own but also used all of his powers of patronage to facilitate the passage of the Thirteenth Amendment (q.v.).

The Emancipation Proclamation has been attacked as a futile measure that freed nobody on the day it was issued. Yet it brought freedom to millions as soon as Union troops entered the areas to which it applied and clearly indicated that the war, officially a struggle to maintain the Union, would also end slavery if the Union won. Lincoln was indeed the Great Emancipator, and after the promulgation of the proclamation, it would be impossible to reconstruct any state without the abolition of slavery.

*See also* Emancipation; Lincoln, Abraham; Thirteenth Amendment.

John Hope Franklin, *The Emancipation Proclamation* (Garden City, N.Y., 1963); Hans L. Trefousse, *Lincoln's Decision for Emancipation* (Philadelphia, 1975).

**ENFORCEMENT ACTS,** three measures to enforce the provisions of the Fourteenth and Fifteenth Amendments (q.v.). The first of these, passed on May 31, 1870, provided for heavy penalties for interference with the right to vote, gave federal courts jurisdiction in cases involving congressional elections, outlawed conspiracies to prevent impartial voting, and empowered the President to employ the armed forces to aid in its execution. The second, passed on February 28, 1871, amended its predecessor by authorizing federal supervision of congressional elections in towns with more than twenty thousand inhabitants and spelled out the powers of supervisory officers. The third, passed on April 20, 1871 (also called the Ku Klux Act), outlawed terrorist conspiracies like the Ku Klux Klan (q.v.) and authorized the President to suspend the writ of habeas corpus in areas where unlawful combinations prevailed.

Constituting an effort to protect the right of blacks (q.v.) to vote, particularly in the South, the measures proved ineffective in the long run. President U. S. Grant (q.v.) invoked the Ku Klux Act in 1871 by suspending the writ of habeas corpus in nine counties in South Carolina, while the Attorney General brought indictments against violators in various Southern states. But by 1876 the determination to enforce the amendments was waning; although in 1875 another Force Bill was passed in the House, it was never considered by the Senate, and in 1876, in *U.S.* v. *Reese et al.* (q.v.) and *U.S.* v. *Cruikshank* (q.v.) the Supreme Court held that parts of the first Enforcement Act were unconstitutional. It declared that the right to vote was a state, not a federal, matter and that the indictments under the statute had been too vague. One last effort to strengthen the laws was made by Henry Cabot Lodge in 1890, when he introduced a new Force Bill into the House only to see it defeated in the Senate, in part by Republicans anxious to gain votes for a silver bill. Not until the 1960s did the federal government finally enforce the post–Civil War Amendments.

*See also* Ku Klux Klan; *U.S.* v. *Cruikshank*; *U.S.* v. *Reese et al.*

William Gillette, *Retreat from Reconstruction, 1869–1879* (Baton Rouge, 1979); Stanley Hirshson, *Farewell to the Bloody Shirt: Northern Republicans and the Southern Negro, 1877–1893* (Bloomington, Ind., 1962).

**EVARTS, WILLIAM MAXWELL** (1818–1901), lawyer, Attorney General, Secretary of State, and U.S. Senator, was born in Boston, the son of an attorney and journalist and the grandson of Roger Sherman of revolutionary renown. Educated at Yale and the Harvard Law School, Evarts settled in New York, where he was admitted to the bar in 1841. He soon gained fame in his profession and from 1849 to 1853 served as assistant district attorney for the Southern District of New York. Although he was a conservative Whig, he contributed $1,000 to the Emigrant Aid Society to fight slavery in Kansas and was one of the founders of the state Republican party. In 1860, as chairman of the New York delegation to the Chicago Republican convention, he worked for the nomination of his friend William H. Seward (q.v.) but then loyally supported the candidacy of Abraham Lincoln (q.v.).

At the outbreak of the Civil War, Evarts served as secretary of the New York Union Defense Committee. He represented the government in the *Prize* cases, which upheld Lincoln's war powers, and was twice sent to Europe by Seward to represent the legal interests of the United States in England and France.

In the postwar era, Evarts, though still a moderate, seemed to favor Congress against Andrew Johnson (q.v.). He was a Republican delegate to the New York constitutional convention of 1867, but he was conservative enough to be chosen one of the defense counsel in the President's impeachment trial. His able speeches contributed to Johnson's acquittal, after which, in June 1868, the President appointed him Attorney General. In this post it fell to him to continue the case against Jefferson Davis (q.v.), with which he had long been associated as a federal prosecutor. But in 1869, after Johnson's last proclamation of amnesty (q.v.), he finally entered a nolle prosequi.

After his return to New York, Evarts became one of the founders and longtime president of the local bar association and took an active part in the fight against the Tweed Ring (Tweed, William Magear, q.v.). In 1874 he was appointed counsel for the United States at the Geneva Tribunal arbitrating the Alabama claims in conformity with the Treaty of Washington (q.v.), yet he failed to obtain the nomination for Chief Justice of the United States, a position for which he had long been mentioned. As counsel for Henry Ward Beecher (q.v.) in the adultery case brought by Theodore Tilton, he succeeded in securing his client's partial vindication by a split jury.

In 1876 Evarts, an unsuccessful candidate for Governor of New York, supported Rutherford B. Hayes (q.v.) for the presidency. When, following the disputed election in November, an electoral commission was appointed, Evarts, as counsel for the Republicans, represented Hayes' claims before it. His eloquence and wit helped Hayes win his case, and the grateful President appointed the attorney Secretary of State. Although because of his identification with Johnson his confirmation was difficult, Evarts carried out his duties with great distinction. At the end of his term he resumed his practice in New York.

Remaining loyal to the party in 1884, Evarts was elected to the U.S. Senate in 1885. A supporter of the Force Bill of 1890 as well as of other measures of the Harrison administration, particularly the McKinley Tariff, his chief contribution was the Evarts Bill for the reorganization of the federal judiciary by the establishment of circuit courts of appeal. He was also interested in historical activities and introduced the measure for the incorporation of the American Historical Society. He was not reelected in 1891, and his failing eyesight, eventually leading to blindness, prevented him from seeking further office. He died in New York. His skillful pleading and legal learning contributed to his success at the bar, and his defense of Andrew Johnson was particularly memorable.

*See also* Electoral Commission; Hayes, Rutherford B.; Johnson, Andrew.

Chester A. Barrows, *William M. Evarts: Lawyer, Diplomat, Statesman* (Berkeley, Calif., 1941); Brainerd Dyer, *The Public Career of William M. Evarts* (Berkeley, Calif., 1933).

# F

FESSENDEN, WILLIAM PITT (1806–1869), Republican Senator and Secretary of the Treasury, was born at Boscawen, New Hampshire, the illegitimate son of the lawyer and later militia general Samuel Fessenden and of Ruth Greene. Taken home to Fryeburg, Maine, by his father shortly after his birth, Fessenden was raised there by his paternal family. He was educated at Bowdoin and in 1827 was admitted to the bar at Portland. In 1835, after brief periods in Bridgton and Bangor, he settled permanently in Portland, where he became a successful attorney. He served in the legislature as a National Republican and Whig in 1832 and 1840; accompanied his godfather, Daniel Webster, on a western trip; and in 1840 was elected to Congress, where he opposed the Gag Rule and other proslavery measures. Returning to Portland in 1843, he was again a member of the legislature in 1845–1846 and 1853–1854, when he was elected to the U.S. Senate. A pronounced opponent of the Kansas-Nebraska Act, he soon joined the new Republican party (q.v.), which reelected him to his seat in 1859.

During the Civil War, Fessenden rendered important service as chairman of the Senate Committee on Finance. In 1864, after the resignation of Secretary Salmon P. Chase (q.v.), Abraham Lincoln (q.v.) appointed him Secretary of the Treasury, an office in which he continued many of Chase's policies. He resigned early in 1865 to reenter the Senate, the Maine legislature having reelected him to his seat.

Always a moderate, after the war Fessenden was one of the leaders of the more conservative faction of his party. Although he sought to prevent a split between Congress and President Andrew Johnson (q.v.), he accepted the chairmanship of the Joint Committee of Fifteen on Reconstruction (q.v.), favored the Freedmen's Bureau Bill (q.v.) and Civil Rights Act (q.v.), and believed the Fourteenth Amendment (q.v.) was an adequate settlement of Reconstruction. As a result, he was lukewarm toward the Reconstruction Acts (q.v.), opposed the Tenure of Office Act (q.v.), and deplored the impeachment of Johnson (q.v.). During the impeachment trial, he resisted popular pressure to become one of the seven "recusants" who voted for the President's acquittal, an action for which he was roundly denounced. Nevertheless, he campaigned loyally for General U. S. Grant (q.v.) and continued to be active in the Republican party. He died in Portland in 1869.

A forceful debater, Fessenden was one of the principal representatives of the moderate faction of the Republican party. His legalistic mind deplored excesses, and he opposed what he considered unconstitutional means to bring about desirable events.

*See also* Impeachment of Andrew Johnson; Johnson, Andrew.

Charles A. Jellison, *Fessenden of Maine: Civil War Senator* (Syracuse, 1962); Francis Fessenden, *Life and Public Services of William Pitt Fessenden* (2 vols., Boston, 1907).

**FIFTEENTH AMENDMENT,** the final measure of constitutional aid to the freedmen during the period of Reconstruction. Providing that "the right of citizens of the United States to vote shall not be abridged by the United States or any State on account of race, color, or previous condition of servitude," the amendment, including an enforcement clause, was adopted by Congress in 1869 and ratified by the states in 1870.

Long the subject of controversy, the demand for black suffrage (q.v.) was tirelessly advanced by the radical Republicans (q.v.). The reform was defeated several times in various Northern states; it was disregarded in the Fourteenth Amendment (q.v.), but the radicals were successful in forcing it upon the South by means of the Reconstruction Acts (q.v.). In the North, however, voting restrictions were retained in many states, and the cause of black enfranchisement received another setback when the Republican platform of 1868 failed to mention it. Yet its advocates did not rest, and following the election of U. S. Grant (q.v.), they finally forced Congress to consider it. After lengthy parliamentary debates and maneuvers, in February 1869 the amendment was passed.

In its final version, however, it represented a conservative rendition of the movement for universal suffrage. The amendment mentioned neither office-holding nor any protection against disfranchisement by subterfuges, such as educational and residence requirements later used by Southern states to subvert it. It also disappointed feminists by failing to prohibit disfranchisement of women.

Historians have emphasized different reasons for the passage of the constitutional change. Some stress the Republicans' interest in securing the black vote in several closely balanced Northern and border states; others, the party's ideological commitment and its desire to protect the freedmen in the South. In later years, it became necessary to pass several Enforcement Acts (q.v.) to give meaning to the amendment, but in 1876, narrowly interpreting it in *U.S.* v. *Reese et al.* (q.v.), the Supreme Court effectively nullified these measures. It was not until the civil rights movement of the twentieth century that the constitutional mandate was finally enforced by the federal government.

*See also* Black Suffrage; Enforcement Acts; Fourteenth Amendment; *U.S.* v. *Reese et al.*

William Gillette, *The Right to Vote: Politics and the Passage of the Fifteenth Amendment* (Baltimore, 1965); LaWanda and John H. Cox, "Negro Suffrage and Republican Politics: The Problem of Motivation in Reconstruction Historiography," *Journal of Southern History*, 33 (1967): 303–30; Glenn M. Linden, "A Note on Negro Suffrage and Republican Politics," *Journal of Southern History*, 36 (1970): 411–20; Michael Les Benedict, *A Compromise of Principle: Congressional Republicans and Reconstruction, 1863–1869* (New York, 1974).

**FINANCE.** *See* GREENBACKS; LEGAL TENDER CASES; OHIO IDEA.

**FISH, HAMILTON** (1808–1893), Governor of New York, Senator, and Secretary of State, was born in New York, the son of a prominent New York lawyer and of the daughter of a descendant of Peter Stuyvesant. Educated at Columbia College, he was admitted to the bar in 1830 and practiced his profession in New York City. In 1841–1843 he served in the House of Representatives as a Whig, was elected Lieutenant Governor in 1847 and was Governor between 1848 and 1850 as well as U.S. Senator between 1851 and 1857. He joined the Republican party (q.v.) after some hesitation but loyally supported its policies by serving on the New York Union Defense Committee in 1861 as well as a commissioner for the investigation of the condition of Union prisoners in 1862.

Always a conservative, Fish supported the Philadelphia National Union Convention (q.v.) in 1866. In spite of his sympathies for the policies of Andrew Johnson (q.v.), however, in 1869 President U. S. Grant (q.v.) appointed him Secretary of State, a position that, with the exception of the first two weeks, he was to occupy during the entire eight years of the Grant administration.

As Secretary of State, Fish established an admirable record. Less expansionist than his predecessor, William H. Seward (q.v.), he was largely responsible for maintaining the peace between the United States and Spain, then endangered by the endemic rebellion in Cuba, and with Great Britain, constantly at odds with America because of fisheries controversies, the *Alabama* Claims, and Fenian raids.

The problems with Spain involved not merely Cuba's desire for independence but also the end of slavery on the island. By adroitly negotiating with succeeding Spanish governments and keeping Grant satisfied by judicious approaches to his various ill-considered schemes, the Secretary of State was able to counteract the interventionists, often the President's close advisers, who wanted to involve the United States in the cause of Cuban independence. On the one hand, he humored Grant by not opposing the President's unrealistic desire for the annexation of the Dominican Republic; on the other hand, he transferred negotiations with Spain from Madrid, where the United States was represented by the irascible Daniel Sickles (q.v.), to Washington. Even during the dangerous crisis following the Spaniards' capture of the *Virginius*, a ship sailing under the American flag, and the execution of some of its officers, he was able to defuse the dangerous war fever. As a result, although Spanish rule in Cuba was not ended until 1898 and slavery not abolished until the 1880s, the United States remained neutral.

The points at issue with Great Britain were more difficult to adjust. The long-standing controversy about the right of American fishermen to cure their catch on Canadian shores had been aggravated by the dispute over the Alabama claims arising from the depredations of Confederate raiders like the *Alabama*, which had been built in England. In addition, the efforts of the Fenians to free Ireland by invading Canada and the dispute about the ownership of the San Juan Islands tended to undermine relations between the two countries.

When during the Johnson administration former Senator Reverdy Johnson (q.v.) attempted to solve the *Alabama* claims by means of the Johnson-Clarendon Convention, the Senate rejected his efforts, and Charles Sumner (q.v.) complicated the problem by demanding that Great Britain pay not only for the actual damage done to American shipping but also for the entire cost of the Civil War following the Battle of Gettysburg, a claim amounting to some $2 billion. These enormous indirect claims could only be met by the cession of Canada, a solution totally unacceptable to Great Britain as long as the Canadians did not desire it.

Fish's attempt to solve these issues was at first severely compromised by the American minister in London, Sumner's friend, the historian John Lothrop Motley. Only after Motley's recall and the Secretary of State's successful delay of negotiations for several years could progress be made. Any treaty would have to be approved by the Senate, and as long as Sumner remained chairman of the Senate's Committee on Foreign Relations, a convention not including his demands was unlikely to pass. But in time the Senator so alienated the administration by his immoderate attacks on the President and his policies, particularly in reference to Santo Domingo, that in 1871 he was deposed from his committee chairmanship. It was then that Fish was able not only to negotiate the Treaty of Washington (q.v.) but to have it accepted. It provided for Canadian concessions to the fishermen, the settlement of the *Alabama* and related claims by an international tribunal, and the appointment of the German Emperor as arbitrator of the San Juan Islands dispute. Although the international tribunal meeting at Geneva almost failed when the indirect claims were again brought forward, in the end the arbitration succeeded and Great Britain had to pay $15.5 million to the United States, partially offset later by the award of some $7.5 million to Britain and Canada for claims by their citizens and the Halifax Commission awarding a payment for the fisheries privileges.

In domestic affairs, Fish, true to his conservative instincts, advised against interference in Southern states, both during the troubles in Louisiana (q.v.) in 1874 and the difficult period following the disputed election of 1876. Continuing in office for the first few days of Rutherford B. Hayes' (q.v.) administration, he urged the new President to withdraw the federal troops from the remaining statehouses in the South. After leaving office he retired to New York and died on his estate at Glenclyffe on Hudson in 1893.

The most prominent member of Grant's cabinet, Fish provided the corruption-plagued Grant administration with some badly needed prestige. His fine diplomatic record established him as one of the most notable American Secretaries of State.

*See also* Foreign Affairs; Grant, Ulysses Simpson.

Allan Nevins, *Hamilton Fish: The Inner History of the Grant Administration* (New York, 1937).


**FLORIDA,** one of the former Confederate states subject to Reconstruction. Lightly settled, the state still exhibited many of the characteristics of the frontier. It contained a large black minority, was bitterly racist, and was often wracked by violence.

In accordance with his plan of Reconstruction, Andrew Johnson (q.v.) on July 12, 1865, appointed William Marvin, a conservative Unionist, Provisional Governor. Marvin called elections for a constitutional convention that abolished slavery but failed to enfranchise a single freedman. Encouraged by the leniency of the President's program, the legislature elected under the amended constitution, while ratifying the Thirteenth Amendment (q.v.), passed a stringent black code remanding the freedmen to a condition little better than slavery. In December 1866 it rejected the Fourteenth Amendment (q.v.).

The Reconstruction Acts (q.v.) returned Florida to military rule. Part of the Third District, it was first commanded by General John Pope (q.v.) and then by George Gordon Meade (q.v.). In accordance with the law, the blacks (q.v.) were enfranchised and a new convention elected. Although the Republicans secured control, they were split into factions. The moderates under Harrison Reed (q.v.) sought to cooperate with some of the more pliant conservatives, whereas the radicals under Liberty Billings, William U. Saunders, and Daniel Richards (the "Mule Team"), were eager to elevate the blacks. Both factions submitted constitutions to Congress that endorsed the moderate one, a document so arranged as to dilute the black vote. Harrison Reed was elected Governor, and the state was readmitted to the Union in July 1868.

During the Reed administration, the Florida Republican party continued to be rent by internal squabbles. The factions now emerging consisted of the moderate Reed wing anxious to harmonize the interests of blacks, white Republicans, and even conservaties, as well as a group of federal officeholders led by U.S. Senator Thomas W. Osborn, a former agent of the Freedmen's Bureau (q.v.), who had considerable influence with the blacks. The Osborn forces tried four times to impeach the Governor, but lack of evidence frustrated their efforts in the long run. In 1872 the moderate Ossian B. Hart was elected Governor, only to die soon afterward and to be succeeded by Reed's opponent, Marcellus L. Stearns, who found it as difficult to end the factionalism as his predecessors.

Although often accused of wastefulness and corruption, the Republican regime in Florida actually succeeded in developing many of the state's resources, in encouraging the building of railroads, in unraveling some of the financial chaos inherited from its predecessors, and in improving the lot of the blacks. In 1873 the legislature, which had already provided for schools for the freedmen, passed a civil rights act, limited, to be sure, but nevertheless providing for equal access to publicly owned facilities. It also enacted various measures for the relief of labor, including lien laws to protect wages and a ten-hour day. But in spite of their efforts, the Republicans were never able to overcome native hostility manifesting itself by continued virulent racism and terrorism.

By 1876 it was clear that the Republican state government was in deep trouble. Detested by large numbers of the party, Governor Stearns was unable to unify the organization behind his candidacy for reelection. It was likely that many Republicans, while remaining loyal to the national ticket, would support George F. Drew, the local Democratic contender. When it became evident that the returns from Florida were among those that would decide the disputed presidential election, the actions of the Returning Board at Tallahassee became crucial. Dominated by the Republicans, it decided in favor of Rutherford B. Hayes (q.v.) as well as of Stearns, but so questionable were the returns from several counties that the decision, particularly in reference to the state election, was challenged in the courts. Although the Electoral Commission (q.v.) in Washington eventually accepted the Hayes returns, local courts overturned the state count, and Drew was inaugurated well before the new President took office. The process of Reconstruction in the state thus ended even before Hayes' withdrawal of the troops from Southern statehouses. The "Redeemers" ("Redemption," q.v.) wrote a new constitution in 1885; Jim Crow laws followed, and the blacks were once again remanded to a position of distinct inferiority.

*See also* Congressional Reconstruction; Electoral Commission; Presidential Reconstruction; "Redemption"; Reed, Harrison.

Jerrell H. Shofner, *Nor Is It Over Yet: Florida in the Era of Reconstruction, 1863–1877* (Gainesville, Fla., 1974); Joe M. Richardson, *The Negro in the Reconstruction of Florida* (Tallahassee, 1965); William Watson Davis, *The Civil War and Reconstruction in Florida* (New York, 1913).


**FORCE ACTS.** *See* ENFORCEMENT ACTS.


**FOREIGN AFFAIRS** during the Reconstruction era was marked by disputes with Great Britain concerning the *Alabama* claims, Fenian raids, border problems with Canada, and the fisheries; with Spain because of the recurrent rebellion in Cuba; and with France because of its efforts to establish a monarchy in Mexico. The period was also characterized by expansionist tendencies resulting in the annexation of Alaska and Midway Island but failing to bring about the incorporation of various Caribbean islands.

During the administration of Andrew Johnson (q.v.), foreign affairs was the province of Secretary of State William H. Seward (q.v.). Diplomatically adroit and animated by a desire for American expansion, Seward was responsible for the purchase of Alaska but was unable to bring about the transfer of the Danish

West Indies to the United States. Not eager to involve the country in renewed warfare, he succeeded in conducting relations with France in such a way as to maintain American nonintervention while Napoleon III was induced to withdraw from Mexico, but he failed to have the Senate accept the Johnson-Clarendon Convention with Great Britain and thus to end the *Alabama* claims controversy.

Seward's eventual successor was U. S. Grant's second Secretary of State, Hamilton Fish (q.v.), whose sagacity and diplomatic finesse prevented war with both Great Britain and Spain. The outstanding differences with the former were the fisheries controversy, arising from American demands that U.S. citizens retain their rights to cure their catch on Canadian shores; the vexed *Alabama* question involving claims for the payment of damages inflicted upon Union shipping by Confederate raiders equipped and built in England; a dispute about the ownership of the San Juan Islands; and the continual raids by Fenians hoping to free Ireland by invading Canada. These problems were further complicated by Charles Sumner's (q.v.) insistence that Great Britain was responsible for prolonging the Civil War by two years and thus owed some $2 billion, a sum that could be met only by the cession of all of British North America. As long as the Canadians were unwilling, Britain refused even to consider these indirect claims.

Nevertheless, Fish proceeded to negotiate. At first handicapped by the presence of Sumner's friend, John Lothrop Motley, as American envoy in London, Fish had to await his recall and the transfer of talks to Washington before he could expect any success. Moreover, Sumner's position as chairman of the Senate Committee on Foreign Relations further complicated matters. It was not until the Senator's removal from his chairmanship following his immoderate attacks on the administration, particularly in respect to Grant's efforts to annex the Dominican Republic, that the Treaty of Washington (q.v.) could be negotiated and accepted by the Senate. Providing for concessions to the fishermen in return for certain Canadian navigation privileges and a just compensation, the treaty mandated the referral of the *Alabama* claims to an international tribunal to meet at Geneva and the appointment of the German Emperor as arbitrator in the San Juan Islands dispute. After a period of renewed anxiety because of the re-emergence of the indirect claims, the Geneva Tribunal excluding these demands, awarded $15.5 million to the United States for the *Alabama* and related claims, while a commission sitting at Halifax assessed the United States $5.5 million for the fisheries and another commission gave Great Britain an additional $1,929,819 for miscellaneous claims.

The troubles with Spain arising from Cuba's striving for independence threatened to involve the United States in the Cuban rebellion of 1868–1878. Secretary of State Fish, however, cleverly maneuvering to keep both American interventionists and Spanish hotheads at bay, succeeded in preserving neutrality, even during the serious *Virginius* affair (1871), when the Spaniards captured an American flagship supplying Cuban rebels and executed several of its officers.

Efforts to buy various Caribbean islands proved unsuccessful. When in 1867 the Danish government sought to cede the Danish West Indies, a treaty was negotiated with the United States. Denmark held a plebiscite on the islands; the inhabitants approved, but the Senate refused to ratify. President Grant was eager to annex Santo Domingo; President Buenaventura Baez offered to cede Samana Bay or sell the whole republic for a handsome consideration. Irregularly concluded by Grant's private emissaries, the original treaty was renegotiated by the State Department. But despite the President's continued efforts to induce the Senate to accept it, he was unable to overcome the opposition to it. Repeatedly attacking the scheme in immoderate language, Charles Sumner dramatized its shortcomings; well-founded rumors of corruption surfaced, and all the President was able to secure from the Senate was an investigation commission that visited the island in 1871 and brought back a glowing report. Without a two-thirds majority, proponents of annexation were powerless, and American expansion into the Caribbean had to await a later time.

Russian America, however, was a different matter. Eager to sell the territory, particularly since the Russian-America Company was in financial trouble, the Russian envoy sounded out the enthusiastic Secretary of State. In spite of the widespread hostility to the Johnson administration, Seward was able to secure congressional support. Many Americans believed that the Tsar had been friendly to the Union during the Civil War; money was used freely, and on the night of March 29–30, the treaty providing for the purchase of the territory for $7.2 million was signed at the State Department. Although it was soon ratified by the Senate, it encountered difficulty in the House, which had to pass on the necessary appropriations. Objections were raised to the purchase of "Seward's icebox," and it was not until 1868 that they were overcome so that Alaska, so named by Sumner, became part of the United States.

*See also* Fish, Hamilton; Seward, William H.; Washington, Treaty of.

Ernest N. Paolino, *The Foundations of the American Empire: William Henry Seward and U.S. Foreign Policy* (Ithaca, N.Y., 1973); Allan Nevins, *Hamilton Fish: The Inner History of the Grant Administration* (New York, 1937); Charles S. Campbell, *The Transformation of American Foreign Relations, 1865–1900* (New York, 1976).


**FOURTEENTH AMENDMENT,** the most notable of the post–Civil War amendments, was passed by Congress on June 13, 1866, and declared ratified on July 28, 1868. Its first section declares all persons born or naturalized in the United States to be citizens of the United States and of the state in which they reside and contains the famous due process and equal protection clauses. These prohibit the states from abridging the privileges and immunities of citizens, from depriving any person of life, liberty, or property without due process of law, and from denying to anyone the equal protection of the laws. Its second part empowers Congress to reduce the representation of any state abridging the suffrage of any portion of its male inhabitants over twenty-one years of age; the third disfranchises certain Confederate officials; and the fourth guarantees the federal while outlawing the Confederate debt. The fifth is an enforcement clause.

The passage of the Thirteenth Amendment (q.v.) rendered the three-fifths compromise obsolete. Thus because there were no longer any slaves to be counted only partially for purposes of representation, as long as the freedmen were kept from voting the conservatives would benefit. Moreover, the *Dred Scott* decision, declaring that blacks (q.v.) were not citizens, required a reversal; Unionists' and freedmen's lives and property were not secure in the South, and there were questions about the constitutionality of the Civil Rights Act (q.v.). Because the Bill of Rights did not apply to the states, some provision for their adherence to due process also had to be made.

Realizing the need for constitutional changes to take care of these problems, in early 1866 Republicans on the Joint Committee on Reconstruction (q.v.) began to frame the necessary amendments. Many of the radicals were in favor of mandating black suffrage (q.v.); because of the difficulty of passing a provision for this purpose, however, the more complicated scheme of reducing representation took its place. At first the House passed a version disfranchising Confederates for ten years, but the Senate substituted the present clause merely affecting those who had previously sworn allegiance to the United States and made provision for congressional amnesty. In this rendition the amendment was passed.

Bitterly opposed by President Andrew Johnson (q.v.), the proposal was rejected by all Southern states with the exception of Tennessee (q.v.). As the election of 1866 had largely turned on the acceptance of the proposed change, the resultant Republican victory enabled Congress in 1867 to enact the Reconstruction Acts (q.v.), which remanded the states to military government and made their ratification of the amendment obligatory. By July 1868 enough states had given their assent to enable the Secretary of State to declare it in force.

In later years, after the Supreme Court in the *Slaughterhouse* cases (q.v.) and in *U.S. v. Cruikshank* (q.v.) had weakened the amendment, its original purpose of protection for the blacks was forgotten, and it was invoked to safeguard corporations from state interference. This interpretation was first suggested by Roscoe Conkling (q.v.), one of the members of the Reconstruction Committee, in 1882, and four years later, in *Santa Clara County* v. *Southern Pacific Railroad Co.*, the Supreme Court seemed to accept this argument. A series of decisions favoring corporations followed, and it was not until the late 1930s, and particularly in the period following World War II, that the court returned to an interpretation favorable to the blacks. In decision after decision, it held that the amendment outlawed segregation, particularly in schools (*Brown* v. *Board of Education of Topeka*, 1954) and that it extended the restrictions of the Bill of Rights to the states. As a result it became one of the principal weapons in the struggle for civil rights.

*See also* Reconstruction Acts; *Slaughterhouse* Cases; *U.S.* v. *Cruikshank*.

Joseph B. James, *The Framing of the Fourteenth Amendment* (Urbana, Ill., 1956); Jacobus tenBroek, *The Antislavery Origins of the Fourteenth Amendment* (Berkeley, Calif., 1951); Bernard Schwartz, ed., *Fourteenth Amendment: Centennial Vol.*, (New York, 1970).

**FREEDMAN'S SAVINGS BANK,** an institution established in March 1865 to provide freed blacks with banking facilities and to teach them the virtues of middle-class thrift. A mutual savings bank, it was to receive the depositors' money at various branches, invest it in government securities, and make no loans. Its headquarters was at first established in New York and then in Washington, and a prestigious Board of Trustees was to supervise its operations.

Eventually setting up some thirty-seven branches, largely in the South, with many black cashiers, the bank, under the direction of its secretary and later president, John W. Alvord, at first appeared to be fulfilling its purpose. It received small sums from its largely impecunious depositors, served some one hundred thousand customers, collected more than $4 million, and cooperated closely with the Freedmen's Bureau (q.v.). In 1870, however, after the trustees succeeded in having Congress change its charter to allow speculative investments for one-half of its assets, under the management of Henry Cooke, William S. Huntington, and D. L. Heaton, it was converted into a speculative enterprise. The resulting dubious investments and regular fraud weakened it greatly. The Panic of 1873 with the collapse of Jay Cooke's banking house affected the institution so badly that it was found to be insolvent. A last-minute effort to restore confidence by appointing Frederick Douglass (q.v.) president could not stave off the disaster, and in July 1874 the bank closed its doors. Not until 1883 had individual depositors realized some 62 cents on the dollar, and all subsequent efforts to have the government assume the remaining debt were unsuccessful.

The failure of the institution had a very bad effect on freedmen's faith in banks. They had been disappointed, had been cheated by alleged philanthropists, and would not soon entrust their hard-earned money to banks again. Thus the institution's original purpose of teaching thrift to former slaves was totally subverted.

*See also* Douglass, Frederick; Freedmen's Bureau.

Carl R. Osthaus, *Freedmen, Philanthropy, and Fraud: A History of the Freedman's Savings Bank* (Urbana, Ill., 1976).

**FREEDMEN'S BUREAU,** a federal agency established in March 1865 for the purpose of supervising and managing "all the abandoned lands in the South and the control of all subjects relating to refugees and freedmen." Charged with giving provisions, clothing, and fuel to the destitute, it was officially called the Bureau of Refugees, Freedmen, and Abandoned Lands, and had the authority to assign up to forty acres of land to its charges, who might buy the land after three years. As a Bureau of the War Department, it was headed by a commissioner with no more than ten assistant commissioners in the various states. General Oliver O. Howard (q.v.) became its head and soon set to work to realize his difficult assignment.

Seeking to carry out the ambitious land policies (q.v.) of its charter, the bureau attempted to lease or convey plots to the freedmen, to some extent continuing experiments initiated earlier on the Sea Islands (q.v.) and on a strip of land along the coast of South Carolina (q.v.) and Georgia (q.v.) set aside for the purpose by General William T. Sherman (q.v.). But its policy fell foul of the Presidential Plan of Reconstruction (q.v.) initiated by Andrew Johnson (q.v.), and in the summer of 1865 Howard received orders to restore all property, including land, to pardoned insurgents. This policy greatly disappointed the blacks (q.v.), and the bureau began to concentrate on its other obligations—relief, education, and legal protection of the freedmen. After Howard had suggested that Congress spell out the bureau's powers more precisely, a Freedmen's Bureau Bill (q.v.) was passed in February 1866. Providing for an indefinite extension of the life of the agency, originally slated to expire one year after the end of the war, the measure extended its jurisdiction over all freedmen and refugees in the country, authorized the increase of the number of assistant commissioners to twelve, and conferred to it jurisdiction in cases in unreconstructed states denying to blacks the equal protection of the laws. In addition, it not only confirmed titles to land in Sherman's coastal strip but also authorized the President to set aside 3 million acres of unoccupied land for distribution to refugees and freedmen. In an open break with Congress, Johnson vetoed the legislation on the grounds that it was a wartime measure, uncalled for in times of peace; that its judicial provisions violated constitutional guarantees; and that no bill affecting them should be passed as long as Southern states remained unrepresented. His veto was sustained, but in July 1866 a new bill, containing clauses for freedmen's education and legal protection, survived Johnson's renewed veto.

In the following two years, the bureau engaged in various educational activities resulting in the establishment of freedmen's schools and colleges. While continuing its relief functions, it established courts to secure for blacks the equal protection of the laws. Some of its agents also became involved in Republican politics, and in July 1868, when its mandate was to expire, Congress extended its life until the end of the forthcoming presidential election. After the inauguration of U. S. Grant (q.v.), the institution was gradually phased out of existence, until by 1872, when it closed its doors, its activities had been practically confined to education and the payment of veterans' claims. A series of investigations into the commissioner's disbursement of funds and the collapse of the walls of Howard University followed, but no wrongdoing was found, at least not by the majority.

If the Freedmen's Bureau was unable to carry out fully its mandate of assisting the integration of the freedmen into society, despite the intense hatred for it in the South it did manage to give substantial aid to the blacks during the first years of freedom. Its ultimate failure was due to the hostility of President Johnson, widespread racial prejudice, and the federal structure of the government.

*See also* Freedman's Savings Bank; Freedmen's Bureau Bill; Howard, Oliver Otis; Land Policies.

George R. Bentley, *A History of the Freedmen's Bureau* (Philadelphia, 1954); Donald G. Nieman, *To Set the Law in Motion: The Freedmen's Bureau and the Legal Rights of Blacks, 1865–1868* (Milwood, N.Y., 1979).

**FREEDMEN'S BUREAU BILL,** a measure passed in February 1866, seeking to extend the powers of the Freedmen's Bureau (q.v.) established during the closing months of the administration of Abraham Lincoln (q.v.). Because President Andrew Johnson (q.v.) had ordered the return of abandoned lands to pardoned insurgents and because the bureau was slated to expire one year after the conclusion of the war, Congress, upon the advice of Commissioner Oliver O. Howard (q.v.), felt constrained to renew the charter of the agency and to spell out its duties in more detail. Accordingly, Senator Lyman Trumbull (q.v.), the chairman of the Senate's Judiciary Committee, framed a measure extending the life of the bureau indefinitely and, among other things, giving it jurisdiction in cases tried in formerly insurgent states denying to freedmen the equal protection of the laws. In addition, he prepared a Civil Rights Bill (Civil Rights Act of 1866, q.v.) as a companion piece. Although the Senator thought he had secured the President's approval, Johnson vetoed it on the grounds that it was unnecessary, denied citizens constitutional rights such as trial by jury, and affected states still unrepresented in Congress. He questioned the propriety of legislation for unrepresented states, thus challenging the powers of the Thirty-ninth Congress. Although his veto was sustained, his subsequent speech on Washington's birthday served to widen the breach between him and Congress, and the Civil Rights Bill was passed over his veto a few weeks later. In July 1866 a similar Freedmen's Bureau Bill became law notwithstanding his veto.

*See also* Freedmen's Bureau; Howard, Oliver Otis.

Patrick Riddleberger, *1866: The Critical Year Revisited* (Carbondale, Ill., 1979); George R. Bentley, *A History of the Freedmen's Bureau* (Philadelphia, 1955).

# G

GARFIELD, JAMES ABRAM (1831–1881), twentieth President of the United States, was born in Orange township, Cuyahoga County, Ohio, the son of a farmer. Losing his father before he was three, Garfield was brought up by his mother in straitened economic circumstances. He worked for a while as a canal boy and carpenter and, after some brief schooling at the Geauga Academy, as a teacher. Baptized by the Disciples of Christ, he enrolled in the denomination's new Western Reserve Eclectic Institute at Hiram. In 1856, having graduated from Williams College, he returned to Hiram to teach and eventually to assume the presidency, while also serving as Campellite preacher and studying law. He was admitted to the bar in 1859.

That same year Garfield was elected as a Republican to the state Senate, and when war broke out, he joined the Forty-second Ohio as a lieutenant colonel. He distinguished himself in the Sandy Valley campaign in eastern Kentucky, was promoted to brigadier general, and took part in the battle of Shiloh. Appointed William S. Rosecrans' chief of staff, he participated in planning the Tullahoma campaign. At Chickamauga, he joined George H. Thomas in his defense of the federal left, but soon afterward, promoted to major general, he left the army to take his seat in Congress, to which he had been elected in 1862.

In the House of Representatives, Garfield at first collaborated with the radicals. A strong supporter of Salmon P. Chase (q.v.), he was critical of Abraham Lincoln (q.v.). After the war, he opposed the policies of Andrew Johnson (q.v.) and favored Congressional Reconstruction (q.v.) but gradually became more moderate. Devoted to hard money and a generally conservative economic policy, in time he emerged as one of the leaders of the Republican party (q.v.), although his involvement in the Crédit Mobilier and the Washington paving scandals tended to stain his reputation.

As a devoted Republican, in 1876 he traveled to Louisiana (q.v.) to assist his party in the disputed election and became a member of the Electoral Commission (q.v.) set up to settle it. He also took part in the Wormley Conference (q.v.) leading to the Compromise of 1877 (q.v.), which, had it been fully carried out, might have resulted in his election as Speaker of the House.

In 1880 Garfield, who had just been sent to the Senate, attended the Republican National Convention at Chicago, ostensibly in the interest of John Sherman (q.v.), whom he nominated for the presidency. But after the convention was deadlocked between the followers of U. S. Grant (q.v.), James G. Blaine (q.v.), and Sherman, Garfield was brought forward as a dark horse and obtained the nomination. In the subsequent campaign, he defeated General Winfield S. Hancock (q.v.), the Democratic candidate.

When Garfield assumed the presidency, the Republican party was split between the Stalwart followers of Roscoe Conkling (q.v.), the Half-Breed partisans of James G. Blaine, and the independents. Despite desperate efforts to harmonize these interests with Blaine as Secretary of State and the Stalwart Chester A. Arthur as Vice President, Garfield was unable to satisfy Conkling, who resigned his Senate seat in a controversy over the New York collectorship. But before the consequences of this split could be assessed, on July 2, 1881, the President was shot by Charles J. Guiteau, a demented disappointed office seeker. After lingering for some two months, Garfield died in Elberon, New Jersey, on September 19, 1881.

An accomplished speaker, though not a particularly efficient parliamentary leader, Garfield was a shrewd politician who used his office to build the foundations for the modern presidency.

*See also* Blaine, James G.; Compromise of 1877; Conkling, Roscoe; Hancock, Winfield Scott; Sherman, John; Wormley Conference.

Allan Peskin, *Garfield* (Kent, Ohio, 1978); John M. Taylor, *Garfield of Ohio: The Available Man* (New York, 1970); Theodore Clarke Smith, *The Life and Letters of James Abram Garfield* (2 vols., New Haven, 1925); Justus D. Doeneke, *The Presidencies of James A. Garfield and Chester A. Arthur* (Lawrence, Kans., 1981).

**GARLAND, EX PARTE** (1867), one of the *test oath* cases in which the Supreme Court held the act of January 1865, barring all who could not take an ironclad oath (q.v.) from practicing in the federal courts. Augustus H. Garland, a Confederate Senator from Arkansas who had been admitted to the Supreme Court in 1860 but fought in the Confederate army afterward, aided by Reverdy Johnson (q.v.) and Matthew H. Carpenter, challenged his exclusion on the grounds of his having received a presidential pardon and the act's being unconstitutional. Justice Stephen Field, speaking for a narrow majority of five, on the same day that he decided *Cummings* v. *Missouri* (q.v.), upheld the petitioner. Declaring that the act violated the constitutional prohibition of bills of attainder and ex post facto laws and that Andrew Johnson's (q.v.) pardon was valid, he held that Garland ought to be admitted to practice. The House attempted to deal with this defiance of its Reconstruction laws by providing that court decisions would henceforth require a two-thirds majority for overriding laws of Congress, but the Senate refused to consider the matter.

*See also Cummings* v. *Missouri*; Johnson, Reverdy; Supreme Court.

Stanley I. Kutler, *Judicial Power and Reconstruction Politics* (Chicago, 1968); Charles Fairman, *Reconstruction and Reunion, 1864–88*, Vol. 6 of the Oliver Wendell Holmes Devise, *History of the Supreme Court of the United States* (New York, 1971).

**GENEVA TRIBUNAL.** *See* WASHINGTON, TREATY OF.

**GEORGIA,** one of the states subject to Reconstruction. After the collapse of the Confederate government, the state was left without a civilian administration until President Andrew Johnson (q.v.) in accordance with his plan of Reconstruction appointed James Johnson Provisional Governor. In compliance with the President's mandate, James Johnson summoned a convention that abolished slavery, repudiated the Confederate debt, and nullified the secession ordinance. In November 1865 a conservative legislature and Governor, Charles J. Jenkins, were elected. Although this legislature ratified the Thirteenth Amendment (q.v.), it refused to confer any political rights on the large number of blacks (q.v.) in the state (about 40 percent of the population) and sent two prominent Confederates, including former Vice President Alexander H. Stephens, to the U.S. Senate.

As in other Southern states, in Georgia conservative rule came to an end after the passage of the Reconstruction Acts (q.v.) in the spring of 1867. It became part of the Third Military District under John Pope (q.v.), and in October a new convention based on black suffrage (q.v.) was elected in which the Republicans obtained a majority. Meeting in Atlanta instead of in the old state capital of Milledgeville, the convention wrote a new state constitution that conferred the suffrage upon the freedmen, set up a free public school system, and granted relief to debtors. Although the delegates voted down an effort to bar blacks from holding office, they refused explicitly to guarantee this right.

A dispute soon arose about a requisition to meet the convention's expenses. When Governor Jenkins refused to honor it, General George G. Meade (q.v.), the new military commander, removed Jenkins and replaced him with Brigadier General Thomas A. Ruger. A subsequent election resulted in the victory of the radical Rufus B. Bullock (q.v.), whose quest for the governorship was aided materially by former Confederate Governor Joseph E. Brown (q.v.), as well as a nominally Republican legislature. The ratification of the Fourteenth Amendment (q.v.) and the readmission of the state (July 1868) followed.

Yet in spite of their tenuous control of the legislature, the Republicans were never firmly in power in Georgia. Split by factionalism and weakened by the all-pervasive racial prejudice, they could not effectively assert themselves. Moderates combined with Democrats to defy the Governor by refusing to disqualify members ineligible under the Fourteenth Amendment, by preventing the election of radical Senators, and finally by expelling all black legislators. The Ku Klux

Klan (q.v.) flourished; massacres of freedmen, such as the Camilla Riot (q.v.), terrorized the blacks (q.v.), and in November led to the loss of the state by General U. S. Grant (q.v.).

To restore the Republicans' power, Bullock asked Congress to remand Georgia to military rule. But this action alienated him from Brown and other moderates, so the party was further weakened. Congress did in fact refuse to seat the state's Senators, but it was not until December 1869 that it complied with the Governor's request. After the legislature was purged of members unable to take the required loyalty oath, the ousted blacks were reinstated, and the Fifteenth Amendment (q.v.) was ratified, the state was fully restored a second time (July 1870). But Congress refused to accede to Bullock's proposal that the legislature elected in 1868 remain in power for two additional years.

This decision made a Democratic victory a certainty, and in December 1870 the conservative party regained control of the legislature. Desperately attempting to retrieve his fortunes, Bullock sought to mollify his enemies by various railroad deals, particularly one involving the lease of the state-owned Western and Atlantic Railroad, which had been mismanaged during the Republican regime. When this effort failed, in October 1871, before the meeting of the new legislature, the Governor resigned, thus securing the succession of the Republican Speaker of the House. However, in December 1871 new elections ordered by the Democratic legislature resulted in the success of the conservative gubernatorial candidate James M. Smith, and the "Redeemers" ("Redemption," q.v.) assumed power. Bullock had left the state but six years later was tried for malfeasance in office, a charge of which he was acquitted.

The conservative role that followed was typical of the "Redeemer" regimes throughout the South. Reduced to sharecropping and utter dependence on merchants and landowners, the freedmen were gradually deprived of political rights and once more relegated to the position of a subordinate race.

*See also* Brown, Joseph Emerson; Bullock, Rufus Brown; Congressional Reconstruction; Presidential Reconstruction; "Redemption."

Elizabeth Studley Nathans, *Losing the Peace: Georgia Republicans and Reconstruction, 1865–1871* (Baton Rouge, 1968); Alan Conway, *The Reconstruction of Georgia* (Minneapolis, 1966); Mildred Thompson, *Reconstruction in Georgia* (New York, 1915).


**GEORGIA v. STANTON,** a suit for an injunction against Secretary of War Edwin M. Stanton (q.v.) and subordinates initiated by Governor Charles J. Jenkins on behalf of Georgia in April 1867 to prevent them from carrying out the Reconstruction Acts (q.v.). Arguing that the state's traditional existence as a sovereign entity was threatened by the legislation, counsel appealed to the Supreme Court to grant relief. The government, represented by Attorney General Henry Stanbery (q.v.), replied that the matter was a political issue over which the Court had no jurisdiction, a contention with which the tribunal agreed. It dismissed the suit in May 1867 but did not render its full decision until February 1868.

*See also Mississippi* v. *Johnson*; Reconstruction Acts; Supreme Court.

Charles Fairbank, *Reconstruction and Reunion, 1864–88*, Vol. 6 of the Oliver Wendell Holmes Devise, *History of the Supreme Court of the United States, 1864–88* (New York, 1971).

**GOULD, JAY** (1836–1892), financier and speculator, was born in Roxbury, New York, the son of a local farmer. At an early age, he acquired an interest in a tannery in the Lehigh Valley but defrauded his associates before moving on to New York to carry on the leather business and to speculate on Wall Street. In 1867 he worked out a scheme to dominate and milk the Erie Railroad in partnership with Daniel Drew and James Fisk. In this endeavor he was opposed by Commodore Cornelius Vanderbilt, with whom he fought the "Erie War" by selling the Commodore stock converted from construction bonds. This transaction led to his flight to Jersey City to escape from Vanderbilt's legal agents in New York. After both men had resorted to bribery to legalize their actions, the "war" ended in a truce, leaving Gould to move on to his next scheme, the cornering of the gold market. Together with Fisk, he enlisted the aid of Abel Corbin, President U. S. Grant's (q.v.) brother-in-law, and sought to induce the administration not to sell gold for a while. The resulting panic drove up the price of gold until on Black Friday (q.v.), September 24, 1869, it reached 164. Then the scheme collapsed; the Secretary of the Treasury, George S. Boutwell (q.v.), intervened and disposed of government bullion. Gould, however, forewarned, had already unloaded his holdings without notifying his partner.

In the 1870s Gould, by shrewdly conducting bearish raids on its securities, secured control of the Union Pacific Railroad and eventually came to dominate important Western lines such as the Missouri Pacific and the Texas and Pacific. He also acquired control of Western Union and the New York elevated lines, while buying the New York *World* to secure newspaper support. During the last years of his life, he fought frequent battles with labor unions, particularly with the Knights of Labor, who in 1885 won a strike against his Missouri Pacific, only to be defeated the next year in a similar contest on the Texas and Pacific. He died in New York in 1892.

A veritable buccaneer, Gould built his fortunes by dubious tactics, often ruining the properties he acquired. In the minds of reformers, he became the symbol of greed and monopoly, although he also furthered railroad construction and by his rate wars sometimes benefited consumers.

*See also* Black Friday; Grant, Ulysses Simpson.

Richard O'Connor, *Gould's Millions* (Garden City, N.Y., 1962); Julius Grodinsky, *Jay Gould: His Business Career, 1867–1892* (Philadelphia, 1957).

**GRAND ARMY OF THE REPUBLIC,** a Civil War veterans' organization professing nonpartisanship but often associated with the Republican party (q.v.). Founded in 1866 by Dr. Benjamin F. Stephenson of Illinois in the interest of Governor Richard J. Oglesby and General John A. Logan (q.v.), it exerted great political influence in many Northern states. Its professed aims were good comradeship, the welfare of veterans, and the retention of the ideals for which they had fought; more specifically, it generally favored bounties, liberal pensions, and preferential employment for former soldiers. After playing a determined part in the struggle against Andrew Johnson (q.v.) and remaining strongly committed until the election of U. S. Grant (q.v.), it became less active, only to reemerge as a strong political force eight years later. The Hayes administration responded with the Arrears Act of 1879, which greatly facilitated the payment of pensions. Although both presidential candidates in 1880 were generals, the veterans tended to favor the Republican, James A. Garfield (q.v.). When in 1884 the Democrats were returned to power, the Grand Army of the Republic (GAR) became involved in bitter disputes with Grover Cleveland, who vetoed pension bills and signed an order to return Confederate battle flags.

With the election of Benjamin Harrison in 1888, the order achieved many of its aims. Its representative, "Corporal" James Tanner, was appointed commissioner of pensions, and in 1890 Congress passed an exceedingly generous pensions act. Tanner, exclaiming, "God help the surplus," liberally distributed funds to his comrades and supporters, while the organization attained its peak with a membership exceeding four hundred thousand.

During the 1890s, the GAR became ever more conservative. Opposing anarchists, socialists, and the Pullman strike, it sought to censor school books deemed pro-Southern and inaugurated the custom of flying the American flag at public school buildings. But as time went on, its influence gradually declined. Death and waning interest decimated its membership, until at its last encampment in 1949 only six survivors attended. It passed into history after functioning for many years as the country's most powerful veterans organization.

*See also* Logan, John A.

Mary R. Dearing, *Veterans in Politics: The Story of the G.A.R.* (Baton Rouge, 1952).

**GRANT, ULYSSES SIMPSON** (1822–1885), eighteenth President of the United States and commanding general of the Union armies, was born at Point Pleasant, Ohio, the son of a tanner. Upon graduation from West Point in 1843, he was stationed at Jefferson Barracks, Missouri, where he met his future wife, Julia Dent. After participating in the Mexican War and distinguishing himself at Molina del Rey and Chapultepec, he was stationed at various Northern posts until in 1852 he was detailed to Ft. Vancouver, Oregon, promoted to captain, and finally sent to Ft. Humboldt, California. In 1854 he resigned his commission and returned to St. Louis to try his hand at farming and real estate, until in 1860 he moved to Galena, Ill., to clerk in his father's leather store.

The outbreak of the Civil War gave Grant his great opportunity. Appointed colonel in the Twenty-first Illinois Volunteers and soon promoted to brigadier general, he engaged the Confederates at Belmont. His capture of Forts Henry and Donelson ended with his demand for the unconditional surrender of Simon B. Buckner. Promoted to major general, he was surprised at Shiloh but succeeded in turning a near disaster into a victory. On July 4, 1863, after a long and skillful campaign, he took Vicksburg. In the fall he was designated commander of all Union forces in the West and in November won the Battle of Chattanooga. When in 1864 Congress restored the rank of lieutenant general, Lincoln appointed Grant to the new grade and made him commanding general of all federal armies.

His new position enabled Grant to draw up an overall plan for victory. He himself would accompany the Army of the Potomac in its move south toward Richmond, while Benjamin F. Butler (q.v.) was to approach the city from the sea, and another force under Franz Sigel was to clear the Shenandoah Valley. At the same time, William T. Sherman (q.v.) was to march upon Atlanta and Nathaniel P. Banks (q.v.) to move toward Mobile.

The plan encountered difficulties. Although Grant, sweeping steadily south, fought the Battles of the Wilderness and Spottsylvania, Butler was unable to take Petersburg, Sherman was delayed in Georgia, Sigel was defeated in the Valley, and Banks was sidetracked at the Red River. Grant then invested Richmond and appointed Philip Sheridan (q.v.) to clean up the valley. Sherman captured Atlanta on September 2 and embarked on his march to the sea; George H. Thomas defeated the Confederates at Nashville in December, and after a long siege, Petersburg and Richmond fell on April 2, 1865. Seven days later Grant accepted Lee's surrender at Appomattox.

After the Civil War, as general-in-chief, Grant was reluctantly drawn into the struggles between the President and Congress. Although at first seemingly supporting Andrew Johnson (q.v.) in a December 1865 report about a trip to the South, the general gradually drew closer to Congress by collaborating with Secretary of War Edwin M. Stanton (q.v.) in implementing policies desired by the Republican majority. Yet, when Johnson dismissed Stanton, the general accepted the position of Secretary of War ad interim, only to break completely with the President upon the Senate's refusal to uphold Stanton's dismissal. Accusing Grant of deceit, Johnson charged that the general had promised not to turn over the office to the ousted Secretary of War, an assertion Grant vigorously denied. His great popularity made him the natural candidate of the Republican party (q.v.), which nominated him for President in May 1868 and in November elected him by defeating the Democrat, Horatio Seymour (q.v.)

Grant's presidency did not serve to enhance his reputation. True, it coincided with the ratification of the Fifteenth Amendment (q.v.) and restoration of all Southern states to their congressional privileges. It also achieved a marked success with the signing of the Treaty of Washington (q.v.) and the maintenance of peace with Great Britain, but it suffered from the President's inexperience in politics, his attraction to men of wealth, and his loyalty to old friends. When his aide, Orville E. Babcock (q.v.), attempted to negotiate a treaty of annexation with the Dominican Republic outside of regular channels, Grant encountered the hostility of Charles Sumner (q.v.), the chairman of the Senate Foreign Relations Committee, and sustained a telling defeat in the Senate's rejection of the scheme. The financiers Jay Gould and James Fisk involved the President indirectly in the Black Friday (q.v.) attempt to corner the New York gold market, and when he appointed the country's first Civil Service Commission, the reformist advocates of Civil Service reform (q.v.) resented his collaboration with spoilsmen such as Roscoe Conkling (q.v.), Benjamin F. Butler (q.v.), Simon Cameron (q.v.), and Oliver P. Morton (q.v.). The result was the organization of the Liberal Republican party (q.v.), which in 1872 nominated Horace Greeley (q.v.) to challenge Grant's reelection. Although the President easily defeated this effort, his second administration proved even more difficult than the first.

Grant's troubles came to light early in 1873 with the revelation of the machinations of the Crédit Mobilier involving the Vice President and a number of congressmen. Then Congress voted itself and the President a rise in salary (the salary grab), with the Whiskey Ring (q.v.), moieties scandal, and the defalcations of Secretary of War William W. Belknap (q.v.), as well as a severe panic, following in short order.

The Southern question also continued to cause trouble. The resurgence of conservatism and the rise of terror in the South made it difficult to enforce the Reconstruction Acts (q.v.). The administration suspended the habeas corpus in South Carolina (q.v.); it sent troops into the Louisiana (q.v.) statehouse to untangle that state's affairs, but it refused to aid Governor Adelbert Ames (q.v.) of Mississippi (q.v.) to stem the tide of violence marking the elections of 1875. As a result, only three Southern states remained in Republican hands until 1877.

In foreign affairs and finance, Grant was more successful. Secretary of State Hamilton Fish (q.v.) kept the country out of war with Spain and lent luster to a cabinet that otherwise was plagued by frequent changes. Grant also garnered some renown for his conservative financial policies, vetoing the 1874 inflation bill and signing the 1875 specie resumption measure.

Following the disputed election of 1876, Grant maintained the national authority. Shocked by the lawlessness in South Carolina, he complied with Governor Daniel Chamberlain's (q.v.) request for aid, but he refused to interfere in Louisiana.

After the inauguration of Rutherford B. Hayes (q.v.), Grant, royally welcomed wherever he went, took a trip around the world. In 1880 Roscoe Conkling and others sought to nominate the general for a third term, but James A. Garfield (q.v.) won the nomination. Thereafter, Grant invested heavily in the Wall Street firm of Grant & Ward, only to lose heavily in the company's collapse. Reduced to straitened circumstances, a situation made worse by his increasingly painful cancer of the throat, the ex-President sought to earn an income by completing his memoirs, a task he completed shortly before his death at Mt. McGregor, New York.

An excellent strategist whose grasp of modern warfare made possible the Union victory in the Civil War, Grant showed great weaknesses as President. His fame as savior of the Union, however, remained undimmed.

*See also* Babcock, Orville E.; Belknap, William Worth; Butler, Benjamin Franklin; Cameron, Simon; Congressional Reconstruction; Conkling, Roscoe; Fish, Hamilton; Johnson, Andrew; Morton, Oliver Perry; Presidential Reconstruction.

William J. McFeely, *Grant: A Biography* (New York, 1974); John A. Carpenter, *Ulysses S. Grant* (New York, 1970); Lloyd Lewis, *Captain Sam Grant* (Boston, 1950); Bruce Catton, *Grant Moves South* (Boston 1960); idem, *Grant Takes Command* (Boston, 1968); William B. Hesseltine, *Ulysses S. Grant, Politician* (New York, 1935); Allan Nevins, *Hamilton Fish: The Inner History of the Grant Administration* (New York, 1936).

**GREELEY, HORACE** (1811–1872), editor and reformer, was born in Amherst, New Hampshire, where he was educated in the public schools. When his family lost its farm, the Greeleys moved to Westhaven, Vermont, and Horace was apprenticed to the publisher of the East Poultney *Northern Spectator*, from whom he learned the printing trade. After a brief stay near Erie, Pennsylvania, where his family finally settled, in 1831 Greeley moved to New York City. Founding a weekly, the *New Yorker*, in 1834, he also became involved with various Whig publications, including the *Jeffersonian*, which he edited. At the same time, he formed a close alliance with Thurlow Weed and William H. Seward (q.v.), whose successful bid for the governorship in 1838 he strongly supported. In 1841 he founded the New York *Tribune*, a Whig newspaper designed to appeal to the mass market. It was to become his mouthpiece and one of the most influential journals in the country.

The New York *Tribune* was dedicated to certain principles that it never abandoned. A pronounced Whig journal, it never failed to further the party's principles of protection and government support of industry. In addition, it opposed the expansion of slave territory, endorsed temperance, and condemned religious bigotry. Greeley's other interests—Fourierism, social uplift, and westward expansion, as well as an insistent nationalism—also found expression in the paper, which at times employed well-known correspondents such as Karl Marx.

Always avid for political office, Greeley served briefly in Congress in 1848–1849 but failed to win the coveted New York senatorship. Disappointed, he broke with his allies Seward and Weed and became active in the new Republican party. In 1860, denied a place in the state's delegation to the Chicago convention, he appeared as a delegate from Oregon and used his influence to undermine Seward, although he was not entirely satisfied with the nomination of Abraham Lincoln (q.v.).

During the secession crisis, at first Greeley wanted to allow the "wayward sisters" to "depart in peace," but after the outbreak of the Civil War, the *Tribune* was foremost in the cry "On to Richmond." The editor, who consistently supported emancipation (q.v.), in the "Prayer of Twenty Millions," urged the President to free the slaves. Not even the Emancipation Proclamation (q.v.), however, induced him to draw close to Lincoln, whose renomination he opposed. In 1864 he sought to involve himself in peace negotiations, met with some Confederates at Niagara Falls, but was unable to accomplish anything. During the same year, he completed the first volume of his *American Conflict*, one of the early histories of the war.

Long devoted to reunion without rancor, during Reconstruction Greeley was identified with a policy of "universal amnesty and impartial suffrage." Although at first sympathetic toward Andrew Johnson (q.v.), because of the President's failure to protect the freedmen the editor broke with the Tennessean, ran unsuccessfully for Congress in 1866, and backed radical policies, including the impeachment. Yet in keeping with his belief in amnesty (q.v.), in 1867 he signed Jefferson Davis's (q.v.) bail bond, an action for which he was widely attacked. In 1868 he supported U. S. Grant (q.v.) for President, only to fall out with the general afterward because of the corruption of the administration and its Southern policy. In addition, Greeley favored the New York Republican faction headed by Reuben E. Fenton, while Grant backed Roscoe Conkling (q.v.), Fenton's bitter antagonist. Thus Greeley drifted into the ranks of the Liberal Republicans (Liberal Republican Movement, q.v.), who in 1872 nominated him for President at their Cincinnati convention. Although many of the Cincinnati reformers deplored the choice of a lifelong protectionist who had never shown much interest in civil service reform (q.v.), the Democrats endorsed Greeley's candidacy. The campaign that followed was marked by incessant abuse of the editor, whose previous statements attacking the Democrats could now be used against him. Discouraged by these onslaughts and the death of his wife, Greeley was decisively defeated and died in Pleasantville, near his longtime home in Chappaqua, New York, soon afterward.

Greeley was one of America's most influential journalists. Although his impact was lessened by his egocentrism and some of his political vagaries, he performed important service in the struggle against slavery and the call for universal amnesty.

*See also* Amnesty; Grant, Ulysses Simpson; Liberal Republicans.

Glyndon G. Van Deusen, *Horace Greeley: Nineteenth Century Crusader* (New York, 1953); William Harlan Hale, *Horace Greeley: Voice of the People* (New York, 1950).

**GREENBACKS,** the noninterest-bearing legal-tender paper currency of the United States originating during the Civil War. Coupled with the suspension of specie payments, the issue of these notes to the amount of some $450 million resulted in fluctuations of their value in relation to gold throughout the following years.

Hugh McCulloch, Andrew Johnson's (q.v.) Secretary of the Treasury, instituted policies designed to contract the paper currency. Although the Contraction Act of 1866 limited his power to do so, he succeeded in reducing the number of greenbacks from $433 million in August 1865 to $399 million in October 1866. In 1868 the Contraction Act was repealed, but in spite of its support by Western agrarian interests, the cause of the greenbacks suffered. Although both political parties contained soft- as well as hard-money wings, the Ohio Idea (q.v.), a proposal that the principal of bonds not specifying payment in gold be redeemed in paper, was rejected by the Republican convention. True, the Democrats adopted it, but their presidential candidate, Horatio Seymour (q.v.), opposed it. Finally, in 1869 a Public Credit Act provided for the redemption of federal bonds in specie.

During the presidency of U. S. Grant (q.v.), the greenbackers, though politically active, were unable to change the President's commitment to hard money. Although two of his appointees to the Supreme Court reversed a decision that held that debts incurred before the passage of the Legal Tender Acts had to be paid in coin, his Secretary of the Treasury, George S. Boutwell (q.v.), sought to maintain the existing equilibrium, and in 1874 Grant vetoed a mild inflation bill. In 1875 Congress passed a resumption measure, and in 1879, after the Treasury had accumulated a gold reserve, specie payments were resumed. Greenback parties under various names, however, contested elections between 1876 and 1884.

An early example of inflationary pressures, the greenback movement in the United States ran counter to the worldwide trend of establishing an international gold standard. Due to the rapidly expanding economy, however, and the hardships caused by deflation, the soft-money advocates were not without provocation.

*See also* Legal Tender Cases; Ohio Idea; Sherman, John.

Irwin Unger, *The Greenback Era* (Princeton, N.J., 1964); Walter T. Nugent, *The Money Question During Reconstruction* (New York, 1967).

**GRIMES, JAMES WILSON** (1816–1872), Governor and Republican Senator from Iowa, was born in Deering, New Hampshire, the son of local farmers. Educated at Hampton Academy and Dartmouth College, he read law in Peterboro, New Hampshire. In 1836 he moved to Burlington, Iowa, where he established a flourishing law practice. Appointed City Solicitor in 1837 and Justice of the Peace one year later, he became active in Whig politics and was elected to the Territorial Assembly in 1838. In 1843–1844 he served a second term in the Assembly and in 1852 was elected to the state legislature. In 1854 Grimes, a firm opponent of the Kansas-Nebraska Act, was elected Governor and later played a decisive role in the founding of the Republican party (q.v.) in Iowa. In 1859 he was elected to the U.S. Senate.

In the Senate, Grimes, a pronounced foe of slavery, was at first known as a radical. He strongly supported the war effort; was an active member of the Committee on Naval Affairs, which he chaired after 1864; and served as chairman of the Committee on the District of Columbia. Reelected in 1864, he became a determined opponent of Andrew Johnson (q.v.), although he long hoped for an adjustment of the differences between President and Congress. In time, he was recognized as one of the leaders of the moderate faction and in the impeachment trial of Johnson was one of the seven "recusants" who voted for the President's acquittal. He did so largely on constitutional grounds and cast his vote in spite of a stroke that had prostrated him. In 1869 he resigned his seat for reasons of health and went on an extended tour of Europe. He died in Burlington in 1872.

Grimes was a typical moderate Republican who disliked Johnson's policies but deplored radical measures. Unlike some of his associates, however, he felt constrained to vote for the President's acquittal.

*See also* Impeachment of Andrew Johnson; Johnson, Andrew.

William Salter, *The Life of James W. Grimes* (New York, 1876); Frederick B. Lewellen, "Political Ideas of James W. Grimes," *Iowa Journal of History and Politics*, 42 (1944): 399–404.

# H

HAHN, MICHAEL (1830–1886), first Free State Governor of Louisiana, was born in Klingenmünster, Rhenish Palatinate, and brought to Louisiana (q.v.) as a child. Educated in the New Orleans public schools and at the University of Louisiana, he was admitted to the bar in 1851. As a determined opponent of secession, in 1860 he supported Stephen A. Douglas and, when Benjamin F. Butler (q.v.) took over the city, in December 1862 was elected to Congress. After a lengthy debate, he was permitted to take his seat the following February but served for only a few weeks in the outgoing Congress. Upon his return to New Orleans, he acquired the *Daily True Delta*, established close relations with Nathaniel P. Banks (q.v.), and in February 1864 was elected Governor by the moderate Unionists. In the subsequent constitutional convention he induced the delegates to endorse emancipation but was unable to persuade them to authorize limited black suffrage (q.v.) as suggested in a letter to him by Abraham Lincoln (q.v.). Only after he published the letter did the convention agree to authorize the legislature to extend the franchise, an action it never took, although it ratified the Thirteenth Amendment (q.v.). Hahn was elected Senator and resigned as Governor but never pressed his claims in Washington.

In the postwar years, appalled by the policies of his successor, J. Madison Wells (q.v.), and those of Andrew Johnson (q.v.), Hahn became increasingly radical. He edited the *Daily Republican*, advocated black suffrage, and was wounded during the 1866 New Orleans riot (q.v.) Moving to St. Charles Parish in 1872, he founded the town of Hahnsville, where he published the St. Charles *Herald*. He was elected to the legislature; served as Speaker of the Assembly, superintendent of the mint, district judge, and state registrar; and in 1884 was sent to Congress as a Republican. He died in Washington in 1886.

Hahn was a nineteenth-century liberal whose contributions to the Reconstruction of Louisiana were considerable. His honest conduct of public affairs marked him as a model reformer during a corrupt era.

*See also* Banks, Nathaniel Prentiss; Butler, Benjamin Franklin; Louisiana; Wells, James Madison.

Amos E. Simpson and Vaughn B. Baker, "Michael Hahn: Steady Patriot," *Louisiana History*, 13 (Summer 1972): 229–52; Peyton McCrary, *Abraham Lincoln and Reconstruction: The Louisiana Experiment* (Princeton, N.J., 1978); LaWanda Cox, *Lincoln and Black Freedom: A Study in Presidential Leadership* (Columbia, S.C., 1981).

**HAMBURG MASSACRE,** a riot instigated by South Carolina (q.v.) "Redeemers" ("Redemption," q.v.) under the leadership of General Matthew C. Butler to disarm the Hamburg black militia. Using the refusal on July 4, 1876, of the militia's commander, Dock Adams, to have his troops give way to two whites in a buggy, Butler, appearing as counsel for the whites in a complaint before Judge Prince Rivers, the town's leading black, demanded that Adams surrender his arms. The case had been postponed until July 8, when large numbers of members of white rifle clubs, the Red Shirts, gathered to take the law in their own hands. Under the circumstances, Adams refused and retired into an armory, where a melee ensued. After the Red Shirts had suffered a casualty, they brought a cannon from nearby Augusta and fired into the building. Storming the armory, they captured twenty-five black militiamen, five of whom they randomly shot.

The affair made it impossible for Governor Daniel H. Chamberlain (q.v.) further to collaborate with Democratic fusionists. The "straightouts" secured control of the party, continued their terror tactics, and nominated Wade Hampton (q.v.) to oppose the Governor. The contest ended in the disputed election of 1876.

*See also* "Redemption"; South Carolina.

Joel Williamson, *After Slavery: The Negroes in South Carolina During Reconstruction, 1861–1877* (Chapel Hill, N.C., 1965); Peggy Lamson, *The Glorious Failure: Black Congressman Robert Brown Elliott and the Reconstruction in South Carolina* (New York, 1973).

**HAMILTON, ANDREW JACKSON** (1815–1875), Texas (q.v.) Unionist and Reconstruction Governor, was born in Madison County, Alabama. After reading law with Judge David Bowen at Weldona, he was admitted to the bar in 1841 and, following his brother Morgan C., moved to Texas in 1846. Appointed Acting Attorney General in January 1850, he lost the August election for that post but served in the legislature from 1851 to 1853. An opponent of secession, in 1859, he successfully ran for Congress on an independent Democratic ticket headed by Samuel Houston. The next year, he supported Stephen A. Douglas and during the secession crisis served on the House Committee of Thirty-three. Although elected to the legislature in March 1861, in 1862 he had to flee to Mexico and eventually made his way to New Orleans. In November 1862 Abraham Lincoln (q.v.) appointed him Military Governor of Texas; he accompanied the expedition to Galveston and in 1864 went to Brownsville to inaugurate his government.

In June 1865 Andrew Johnson (q.v.) appointed Hamilton Provisional Governor of Texas. Because of the disorder and the great distances in the state, the constitutional convention did not meet until February 1866, when it framed a conservative constitution with an electorate based on white suffrage and shielding ex-Confederates from damage suits. In the subsequent election, the conservative James W. Throckmorton was elected Governor. Hamilton, offended by the conservative nature of the constitution, turned against Johnson when he accepted it, and in September 1866 the former Governor was one of the participants in the Southern Loyalist Convention (q.v.) at Philadelphia.

Yet Hamilton, unlike his brother, was no radical. Returning to Texas after serving as register of bankruptcy in Mississippi, he was appointed Associate Justice of the Supreme Court and played a prominent role in the convention of 1868. After he had opposed radical measures such as the division of the state and the disfranchisement of former Confederates, he became the moderates' candidate for Governor but lost by a small margin to the radical Edmund J. Davis, although he always believed he had won. A member of the conservative taxpayers convention in 1871, he supported the Liberal Republicans (Liberal Republican Movement, q.v.) in the following year. Later he was engaged in various railroad enterprises and died in Austin in 1875.

*See also* Johnson, Andrew; Presidential Reconstruction; Texas.

John L. Waller, *Colossal Hamilton of Texas: A Biography of Andrew Jackson Hamilton, Militant Unionist and Reconstruction Governor* (El Paso, Tex., 1968).

**HAMPTON, WADE** (1818–1902), Confederate general, Governor, and Senator from South Carolina (q.v.), was born at Charleston, the scion of one of the richest families in the South. Educated at South Carolina College, he studied law but became a planter with properties in South Carolina, Mississippi, and Louisiana, owning some three thousand slaves. In 1852 and 1854 he was elected to the lower house of the South Carolina legislature and in 1858 and 1860 to the upper house, where he opposed the reopening of the slave trade and deplored secession. But when the state seceded, he heartily supported it. He joined the army as a colonel, was promoted to brigadier general in May 1862, to major general in September 1863, and to lieutenant general in January 1865. Taking part in the Battles of Bull Run, Seven Pines, Brandy Station, and Bentonville, as well as the operations against Philip H. Sheridan (q.v.) at Trevilian and the Petersburg campaign, he was repeatedly wounded. An intrepid cavalry leader, he accompanied J.E.B. Stuart on his raids and in 1864 became chief of cavalry. At the end of the war, he counseled flight into Texas and continued resistance but eventually stayed in South Carolina.

Naturally supporting the policies of Andrew Johnson (q.v.), Hampton ran unsuccessfully for Governor in 1865 but continued to play an active role in conservative and Democratic politics. In 1868 he was a member of the New

York Democratic national convention; in 1872 he supported Horace Greeley (q.v.), and in 1876, after the failure of an attempted fusion with moderate Republicans, he became the candidate of the straightout conservative ticket in South Carolina. After a campaign marked by violence, particularly by the Democratic Red Shirts, he claimed a victory over his Republican opponent, Daniel H. Chamberlain (q.v.), but the result was disputed by the returning board, and for a time two administrations contested the government of the state. When Rutherford B. Hayes (q.v.) assumed the presidency, he withdrew his support from Chamberlain, and Hampton was able to take undisputed possession of the state government.

The "Redeemer" ("Redemption," q.v.) regime under Hampton at first sought to honor its promises of fair treatment of the blacks (q.v.). Some of these had even voted for the Governor, who was known to be an advocate of impartial black suffrage (q.v.) (restricted by educational qualifications). But his opponents within the party, at first led by Martin W. Gary and then by Benjamin R. Tillman, were instrumental in gradually whittling down remaining black privileges. Hampton himself was elected a U.S. Senator in 1879. Tillman's forces were too strong for him, however, and he had to retire in 1891. Two years later Grover Cleveland appointed him commissioner of railroads. He died in Columbia in 1902.

A relatively moderate among the "Redeemers," Hampton advocated the faithful observance of constitutional obligations toward the freedmen. Not even his great prestige, however, was able to counteract the reactionary policies of his associates.

*See also* Chamberlain, Daniel Henry; Hayes, Rutherford B.; "Redemption"; South Carolina.

Manly Wade Wellman, *Giant in Grey: A Biography of Wade Hampton of South Carolina* (New York, 1949); Hampton M. Jarrell, *Wade Hampton and the Negro: The Road Not Taken* (Columbia, S.C., 1949).


**HANCOCK, WINFIELD SCOTT** (1824–1886), Union general and Democratic presidential candidate, was born at Montgomery Square, Pennsylvania, the son of a teacher and lawyer. A member of the West Point class of 1844, he served with the infantry in the Indian Territory before distinguishing himself during the Mexican War. After service in Missouri, Florida, and the Western frontier, he was sent to California, where he found himself at the outbreak of the Civil War.

Appointed brigadier general in September 1861, Hancock was one of the most successful Union commanders. Winning laurels during the Peninsular campaign, where George B. McClellan called him "superb," he distinguished himself again at Antietam, was promoted to major general in September 1862, and fought brilliantly at Fredericksburg, at Chancellorsville, and particularly at Gettysburg. Commanding the Second Corps, he chose the ground for the Union line, kept it intact, and successfully repulsed the Confederate charge on the third day, when he was severely wounded. Restored to his corps in time to take part in the campaigns in Virginia in 1864, he again rendered exemplary service at the Wilderness, Spottsylvania, and Cold Harbor.

At the end of the war, he was in command of the Department of West Virginia and the Middle Military Division, which included Washington, so that he had to supervise the execution of the assassins of Abraham Lincoln (q.v.), including that of the unfortunate Mary Surratt (q.v.), a miscarriage of justice for which he was often unjustly held responsible. Appointed commander of the Military Department of Missouri in 1866, in the following year he conducted a campaign against Indians in Kansas.

Always a Democrat, General Hancock disapproved of radical measures of Reconstruction. His support of Andrew Johnson (q.v.) caused the President in August 1867 to appoint him commander of the Fifth Military District consisting of Louisiana (q.v.) and Texas (q.v.). Here Hancock endeared himself to conservatives by issuing General Orders No. 40, stressing the supremacy of the civilian government, which so pleased Johnson that he asked Congress for a vote of thanks to the general but incurred the enmity of the radicals. The general persevered in his course by halting the removal of conservative officeholders and facilitating the voter registration of former Confederates. When he reversed the actions of a radical Board of Aldermen in New Orleans, General U. S. Grant (q.v.) overruled him, and he asked to be relieved. In March 1868 he returned north to assume command of the Military Division of the Atlantic.

When Grant was elected President, he sent Hancock to Minnesota to take over the Department of Dakota, a position he held until 1872. Then he was transferred to the Division of the Atlantic with headquarters on Governor's Island, New York.

Because of Hancock's enviable military reputation and his steadfast adherence to the principles of the Democratic party (q.v.), he was seriously considered for the presidential nomination in 1868. Defeated at the New York national convention by Horatio Seymour (q.v.), he tried again in 1876 and was finally nominated in 1880, when, together with William H. English, he campaigned against the Republican candidate, James A. Garfield (q.v.). Hancock lost by a narrow margin and remained in New York, where he died in 1886.

An able soldier, Hancock's political experience was limited. But he enabled the Democrats to counter Republican charges of disloyalty and to blunt the tactics of waving the "bloody shirt" (q.v.).

*See also* Garfield, James Abram; Johnson, Andrew; Louisiana.

David M. Jordan, *Winfield Scott Hancock: A Soldier's Life* (Bloomington, Ind., 1988); Glenn Tucker, *Hancock the Superb* (Indianapolis, 1960).

**HAYES, RUTHERFORD B.** (1822–1893), nineteenth President of the United States, was born in Delaware, Ohio, the posthumous son of Rutherford Hayes, a farmer, and Sarah Birchard Hayes. Brought up by his mother and wealthy uncle Sardis Birchard, he was educated at Kenyon College and Harvard Law School, from which he graduated in 1845. After practicing law in his uncle's town of Upper Sandusky (now Fremont), Ohio, in 1850 he moved to Cincinnati, where he established a law practice. An antislavery Whig, he defended fugitive slaves and from 1858 to 1861 served as City Solicitor.

During the Civil War, Hayes saw service in West Virginia and the Shenandoah Valley, was wounded four times, and rose to the rank of major general. Elected to Congress in 1865, he opposed the Reconstruction policies of Andrew Johnson (q.v.). His fellow citizens rewarded him by making him Governor of Ohio in 1867, in an election in which the Democrats captured the state legislature, and reelected him two years later. In 1872 he helped write the national Republican platform but was defeated in a race for Congress. After returning to Fremont, he won reelection as Governor in 1875 against the formidable opposition of the inflationist William Allen. Overcoming powerful rivals such as James G. Blaine (q.v.), Benjamin Bristow (q.v.), and Oliver P. Morton (q.v.), he was nominated for President at the 1876 Cincinnati Republican National Convention. William Wheeler of New York was his running mate.

Hayes was opposed by Governor Samuel J. Tilden (q.v.) of New York, a reform candidate like himself. After a spirited campaign, Tilden received 174 undisputed electoral votes and Hayes 165, but 185 were needed for election. Because the three remaining Republican states in the South sent in two sets of returns and one of the electors in Oregon was found to be ineligible, 20 votes were disputed. Thus the result was in doubt, and politicians of both political parties traveled south to influence the returning boards. Congress, split between a Democratic House and a Republican Senate, had difficulty in finding a solution until it established an Electoral Commission (q.v.) of five senators, five congressmen, and five Supreme Court justices, evenly divided between the parties. The deciding vote was expected to be cast by Justice David Davis (q.v.), an independent, but at the last moment he was elected a Democratic Senator from Illinois, and Justice Joseph P. Bradley of New Jersey, a Republican, took his place. Thereupon, the commission, by a partisan vote of eight to seven, decided not to go behind the returns and declared Hayes the winner. A series of deals, the Compromise of 1877 (q.v.), which involved promises to the South of economic support as well as of the withdrawal of the remaining federal troops from the statehouses, facilitated the settlement. Yet Hayes' title to the presidency remained clouded, although he would have won had blacks not been kept from the polls in a number of Southern states.

As President, Hayes sought to unify the party and the country by giving recognition to reformers such as William Evarts (q.v.) and Carl Schurz (q.v.) and by appointing a Southerner, David M. Key of Tennessee, Postmaster General. But this policy only alienated the Stalwarts, particularly Roscoe Conkling (q.v.), without winning over most of the Half-Breeds. The disgust of the former was heightened when the President honored the promise of withdrawing the troops from the remaining statehouses, so Governor Daniel Chamberlain (q.v.) of South Carolina and Governor Stephen B. Packard (q.v.) of Louisiana were superseded by their Democratic rivals, and federal efforts to enforce Reconstruction for all practical purposes came to an end. The blacks (q.v.) were gradually reduced to second-class citizenship while former Confederates took over. Hayes himself remained devoted to black rights, but aside from vetoing Democratic efforts to repeal the Enforcement Acts (q.v.) by riders to appropriation bills and presiding over philanthropic efforts to educate the freedmen, he could do little to help them.

Hayes also attempted to further civil service reform (q.v.). Although it was introduced in some departments, particularly in Carl Schurz's Department of the Interior, the reform met with determined opposition, especially by the New York machine of Roscoe Conkling. When Hayes attempted to replace Conkling's supporters in the New York Customs House, Collector Chester A. Arthur and naval officer Alonzo B. Cornell, the Senate refused to confirm their successors, and it took the President more than a year to have new appointees to their positions confirmed. Conkling remained his implacable enemy.

Taking office in the midst of the Panic of 1873, in the summer of 1877 the administration was faced with serious railroad strikes in Maryland, Pennsylvania, West Virginia, and elsewhere. Although not willing to take the extreme measures demanded by the employers, Hayes did help break the strikes by authorizing the army to restore law and order. A fiscal conservative, he vetoed the 1878 Bland-Allison Act for the coinage of silver and, when his veto was overridden, kept purchases at a minimum while taking great pride in the resumption of specie payments in 1879.

Having opted for a single term, Hayes retired after the election of James A. Garfield and returned to his home at Spiegel Grove in Fremont. He died there in 1893.

An honest, well-meaning statesman, Hayes has been blamed for abandoning the freedmen and Reconstruction by the withdrawal of federal troops from Southern statehouses. Probably unable to prevent this development, he did his best to give the country a decent administration.

*See also* Civil Service Reform; Compromise of 1877; Conkling, Roscoe; Electoral Commission.

Charles Richard Williams, *The Life of Rutherford Birchard Hayes: Nineteenth President of the United States* (2 vols., Columbus, Ohio, 1914); Harry Barnard, *Rutherford B. Hayes and His America* (Indianapolis, 1954); Kenneth E. Davison, *The Presidency of Rutherford B. Hayes* (Westport, Conn., 1972); Ari Hoogenboom, *The Presidency of Rutherford B. Hayes* (Lawrence, Kans., 1988).

**HENDERSON, JOHN BROOKS** (1826–1913), Senator from Missouri (q.v.), was born near Danville, Virginia. Taken by his parents to Lincoln County, Missouri, in 1832, he was orphaned soon thereafter but was able to study law and was admitted to the bar in 1848. He established a flourishing practice in Louisiana, Missouri, was elected to the state legislature in 1848 and 1856, and served as a Buchanan elector. A delegate to the Charleston Convention, in 1860 he supported Stephen A. Douglas, ran for Congress, but was defeated by James S. Rollins. Although he was a Southerner and a slaveholder, in 1861 he became a strong Unionist member of the state convention in which he exerted effective leadership.

In 1861, upon the expulsion of Senator Trusten Polk, Henderson was appointed to complete the vacant term and then was elected to the full Senate term commencing in 1863. A proponent of emancipation, he helped frame the Thirteenth Amendment (q.v.), which he introduced in the Senate. Although believing that Congress ought to take charge of Reconstruction and favoring black suffrage (q.v.), he remained a moderate, convinced that the states had never been out of the Union. He represented the state in the *test oath* case of *Cummings* v. *Missouri* (q.v.); yet in 1868 he was one of the seven "recusant" Republicans who voted to acquit Andrew Johnson (q.v.), an action that made his reelection impossible. Moving to St. Louis at the end of his term, he reestablished himself as a prominent lawyer. In 1875 President U. S. Grant (q.v.) appointed him a prosecutor of the Whiskey Ring (q.v.), only to dismiss him when he probed too deeply. An unsuccessful Republican candidate for Governor in 1872 and for Senator in 1873, he presided over the Republican Convention in Chicago in 1884. He served as a delegate to the 1889 Pan-American Convention, moved to Washington, and in his later years was an active anti-imperialist. He died in Washington in 1913.

A principled border-state moderate, Henderson rendered important service in keeping Missouri in the Union. His later career belies the theory that the "recusants" were never forgiven by the Republican party (q.v.).

*See also* Johnson, Andrew; Thirteenth Amendment.

F. A. Sampson, "Hon. John Brooks Henderson," *Missouri Historical Review*, 7 (1913): 237–41; William E. Parrish, *Missouri Under Radical Rule, 1865–1870* (Columbia, Mo., 1965).


**HOLDEN, WILLIAM WOODS** (1818–1892), Governor of North Carolina (q.v.), was born at Hillsboro, the illegitimate son of a grist mill operator. Raised by his mother until the age of six, Holden was then taken into the household of his father, who had married, and was raised together with his half-brothers and sisters. He was apprenticed to a newspaper editor at age ten; settled in Raleigh to become a printer at the local Whig paper, the *Star*; and in 1843 assumed the editorship of the Democratic Raleigh *Standard*, which he retained until 1868. In spite of his Whig past, Holden soon became a power within the Democratic party (q.v.), which in 1846 elected him to the state legislature and which to him seemed to be the proper vehicle for his populist aims of public education and universal white suffrage. Appointed state printer, in 1858 he sought the Democratic nomination for Governor but was defeated by the large planting interest that was afraid of his Populist notions. Yet he continued to wield power in the party and was closely identified with its states rights faction.

In 1860 Holden was a delegate to the Democratic National Convention in Charleston, but despite his previous extremism, he refused to join in the walkout led by William L. Yancey. Although in the end he supported John C. Breckinridge for the presidency, he became less and less radical as the secession crisis developed and identified with the Unionists. True, after the Fort Sumter crisis, as a delegate to the secession convention, he reluctantly voted for the break with the Union; within two years, however, he was one of the founders of the Conservative party opposing the Jefferson Davis (q.v.) administration. In 1862 he backed Zebulon Vance (q.v.) for Governor, only to turn against Vance by running for Governor himself in 1864 on an unsuccessful peace ticket.

In 1865 Andrew Johnson (q.v.), whose views had often paralleled Holden's, appointed him Provisional Governor of North Carolina. He attempted to carry out faithfully Presidential Reconstruction (q.v.) by reorganizing county governments and summoning a constitutional convention that outlawed slavery and repealed the secession ordinance. In the subsequent elections, however, he was defeated by the more conservative Jonathan Worth. Disappointed in the results of Johnson's policies, Holden became one of the founders of the state's Republican party and in 1868, after the introduction of black suffrage (q.v.), was elected Governor.

The Holden administration was beset by difficulties from the start. It established a free public school system but soon found itself mired in various railroad scandals, which the Governor, though personally honest, could not prevent. In addition, the Ku Klux Klan (q.v.) committed depredations and crimes against freedmen and Republicans. To stop this violence, Holden declared two counties to be in a state of insurrection and mobilized state troops under the command of George W. Kirk in the Unionist western counties and in Tennessee to counteract the terror. During the consequent Kirk-Holden War (q.v.), a number of Klansmen and their supporters, including the Governor's bitter opponent, Josiah Turner, were arrested. Determined to try the prisoners by military commission, Holden refused to honor their writs of habeas corpus. But the federal government did not support him; a federal court freed the detainees, and in 1870 the Republicans lost the state election. The new conservative legislature impeached the Governor and, after a predetermined trial, convicted and removed him from office.

In 1872 President U. S. Grant (q.v.) appointed Holden postmaster of Raleigh, a position he held until 1881. Always hoping for a vindication and a reversal of the unfair verdict against him, he died in Raleigh in 1892.

Holden's frequent changes of party allegiance seemed opportunistic to many, although he never wavered in his support of popular democracy. His efforts to suppress the Ku Klux Klan, though only partially successful, were wholly justified.

*See also* Kirk-Holden War; North Carolina; Presidential Reconstruction; Vance, Zebulon.

Horace W. Raper, *William W. Holden: North Carolina's Political Enigma* (Chapel Hill, N.C., 1985).

**HOLT, JOSEPH** (1807–1892), cabinet member and Judge Advocate General, was born in Breckinridge County, Kentucky. Educated at St. Joseph's and Centre Colleges, he studied law in Lexington. After practicing briefly in Elizabethtown, in 1832 he established himself in Louisville, became active in Jacksonian politics, and between 1833 and 1835 served as commonwealth attorney. In 1835 he moved to Mississippi but returned in 1842. After the death of his first wife, in 1850 he married Margaret Wickliffe, the daughter of a former Governor of Kentucky, and, a few years later, settled in Washington. In 1857 James Buchanan appointed him commissioner of patents and in 1859 Postmaster General. During the secession crisis, Holt, though a longtime advocate of states rights, nevertheless became a firm Unionist and in December 1860 took over John B. Floyd's portfolio of Secretary of War. Using all his influence to save Kentucky for the Union, he impressed Abraham Lincoln (q.v.), who in September 1862 appointed him Judge Advocate General, a position in which he made a name for himself by systematically arranging his opinions, which were printed in order, to standardize legal proceedings in the army.

After the assassination of Lincoln, Holt, convinced of the culpability of the leaders of the Confederacy, influenced Andrew Johnson (q.v.) to issue the proclamation of May 2, 1865, implicating Jefferson Davis (q.v.) and some associates. As chief prosecutor of the assassins, he procured death sentences for the principal conspirators. But he became involved in a bitter controversy with Johnson concerning the recommendation of mercy for Mrs. Mary Surratt (q.v.), the President maintaining that Holt had withheld it from him and Holt denying the accusation. In the absence of conclusive evidence, it is difficult to assess the merits of the case. Holt submitted the court's findings to Johnson on July 5, 1865; both men agreed that mercy was not appropriate, but whether the President, who was ill at the time, saw the recommendation or whether Holt did indeed withhold it is not clear, particularly since there were no witnesses present. Holt never ceased to attempt to refute Johnson's charges; he continued to serve as Judge Advocate General until 1875, when he retired, and died in Washington in 1892.

*See also* Davis, Jefferson; Johnson, Andrew; Stanton, Edwin M.; Surratt, Mary Eugenia Jenkins.

Roger J. Bartman, "The Contribution of Joseph Holt to the Political Life of the United States" (Ph.D. diss., Fordham University, 1958); Mary Bernard Allen, "Joseph Holt" (Ph.D. diss., University of Chicago, 1927); Benjamin P. Thomas and Harold M. Hyman, *Stanton: The Life and Times of Lincoln's Secretary of War* (New York, 1962).

**HOMESTEAD ACT OF 1866,** the Southern Homestead Act, a measure passed on June 21, 1866, opening public lands in Alabama (q.v.), Mississippi (q.v.), Arkansas (q.v.), Louisiana (q.v.), and Florida (q.v.) to homesteaders. Long urged by advocates of land reform, particularly George W. Julian (q.v.), the law enabled actual settlers to procure eighty acres for a fee of $5. By stipulating that until January 1, 1867, entrants had to swear that they had always been loyal to the United States, Congress hoped to reserve the land for the freedmen. Blacks (q.v.) did take up some acreage, but the land was often inferior and the freedmen were too short of capital to farm it successfully. When the measure was repealed in 1876, only a few thousand acres had been cultivated by the freedmen.

*See also* Julian, George W.; Land Policies.

Christie Farnham Pope, "Southern Homesteads for Negroes," *Agricultural History*, 44 (April 1970): 201–12.

**HOWARD, OLIVER OTIS** (1830–1909), major general and commissioner of the Freedmen's Bureau (q.v.), was born in Leeds, Maine. Educated at Bowdoin College and a member of the West Point class of 1854, Brigadier General Howard took part in the first Bull Run and the Peninsular Campaign, in which he lost an arm at Fair Oaks. Returning to active service, he fought at Antietam, was promoted to major general, and commanded XI Corps at Chancellorsville and Gettysburg before being sent to the West to participate in the actions around Chattanooga. During the later part of the Georgia and Carolina campaigns, he commanded the Army of Tennessee.

In 1865 Howard, whom Lincoln (q.v.) had earmarked for the post, was appointed commissioner of the Freedmen's Bureau, an agency he headed during the entire time of its existence. A devout Christian who sympathized with the aspirations of the freedmen, he attempted to use the bureau to educate them, provide them with judicial protection, and facilitate their acquisition of land. But he was hampered in his efforts by President Andrew Johnson (q.v.), whose policy of restoring land to pardoned insurgents forced the commissioner to issue Circular No. 15, making it impossible to carry out his previous Circular No. 13 for the distribution of forty acres each to the blacks (q.v.). Because it fell to Howard to carry out Johnson's orders he has been severely criticized; yet it is difficult to see how he could have refused to do so without losing his position and all influence.

One of Howard's principal goals as commissioner of the Freedmen's Bureau was the encouragement of black education, not merely in the lower grades but up to and including college. He was instrumental in the founding of Howard University, of which he became president in 1869. Other black colleges also received his support.

During the last years of the Freedmen's Bureau, Howard was the subject of various investigations into his disbursement of funds. They all ended in his favor, although it was evident that his administrative methods had been somewhat lax.

In 1872 Howard succeeded in making peace with the Apache leader Cochise, and after the Freedmen's Bureau was phased out, he was sent to the Department of the Columbia. There he became involved in the Nez Percé War of 1877 and the lengthy pursuit of Chief Joseph, as well as in the hostilities with the Bannocks. In 1881 he was appointed superintendent of West Point; in 1882, commandant of the Department of the Platte; and in 1886, he was promoted to major general in the regular army, as commander of the Division of the Pacific. In 1888 he was transferred to the Military Division of the Atlantic with headquarters in New York, where he stayed until his retirement in 1894.

After his retirement Howard moved to Burlington, Vermont; wrote and lectured extensively; and was one of the founders of Lincoln Memorial University at Harrogate, Tennessee. He died in Burlington in 1909.

*See also* Freedmen's Bureau; Indians; Land Policies.

John Carpenter, *Sword and Olive Branch: Oliver Otis Howard* (Pittsburgh, 1964); William S. McFeely, *Yankee Stepfather: General O. O. Howard and the Freedmen* (New Haven, 1968).

# I

---

**IMPEACHMENT OF ANDREW JOHNSON,** the ultimate effort of the Republicans to rid themselves of President Andrew Johnson (q.v.). Long differing with the President on the question of Reconstruction, Congress had sought to deprive him of his patronage with the Tenure of Office Act (q.v.) and sought to deprive him of his powers as commander-in-chief of the army with the command of the army provisions of the Appropriations Act of 1867–1868 by requiring him to transmit all orders through the general of the army. Then, in December 1867, the House of Representatives actually attempted unsuccessfully to impeach him. In February 1868, after the Senate had reinstated Secretary of War Edwin M. Stanton (q.v.), who had been dismissed by Johnson in August 1867, the President defied the Tenure of Office Act by again dismissing Stanton and appointing Lorenzo Thomas Secretary ad interim. Thereupon the House, by a strict party vote, passed the Covode Resolution, impeaching the chief executive of high crimes and misdemeanors, and appointed a committee to draw up the charges.

The eleven articles that were finally adopted accused Johnson of having violated the Tenure of Office Act, the command of the army provisions, and the Conspiracy Act of 1861. He was also charged with attempting to prevent the execution of the Reconstruction Acts, delivering speeches tending to bring Congress into disrepute, and denying the legitimacy of both Houses. A Board of Managers consisting of both moderates and radicals represented the prosecution; the defense included eminent legal talent such as former Associate Justice Benjamin R. Curtis, future Secretary of State William M. Evarts (q.v.), and Attorney General Henry S. Stanbery (q.v.), and the trial opened on March 29. Because the case was essentially political, the proceedings yielded few surprises, but during the trial, Johnson gave assurances to Senator James W. Grimes (q.v.)

that he would abide by the Reconstruction Acts, obliged Senator Edmund G. Ross (q.v.) by transmitting the constitutions of Arkansas (q.v.) and South Carolina (q.v.), and, in accordance with an agreement, appointed General John M. Schofield (q.v.) Secretary of War.

These deals contributed to the final outcome. When on May 16 the Senate voted on the eleventh catch-all article, the President was acquitted by one vote, seven Republican "recusants" deserting their party to vote "not guilty." The ballot on May 26 on the second and third article, dealing with the appointment of Thomas, produced the same result.

The outcome of the trial determined that no President could be impeached for mere political differences with Congress, thus safeguarding the system of checks and balances embedded in the Constitution. It also heartened Southern conservatives in their resistance to Reconstruction.

*See also* Evarts, William M.; Johnson, Andrew; Stanton, Edwin M.; Tenure of Office Act.

Hans L. Trefousse, *Impeachment of a President: Andrew Johnson, the Blacks, and Reconstruction* (Knoxville, Tenn., 1975); Michael Les Benedict, *The Impeachment and Trial of Andrew Johnson* (New York, 1973).


**INDIANS.** During the period of Reconstruction, native American resistance to white settlement caused several wars and massacres. Threatened by settlers on the Great Plains and prospectors in the mountains, various Indian nations sought to protect their interests by force; the government, convinced that the native Americans must either be settled on reservations, policed by the army, or assimilated, countered with military measures. After the Sioux, resentful of the opening of the Bozeman Trail, massacred Captain William J. Fetterman and his command in 1866, a peace commission succeeded in 1867 in establishing a temporary agreement with the Southern Indians at Medicine Lodge and in 1868 with the Sioux at Fort Laramie. Yet the arrangements did not last; fighting resumed, and in 1868 General George A. Custer destroyed the Cheyenne at Washita.

When General U. S. Grant (q.v.) became President, he sought to inaugurate what he called a "peace policy" and appointed the Seneca Indian General Ely S. Parker Indian Commissioner, but he was no more able than his predecessors to come to terms with the rebellious tribes. In the Apache War of 1871–1886, in which black troops played a significant role, the followers of Geronimo were finally settled on reservations; in the Red River War of 1874–1875, other southwestern Indians were scattered, and in 1875 the Second Sioux War broke out. In this engagement, caused by white incursions into the Black Hills, Sitting Bull and Crazy Horse defeated and killed General Custer (q.v.) and his troops at the Little Big Horn, only to be themselves vanquished by General Alfred H. Terry later that year (1876).

The Indian wars did not cease during subsequent administrations. Made desperate by the destruction of the great buffalo herds and goaded to despair by advancing railroads and settlers, several nations vainly attempted to resist. In 1877 the Nez Percé under Chief Joseph fought Generals O. O. Howard (q.v.) and Nelson P. Miles, only to be overcome after a long chase and removed to the Indian Territory. The Bannocks and Utes rose in 1878 and 1879 with similar results, and it was not until 1890 that Indian fighting finally came to an end.

Government policies in the 1870s and 1880s tended increasingly toward efforts at assimilation. Secretary of the Interior Carl Schurz (q.v.), after first continuing the practice of settling whole tribes in large reservations, later gave up this proceeding and strongly advocated a policy of breaking up the tribal system by introducing landholding in severalty, an approach given legislative sanction in 1886 with the Dawes Act. It was no more successful than previous attempts, however, and the basic problem of a clash between land-hungry whites and nomadic Indians remained insoluble.

*See also* Custer, George Armstrong; Howard, Oliver Otis; Schurz, Carl.

Robert M. Utley, *Frontier Regulars: The United States Army and the Indian, 1866–1890* (New York, 1973); Henry E. Fritz, *The Movement for Indian Assimilation, 1860–1890* (Philadelphia, 1963); Loring Benson Priest, *Uncle Sam's Stepchildren: The Reformation of United States Indian Policy, 1865–1887* (New Brunswick, N.J., 1942).

**IRONCLAD OATH,** an oath of loyalty devised by Congress on July 2, 1862. Requiring prospective federal officeholders to swear not only that they promised to be loyal to the United States in the future but also that they had never in the past voluntarily supported the insurgents, this test was widely used during Reconstruction to insure the supremacy of the Republican party (q.v.). In 1865 it was extended to attorneys in the federal courts, but this provision as well as state loyalty tests for ministers were found unconstitutional in the *test oath* cases of 1867. The oath formed part of the Wade-Davis Bill (q.v.), which required it of all voters for the proposed state conventions, and during the administration of Andrew Johnson (q.v.), it loomed as one of the obstacles to Presidential Reconstruction (q.v.). In 1867 it was included in the second and third Reconstruction Acts (q.v.) to qualify registrars. Although in 1868 it was modified to some extent, it was not finally repealed until 1884.

*See also* Johnson, Andrew; Presidential Reconstruction; Reconstruction Acts; Wade-Davis Bill.

Harold Melvin Hyman, *The Era of the Oath: Northern Loyalty Tests During the Civil War and Reconstruction* (Philadelphia, 1954).

# J

JOHNSON, ANDREW (1808–1875), seventeenth President of the United States, was born in Raleigh, North Carolina, the son of poor white working people. Apprenticed to a tailor at an early age, Johnson never had a day's schooling in his life. After running away from his employer who advertised for his recapture, he finally settled in Greeneville, Tennessee, where he established a tailor shop and married Eliza McCardle, a shoemaker's daughter. Elected an alderman in 1829, mayor in 1834, state representative in 1835 and 1839, and state Senator in 1841, he was sent to Congress in 1843. A convinced Jacksonian Democrat, in 1853 and 1855 he was elected Governor and in 1857 U. S. Senator.

The secession crisis faced Johnson with a difficult decision. Most of the Democrats in Tennessee (q.v.) were secessionists, but he had long clashed with many of the Southern leaders in Congress about his advocacy of populist measures, particularly his sponsorship of the Homestead Act. Moreover, he came from Unionist East Tennessee, and on December 18 and 19, 1860, he delivered a strong Unionist speech in the Senate denouncing secession. Cooperating with his former Whig opponents, in February 1861 he worked hard to defeat the secession movement, and when, after Fort Sumter, Tennessee left the Union, he stood out as the only Senator from a seceding state to remain loyal.

In 1862 Abraham Lincoln (q.v.) appointed Johnson Military Governor of Tennessee. He ruled the state with an iron hand, but it was not until after his conversion to emancipation (q.v.) in 1863 and his nomination and election as Vice President on the Union ticket that he finally succeeded in establishing a Reconstruction government that abolished slavery.

The assassination of Abraham Lincoln made Johnson President. Although he sounded vindictive at first, in reality he had not wavered in his belief that the seceded states had never left the Union and that, as soon as they ceased to resist federal authority, they ought to be restored as outlined in the Johnson-Crittenden Resolutions. Consequently, on May 29, 1865, he issued a Proclamation of Amnesty (q.v.), in effect promising amnesty to all but high officers of the Confederacy and those with property of more than $20,000. On the same day he published another proclamation appointing William W. Holden (q.v.) Provisional Governor of North Carolina (q.v.) and calling for the restoration of the state on the basis of white suffrage. The proclamation served as a model for all other Southern states. Johnson asked them to abolish slavery, repudiate the Confederate debt, and nullify the secession ordinances, but he did not always insist even upon these mild conditions.

The result of this policy of Presidential Reconstruction (q.v.) was the election of conservative legislatures and members of Congress as well as the passage of onerous black codes (q.v.). Congress, perturbed about these proceedings, in December 1865 refused to seat any of the newly elected Southern members and appointed a Committee of Fifteen to deal with all questions of Reconstruction. The rift between the President and Congress widened when in early 1866 he vetoed the Freedmen's Bureau and Civil Rights Bills (q.v.); yet, though accused of deserting his party, Johnson had never been a Republican; he represented the War Democratic element in the Union party and was elected as such.

In the summer of 1866, Johnson, totally rejecting the Fourteenth Amendment (q.v.), sought to create a new conservative party, and supported the Philadelphia National Union Convention (q.v.). Campaigning strenuously but ineffectively in the "swing around the circle" (q.v.), he was unable to prevent his opponents' sweeping victory.

In 1867 the differences between Congress and the President became worse. Violently opposed to the Reconstruction Acts (q.v.), he nevertheless complied with them but gradually replaced radical commanding generals with moderates. Although he was hampered by the Tenure of Office (q.v.) and "command of the army" acts, he sought to remodel his cabinet by dismissing Secretary of War Edwin M. Stanton (q.v.) and replacing him with General U. S. Grant (q.v.). Congress, which had already initiated an impeachment investigation and actually sought to impeach him in December 1867, did not approve, and in January 1868 the Senate refused to uphold Stanton's dismissal. Because Grant refused to cooperate with the President, a break developed between the two men, and when in February Johnson once more discharged Stanton, this time in defiance of the Tenure of Office Act, and appointed Lorenzo Thomas Secretary ad interim, the House impeached him for high crimes and misdemeanors. During the subsequent trial lasting until May 26, he made several deals with Senators and others, which contributed to his acquittal by one vote, but he was rendered powerless for the remainder of his term. His efforts in July 1868 to capture the Democratic nomination were unsuccessful.

After his retirement from the presidency, Johnson returned to Tennessee. In 1869 he vainly sought reelection to the Senate; in 1872 he contested unsuccessfully for congressman-at-large, and it was not until 1875 that he finally realized his ambition of returning to the Senate. After briefly taking his seat, he died near Carter Station, Tennessee, later that year.

An adept Democratic politician who succeeded in defeating both his Whig and Democratic opponents in Tennessee, Johnson found himself in an unfamiliar milieu when he became President. His populist agrarian appeals did not have the same electrifying effects in the country at large as in his home state, and his immediate policies were a failure. Nevertheless, by refusing to exploit the opportunities to reform the South immediately after the war and by giving hope to Southern conservatives, he so undermined Reconstruction that his racist notions of keeping the South "a white man's country" were realized.

*See also* Amnesty; Congressional Reconstruction; Impeachment of Johnson; Presidential Reconstruction.

Hans L. Trefousse, *Andrew Johnson: A Biography* (New York, 1989); James E. Sefton, *Andrew Johnson and the Uses of Constitutional Power* (Boston, 1980); Lately Thomas, *The First President Johnson: The Three Lives of the Seventeenth President of the United States of America* (New York, 1968); Eric L. McKitrick, *Andrew Johnson and Reconstruction* (Chicago, 1960); Albert Castel, *The Presidency of Andrew Johnson* (Lawrence, Kans., 1979).

**JOHNSON, REVERDY** (1796–1876), Maryland (q.v.) jurist, Senator, and U.S. Attorney General, was born in Annapolis, the son of John Johnson, a lawyer. Educated at St. John's College and trained in the law by his father, he was admitted to the bar in 1816. He settled briefly in Upper Marlborough but then moved to Baltimore, which became his permanent home.

Johnson soon achieved prominence at the bar and in politics. He served in the state Senate from 1821 to 1828, became a Whig, and was sent to the U.S. Senate in 1845. In 1849 Zachary Taylor appointed him Attorney General, but after his retirement in 1850 and the collapse of the Whig party, he became a reluctant Democrat and was one of the attorneys for the defense in the *Dred Scott* case.

During the secession crisis and the Civil War, Johnson was a strong Unionist. He was a member of the Washington Peace Conference in 1861 and reentered the state Senate later that year. In 1863 he returned to U.S. Senate, favored George B. McClellan in 1864, but supported the Wade-Davis Bill (q.v.) and the Thirteenth Amendment (q.v.).

After the war, Johnson defended Mary E. Surratt (q.v.), supported Andrew Johnson (q.v.), and represented the Senate minority on the Joint Committee of Fifteen on Reconstruction (q.v.). He also appeared successfully in *ex parte Milligan* (q.v.), *ex parte Garland* (q.v.), and *Cummings* v. *Missouri* (q.v.). Opposed to most measures of Congressional Reconstruction (q.v.), he participated in the National Union Convention (q.v.) in Philadelphia. Nevertheless, he was so eager to restore the Southern states to representation that, alone among the Democrats, he voted for the first two Reconstruction Acts (q.v.). During the impeachment trial of Andrew Johnson, he arranged a meeting between the President and Senator James W. Grimes (q.v.) during which the President promised not to interfere further with Reconstruction, a pledge that enabled Grimes and others to vote for Johnson's acquittal.

In July 1868 the President appointed Johnson minister to Great Britain. During his stay in England he negotiated the Johnson-Clarendon Convention seeking to settle outstanding disputes between the United States and the United Kingdom, including the *Alabama* claims, but the treaty was rejected by the Senate. Johnson returned to Baltimore, resumed his practice, and in 1875 successfully represented the defendant in *U.S.* v. *Cruikshank* (q.v.). He died in Annapolis in 1876.

*See also Cummings* v. *Missouri*; *Garland, Ex Parte; Milligan, Ex Parte*; Reconstruction, Joint Committee on; *U.S.* v. *Cruikshank*.

Bernard C. Steiner, *A Life of Reverdy Johnson* (Baltimore, 1914, New York, 1970).

**JULIAN, GEORGE WASHINGTON** (1817–1899), radical congressman from Indiana, was born in Centerville, Indiana, the son of Quaker parents active in politics. Admitted to the bar in 1840, he began the practice of law in Newcastle and eventually returned to his home town. A Whig, he was elected to the assembly in 1845 but was defeated for the state Senate two years later. In 1849 he was one of the few Free Soilers elected to Congress, where he denounced slavery in no uncertain terms. Defeated for reelection, in 1852 he was nominated Vice President on the Free Democratic ticket headed by John P. Hale. After the passage of the Kansas-Nebraska Act, he joined the People's and Republican parties and in 1860 was reelected to Congress, to which he was regularly returned until 1870.

A forceful advocate of antislavery measures, who married the daughter of Joshua R. Giddings, Julian was a member of the Joint Committee on the Conduct of the War and the chairman of the Committee on Public Lands. He was particularly interested in land reform, which he believed to be essential for the reconstruction of the seceded states, and in 1864 sponsored a bill for the distribution of homesteads to veterans in the South. This measure was in line with his belief in the territorialization of the insurgent states coupled with land for the freedmen. He also supported women's suffrage.

During the impeachment of Andrew Johnson (q.v.), Julian served on the committee to draw up charges. In 1868, despite his distrust of generals, he supported U. S. Grant (q.v.) but became alienated from the administration, in part because of his longtime rivalry with Oliver P. Morton (q.v.), the President's Stalwart supporter. Defeated for reelection in 1870, two years later he campaigned for the Liberal Republicans (Liberal Republican Movement, q.v.). After moving to Irvington, he endorsed the Democrats, who in 1876 sent him to Louisiana to observe the actions of the returning board in that year's disputed election. In 1885 Grover Cleveland appointed him surveyor general of New Mexico, a post he held until 1889, when he returned to Indiana. He died in Irvington in 1899.

*See also* Land Reform; Morton, Oliver Perry.

Patrick W. Riddleberger, *George Washington Julian: Radical Republican* (Indianapolis, 1866).

# K

KELLEY, WILLIAM DARRAH (1814–1890), radical congressman from Pennsylvania, was born in Philadelphia, the son of a watchmaker and jeweler. Apprenticed to a jeweler, in 1835 he moved to Boston to practice his craft but within a few years returned to Philadelphia to study law and was admitted to the bar in 1841. In 1845 he was appointed prosecuting attorney and in 1843 judge of the Court of Common Pleas.

A longtime Democrat, Kelley had strong antislavery convictions, which after 1854 led him into the Republican party (q.v.). Although defeated for Congress in 1856, he was elected in 1860 and for almost thirty years served uninterruptedly as a delegate from his Philadelphia district.

Kelley, so extreme a protectionist that he was called ''Pig Iron Kelley,'' was a radical in every respect. He opposed capital punishment, befriended labor, and favored inflation. Above all, however, he was a spokesmen for the attainment of rights for the blacks. In the belief that the Southern states were ''alien enemies,'' he not only supported the Wade-Davis Bill (q.v.) but fully endorsed black suffrage (q.v.), a reform he advocated in Congress as early as January 1865. Justifying his insistence on votes for freedmen with Article IV, Section 4 of the Constitution, guaranteeing every state a republican government, he held that the federal government should bestow the ballot on blacks everywhere. In 1867 his appearance at Mobile so infuriated local conservatives that it instigated a riot, but he refused to compromise. His efforts were crowned with success with the passage of the Fifteenth Amendment (q.v.), which he had helped formulate.

In his later years, Kelley became more and more identified with protectionism. Despite a brush with the Crédit Mobilier scandal, he was regularly returned to Congress until 1890, when he died in Washington.

*See also* Radical Republicans.

Ira V. Brown, "William D. Kelley and Radical Reconstruction," *Pennsylvania Magazine of History and Biography*, 85 (1961): 45–57; Hans L. Trefousse, *The Radical Republicans: Lincoln's Vanguard for Racial Justice* (New York, 1969).

**KELLOGG, WILLIAM PITT** (1830–1918), carpetbag Governor and Senator from Louisiana, was born in Orwell, Vermont, the son of a Congregational minister. Moving to Illinois in 1846, he was admitted to the bar seven years later and practiced in Canton. Active in the organization of the Republican party (q.v.), he was a delegate to the 1856 Bloomington and 1860 Chicago conventions and an Abraham Lincoln (q.v.) elector. In 1861 he was appointed Chief Justice of Nebraska territory and in 1865, after serving as brigadier general, was named collector of the Port of New Orleans. As one of the mainstays of the local Republican party, he attended the 1868 Chicago convention and was rewarded with a seat in the U.S. Senate.

The troubles of the Louisiana (q.v.) Republicans cut short his stay in Washington. After cooperating with Governor Henry Clay Warmoth (q.v.), he broke with his fellow carpetbagger, who, in a Fusion movement, sought conservative support and in the disputed election of 1872 claimed victory in the race for Governor against the Democrat John McEnery (q.v.). The result was the emergence of two rival governments, one headed by Kellogg and the other by McEnery. After appeals to Congress, which recommended new elections, Kellogg, propped up by the administration of the U. S. Grant (q.v.), gained control, but the disaffected conservatives resorted to tax revolts and violence, particularly in Colfax (Colfax Riot, q.v.), Coushatta (Coushatta Massacre, q.v.), and New Orleans, to overthrow the regime. A similar disputed election in 1874 brought about federal intervention. General P. Regis de Trobriand expelled certain McEnery delegates from the legislature, and Congress again sent an investigating committee. One of its members, William A. Wheeler, arranged a compromise, but peace was elusive. In violation of the agreement, the House impeached Kellogg, although the Senate quickly acquitted him.

In 1876 the result was again in dispute. Yet Kellogg was not affected; he was elected to the U.S. Senate, and although the Democrats took over the state after Rutherford B. Hayes (q.v.), with the aid of Louisiana's disputed votes, had become President, the Senator not only was able to serve out his term but at its conclusion was able to secure election as a Republican to the House of Representatives. After the expiration of his term, he moved to Washington, remained active in Republican politics, and died in the capital in 1918.

*See also* Carpetbaggers; Colfax Riot; Coushatta Massacre; Louisiana; Warmoth, Henry Clay.

John Edmund Gonzales, "William Pitt Kellogg, Reconstruction Governor of Louisiana, 1873–77," *Louisiana Historical Quarterly*, 29 (1946): 394–495; Richard Nelson Current, *Those Terrible Carpetbaggers: A Reinterpretation* (New York, 1988).

**KENTUCKY,** a border state not subject to Reconstruction. Unlike other slave states, Kentucky, which had remained loyal during the Civil War, emerged from the conflict with slavery still legal. Yet although it had furnished sixty-four thousand troops to the federal, and only thirty thousand to the Confederate army, the population, including the Unionists, resented various antislavery measures. Kentuckians deplored the Emancipation Proclamation (q.v.), from which the state was exempt; the recruitment of black troops; and the bill freeing the families of Union soldiers. Moreover, they were deeply offended by the imposition of martial law in 1863. Nevertheless, the presence of Union troops had already influenced many slaves to seek their freedom, so by the spring of 1865 only about sixty-five thousand blacks (q.v.) remained in bondage.

The politics of the state were not conducive to emancipation. Strongly racist, the whites were determined to keep the blacks in subjection, an attitude particularly cultivated by the Democratic party, an organization consisting of both Union and states rights elements, and led by Garrett Davis, Charles Wickliffe, and W. F. Bullock. But not only the Democrats were hostile to Congressional Reconstruction (q.v.); many of the Unconditional Unionists and Republicans, while supporting the ratification of the Thirteenth Amendment (q.v.), were often also opposed to increases in federal power. Represented by men like the reformer Benjamin H. Bristow (q.v.), they generally supported the moderate policies of Andrew Johnson (q.v.). A third grouping of conservatives like Thomas E. Bramlette, R. T. Jacobs, and J. H. Harney complicated the political picture.

The results of this conservatism long affected developments in Kentucky. Capturing the state legislature in 1865, the Democrats relieved former insurgents of their disabilities and refused to ratify the Thirteenth Amendment, so slavery did not come to an end until December 1865. Black testimony was not admitted in the courts until 1874, and black suffrage (q.v.) had to await the passage of the Fifteenth Amendment (q.v.), which the state also rejected. Although Johnson lifted martial law in October 1865, the continuing persecution of the blacks led to the extension of the jurisdiction of the Freedmen's Bureau (q.v.) to Kentucky. Furious white reaction to this alleged violation of states rights resulted in the strengthening of the Democratic party, and widespread terrorist Ku Klux Klan (q.v.) activity harassed the freedmen. So strong were the conservatives and Democrats that it was not until 1896 that a Republican presidential candidate was able to carry the state.

Unlike their counterparts in the deep South, the blacks in Kentucky tended to become wage laborers instead of sharecroppers. Although some schools, including a college, were established for them, their social and economic position remained depressed. The state joined others in furthering the construction of railroads; it established profitable distilleries and began to exploit its timber and mining riches, but it remained largely agrarian. Although it is not true that Kentucky simply revealed its long-standing Confederate sympathies during the period of Reconstruction, it did manifest its opposition to federal interference with the established rights of the states.

*See also* Thirteenth Amendment.

Ross A. Webb, *Kentucky in the Reconstruction Era* (Lexington, Ky., 1979); Victor B. Howard, *Black Liberation in Kentucky: Emancipation and Freedom, 1862–1884* (Lexington, Ky., 1983); E. Merton Coulter, *Civil War and Readjustment in Kentucky* (Chapel Hill, N.C., 1926).

**KIRK-HOLDEN WAR,** an effort in 1870 to suppress the Ku Klux Klan (q.v.) in North Carolina (q.v.). After a series of violent outrages and assassinations, Governor William W. Holden (q.v.), who at first had tried to reach an accommodation with the instigators of terror in the state, determined to rely on the powers conferred upon him by the legislature to suppress the Klan by declaring counties in a state of insurrection and to use the militia to restore order. He invoked this law, the so-called Shoffner Act, first in Alamance and then in Caswell County; recruited troops from the Unionist western part of the state and from Tennessee; and placed them under the command of George W. Kirk, a former federal officer. The troops arrested a number of members and supporters of the Klan, including the Governor's bitter opponent, Josiah Turner, the Democratic editor of the Raleigh *Sentinel*, whom Holden sought to try by military commission. He refused to comply with a writ of habeas corpus issued by Chief Justice Richmond M. Pierson, but when the federal government failed to sustain the Governor, the prisoners obtained a writ of habeas corpus from federal judge George W. Brooks in Salisbury and Holden had to free them. The result was the loss of the August election and the impeachment and removal of Holden by the new Democratic majority.

*See also* Holden, William Woods; Ku Klux Klan; North Carolina.

Allen W. Trelease, *White Terror: The Ku Klux Klan Conspiracy and Southern Reconstruction* (New York, 1971); Horace W. Raper, *William W. Holden: North Carolina's Political Enigma* (Chapel Hill, N.C., 1985).

**KU KLUX KLAN,** a secret terrorist organization designed to overawe blacks and Republicans, particularly at election time, in order to frustrate Congressional Reconstruction (q.v.). Founded in Pulaski, Tennessee, in May 1866, it was at first a social club but soon assumed a political character. It was organized into dens headed by a Grand Cyclops, provinces by a Grand Dragon, and dominions by a Grand Titan; the order as a whole was commanded by a Grand Wizard of the Empire. These officers were assisted by Night Hawks, Goblins, Furies, Hydras, and Genii, with ordinary members called Ghouls. In spite of this elaborate structure, the actual organization was comparatively loose, and many similar bands, like the Knights of the White Camelia in Louisiana and neighboring states as well as others had an independent existence.

The Klan's methods of intimidation consisted of night riding by hooded, often white-robed bands in fantastic costumes, who intimidated, whipped, tortured, and sometimes murdered their opponents, particularly freedmen, whom they occasionally sought to frighten by pretending to be the ghosts of Confederates killed during the Civil War. Their reign of terror was so pronounced that they did not hesitate to kill members of state legislatures and other officials, especially leaders of the black community. Representing a broad segment of the white population, including members of the upper as well as the lower classes, they often also attracted local criminal elements, so the more prominent leaders, like Imperial Wizard General Nathan Bedford Forrest, could disavow the brutal deeds of some of the bands. In fact, Forrest dissolved the order in 1869, but his rescript had little effect.

In many respects, the Ku Klux Klan and related organizations functioned as the terrorist arm of the Democratic party. Effective in diminishing the Republican vote at election time, it was not able to overthrow the Reconstruction regimes, although in Georgia (q.v.) it contributed to the return of conservative government. In Arkansas (q.v.), Governor Powell Clayton (q.v.) successfully employed the militia against it; in North Carolina (q.v.), however, Governor William W. Holden (q.v.), attempting to do the same thing in the Kirk-Holden War (q.v.), was less effective. Finally, in 1870 and 1871 the federal government brought its power to bear, and Congress passed the Enforcement Acts (q.v.), particularly the third Force or Ku Klux Act, which was specifically directed at the order and empowered the President to suspend the writ of habeas corpus in areas affected by the Klan. President U. S. Grant (q.v.) in 1871 did so in several South Carolina (q.v.) counties; indictments were brought elsewhere also, and Klan activity subsided. The terror the organization had sponsored, however, continued under other forms and contributed to the overthrow of several Reconstruction regimes, especially in Mississippi (q.v.).

The myth of the Klan's noble deeds as a defender of white civilization arose at the turn of the century, particularly with the publication of Thomas Dixon's novel, *The Klansman*, which was made into a moving picture by D. W. Griffith in his epochal film, *The Birth of a Nation*. Subsequently, the Klan was reorganized as an ostensibly superpatriotic organization, now directed against Catholics, Jews, and foreigners as well as blacks (q.v.), but it was greatly weakened during the 1920s because of various financial scandals.

*See also* Clayton, Powell; Enforcement Acts; Holden, William Woods; Kirk-Holden War.

Allen W. Trelease, *White Terror: The Ku Klux Klan Conspiracy and Southern Reconstruction* (New York, 1971); George C. Rable, *But There Was No Peace: The Role of Violence in the Politics of Reconstruction* (Athens, Ga., 1984); David M. Chalmers, *Hooded Americanism: The History of the Ku Klux Klan* (New York, 1951).

# L

---

**LABOR,** during 1865 to 1873 benefited by a considerable increase in real wages chiefly affecting skilled workers. Strongly influenced by America's free-labor ideology stressing a community of interest between employer and employee and the ability of every person to rise, labor did not constitute a united front. Yet unions did show some strength and in 1866 even combined to form the National Labor Union led by Ira Stewart. The organization was especially committed to the eight-hour day, and an ineffectual measure calling for the reform passed in 1868.

The Panic of 1873 seriously undermined the free-labor ideology. Hard hit by unemployment and depressed wages, labor became more militant. Demonstrations were held in many cities, and in January 1874 police forcibly dispersed some seven thousand workers who had gathered at Tompkins Square in New York City. Later that year the anthracite miners of Pennsylvania went on strike, a dispute complicated by the activities of the Ancient Order of the Hibernians with its violent offspring, the Molly Maguires, who were accused of various murders until infiltrated and destroyed by Pinkerton detectives. The strike was crushed, twenty miners were hanged, and the mine owners were able to use the popular revulsion to break down the Workingmen's Benevolent Association, which had no connection with the Mollies. Then in 1877 a great strike wave engulfed the railroads, which had sought to cut back wages. Workers on the Baltimore and Ohio, Pennsylvania, and other lines halted traffic and destroyed rolling stock until President Rutherford B. Hayes (q.v.) sent federal troops to "restore order."

Labor also ventured into politics during this period. In Massachusetts, Wendell Phillips (q.v.) ran unsuccessfully for Governor in 1870 on a Labor Reform ticket. In 1872 the Labor Reform party nominated Justice David Davis (q.v.) for President, only to see its efforts wasted when the candidate withdrew. In 1876 labor endorsed the Greenback or National Independent party, which backed the aged iron manufacturer Peter Cooper. The Socialist Labor party, a Marxist organization, also made its appearance but had few followers, and by and large, labor tended to support the major political organizations.

Labor showed little enlightenment in its attitude toward Reconstruction. Deeply racist, it either rejected potential black supporters or caused them to be organized in segregated units. In addition, it was in the forefront of the opposition to Chinese immigration, particularly in California, where Dennis Kearney instigated riots against the Orientals. Not until the 1880s did the Knights of Labor finally welcome black members.

*See also* Davis, David; Hayes, Rutherford B.; Phillips, Wendell.

David Montgomery, *Beyond Equality: Labor and the Radical Republicans, 1862–1872* (New York, 1967); Eric Foner, *Reconstruction: America's Unfinished Revolution* (New York, 1988).

**LAMAR, LUCIUS QUINTUS CINCINNATUS** (1825–1893), secessionist, congressman, and Senator from Mississippi (q.v.), Secretary of the Interior and Associate Justice of the Supreme Court, was born in Putnam County, Georgia, the son of a lawyer. Educated at Emory College, he practiced law in Covington but in 1849 moved to Mississippi (q.v.) to pursue his profession and to teach mathematics at the university in Oxford, of which his father-in-law was president. He returned to Georgia in 1852, where the next year he was elected to the legislature as a states rights Democrat. In 1855 he established a permanent residence in Mississippi, this time on a plantation north of Oxford, and practiced law in Holly Springs. Elected to Congress in 1857 and 1859, he was preparing to resign to become a professor of mental and moral philosophy at the University of Mississippi when the secession crisis interfered. Close to Jefferson Davis (q.v.), he took part in framing the secession ordinance, and when war broke out, he became lieutenant colonel of the Nineteenth Mississippi Regiment, which saw action at Williamsburg. Bad health interrupted his military service, but he performed various missions for Davis, including one as diplomatic agent to Russia. Recalled from Europe before he ever reached St. Petersburg, in 1864 he rejoined the army as Judge Advocate.

After the war, Lamar was appointed professor of ethics and metaphysics and then of law at the University of Mississippi. Elected to Congress in 1872, he made a name for himself with a eulogy on Charles Sumner (q.v.) in which he extolled sectional reconciliation. Nevertheless, he was active in the violent 1875 campaign in Mississippi, which "redeemed" ("Redemption," q.v.) the state and participated in negotiations for the resignation of Governor Adelbert Ames (q.v.) in return for dropping impeachment charges. Although his main concern was always the restoration of Democratic rule in the South, he also endorsed various government measures to bolster the economy, particularly subsidies for railroads. In 1875 he became chairman of the Democratic caucus and in 1876 took a hand in the arrangements leading to the Compromise of 1877 (q.v.), which seemed to fulfill not only his desire for an end to federal interference in the South but also his hope for the construction of the Texas Pacific Railroad. Although he disregarded the instructions of the legislature to support the inflation bill of 1874, he secured election to the Senate in 1877 and 1882. In 1885 Grover Cleveland appointed him Secretary of the Interior and in 1888 Associate Justice of the Supreme Court. He died in Georgia in 1893.

Lamar liked to speak of sectional reconciliation and of fairness to the blacks (q.v.) and was long regarded as the embodiment of the finest example of Southern desire for reunion. In reality, he supported every measure designed to restore and then maintain white supremacy in the South.

*See also* Compromise of 1877; "Redemption"; Sumner, Charles.

James B. Murphy, L.C.Q. Lamar, *Pragmatic Patriot* (Baton Rouge, La., 1973); Wirt Armistead Cate, *Lucius Q. C. Lamar: Secession and Reunion* (Chapel Hill, N.C., 1935).

**LAND POLICIES,** a major issue during Reconstruction. The problem of the freedmen's future inevitably raised the question of possible black landownership. During the Civil War, Abraham Lincoln (q.v.) attempted to enable freedmen by preemption to secure Sea Island lands forfeited by nonpayment of taxes, only to encounter the objections of tax commissioners. Experiments in black land-owning were instituted at Davis Bend, Mississippi, and elsewhere, until on January 16, 1865, William T. Sherman (q.v.) set aside the Sea Islands (q.v.) and a strip on the mainland thirty miles wide between Charleston and the St. Johns River in Florida for the exclusive use of blacks (q.v.). Shortly afterward, in March 1865, Congress passed a bill establishing the Freedmen's Bureau (q.v.), which it empowered to allot forty acres of abandoned land or tracts to which the United States had acquired title to refugees and freedmen. The uncertainty of titles, however, especially in consequence of the Second Confiscation Act limiting forfeiture to the owner's lifetime, as well as the bureau's lack of funds, complicated the execution of the law.

Nevertheless, the Freedmen's Bureau, particularly after the promulgation of General Oliver O. Howard's (q.v.) Circular No. 13, conveyed land to some blacks (q.v.). Because this policy conflicted with the President's amnesty policy, Andrew Johnson (q.v.) reversed this directive and in September 1865 ordered Howard to publish Circular No. 15, in effect retracting it. Blacks were again deprived of land that was restored to pardoned insurgents. Partially to counteract this development, in February 1866 Congress enacted a bill extending the powers of the Freedmen's Bureau, which the President vetoed. But in June 1866 Congress passed a Southern Homestead Act (q.v.), which set aside public lands in the South and gave preference to freedmen, and the next month enacted another Freedmen's Bureau Bill notwithstanding the President's objections. Because of lack of capital and bureaucratic difficulties, however, few blacks were able to take advantage of the Homestead law, and the land provisions of the Freedmen's Bureau Bill also met with obstacles.

Several radical members of Congress, particularly Thaddeus Stevens (q.v.)

and George W. Julian (q.v.), favored widespread confiscations to reform the Southern land system. But the prevailing attitude concerning the sanctity of private property made it impossible for them to convince their colleagues to follow suit. Although the Republican government of South Carolina (q.v.) did distribute some land, in general the blacks remained landless. The result was that most of them became tenants or sharecroppers on farms owned by whites.

*See also* Freedmen's Bureau; Homestead Act of 1866; Howard, Oliver Otis; Sea Islands; Sherman, William Tecumseh; Stevens, Thaddeus.

Claude F. Oubre, *Forty Acres and a Mule: The Freedmen's Bureau and Black Land-ownership* (Baton Rouge, 1978); Roger L. Ranson and Richard Sutch, *One Kind of Freedom: The Economic Consequences of Emancipation* (New York, 1977); Willie Lee Rose, *Rehearsal for Reconstruction: The Port Royal Experiment* (Indianapolis, 1964); LaWanda Cox, *Lincoln and Black Freedom: A Study in Presidential Leadership* (Columbia, S.C., 1981); Eric Foner, *Reconstruction: America's Unfinished Revolution, 1863–1867* (New York, 1988).

**LEGAL TENDER CASES,** Supreme Court decisions concerning the constitutionality of the wartime Legal Tender Acts making greenbacks legal tender. In *Hepburn* v. *Griswold* (1870), the court, by a narrow majority including Chief Justice Salmon P. Chase (q.v.), decided that the notes were not valid for debts incurred before the passage of the laws. Welcomed by bankers and creditors, this decision was unpopular with railroads and debtors, and after President U. S. Grant (q.v.) appointed two new justices, Joseph P. Bradley of New Jersey and William Strong of Pennsylvania, the court, in *Knox* v. *Lee* (1871) reversed itself. Holding that the Legal Tender Acts were constitutional, it ruled that greenbacks were legal tender for all debts, even those incurred before the enactment of the legislation.

It has been charged ever since that Grant deliberately packed the court to obtain this decision; yet no proof of the contention has ever been found, and it is now generally discounted.

*See also* Chase, Salmon Portand; Grant, Ulysses Simpson; Greenbacks.

Charles Fairman, *Reconstruction and Reunion, 1864–88*, Vol. 6 of the Oliver Wendell Holmes Devise, *History of the Supreme Court of the United States* (New York, 1971); Stanley L. Kutler, *Judicial Power and Reconstruction Politics* (Chicago, 1968).

**LIBERAL REPUBLICAN MOVEMENT,** the reform effort to displace President U. S. Grant (q.v.), cleanse the Republican party of corruption, and end its reliance upon spoilsmen. Various Republican leaders, disaffected because of the scandals of the Grant administration, sought to reform the Republican party from within. Deploring the President's effort to annex the Dominican Republic, his failure to institute meaningful civil service reform (q.v.), and his Southern policy, Senators like Carl Schurz (q.v.) were joined by newspaper editors, free traders, and disappointed politicians to lay the groundwork for a new political organization when their attempts to capture the Republican party failed.

It was in Missouri (q.v.) that the Liberals achieved their first success. Carl

Schurz and B. Gratz Brown (q.v.), though eventually antagonistic toward each other, managed to overcome the proadministration faction, promise amnesty, and elect Brown Governor. The movement spread to other states, and in 1871 the Democrats proved receptive to Liberal overtures, particularly after Clement L. Vallandigham (q.v.), the wartime Copperhead, endorsed a "new departure" policy including the acceptance of the Reconstruction amendments. The Liberals began to woo the South, and a convention was called to meet in Cincinnati in May 1872 to nominate a President. It was expected that the Democrats would endorse the candidate.

The Cincinnati convention proved anticlimactic. Urged by the permanent chairman, Carl Schurz, to crush corruption and give the Republic a pure and honest government, the delegates wrote a platform stressing amnesty, local self-government, civil service reform, and a commitment to equal rights. On the tariff question, they adopted a compromise leaving the matter to each congressional district. Then they turned to the nomination of a promising candidate. Charles Francis Adams, David Davis (q.v.), and Lyman Trumbull (q.v.) seemed to be in the lead. Davis, however, was undercut by the "quadrilateral," the editors of four newspapers, who published scathing editorials about him. The arrival of B. Gratz Brown and Francis P. Blair (q.v.), anxious to sidetrack their opponent Carl Schurz, heralded a combination with Whitelaw Reid, the managing editor of the New York *Tribune*, who was promoting the candidacy of his chief, Horace Greeley (q.v.). Brown withdrew in favor of the editor, and Greeley was nominated with Brown as a running mate.

The nomination of the New York editor was disastrous. A lifelong protectionist not particularly interested in civil service reform, he had denounced the Democrats for decades. In addition, he favored temperance, a stand sure to alienate the important German-Americans. As expected, the Republicans renominated the President; the Democrats, eager to beat Grant under any circumstances, had no choice but to endorse their old enemy. Many Liberals were unhappy about the candidate; some hoped to induce him to withdraw, but in the end most had to back him. In the campaign that followed, Greeley and his supporters were savagely attacked for their alleged abandonment of the freedmen; three-quarters of the old abolitionists and almost all blacks (q.v.) refused to heed Charles Sumner's (q.v.) advice favoring the editor, and Grant won by an overwhelming majority. The heartbroken Greeley died before the electoral vote could even be counted.

Although the Liberal Republican movement was at first unsuccessful and many of its leaders eventually joined the Democrats, it nevertheless helped to undermine Reconstruction and ushered in the gradual end of Republican rule in the South.

*See also* Amnesty; Civil Service Reform; Greeley, Horace; Schurz, Carl; Trumbull, Lyman.

Richard Allan Gerber, "The Liberal Republicans of 1872 in Historiographical Perspective," *Journal of American History*, 42 (1975): 40–73; James M. McPherson, "Grant or Greeley? The Abolitionist Dilemma in the Election of 1872," *American Historical Review*, 71 (1963): 43–61; Earle Dudley Ross, *The Liberal Republican Movement* (New York, 1919).


**LINCOLN, ABRAHAM** (1809–1865), sixteenth President of the United States, was born near Hodgenville, Kentucky, the son of a farmer. Taken by his family to Southern Indiana and then to central Illinois, he settled in New Salem, where he held a number of odd jobs, including those of postmaster and surveyor. After taking part in the Black Hawk War and suffering defeat in the election of 1832, he was returned as a Whig to the state Assembly two years later. In 1836 he was admitted to the bar and in 1837 settled in Springfield, where he practiced his profession until 1861. He married Mary Todd in 1842.

Always opposed to slavery, in 1837 Lincoln was one of two members of the legislature to sign a protest against the institution. Elected to Congress in 1846, he opposed the Mexican War and was one of the framers of a scheme for emancipation in the District of Columbia. He was not returned to Congress.

After the passage of the Kansas-Nebraska Act, Lincoln denounced it so effectively that he soon assumed leadership in the new Republican party (q.v.). Running for the Senate against Stephen A. Douglas in 1858, he attained national prominence, and although he lost, the Republicans obtained a plurality of the votes and in 1860 nominated him for President.

Lincoln's subsequent election resulted in the secession crisis. Refusing to countenance any further extension of slavery, he rejected various compromises and, after his inauguration, sought to send supplies to the beleaguered federal garrison at Fort Sumter. When the Confederates replied by firing upon the installation, civil war broke out.

Lincoln proved to be an outstanding war leader. Marshaling public opinion behind the government and, after some setbacks, successfully directing military efforts, he saw the Union through to victory. A master of political finesse, in 1863 he issued the Emancipation Proclamation (q.v.) at exactly the right time. Subsequently, he exerted his influence to end slavery where it still existed and, finally, by the use of patronage, made possible the passage of the Thirteenth Amendment (q.v.). He was indeed the Great Emancipator.

On Reconstruction, Lincoln, a supreme pragmatist, changed his views as time went on. At first committed to the mere suppression of the rebellion without necessarily abolishing slavery, he gradually shifted his position to include confiscation of enemy property, including slaves, as well as total emancipation. In March 1862 he appointed Andrew Johnson (q.v.) Military Governor of Tennessee (q.v.) to facilitate the state's return to the Union and then took similar steps in Arkansas (q.v.), Louisiana (q.v.), and North Carolina (q.v.). Always eager to use Reconstruction measures to further the war effort, he issued his Proclamation of Amnesty and Reconstruction in December 1863. Offering pardons to all insurgents except some high Confederate officials if they took an oath of allegiance, he empowered them to set up loyal governments that would end slavery as soon as 10 percent of the voters of 1860 had accepted his terms. This Ten Percent Plan (q.v.) was put into effect in Louisiana after Lincoln placed General Nathaniel P. Banks (q.v.) in charge of the process, which resulted in the election of Michael Hahn (q.v.) as Governor. The subsequent constitutional convention abolished slavery but failed to heed Lincoln's private admonition to Hahn to enfranchise some freedmen. In Arkansas, too, a new state government with Isaac Murphy as Governor was inaugurated in accordance with Lincoln's plan.

In Congress, the scheme encountered serious opposition. Objecting to the 10 percent provision as well as to executive leadership in the Reconstruction process, Henry Winter Davis (q.v.) in the House and Benjamin F. Wade (q.v.) in the Senate framed the Wade-Davis Bill (q.v.), which passed during the last days of the congressional session in July 1864. It provided for the election of constitutional conventions after 50 percent of the citizens of the United States had taken the loyalty oath and required all prospective electors to subscribe to the Iron Clad Oath (q.v.) attesting to past loyalty while mandating the end of slavery. Not wishing to undo his work in Louisiana and Arkansas, Lincoln pocket-vetoed the bill, although he called it "one very popular plan for the loyal people of any State choosing to adopt it." This action infuriated its authors, who issued the intemperate Wade-Davis Manifesto (q.v.), bitterly attacking the President in the midst of his reelection campaign. But Union successes in the field and the necessity of beating George B. McClellan, the Democratic candidate, finally convinced them as well as other critics to rally to the President who was triumphantly reelected in November 1864.

When Congress met again in December, the Reconstruction question once more engaged its attention. After a compromise proposal envisaging the admission of Louisiana and a plan similar to the Wade-Davis Bill for other states failed, chiefly because of Louisiana's refusal to grant black suffrage (q.v.), the lawmakers adjourned without taking any action. But in the final days of his administration, Lincoln sought to close the gap by publicly endorsing the limited enfranchisement of blacks in Louisiana. Three days later, on April 14, 1865, he was assassinated by John Wilkes Booth at Ford's Theater in Washington.

What Lincoln's policy would have been after the war has long been a subject of speculation. The few clues available indicate that he would have been as flexible as always. When after the fall of Richmond overtures were made to reassemble the Confederate legislature of Virginia (q.v.) to take the state out of the war, he gave his permission. But a few days later General Robert E. Lee surrendered at Appomattox, and the President, pressed by radical critics, withdrew his consent. On the last day of his life, he was contemplating a scheme for the government of North Carolina and Virginia.

Perhaps the most successful of all American Presidents, Lincoln dealt with the problem of Reconstruction with the same skill with which he handled other matters. Because his policies were designed for wartime conditions, it is difficult to compare them with those of his successor. But that he would have permitted former Confederates once more to reduce the freedmen to a condition little better than slavery and the Democrats to resume control with the aid of the restored Southern states is highly unlikely.

*See also* Banks, Nathaniel Prentiss; Johnson, Andrew; Lincoln, Abraham, Assassination of; Ten Percent Plan; Wade-Davis Bill; Wade-Davis Manifesto.

Stephen B. Oates, *With Malice Toward None: The Life of Abraham Lincoln* (New York, 1971); Peyton McCrary, *Abraham Lincoln and Reconstruction: The Louisiana Experiment* (Princeton, N.J., 1978); Herman Belz, *Reconstructing the Union: Theory and Policy During the Civil War* (Ithaca, N.Y., 1969); LaWanda Cox, *Abraham Lincoln and Black Freedom: A Study in Presidential Leadership* (Columbia, S.C., 1981); Hans L. Trefousse, *The Radical Republicans: Lincoln's Vanguard for Racial Justice* (New York, 1969); William B. Hesseltine, *Lincoln's Plan of Reconstruction* (Tuscaloosa, 1960).

**LINCOLN, ABRAHAM, ASSASSINATION OF** (1865), was the result of a plot perfected by the actor John Wilkes Booth, who strongly sympathized with the Confederate cause. Conspiring with his Baltimore friends Samuel B. Arnold and Michael O'Laughlin, he recruited a number of others, including David E. Herold, a pharmacist's clerk; Lewis Paine, a former Confederate soldier; George A. Atzerodt, a wagon painter; and John H. Surratt, a Confederate spy, whose, mother, Mary E. Surratt (q.v.), kept a boardinghouse where his associates met. At first, the actor planned to kidnap the President and to abduct him to the Confederacy, a scheme he tried to carry out on March 17, 1865, on the road from the Soldiers Home near Washington, but Lincoln failed to appear. O'Laughlin and Arnold became inactive and John Surratt left for Canada.

With the fall of the Confederacy, the kidnapping plot became moot. Consequently, Booth decided to kill the President instead. He was in the audience when Lincoln delivered his April 11 speech at the White House, and, hearing him advocate limited black suffrage (q.v.) for Louisiana (q.v.), he vowed that this would be the last speech the President would ever make. Learning that Lincoln would attend the performance of the play *My American Cousin* at Ford's Theater on April 14, he determined to murder his victim there. Paine was to assassinate Secretary of State William H. Seward (q.v.), laid up at his house after a carriage accident, and Atzerodt was to strike Vice President Andrew Johnson (q.v.) at his hotel, the Kirkwood House.

At 10:15 that night, Booth carried out his plan. Entering the President's box— the guard had abandoned his post—the assassin shot Lincoln. Then he jumped down upon the stage and, though he had broken his leg, raised himself while flashing a dagger and shouted, "Sic semper tyrannis," the motto of the state of Virginia. With the aid of the stagehand Edman Spengler, he mounted a horse and escaped.

In the meantime, Paine had attacked both Seward and his son, injuring them severely but failing to kill them. Atzerodt, however, had lost courage, and the Vice President was not assaulted.

Pandemonium followed. No one knew the extent of the conspiracy, and many feared the worst. The President, mortally wounded, was carried across the street to the home of William Petersen, where he died the next morning. Secretary of

War Edwin M. Stanton (q.v.) took charge of ferreting out the conspirators, all of whom were soon apprehended. Booth and Herold, who had joined the fugitive assassin, were found hiding in Richard Garrett's barn near Port Royal, Virginia. After the pursuing soldiers set fire to the barn, Booth, who refused to come out, was killed by Sergeant Boston Corbett. Herald was captured and tried together with the other conspirators by a military commission, which found them guilty. Atzerodt, Herold, Paine, and Mrs. Surratt were condemned to death, and the others, including Dr. Samuel A. Mudd, who had set Booth's leg, to various terms of imprisonment.

The assassination of the President created a revulsion of feeling in the North. Johnson issued a proclamation offering rewards for the capture of Jefferson Davis (q.v.) and other Confederate leaders who were erroneously believed to be implicated in the crime, and he refused to commute the sentence of Mrs. Surratt, whose guilt was problematical. Countless conspiracy theories, including one implicating the Secretary of War, surfaced afterward, but they were generally found to be without substantiation.

Lincoln's death brought Andrew Johnson to the presidency, thus substituting a man of narrow views about the Constitution and race for a statesman of far-reaching ability unhampered by ancient prejudices. The struggle between President and Congress and the consequent Reconstruction problems were the result.

*See also* Davis, Jefferson; Johnson, Andrew; Lincoln, Abraham; Surratt, Mary Eugenia Jenkins.

William Hanchett, *The Lincoln Murder Conspiracies* (Urbana, Ill., 1983); Thomas R. Turner, *Beware of the People Weeping: Public Opinion and the Assassination of Abraham Lincoln* (Baton Rouge, 1982); George S. Bryan, *The Great American Myth* (New York, 1940).

**LITTLEFIELD, MILTON SMITH** (1830–1899), Union general and Reconstruction railroad lobbyist, was born in Ellisburg, New York, the son of a Baptist preacher, miller, and politician, and brought up in Cicero near Syracuse. He taught school in Grand Rapids, Michigan, until the late 1850s, when he moved to Jerseyville, Illinois. Interested in the law, in 1859 he clerked in Abraham Lincoln's (q.v.) Springfield office.

During the Civil War, Littlefield served in the army, saw action at Shiloh, and in 1863 was sent by Abraham Lincoln to Hilton Head, South Carolina, to organize black troops. After accompanying the expedition to Florida that ended in the defeat at Olustee, in 1864 Littlefield was breveted a brigadier general and in 1865 accepted the surrender of Charleston.

During the next year, Littlefield engaged in the lumber and oil business in Philadelphia. In 1867 he went south and in North Carolina (q.v.) became associated with the local banker and speculator George W. Swepson (q.v.). Soon emerging as the foremost lobbyist in the state, he influenced the radical convention and legislature of 1868, from which he secured passage of various railroad measures advocated by the ring of which he was part. The state, interested in railroad development, exchanged its bonds for those of railroads controlled by Littlefield and his associates, and the insiders reaped substantial profits. In 1869 he became president of the Western Division of the North Carolina Railroad.

In that same year, Littlefield, already under suspicion in North Carolina, transferred his operations to Florida (q.v.), where he repeated the railroad speculations in which he had engaged so successfully before. The legislature passed bills favorable to the lines for which he was the chief lobbyist; he himself was elected president of the Jacksonville, Pensacola and Mobile Railroad, and he disposed of the state's railroad bonds in Europe even after the exposure of his speculations by the New York *World*, so he was able to reap the rewards of these dubious activities.

Littlefield's success as a lobbyist with Reconstruction governments was not only due to his ingratiating personality and good looks but also to his connections with leading Republicans. As President of the North Carolina Union League and presiding officer of the League's national convention in Long Branch, N.J., in 1870, he wielded considerable influence. To have a mouthpiece in North Carolina, he bought the Raleigh *Standard*, and in 1868 Governor William W. Holden (q.v.) appointed him state printer. Even after his speculations went sour and he left the South, he succeeded in thwarting investigators and in foiling the efforts of the Governor of North Carolina to have him extradited.

After 1878 Littlefield returned to the North. For a while, he lived in Morristown, New Jersey, and then in New York, where he died in 1899.

Often cited as proof of the corruption of the carpetbaggers (q.v.), Littlefield was not typical of this group. His operations were supported by a number of conservatives, and the general indictment of carpetbaggers for corruption cannot be sustained.

*See also* Carpetbaggers; Corruption; Swepson, George.

Jonathan Daniels, *Prince of Carpetbaggers* (Philadelphia, 1958); Horace W. Raper, *William W. Holden: North Carolina's Political Enigma* (Chapel Hill, N.C., 1985); Paul E. Fenlon, "The Notorious Swepson-Littlefield Fraud," *Florida Historical Quarterly*, 32 (April 1954): 231–61.


**LOGAN, JOHN ALEXANDER** (1826–1889), Union general and Stalwart Republican leader, was born near Murphysboro, Illinois, the son of a doctor who was an active Democrat. Educated at Shiloh Academy and, after service in the Mexican War, at the Louisville Law School, he practiced law in his hometown and nearby Benton. He was a convinced Democrat, was elected to the Assembly in 1854 and 1856 and served as one of James Buchanan's presidential electors. In 1858 and 1860 he was sent to Congress, where he backed Stephen A. Douglas. During the secession crisis he severely criticized the Republicans for their allegedly aggressive policies but, after coming close to sympathizing with secession, in June 1861 finally cast his lot with the Union. He entered the army; established a good record at Fort Donelson, in northern Mississippi and Vicksburg, as well as in the battles leading to the capture of Atlanta; and became one of the most successful political generals of the war. Promoted to major general in 1863, he commanded XV Corps and, for a short time, the Army of Tennessee, until William T. Sherman (q.v.) superseded him and returned him to his corps. This action turned him against Sherman as well as against West Point, but he finished the war in the final campaigns leading to Joseph E. Johnston's surrender.

After the war, Logan at first supported Andrew Johnson (q.v.) but in 1866 joined the radical Republicans (q.v.). A cofounder and for several years commander of the Grand Army of the Republic (q.v.), he was responsible for the introduction in 1868 of Memorial Day and, after his election to Congress in 1866, remained a spokesman for veterans' rights. In the House, to which he was reelected in 1868 and 1870, he made a name for himself as an advocate of the impeachment of Johnson (q.v.) and a member of the Board of Managers, as a Stalwart Republican, and as a fiery orator adept in the waving of the "bloody shirt" (q.v.). In spite of his prewar Negro-baiting, he was now a steadfast defender of black rights.

A skillful politician, Logan built up a powerful machine in Illinois. Elected to the Senate in 1871, he moved to Chicago and, although defeated for reelection in 1877, made a comeback two years later, when he returned to the Senate. With some exceptions, he backed the policies of President U. S. Grant (q.v.) and in 1880 was one of the general's main supporters for a third term, although he later loyally campaigned for James A. Garfield (q.v.). In 1884 he was his party's vice presidential candidate on the unsuccessful ticket with James G. Blaine (q.v.), had difficulty in securing reelection to the Senate in 1885, but at length prevailed. Continuing his Stalwart stand, during his later years in the Senate he fought incessantly against efforts to reinstate General Fitz-John Porter and in 1886 published his polemical book, *The Great Conspiracy*. His wife, Mary Simmerson Cunningham, was an active participant in his campaigns and long after his death in Washington published her memoirs under the title *Reminiscences of a Soldiers' Wife*.

An able general and politician, Logan was often accused of corruption and spoilsmanship. In view of the fact that he was never wealthy and that no proof of wrongdoing was ever found, it is more likely that he was simply a shrewd organizer of a political machine who benefited by its practices.

*See also* Grand Army of the Republic; Grant, Ulysses Simpson.

James Pickett Jones, *John A. Logan: Stalwart Republican from Illinois* (Tallahassee, Fla., 1982); James P. Jones, *"Black Jack": John A. Logan and Southern Illinois in the Era of the Civil War* (Tallahassee, Fla., 1967).

**LOUISIANA,** one of the states subject to Reconstruction. Because federal troops conquered Southern Louisiana early in the war, the Reconstruction process there began sooner than in most other areas. Elections for Congress, based on the comparatively large number of white Unionists, were held in December 1862 in two New Orleans districts, where Michael Hahn (q.v.) and Benjamin F. Flanders were returned to the House of Representatives and briefly seated. But it was not until Abraham Lincoln (q.v.) published his Proclamation of Amnesty that Reconstruction really got under way. Eager to abolish slavery and to re-establish loyal government as quickly as possible, the President turned a deaf ear to conservative Unionists who had elected their own congressmen and to radicals anxious for delay. He entrusted the process to General Nathaniel P. Banks (q.v.) who called for an election under the state's old constitution of 1852, although he did not recognize its sanction of slavery. The result was the election in February 1864 of Michael Hahn as Governor.

Elections for a constitutional convention followed. This body met, abolished slavery, and wrote a constitution leaving the matter of black suffrage (q.v.) to the discretion of the legislature. Because of the latter's failure to act upon the subject, the congressional representatives elected under the new charter were never seated.

The inauguration of Andrew Johnson (q.v.) boded ill for the Louisiana experiment. Governor Hahn, who had been elected to the Senate, turned over his office to Lieutenant Governor J. Madison Wells (q.v.), a scalawag who sought to ally himself with conservatives and former Confederates. Stringent Black Codes (q.v.) were passed, and, with the President's blessing, the old ruling elite regained much of its power. When this group finally tried to scrap the constitution of 1864, Wells, realizing that his efforts at reconciliation had failed, countenanced the recall of the constitutional convention. This attempt in July 1866 was frustrated by the New Orleans riot (q.v.), a merciless massacre of black and white Unionists.

The revulsion caused in the North by this atrocity contributed to the defeat of the Democrats and Johnson's policies. After the passage of the Reconstruction Acts (q.v.), Louisiana was once again placed under military rule. In compliance with the law, the state, with its large black population, elected a constitutional convention that framed a new constitution conferring the suffrage upon the blacks (q.v.), disfranchising a number of former insurgents, and mandating integration. In the subsequent elections, the carpetbagger Henry Clay Warmoth (q.v.) was chosen Governor, the former slave Oscar J. Dunn became Lieutenant Governor, and the legislature was safely Republican. It ratified the Fourteenth Amendment (q.v.), and in June 1868 Louisiana was readmitted.

Yet the opposition of the entrenched whites made it difficult for any radical regime to function, and because of the incessant intimidation of the blacks, in the presidential election of 1868 the state was carried by the Democrats. To prevent similar tactics, the Republicans established a Returning Board with the power to pass on disputed election returns, and in time, the Governor's control of the election machinery and the passage of the Enforcement Acts (q.v.) strengthened the Republicans' position. The charges of corruption brought against the radical regimes were partially justified, although dishonesty neither started nor ended with the Republicans. In 1870 they succeeded in recapturing the legislature; however, Warmoth now faced opposition not only from the conservatives but also from the Republican Custom House faction headed by U.S. marshal Stephen

B. Packard (q.v.) and favored by collector James F. Casey, President U. S. Grant's (q.v.) brother-in-law.

Beset by continuing corruption, the Republican regime experienced further trouble in 1872, when Warmoth, seeking to ally himself with the moderate opposition, joined the Liberal Republicans (Liberal Republican Movement, q.v.). The Democrats and eventually the Liberals nominated the former Confederate John McEnery (q.v.) for Governor, and the regular Republicans put up the carpetbagger William Pitt Kellogg (q.v.). The resulting disputed election led to the emergence of two rival returning boards and legislatures. When the Republican board sought relief from federal Judge Edward H. Durell, he ordered the seizure of the statehouse and recognized the Republican legislature, which then impeached Warmoth. Accusing him of having tried to bribe Lieutenant Governor P.B.S. Pinchback (q.v.), it made the latter, a well-educated mulatto, Governor for the short period before Kellogg's inauguration.

Although in the long run the Kellogg government rather than its Democratic rival was recognized by the federal government, the emergence of the terrorist White League (q.v.) made the normal functioning of the Republican administration impossible. Bloody massacres of blacks occurred in 1873 at Colfax (Colfax Riot, q.v.) and in 1874 at Coushatta (Coushatta Massacre, q.v.), and the election of 1874 again ended in a disputed verdict. This time Colonel P. Regis de Trobriand with federal troops ejected several Democratic members of the legislature whose seats were contested, and their Republican rivals took their places. This action was upheld by General Philip H. Sheridan (q.v.), who sent a telegram to Washington suggesting that members of the White League be treated as "banditti."

Such a military incursion into the legislature raised spectors of Caesarism. Seeking to resolve the issue, a congressional subcommittee arranged for a compromise named for William A. Wheeler, which permitted the Kellogg regime to continue but surrendered the lower house of the legislature to the Democrats. The latter promptly impeached the Governor, but the Senate immediately dismissed the charges.

Against this background, it was not surprising that the crucial election of 1876 was again contested. After considerable intimidation, the results seemed to favor the Democrats. The Republican Returning Board, however, maintaining that terror had rendered the returns from several parishes invalid, disallowed them and declared the presidential electors of Rutherford B. Hayes (q.v.) and the Republican candidate for Governor, Stephen B. Packard (q.v.), the victors. But as a result of the Compromise of 1877 (q.v.), Hayes' claims were recognized, while the Democrat Francis T. Nicholls (q.v.) became Governor, and Reconstruction came to an end.

In Louisiana as elsewhere, "Redemption" (q.v.) ushered in an age of increasing disabilities for the blacks. Already largely sharecroppers, they were gradually stripped of their political rights until the Constitution of 1898 legalized the various subterfuges nullifying the Fourteenth and Fifteenth Amendments (q.v.).

*See also* Congressional Reconstruction; Hahn, Michael; Kellogg, William Pitt; Nichols, Francis Tillou; Packard, Stephen B.; Pinchback, Pinckney Benton Stewart; Presidential Reconstruction; Warmoth, Henry Clay; Wells, James Madison.

Joe Gray Taylor, *Louisiana Reconstructed, 1863–1877* (Baton Rouge, 1974); Willie M. Caskey, *Secession and Reconstruction of Louisiana* (Baton Rouge, 1938); Peyton McCrary, *Abraham Lincoln and Reconstruction: The Louisiana Experiment* (Princeton, N.J., 1978).

**LOYAL LEAGUE.** *See* UNION LEAGUE.

**LYNCH, JOHN ROY** (1847–1939), congressman from Mississippi (q.v.) and Republican leader, was born into slavery in Concordia Parish, Louisiana. Sold with his mother across the river to Natchez, he remained in the Mississippi city after emancipation, when he became a photographer and acquired some education by attending evening school. In 1869 Governor Adelbert Ames (q.v.) appointed him Justice of the Peace, and later that year he was elected to the legislature. He served until 1873, occupying the position of Speaker of the House during his second term. In 1873 he went to Congress, was reelected in 1875, but was defeated in 1876 by the Democrat James R. Chalmers. In 1880 he again challenged Chalmers, who claimed victory; Lynch contested the result, however, and in the spring of 1882 was seated. In November he was finally defeated for reelection.

While in Congress, Lynch distinguished himself by his probity, his oratorical ability, and his strong advocacy of the Civil Rights Bill (Civil Rights Acts, q.v.). Chairman of the Republican State Executive Committee between 1881 and 1889, he attended his party's national conventions in 1872 and in 1884, when upon Theodore Roosevelt's nomination he became temporary chairman, as well as in 1888, 1892, and 1900.

In the mid–1880s, Lynch, a successful planter and businessman, retired to one of his properties in Adams County and engaged in agriculture. He returned to Washington in 1889, when he was appointed fourth auditor of the Treasury by President Benjamin Harrison. After studying law, he was admitted to the Mississippi bar in 1896 and practiced in Washington. In 1898 President William McKinley commissioned him a major and paymaster in the army. He remained in the service after the Spanish-American War, traveled widely, and did not retire until 1911. Afterward, he moved to Chicago, where he resumed his legal work. In 1913 he wrote his *Facts of Reconstruction* to correct the prevailing proconservative view, and shortly before his death in 1939 he completed his autobiography, *Reminiscences of an Active Life*.

An able politician and man of affairs, Lynch was one of the most successful black legislators during Reconstruction and was generally esteemed by his colleagues.

*See also* Ames, Adelbert; Mississippi.

John Hope Franklin, "John Roy Lynch: Republican Stalwart from Mississippi," in Howard N. Rabinowitz, ed., *Southern Black Leaders of the Reconstruction Era* (Urbana, Ill., 1982); John Roy Lynch, *Reminiscences of an Active Life: The Autobiography of John Roy Lynch* (Chicago, 1970).

# M

**McCARDLE, EX PARTE,** a Supreme Court case that Congress withdrew from the court's jurisdiction because it involved the constitutionality of the Reconstruction Acts (q.v.). In November 1867 William H. McCardle, the editor of the Vicksburg *Times*, was arrested and remanded to military custody by General Edward O. C. Ord for publishing certain editorials inciting to insurrection and impeding Reconstruction. After McCardle's application to the Federal Circuit Court in Mississippi (q.v.) for a writ of habeas corpus was denied, he appealed to the Supreme Court of the United States under the Habeas Corpus Act of 1867 authorizing such actions.

When in early 1868 the case reached the Supreme Court, the Republicans in Congress, afraid that the Reconstruction Acts under with McCardle had been arrested might come under scrutiny and be held unconstitutional, hurriedly passed legislation specifically repealing the appeal provisions of the 1867 statute. President Andrew Johnson's veto was overridden, and on March 27, 1868, the bill became law. The Court postponed action until April 1869, when it decided that Congress possessed the power to curtail appellate jurisdiction while a case was pending. Although the case has long been cited as proof of the court's yielding to Congress during Reconstruction, in view of the contrary decision in *ex parte Yerger* (q.v.), decided soon afterward, this interpretation has been generally abandoned.

*See also* Reconstruction Acts; Supreme Court.

Charles Fairman, *Reconstruction and Reunion, 1864–88*, Vol. 6 of the Oliver Wendell Holmes Devise, *History of the Supreme Court of the United States* (New York, 1971); Stanley Kutler, *Judicial Power and Reconstruction Politics* (Chicago, 1968).

**McENERY, JOHN** (1833–1891), unrecognized conservative Governor of Louisiana (q.v.) was born in Virginia in 1833 and taken to Monroe, Louisiana, when
he was two years old. Educated at Hamilton College, Indiana, he was admitted
to the North Louisiana bar and established a legal practice. Joining the Ouchita
Blues at the outbreak of the war, he rose to the rank of lieutenant colonel in the
Fourth Louisiana.

After the war, McEnery, a thorough conservative, was appointed district judge
and elected to the legislature. In 1872 he was the candidate of the Liberals and
conservatives against the regular Republican William Pitt Kellogg (q.v.) The
campaign resulted in a dispute; McEnery claimed victory and was upheld by a
returning board, which had been changed by his ally Henry Clay Warmoth (q.v.),
but Kellogg challenged this decision, and a Republican returning board upheld
him. To settle the matter, the Republicans applied to federal judge Edward H.
Durell who sided with them and issued an order to the federal marshal to seize
the statehouse in their interest. Yet the conservatives persisted; their legislature
continued to defy the Republican government.

In January 1873 both Governors were installed, and the rival legislatures met.
Although the federal government recognized the Republican regime, McEnery
refused to yield. He appointed his own militia, issued a proclamation forbidding
the payment of taxes to his opponents, and relied on the White League (q.v.)
for support. The Colfax Riot (q.v.) followed, as did the Coushatta Massacre of
1874 (q.v.). In September the McEnery forces seized the statehouse, the city
hall, and the police stations in New Orleans, killing thirty-two and wounding
thirty-nine persons. Summoned to the city, McEnery arrived simultaneously with
General William H. Emory, to whom he finally surrendered the seized public
property. The election of 1874 again resulted in a disputed outcome. McEnery's
supporters tried to take over the legislature but were halted by federal troops
who ejected those holding contested seats. The matter was finally settled by a
congressional compromise turning over the lower house to the Democrats but
allowing Kellogg to stay in power. McEnery withdrew and resumed his legal
practice. He died in New Orleans in 1891.

*See also* Colfax Riot; Coushatta Massacre; Kellogg, William Pitt; Louisiana.

Joe Gray Taylor, *Louisiana Reconstructed, 1863–1877* (Baton Rouge, 1974); Obituary,
*New York Times*, March 29, 1891.

**McPHERSON, EDWARD** (1830–1895), clerk of the House of Representatives
and Republican leader, was born in Gettysburg, the son of a banker. Educated
at Pennsylvania (now Gettysburg) College, McPherson read law with Thaddeus
Stevens (q.v.), with whom he became closely associated. He then turned to
journalism, served as a reporter at the state legislature, and edited the *Harrisburg
Daily American* as well as the Lancaster *Independent*. A determined foe of slavery
and active Republican, he was elected to Congress from his home district in
1858, made common cause with the radicals, and was reelected in 1860. Defeated
in 1862, he was appointed deputy commissioner of internal revenue but soon

afterward secured election as clerk of the House of Representatives, a position he was to hold continually, whenever the Republicans were in power, between 1863 and 1891.

The office of clerk of the House conferred considerable power upon the occupant, particularly at the beginning of each session. By custom and after 1863 by law the clerk had the duty of reading the roll of members-elect before the organization of the chamber, listing only those who had been chosen regularly. Because of the controversy concerning Andrew Johnson's (q.v.) plan of Reconstruction, this function would be vital in 1865. McPherson's great moment came on December 4, when by prearrangement he left out all members-elect from states that had seceded, including Horace Maynard, the steadfast Unionist from Tennessee. He refused to entertain Maynard's protest, and none of the Southerners was admitted. The President had suffered his first defeat in the struggle with Congress.

McPherson's power soon increased. In 1867 the House conferred upon the clerk the right to select local newspapers to publish the laws, a privilege he used to the advantage of the Republican party. It was he who on February 24, 1868, finished reading Stevens' final impeachment speech, and it was he who in 1873 presented Oakes Ames' explanation of his connection with the Crédit Mobilier. In the meantime, he had acquired the Gettysburg *Star and Sentinel*, and after he lost his clerkship to the Democrats in 1875, he became permanent chairman of the 1876 Republican National Convention. Although he strongly favored the nomination of James G. Blaine (q.v.), he loyally supported the winner, Rutherford B. Hayes (q.v.), who in 1877 appointed him chief of the Bureau of Printing and Engraving.

McPherson resigned his position in 1878 to assume the editorship of the Philadelphia *Press*, which he retained until 1880, when he was designated secretary of the Republican Congressional Committee, a post he also held in 1884. While continuing his journalistic activities in Gettysburg, he was again elected clerk of the House when in 1881 and 1887 the Republicans recaptured it.

McPherson's most lasting endeavor was the publication of his famous political manuals, compendia of the important political events and votes of Congress from year to year. The first of these, covering the period of the Civil War, was called *The Political History of the United States of America During the Great Rebellion, 1860–1865*; the following yearbooks were combined into *The Political History of the United States of America During the Period of Reconstruction, 1865–1870*, and thereafter the *Handbooks of Politics* generally appeared every two years until 1894. A rich source of statistics and facts, they constitute an important tool for the study of the time. McPherson also contemplated a biography of Thaddeus Stevens but never finished it. He died in Gettysburg in 1895.

*See also* Johnson, Andrew; Stevens, Thaddeus.

Harold M. Hyman and Hans L. Trefousse, *New Introduction to Edward McPherson, ed., The Political History of the United States During the Great Rebellion, 1860–1865* (New York, 1872).

**MAHONE, WILLIAM** (1826–1895), Confederate general, railroad builder, and Virginia (q.v.) political leader, was born in Monroe, Virginia, the son of a tavernkeeper. Educated at Virginia Military Institute, he became a civil engineer, was active in railroad construction, and in 1860 was elected president of the Norfolk and Petersburg Railroad. He participated in most of the engagements of the Army of Northern Virginia and so distinguished himself at the Battle of the Crater that he was promoted to the rank of major general. Robert E. Lee is said to have considered him the most talented of the younger leaders of the army.

Returning to the presidency of his railroad in 1865, he also headed the neighboring Southside Railroad and became the chief advocate of the consolidation of these and other lines to forge a direct link between Norfolk and Bristol—the Atlantic, Mississippi and Ohio Railroad. This project was designed to foil the ambitions of John W. Garrett of the Baltimore and Ohio, who sought to funnel the trade of Virginia through Baltimore rather than through Norfolk. In pursuit of this design, in 1868 Mahone was at first not unfriendly toward the gubernatorial ambitions of the radical Henry H. Wells. When Wells proved hostile to his plans, however, the general turned against him and in 1869 backed the moderate Gilbert C. Walker. Walker won; his legislature fully authorized Mahone's consolidation plans, and he became president of the Atlantic, Mississippi and Ohio at a salary of $25,000 per annum. In fact, his interest in Reconstruction seems to have been more closely connected with his struggle with the Baltimore and Ohio than with conventional issues.

After losing his railroad following the Panic of 1873, Mahone turned to direct political involvement. Although he failed to obtain the nomination for Governor in 1877, he became one of the founders of the Readjuster (q.v.) movement, which proposed to scale down Virginia's debt by lowering the interest paid on it and use the proceeds for social improvement. When in 1879 the Readjusters captured the legislature, they elected the general to the U.S. Senate. He took his seat in the evenly divided upper house in 1881 and, by cooperating with the Republicans, enabled them to organize the chamber.

From 1879 to 1883 Mahone's machine was dominant in Virginia. He used his power to further education, scale down the debt, and abolish the poll tax and whipping post. His strength lay with the small farmers of the Piedmont and the West, as well as with the tidewater black voters, who appreciated his effort to break the power of the Bourbons. In 1884 he affiliated with the Republican party (q.v.) but he was unable to secure reelection to the Senate either in 1885 or 1887 or win the governorship in 1889. He died in Washington in 1895.

The diminutive Mahone was a capable railroad builder and skillful politician. If he was imperious, he nevertheless succeeded in benefiting disadvantaged farmers of both races.

*See also* Readjusters; Virginia.

Nelson Morehouse Blake, *William Mahone of Virginia: Soldier and Political Insurgent* (Richmond, Va., 1935); Virginius Dabney, *Virginia: The New Dominion* (Garden City, N.Y., 1971).

**MARYLAND,** one of the boarder states that did not secede. Although remaining loyal, Maryland was deeply divided, with the plantation counties in the South and on the Eastern Shore favoring the South and those in the North and West supporting the Union. In 1863, the Unconditional Unionists, led by Henry Winter Davis (q.v.), were able to score important gains, and the Unionist legislature authorized the election of a constitutional convention. Meeting in 1864, this body framed a charter that abolished slavery, lessened the influence of southern and Eastern shore counties, disfranchised secessionists, and made provisions for education. The constitution was adopted by a narrow vote dependent on soldiers' ballots, so in November 1864 slavery was abolished. In the same month, Abraham Lincoln (q.v.) was able to carry the state.

In 1865 the Unionist legislature enacted a stringent Registry Act to keep insurgents from voting, ratified the Thirteenth Amendment (q.v.), and elected the radical John A. Creswell to the Senate. But the conservatives were restive. Unwilling to adjust to emancipation, they sought to perpetuate some form of slavery, particularly by apprenticing minors, a custom that died out only gradually after the Freedmen's Bureau (q.v.) and the judiciary condemned it. In addition, the opposition was able to take advantage of the prevailing racism and a split in the Union party, in which the moderates parted company with their more radical associates. Thomas Swann, the Governor inaugurated early in 1866, endorsed the policies of Andrew Johnson (q.v.) and reached an accommodation with the conservatives. Actively seeking their support for his election to the Senate, by appointing new registrars and police commissioners he enabled the conservatives to win the election of November 1866. In return, they elected him to the Senate, although at the last moment he refused to serve.

In the spring of 1867, after repealing the Registry Act, the conservative, soon to be called Democratic, convention called an election for another constitutional convention. This assembly framed a basic law that abolished all test oaths, denied the vote to the blacks (q.v.), and restored the dominance of the plantation counties. Although it authorized the admission of black testimony in the courts, it permitted the legislature to reverse this provision. Adopted shortly afterward, the constitution of 1867 deprived all officeholders but the Governor of their positions and perpetuated conservative rule.

In keeping with its conservative attitude, Maryland failed to ratify the Fourteenth and Fifteenth Amendments (q.v.). Firmly Democratic, it was carried by Horatio Seymour (q.v.) in 1868, by Horace Greeley (q.v.) in 1872, and by Samuel J. Tilden (q.v.) in 1876. Only the introduction of black suffrage (q.v.) in 1870 following the passage of the Fifteenth Amendment enabled the Republican party to make something of a comeback, although until the 1890s the state remained under Democratic domination.

*See also* Davis, Henry Winter.

Charles A. Wagandt, "Redemption or Reaction? Maryland in the Post-Civil War Years," in Richard O. Curry, ed., *Radicalism, Racism, and Party Realignment: The Border States During Reconstruction* (Baltimore, 1969); Barbara Fields, *Slavery and Freedom on the Middle Ground: Maryland During the Nineteenth Century* (New Haven, 1985).

**MEADE, GEORGE GORDON** (1815–1872), Union general and military commander of the Third Military District, was born in Cadiz, Spain, the son of an American merchant. Educated in Washington and Philadelphia, he graduated from West Point in 1835 and served for one year in the army as an artillery officer. Until 1842, when he rejoined the army, he was active as a topographical engineer. After service in the Mexican War, he resumed his profession as an officer, carrying out surveys of various coastlines and borders. Promoted to brigadier general in 1861, he took part in the Peninsular Campaign, where he was wounded; the second Battle of Bull Run; Antietam; and Fredericksburg. A major general in command of V Corps at Chancellorsville, he was not permitted to make full use of his capabilities, but in June 1863 he was appointed commanding general of the Army of the Potomac, which he led to victory at Gettysburg. His success, however, was clouded by his allowing Lee's army to escape across the swollen Potomac. During the subsequent Bristoe and Mine Run campaigns, he failed to overcome Lee; yet he remained in charge of the Army of the Potomac for the remainder of the war, serving under U.S. Grant (q.v.) after the latter's elevation to general-in-chief.

After Appomattox, Meade became the commander of the Division of the Atlantic and in 1867 was appointed in General John Pope's (q.v.) place to take over the Third Military District, consisting of Georgia (q.v.), Alabama (q.v.), and Florida (q.v.). A political moderate, he was at first welcomed by the white population, but his removal of the Governor and Treasurer of Georgia for withholding funds from the radical constitutional convention soon earned him the conservatives' censure. Nevertheless, he allowed conservative newspapers to benefit from official announcements, enabled the more conservative faction of the Florida constitutional convention to prevail, and sought to restrain registrars from participating in politics. In addition, after the new constitution of Alabama was defeated because of the failure of the majority of registered voters to participate, he certified that it had been rejected "on its merits."

After his deep disappointment at having been passed over for promotion, in 1869 Meade returned to the Division of the Atlantic in Philadelphia. In 1870 he was elected president of the Society of the Army of the Potomac, and in 1872 he supported Grant for reelection. He died in Philadelphia in 1872.

*See also* Alabama; Congressional Reconstruction; Florida; Georgia; Grant, Ulysses Simpson.

Freeman Cleaves, *Meade of Gettysburg* (Norman, Okla., 1960); James E. Sefton, *The United States Army and Reconstruction, 1865–1877* (Baton Rouge, 1967); Martin E. Mantell, *Johnson, Grant, and the Politics of Reconstruction* (New York, 1973).

**MEMPHIS RIOT,** a racial affray between blacks (q.v.) and whites on May 1–3, 1866. Its black population swollen by the influx of freedmen and discharged soldiers, Memphis constituted a powderkeg in the spring of 1866. After some black troops were mustered out on April 30, a melee broke out on May 1 between blacks, both soldiers and civilians, and the largely Irish police, which were trying to arrest two black veterans. Both active and discharged troops were then concentrated in nearby Fort Pickering, but that night a white mob invaded the black section and began a wanton round of murder, rape, robbery, and arson. Requested to send troops the next day, General George Stoneman, conscious of past criticism of military interference, delayed for twenty-four hours, by which time the rioters, including the police, had inflicted great damage. Forty-six blacks and two whites had been killed, seventy-five persons injured, one hundred robbed, five black women raped, ninety-one homes burned, and twelve schools as well as four churches destroyed. A congressional investigation resulted in a devastating report.

Partially due to economic as well as racial tensions, the Memphis riot created sympathy for more thoroughgoing policies toward the South and strengthened Congress in its struggle with Andrew Johnson (q.v.).

*See also* Johnson, Andrew.

Bobby L. Lovett, "Memphis Riots: White Reaction to Blacks in Memphis, May 1865–July 1866," *Tennessee Historical Quarterly*, 38 (1979): 9–33; James Gilbert Ryan, "The Memphis Riot of 1866: Terror in a Black Community During Reconstruction," *Journal of Negro History*, 62 (1977): 243–57; Altina L. Waller, "Community, Class and Race in the Memphis Riot of 1866," *Journal of Social History*, 18 (1984): 233–46; Rembert W. Patrick, *The Reconstruction of the Nation* (New York, 1967).

**MEXICO.** *See* FOREIGN AFFAIRS.

**MILITIA,** state forces organized during the Reconstruction by both conservatives and radicals to support their respective administrations. During the period of Presidential Reconstruction (q.v.) governors appointed by Andrew Johnson (q.v.) sought to raise militias to enforce conservative rule. In Mississippi, (q.v.) Governor William L. Sharkey (q.v.) activated a force contrary to the wishes of General Henry W. Slocum, the federal commander. But although Slocum was supported by Carl Schurz (q.v.), then on his trip of inspection through the South, the President supported Sharkey who employed the militia in overawing and disarming blacks (q.v.). As in other states, it was made up largely of former Confederate soldiers and upheld the reactionary regime of the Johnson governor.

Because of these characteristics, the Southern militia was specifically outlawed by the Military Appropriation Act of 1867. But during Congressional Reconstruction (q.v.), it became apparent that militia forces might again be used, this time by Republican governments, and in March 1869 the prohibition was withdrawn in the reconstructed states. Thereupon, various militias were organized. Although not all members were blacks, many freedmen served in these forces, which soon became known as the "Negro Militia." Most determinedly employed in Arkansas (q.v.), they were involved in the Brooks-Baxter War (q.v.). In North Carolina (q.v.), they furnished manpower for the Kirk-Holden War (q.v.), and in Louisiana (q.v.) they were active in the controversies between the various rival governments. Badly trained and bitterly resented by the white conservatives, they faced an impossible task, and their employment was not very effective. By

1875 white counterforces were organized, black militiamen were harassed and even murdered, and, in the end, the militia movement failed at the same time that the governments employing it were overthrown.

*See also* Brooks-Baxter War; Kirk-Holden War.

Otis Singletary, *Negro Militia and Reconstruction* (New York, 1957).

**MILLIGAN, EX PARTE,** 1866 Supreme Court decision holding that military tribunals were unconstitutional when the civil courts were open. In 1864 Lambdin P. Milligan and several associates, officers in a pro-Confederate organization in Indiana, were arrested, tried by a military commission for various capital crimes against the government, and sentenced to be hanged. Abraham Lincoln (q.v.) delayed the execution of the verdict, but after his assassination, his successor, Andrew Johnson (q.v.) ordered Milligan to be executed in May 1865. On the grounds that in the meantime a grand jury had failed to indict him as required under the Habeas Corpus Act of 1863, Milligan applied for a writ of habeas corpus from the Circuit Court in Indiana. Dividing on the question of its jurisdiction in appeals from military tribunals, the court certified the case to the Supreme Court for a decision, and the prisoner's sentence was commuted to life imprisonment.

In the subsequent hearing, Milligan's side was argued by distinguished counsel such as James A. Garfield (q.v.), Jeremiah S. Black, and David Dudley Field, while the government's case was presented by Attorney General James Speed (q.v.), Henry Stanbery (q.v.), and Benjamin F. Butler (q.v.). Giving notice in April 1866 that the writ had been granted, in December the court rendered its decision. It held unanimously that Milligan's right to trial by jury had been violated by his trial by military commission when the civil courts were open, but in an obiter dictum divided five to four on the question of whether Congress possessed the right to establish such tribunals, with the majority in the negative.

Widely denounced at the time because it seemed to put into question Congressional plans of Reconstruction, today the decision is considered one of the cornerstones of American liberty.

*See also* Supreme Court.

Charles Fairman, *Reconstruction and Reunion, 1864–88*, Vol. 6 of the Oliver Wendell Holmes Devise, *History of the Supreme Court of the United States, 1864–88* (New York, 1971); Stanley I. Kutler, *Judicial Power and Reconstruction Politics* (Chicago, 1968).

**MISSISSIPPI,** one of the states reconstructed by Congress. After an unsuccessful attempt of the last Confederate Governor to call a convention, on June 13, 1865, President Johnson (q.v.) appointed William L. Sharkey (q.v.), a prewar Whig, Provisional Governor. The convention elected in accordance with the Presidential Plan of Reconstruction (q.v.) abolished slavery, nullified the secession ordinance, and provided for the election of a new legislature. In spite of the President's warning to enfranchise at least a few blacks (q.v.), however, it refused to do so.

When in October the legislature met, it passed one of the most stringent black codes (q.v.) in the South, failed to ratify the Thirteenth Amendment (q.v.), and sent Governor Sharkey and James Lusk Alcorn (q.v.), a Unionist Whig who had served briefly as a brigadier general in the Confederate state forces to the Senate. Another prewar Whig, Benjamin G. Humphries, who had also been a Confederate general, was elected Governor.

Mississippi's contumacy was one of the most glaring examples of the failure of Presidential Reconstruction. The refusal of the state legislature to ratify not only the thirteenth but also the Fourteenth Amendment (q.v.) and its reduction of the freedmen to a status little removed from slavery facilitated the passage of the Reconstruction Acts (q.v.), which finally conferred political rights on the state's black majority.

The new constitution framed in 1868 by the convention mandated by the law not only sought to secure the freedmen's rights but also provided for a public school system for both races. Because of clauses disfranchising large number of ex-Confederates, however, the voters rejected it. During the election, General Irvin McDowell, the military commander of the state, removed Governor Humphreys and appointed General Adelbert Ames (q.v.) Military Governor. The constitution was finally accepted in 1869 after it was resubmitted with the disenfranchisement clauses to be voted on separately, and Alcorn, who had joined the Republicans, became Governor. According to a supplementary act by Congress, the newly elected legislature had to ratify the Fifteenth as well as the Fourteenth Amendment before the state could be readmitted, a condition it quickly fulfilled. Hiram Revels (q.v.) and Ames became Senators, Revels being the first black man so honored.

The Alcorn administration distinguished itself by establishing the new public school system and by the appointment of an able judiciary. In 1871 the Governor was elected to the Senate, where he soon fell out with his colleague Ames, and in 1873, the two Senators ran against each other for Governor, Alcorn relying on the moderates and scalawags (q.v.) and Ames on the carpetbaggers (q.v.) and blacks, who insured his victory.

But the Ames administration was short-lived. Unable to effect needed economies and hated by the conservatives, Ames fell victim to the Mississippi Plan, a scheme of violence and intimidation designed to restore white Democratic rule. After a series of riots, the systematic repression of the blacks, and the Grant administration's refusal to intervene, in 1875 the conservatives recaptured the legislature. Early in 1876, they brought trumped-up charges of impeachment against the Governor, who resigned after these accusations were withdrawn and left the state for good. The "Redeemers" ("Redemption," q.v.) now in power drastically reduced expenditures, particularly in education, and gradually diminished the black vote by redistricting and instituting more complicated methods of registration. It was not until 1890, however, that the constitution of 1868 was discarded and the blacks, by then largely sharecroppers, were increasingly disfranchised by means of a clause requiring the understanding of the basic document.

*See also* Alcorn, James Lusk; Ames, Adelbert; Bruce, Blanche Kelso; Congressional Reconstruction; Presidential Reconstruction; "Redemption"; Sharkey, William Lewis.

James Wilford Garner, *Reconstruction in Mississippi* (New York, 1901); William C. Harris, *Presidential Reconstruction in Mississippi* (Baton Rouge, 1967); William C. Harris, *The Day of the Carpetbagger: Republican Reconstruction in Mississippi* (Baton Rouge, 1979); Vernon Lane Wharton, *The Negro in Mississippi, 1865–1890* (Chapel Hill, N.C., 1947).

**MISSISSIPPI v. JOHNSON,** a suit by the state of Mississippi for an injunction to prevent President Andrew Johnson (q.v.) from carrying out the Reconstruction Acts (q.v.). Presented by William L. Sharkey (q.v.) in April 1867, it was opposed by Attorney General Henry Stanbery (q.v.), appearing for the government on the grounds that the Supreme Court could not enjoin the President, a contention the court upheld by refusing leave to file the bill. At the same time it allowed the parallel case of *Georgia* v. *Stanton* (q.v.) to be heard. It too was opposed by the Attorney General who was sustained by the court. The old notion that in these two cases the Supreme Court sought to avoid involvement in Reconstruction is no longer generally held.

*See also Georgia* v. *Stanton*; Reconstruction Acts; Sharkey, William L.; Supreme Court.

Stanley I. Kutler, *Judicial Power and Reconstruction Politics* (Chicago, 1968); Charles Fairman, *Reconstruction and Reunion, 1864–88*, Vol. 6 of the Oliver Wendell Homes Devise, *History of the Supreme Court of the United States, 1864–88* (New York, 1971).

**MISSOURI,** one of the border states that remained loyal during the Civil War. The state's Unionists were divided; the conservatives, called Claybanks, wanting to move slowly on the matter of emancipation (q.v.), and the radicals, called Charcoals, favoring immediate action. When the legislature of 1862 was deadlocked about this question, Governor Hamilton R. Gamble reconvened the 1861 convention, in which the Claybanks prevailed and passed a measure for gradual emancipation starting in 1870. They won again in the bitterly contested judicial election of 1863; the radicals, however, were able to elect Benjamin Gratz Brown (q.v.) to the Senate. In 1864, despite their opposition to the renomination of Abraham Lincoln (q.v.), the radicals succeeded in seating their delegates at the Union National Convention in Baltimore and eventually agreed to support the President's ticket.

In the fall of 1864 Lincoln carried the state; the radical Thomas C. Fletcher was elected Governor, and both houses of the legislature were under Charcoal control. A constitutional convention elected at the same time met in January 1865, freed the slaves, and proceeded to frame a new basic law for the state. Largely inspired by Charles D. Drake, it provided for stringent test oaths not only for voters but also for certain professionals and the ousting of most incumbent officials. Authorizing education for both races, it secured civil rights for blacks but failed to give them the suffrage. Ratification was secured only after a hard contest in which Francis P. Blair, Jr. (q.v.) led the opposition.

In 1866 another contest loomed. Aided by Andrew Johnson (q.v.), the conservatives sought to gain control of the legislature. But the rigorous disfranchisement rules enabled the radicals to prevail again, although in the next year the Supreme Court, in *Cummings* v. *Missouri* (q.v.) and *ex parte Garland* (q.v.), declared some of the test oaths unconstitutional. The radicals elected Drake to the Senate and provided the state with a progressive administration. Strengthening the economy, they built railroads, introduced a general incorporation law, and sanctioned the eight-hour day. In addition, they improved the public school system and in 1868 enabled U.S. Grant (q.v.) to win in Missouri.

Nevertheless, its proscriptive measures rendered the radical administration unpopular. In 1869 the German-American leader Carl Schurz (q.v.), who had come to St. Louis barely two years earlier to edit the *Westliche Post*, despite Drake's opposition, was elected U.S. Senator. But he soon fell out with the national administration. Differing on foreign policy, civil service reform (q.v.), and Reconstruction, he was one of the founders of the Liberal Republican movement (q.v.), and when the Republicans met in convention in 1870, the Liberals, unable to secure their platform, bolted and made common cause with the Democrats. The coalition won, elected Brown Governor, and brought about the repeal of the test oaths. Even though Missouri ratified the Fifteenth Amendment (q.v.), and the blacks (q.v.) obtained the vote, the Democrats reemerged as the strongest party in the state. In 1871 they sent Blair to the Senate; in 1872 they carried Missouri for Horace Greeley (q.v.), and in 1874 they elected a former Confederate general to take the place of Carl Schurz. Writing a new constitution in 1875, they continued to dominate the state until the beginning of the twentieth century.

*See also* Brown, Benjamin Gratz; *Cummings* v. *Missouri*; *Garland, Ex Parte*; Schurz, Carl.

William E. Parrish, *Missouri Under Radical Rule, 1865–1870* (Columbia, Mo., 1965); Edwin C. McReynolds, *A History of the Crossroads State*, (Norman, Okla., 1967).

**MORGAN, ALBERT TALMON** (1843–1922), Mississippi Republican, was born in northern New York, the son of a pioneering family that later moved to Wisconsin. Educated in Oberlin, Ohio, Morgan entered the army at age eighteen, was severely wounded at Gettysburg, and rose to the rank of brevet lieutenant colonel. After the war, he joined his brother in a planting venture at Yazoo City, Mississippi (q.v.), but was unsuccessful, partly because of the hostility of his neighbors. Elected to the constitutional convention of 1868, he displayed signs of political leadership and was an advocate of stringent disfranchising clauses. In 1869 he was elected state Senator and was instrumental in effecting the repeal of the prohibition against mixed marriages. Then he himself married a quadroon from New York, an action that rendered him, already despised as a carpetbagger (q.v.), totally unacceptable in Southern society. Governor Adelbert Ames (q.v.)

also appointed him to the Yazoo County Board of Supervisors, which elected him president. In this position, he was active in securing new public buildings, schoolhouses, and bridges, and in 1873 he was elected sheriff. When under a legal pretext his predecessor refused to give up office, a melee ensued in which Morgan, in self-defense, allegedly killed his opponent. Arrested and brought to Jackson, he was freed by an official appointed by Governor Ames and finally assumed his office. In 1875, however, like other Republicans, he fell victim to the violence of the conservative opposition and left Mississippi for good. Practicing law and clerking at the pension office in Washington, he was dismissed when Lucius Q. C. Lamar (q.v.) became Secretary of the Interior in 1885. After publishing his book *Yazoo; or On the Freedom Line in the South*, he left for Lawrence, Kansas. Eventually, he sought his fortune, unsuccessfully, by prospecting in Colorado, published books advocating inflation, and died in Denver in 1922.

*See also* Ames, Adelbert; Carpetbaggers; Mississippi.

Richard N. Current, *Those Terrible Carpetbaggers: A Reinterpretation* (New York, 1988); Hodding Carter, *The Angry Scar* (New York, 1959).

**MORTON, OLIVER PERRY** (1823–1877), Civil War Governor and radical Senator from Indiana, was born in Salisbury near Centerville, Indiana, the son of a shoemaker who also kept a tavern. Orphaned in 1826 by the death of his mother, he was raised by two maternal aunts in Springdale, Ohio, but in 1838 moved back to Centerville, where his father was living. He attended Wayne County Seminary, took odd jobs as a clerk and hatter and then studied at Miami University and read law. Admitted to the bar, he began his legal practice in Centerville. In 1852 the Democratic legislature elected him to serve a few months as a county judge, but at the end of his term, feeling the need for further study, he enrolled at the Cincinnati Law School before resuming his practice, which soon yielded him a good income.

The Kansas-Nebraska Act caused Morton to leave the Democratic party (q.v.), and for the rest of his life he became an ardent Republican. Defeated for Governor in 1856, in 1860 he was elected Lieutenant Governor, and early in 1861, upon Governor Henry S. Lane's elevation to the Senate, assumed the higher office.

An energetic executive, Morton was an effective war Governor who employed all the means at his command to counteract the obstructionist tactics of the Democratic legislature and the Copperhead conspiracies threatening the state. He was reelected in 1864 and contributed to Abraham Lincoln's (q.v.) victory in Indiana.

After the war, Morton at first approved of Andrew Johnson's (q.v.) policies. Seeking relief in Paris from a serious stroke that had crippled him, he undertook a diplomatic mission for the President, who wanted Napoleon III to withdraw his troops from Mexico. But when the Governor returned and Johnson refused to heed his advice to sign the Civil Rights Bill (Civil Rights Acts, q.v.), he broke with the administration. Taking part in the Southern Loyalist Convention at Philadelphia (q.v.), he was active in the 1866 campaign and was elected to the Senate in 1867.

It did not take long for Morton to become one of the radical leaders in the upper house. He favored the impeachment of Johnson (q.v.) and black suffrage (q.v.), was a strong supporter of Ulysses S. Grant (q.v.), and proposed an amendment (q.v.) that would have safeguarded the freedmen's right to vote by affirmative language. Nevertheless, he worked arduously for the ratification of the less radical constitutional change and later insisted that its ratification be made one of the conditions for readmission of the remaining unreconstructed states. As one of the principal Stalwart upholders of the Grant regime, he sustained its effort to annex the Dominican Republic; defended it against attacks involving arms sales to France, Reconstruction policies, and corruption; and sanctioned its deposition of Charles Sumner (q.v.) as chairman of the Foreign Relations Committee. At the same time, he opposed civil service reform (q.v.) and general amnesty (q.v.).

Reelected in 1872, Morton's support of the administration continued. He defended the Republican government of William Pitt Kellogg (q.v.) in Louisiana (q.v.), sought to seat P.B.S. Pinchback (q.v.) in the Senate, and never failed to denounce the outrages in the South, particularly the violent election of 1875 in Mississippi (q.v.). His only difference with the President concerned the money question. Although he had formerly been in favor of hard money, after the Panic of 1873 he endorsed a mild form of inflation and regretted Grant's veto of the inflation bill of 1874.

At the Cincinnati Convention of 1876, Morton was one of the candidates for the presidency but loyally supported the actual nominee, Rutherford B. Hayes (q.v.). During the struggle about the disputed election, he never doubted that Hayes had won. Consequently, he opposed the creation of an Electoral Commission (q.v.). Nevertheless, he served upon it and contributed to its decision in favor of the Republicans. Afterward, he reluctantly sustained Hayes' Southern policy as inevitable. He died in Indianapolis in 1877.

A radical of radicals, Morton was an ardent defender of the rights of blacks (q.v.) and the concept of human equality. Politically astute, he dominated Indiana politics for many years. Often accused of opportunism—he changed his views upon the tariff, currency, and Reconstruction—he always held that he was open-minded and in an age of corruption maintained his personal honesty.

*See also* Grant, Ulysses Simpson; Louisiana; Pinchback, Pinckney Benton Stewart.

William Dudley Foulke, *Life of Oliver P. Morton* (2 vols., Indianapolis, 1899).

# N

NAST, THOMAS (1840–1902), political cartoonist, was born in Landau, Germany, the son of a musician in a Bavarian military band. Brought to New York in 1846, he began sketching for *Frank Leslie's Illustrated Newspaper* in 1855, then undertook missions for the New York *Illustrated News*, and in 1860 accompanied Giuseppe Garibaldi's expedition to Sicily as an artist. In 1862 he joined *Harper's Weekly*.

As a cartoonist for the popular weekly, Nast stressed patriotic, Unionist values during the Civil War and radical Republicanism afterward. His incisive drawings lambasted Andrew Johnson (q.v.), the Democratic party, and the Southern Bourbons while extolling Republican heroes, particularly Ulysses S. Grant (q.v.), whose administration Nast supported with many telling cartoons disparaging its enemies. A foe of corruption, he contributed to the downfall of William M. Tweed (q.v.) by inventing the symbol of the Tammany tiger and pilloring the Democratic boss.

Nast's support of radicalism and Congressional Reconstruction (q.v.) made him a strong defender of the blacks (q.v.). His tolerance extended to other oppressed minorities such as the Chinese and the Indians but was marred by a strong antagonism against Roman Catholics, whom he savagely cartooned in his campaign against the Democrats. In 1872 he played an important role in the defeat of Horace Greeley (q.v.), whose Liberal Republicans (Liberal Republican Movement, q.v.) he unsparingly castigated in merciless cartoons. It was during the 1870s that he invented the symbols of the Republican elephant and the Democratic donkey, popularized the concept of the "rag baby" in the struggle against inflation, and enlisted his pen in the fight against "demon rum." In 1884, repelled by James G. Blaine's (q.v.) unsavory past, he supported Grover Cleveland.

But Nast's most active career was over. In 1886, alienated by the magazine's lessening emphasis on issues that interested him and at odds with editor George William Curtis (q.v.), Nast left *Harper's Weekly*. In 1894 he briefly sought to establish his own magazine, *Nast's Weekly*; however, his pen was no longer as influential as before, partially because of the change in the major parties' identification with clear causes, partially because of the introduction of new technology. The invention of photochemical reproduction was simply not as suited to his art as the old engraved wooden blocks. In 1902 Theodore Roosevelt appointed him consul at Guyaquil, Ecuador, but he died of yellow fever soon after his arrival.

*See also* Grant, Ulysses Simpson; Greeley, Horace; Johnson, Andrew; Liberal Republican Movement; Radical Republicans.

Morton Keller, *The Art and Politics of Thomas Nast* (New York, 1968); J. Chalmers Vinson, *Thomas Nast: Political Cartoonist* (Athens, Ga., 1967); Albert Bigelow Paine, *Th. Nast: His Period and His Pictures* (New York, 1904).

**NATIONAL LABOR UNION,** a labor organization with a political orientation founded at Baltimore in 1866. From the beginning, the National Labor Union (NLU) was primarily interested in the legal establishment of the eight-hour day and later in currency reform favoring greenbacks (q.v.). Its first national congress was attended by more than sixty-five delegates from unions, trade assemblies, and eight-hour leagues. It elected a president, initiated the preparation of an Address to the Workingmen of the United States, favored producers and consumers cooperatives, and endorsed the organization of black workers. Its political orientation was further underlined by the election in 1868 of William H. Sylvis of the Molders International Union as president. Both he and his successor, Richard F. Trevellick, who took over after Sylvis's death in 1869, stressed political action.

The NLU's political orientation alienated several trade unions, a trend that became even more marked after the establishment in 1872 of the Labor Reform party. Many unions had prohibitions against party politics in their constitutions, and the blacks (q.v.) preferred to remain affiliated with the Republicans. Weakened by the withdrawal of Justice David Davis (q.v.), whom it had nominated for President, the Labor Reform party proved short-lived and ineffective. Although the NLU, under the name of Industrial Congress, lived on until 1875, it was clearly losing its importance, and the eight-hour laws that it had promoted were generally unavailing.

*See also* Davis, David.

David Montgomery, *Beyond Equality: Labor and the Radical Republicans, 1862–1872* (New York, 1967); Foster Rhea Dulles, *Labor in America* (New York, 1949); John R. Commons et al., *History of Labor in the United States* (2 vols., New York, 1918).

**NATIONAL UNION CONVENTION,** a meeting of supporters of Andrew Johnson (q.v.) in Philadelphia in August 1866. Johnson, increasingly at odds with Congress about Reconstruction, sought to strengthen his position by forming a new political grouping consisting of conservative Republicans and moderate Democrats. After the failure of Congress to sustain his veto of the Civil Rights Bill (Civil Rights Acts, q.v.), in April 1866 a National Union Executive Committee was established, which, under the leadership of Montgomery Blair and Alexander W. Randall, in May gave rise to the National Union Club to promote the movement.

In June, Johnson and his friends decided to call a national convention. Senators James R. Doolittle (q.v.), Edgar Cowan, former Senator Orville H. Browning (q.v.), and Randall, as well as several cabinet members, including William H. Seward (q.v.), Hugh McCulloch, and Gideon Welles (q.v.), took the lead in drawing up the call for the convention. Secretary of the Interior James Harlan, Postmaster General William Dennison, and Attorney General James Speed (q.v.) refused to subscribe to it and resigned, while Secretary of War Edwin M. Stanton (q.v.) also failed to endorse it but remained in office. The resulting document was also signed by a number of other supporters of the President.

Preparations for the meeting proceeded everywhere, North and South. Soon it became apparent, however, that it would be difficult to keep the Democrats from becoming too prominent. This problem, which was never resolved, caused great embarrassment to Johnson's Republican allies, particularly to Henry J. Raymond (q.v.), the national chairman of the Republican party (q.v.), who supported the convention. Nevertheless, when on August 14 the delegates convened in a newly built Wigwam in Philadelphia, unity seemingly prevailed. General John A. Dix delivered the keynote address; Governor James Orr of South Carolina and General Darius N. Couch of Massachusetts and their fellow delegates entered arm-in-arm (hence the name, "Arm-in-Arm" Convention), and Doolittle was made permanent president. Although a jarring note was provided by the notorious Copperhead Clement L. Vallandigham (q.v.), who with great difficulty was kept from disturbing the proceedings, in the end harmonious resolutions were passed. Glorying in the restoration of the Union and praising Johnson's policies, they asserted the right of every state to representation in Congress. A longer address amplifying these doctrines was also prepared, and upon adjournment, a committee waited upon the President to present the resolutions to him. He received them with fulsome praise.

Despite Johnson's enthusiasm, the National Union Convention proved abortive. The split between its Republican and Democratic members weakened it, and the prominence in it of former Confederates rendered it suspect in the minds of the majority of Republicans. In November the National Union movement received a serious blow because of the radical victory, and although Johnson continued to promote its goals, it gradually passed from the scene.

*See also* Doolittle, James Wood; Johnson, Andrew; Raymond, Henry Jarvis.

Thomas Wagstaff, "The Arm-in-Arm Convention," *Civil War History*, 14 (June 1968): 101–19; Patrick W. Riddleberger, *1866: The Critical Year Revisited* (Carbondale, Ill., 1979).

**NEW ORLEANS RIOT,** a massacre of Unionists, mostly black, at New Orleans on July 30, 1866. After a conservative victory in Louisiana (q.v.) in November 1865, the restive Unionists, both moderate and radical, hoped to regain political power by extending the suffrage to the blacks (q.v.) and disfranchising leading former Confederates. To accomplish this aim, following the passage of the Civil Rights Bill (Civil Rights Acts, q.v.) over the President's veto, in June 1866 they attempted to recall the adjourned constitutional convention of 1864. This move, of dubious legality, had the support of Governor J. Madison Wells (q.v.), although it was opposed by Lieutenant Governor Albert Voorhees and the presiding judge of the First District Court of New Orleans, Edmund Abell. Encouraged by the Governor's support, the Unionists, acting through Rufus K. Howell, the president pro tem of the body, called for a meeting of the adjourned convention on July 30.

This project caused great apprehension among the conservatives. Judge Abell, in a charge to a grand jury, declared it illegal, and on July 25, Mayor John T. Monroe informed the commanding general, Absalom Baird, that he intended to disperse it. Replying that the army would not interfere in political matters, Baird nevertheless stated that the delegates had the right to assemble. A mass meeting of Unionists at Mechanics Hall on July 27 further alarmed the conservatives who considered the speeches delivered there, particularly one by Dr. Anthony P. Dostic (q.v.), inflammatory. On July 28 the Lieutenant Governor wired for information about the army's intentions to President Andrew Johnson (q.v.), who answered that the military would sustain the courts, while Baird asked for instructions from Secretary of War Edwin M. Stanton (q.v.), who failed to reply.

Thus when the delegates met at Mechanics Hall on July 30, no troops were present. A procession of blacks carrying an American flag was fired upon; a riot started, and police, firemen, and bystanders not only attacked the procession but began to fire indiscriminately into the hall. More than thirty-five persons, mainly blacks but including Dostie, were killed and more than one hundred, among them former Governor Michael Hahn (q.v.), wounded. As General Philip H. Sheridan (q.v.), returning to his command in New Orleans shortly after the riot, described it, it was an ''absolute massacre,'' and the country was stunned by the renewed violence in the South.

Occurring shortly before the National Union Convention (q.v.) in Philadelphia, the riot had a profound influence upon the elections of 1866. Although Johnson attempted to blame it upon the radicals and Stanton was criticized for his failure to respond to Baird, the President's opponents used it to discredit his plan of Reconstruction, and it contributed significantly to the Republican victory in the fall elections.

*See also* Dostie, Anthony P.; Johnson, Andrew; Louisiana; Wells, James Madison.

Gilles Vandal, *The New Orleans Riot of 1866: Anatomy of a Tragedy* (Lafayette, La., 1983).

**NICHOLLS, FRANCIS TILLOU** (1834–1912), ''Redemption'' Governor and later Chief Justice of Louisiana (q.v.), was born at Donaldsonville, the son of Judge Thomas Clark Nicholls and Louisa Drake Nicholls, a member of a prominent New York family. Educated at the local schools and at Jefferson Academy, he entered West Point in 1851. After graduation in 1855, he was assigned to a post at Fort Yuma, California, but resigned because of poor health. He studied at the University of Louisiana (now Tulane) law school, was admitted to practice in 1858, and established himself as a lawyer in Assumption Parish, where he married Caroline Z. Guion, the daughter of a sugar planter. Entering the Confederate army at the outbreak of war, he was wounded at Winchester and Chancellorsville and rose to the rank of brigadier general. Toward the end of the conflict, having lost both an arm and a leg, Nicholls was sent to an administrative post in Texas.

When the war was over, Nicholls returned to Napoleon, Louisiana, to resume the practice of law. Disfranchised, he served as president of the Democratic parish committee.

In 1876 the Conservative-Democratic party nominated Nicholls for Governor. After a hard-fought campaign against Stephen B. Packard (q.v.), in which he sought to assure the blacks (q.v.) of his goodwill, he claimed victory, but in the midst of the disputed election the result remained unclear. Consequently, two legislatures and governors took office in January, but Nicholls was helped by the unexpected support of Pinckney B. S. Pinchback (q.v.), who was disappointed at his failure to be elected Senator. When in April 1877 President Rutherford B. Hayes (q.v.) withdrew the federal troops from the statehouse, the Confederate general and his legislature assumed uncontested control of the government. ''Redemption'' had begun.

During his term of office, Nicholls sought to redeem his pledges to the blacks, some of whom he even appointed to office. But the Democratic-Conservative victory resulted in random violence against the freedmen, persecutions that the Governor was unable to stop. Reelected in 1878, he reluctantly endorsed the call for a constitutional convention, but when that body shortened his term, he did not run for reelection. He practiced law in New Orleans until he was nominated and elected Governor again in 1888. In his new term of office, he became involved in a struggle to break the power of the Louisiana Lottery Company, a contest in which he emerged victorious. Appointed Chief Justice of Louisiana in 1892, he served until the end of his term in 1904, when he became an associate justice. He retired in 1911 and died at Ridgefield Plantation in Thibodaux in 1912.

*See also* Louisiana; Packard, Stephen B.; Pinchback, Pinckney Benton Stewart; ''Redemption.''

Hilda Mulvey McDaniel, ''Francis Tillou Nicholls and the End of Reconstruction,'' *Louisiana Historical Quarterly*, 32 (1949): 357–513; William Ivy Hair, *Bourbonism and Agrarian Protest: Louisiana Politics, 1877–1900* (Baton Rouge, 1969); C. Vann Woodward, *Origins of the New South: 1877–1913* (Baton Rouge, 1951).

**NORTH CAROLINA,** one of the states subject to Reconstruction. One of the last states to secede, North Carolina was one of the first to be subject to attempts at Reconstruction, when, after the capture of Forts Hatteras and Clark in August 1861, Henry Foster and Marble Nash Taylor attempted to revive a loyal state government in the Pamlico Sound area. Foster was even elected to Congress, but the House refused to seat him. Then, in May 1862, Abraham Lincoln (q.v.) appointed Edward Stanley, a conservative Unionist, Provisional Governor. Stanley, however, sought to enforce the Fugitive Slave Law and closed black schools, actions that caused him to be denounced in Congress, and he resigned in January 1863.

The next attempt at Reconstruction occurred after the end of the war. In May 1865 Andrew Johnson (q.v.) published his Proclamation of Amnesty (q.v.) and appointed William W. Holden (q.v.) Provisional Governor of the state, the first instance of the implementation of the Presidential Plan of Reconstruction (q.v.), which was to be applied to the other Southern states as well. Holden called an election for a constitutional convention. Meeting in October, the convention abolished slavery, nullified the secession ordinance, and, after considerable pressure, repealed the Confederate debt. It failed to extend the suffrage to any blacks (q.v.), so that in the subsequent elections a conservative legislature was chosen and Holden defeated for Governor by Jonathan Worth, a former Whig acceptable to the conservatives. The legislators ratified the Thirteenth Amendment (q.v.), and although they enacted a black code less severe than that of neighboring states, in spite of a petition of a Negro convention, they refused to accord full civil rights to the freedmen.

The Reconstruction Acts (q.v.) remanded North Carolina to military rule. In November 1867 an election based on universal male suffrage with the exception of certain leading former Confederates resulted in the convocation of a Republican constitutional convention, which, influenced by carpetbaggers (q.v.) like Albion W. Tourgée (q.v.), framed a charter for a new government based on equal rights for the blacks and embodying reforms in local government as well as in the judiciary. When it was adopted by the people, Holden was elected Governor, and a Republican legislature was returned. After it ratified the Fourteenth Amendment (q.v.), the state was readmitted to the Union (June 1868).

Republican dominance in North Carolina proved to be of short duration. Struggling with corruption (q.v.), particularly in regard to the financing of railroads controlled by George W. Swepson (q.v.) and Milton S. Littlefield (q.v.), the Republican regime soon found itself under attack by especially violent secret societies including the Ku Klux Klan (q.v.). To frustrate the night riders, Holden, after the legislature passed the Shoffner Act authorizing him to do so, declared Alamance and Caswell Counties to be in a state of insurrection. He summoned the militia, placed it under the command of George W. Kirk, and began the so-called Kirk-Holden War (q.v.), an effort to restore order and to arrest the ring leaders of the rebellious element. But in spite of appeals for federal support, Holden never received the full backing he requested. On the contrary, he fell afoul of the federal courts when federal Judge George Washington Brooks released the Governor's prisoners, including his chief opponent, Josiah Turner, by invoking the Fourteenth Amendment and the Habeas Corpus Act. The result was that in the elections of 1870 the conservatives gained a majority of the legislature, which promptly impeached and removed Holden. The end of Reconstruction was in sight.

It is true that Holden's successor, Lieutenant Governor Tod R. Caldwell, was able to win election in his own right in 1872 and that efforts to suppress the Klan continued, but the conservatives retained control of the legislature. Strengthening their hold on the state government in 1874, in the next year they convened a convention to revise the constitution. These changes gave them greater influence over local government and the judiciary, and in 1876 Zebulon Vance (q.v.), the wartime Confederate Governor, defeated his Republican rival and regained control of the executive office. "Redemption" (q.v.) was in full swing, and although North Carolina continued to retain a relatively strong Republican minority, its racial policies differed little from those of neighboring states.

*See also* Congressional Reconstruction; Holden, William Woods; Presidential Reconstruction; Tourgée, Albion Winegar.

J. G. de Roulhac Hamilton, *Reconstruction in North Carolina* (New York, 1914); Horace W. Raper, *William W. Holden: North Carolina's Political Enigma* (Chapel Hill, N.C., 1985); Otto H. Olson, *Carpetbagger's Crusade: The Life of Albion Winegar Tourgée* (Baltimore, 1965); Michael Perman, *The Road to Redemption: Southern Politics, 1869–1879* (Chapel Hill, N.C., 1984); William Gillette, *Retreat from Reconstruction, 1869–1879* (Baton Rouge, 1979).

**NORTH CAROLINA PROCLAMATION** (1865), President Andrew Johnson's (q.v.) order for the restoration of North Carolina that inaugurated the process of Presidential Reconstruction (q.v.) and became a model for it in other states. Issued on May 29, 1865, in conjunction with the President's Proclamation of Amnesty (q.v.) and citing the constitutional guarantee of republican government to the states, the proclamation provided for the appointment of William W. Holden (q.v.) as Provisional Governor of North Carolina. His duty would be to convene a convention to amend the state constitution and to take charge of the process of restoration. The President, who acted under his powers as President of the United States and commander-in-chief of the army and navy, also confined the right to vote to those who had taken his oath of amnesty and who had been electors in 1861, thus disfranchising the freedmen.

Although not specifically stated in the proclamation, it was known that Johnson expected the convention to abolish slavery. He also hoped for the ratification of the Thirteenth Amendment (q.v.), the nullification of the ordinance of secession, and the repudiation of the Confederate debt, a condition he later conveyed to the state authorities.

The result of this proclamation and parallel provisions for other states was the emergence of conservative governments throughout the South, the passage of the black codes (q.v.), and the election to Congress of former ranking Confederates. These developments then led to the breach between Congress and the President.

Although it has been asserted that in issuing his proclamation Johnson was merely following the example of Abraham Lincoln (q.v.), it must be remembered that Lincoln promulgated his Ten Percent Plan (q.v.) in time of war to weaken the enemy. What he would have done in time of peace is unknown, but it is unlikely that he would have permitted the strengthening of the Democratic party by the reemergence of former leaders of the Confederacy or the virtual reestablishment of slavery with the black codes.

*See also* Amnesty; Johnson, Andrew; Lincoln, Abraham; Presidential Reconstruction; Ten Percent Plan.

Hans L. Trefousse, *Andrew Johnson: a Biography* (New York, 1989); Eric L. McKitrick, *Andrew Johnson and Reconstruction* (Chicago, 1960).

# O

OHIO IDEA, a proposal to pay the principal of bonds not specifying redemption in coin in greenbacks, so named because of its advocacy in 1867 by the Ohio politician George H. Pendleton. Endorsed by the Democratic party (q.v.) in 1868, it was considered a mild form of inflation, although this was denied by its supporters. It appealed to debtor and agrarian interests, especially in the West, who believed it unfair that bondholders should be able to collect coin for securities they had originally bought in depreciated greenbacks.

*See also* Greenbacks.

Irwin Unger, *The Greenback Era* (New York, 1964).

ORD, EDWARD OTHO CRESAP (1818–1883), Union general and commander of the Fourth Military District, was born in Cumberland, Maryland, the son of a former midshipman and army lieutenant and of Rebecca Cresap, a member of a prominent Western Maryland family. Educated in Washington and at West Point, he graduated in 1839. Afterward he served in the Seminole War, at various eastern posts, in California, and in the Northwest. In 1858 Captain Ord was detailed as an artillery instructor to Fortress Monroe, from where he was ordered to Charlestown as part of the detachment sent to provide security for the execution of John Brown. By 1860 he was back in California.

Although a Democrat of Southern birth, Ord was a strong Unionist who was appointed a brigadier general in September 1861. Distinguishing himself in the engagement at Dranesville, Virginia, he was promoted to major general and sent west, where he participated in the battles at Iuka and Corinth and was severely wounded at Hatchie. After his recovery, he took part in the siege of Vicksburg, where he commanded XIII Corps. In 1864, in charge of the VIII and then XVIII Corps, he again won laurels in the capture of Fort Harrison. Wounded a second time, he recovered to be placed in command of XXIV Corps and then the Army of the James as well as the Department of Virginia and North Carolina. The campaigns leading to the capture of Petersburg and the surrender at Appomattox formed the climax of his Civil War career.

Finding himself in charge of Richmond after its capture, Ord, long anxious for a mild peace and distrustful of black troops, removed the latter from the city. In June 1865 he was recalled from Richmond and assigned to the Department of the Northwest. From there he was sent to Arkansas (q.v.), where he became assistant commissioner of the Freedmen's Bureau (q.v.) and after the passage of the Reconstruction Acts (q.v.) was appointed commanding general of the Fourth Military District, comprising Arkansas and Mississippi (q.v.).

As one of the generals charged with military Reconstruction, Ord was attacked by radicals as a conservative and by conservatives for the opposite reason. In reality, he sought to keep an even course. Thus he removed the politically unreliable Treasurer of Arkansas and prohibited the reassembly of the state's old legislature. In the case of the Camden *Constitutional Eagle*, sacked by a local commander after scurrilous attacks on the army, he upheld the freedom of the press by censuring and court-martialing the guilty parties. However, in the case of William H. McCardle (*McCardle, ex parte*, q.v.) of the Vicksburg *Daily Times*, he took the opposite approach by arresting the editor for obstructing the laws and encouraging violence. He successfully initiated and supervised the registration and election process in the two states but was recalled in December 1867 and transferred to the Department of California. There he fought against Cochise and his Apaches in Arizona. In 1871 he took over the Department of the Platte at Omaha and in 1875 was put in command of Texas. Because of the difficulty of controlling armed parties and Indians raiding across the Rio Grande, he became involved in their pursuit across the international border. This delicate diplomatic issue created many problems, but in the end Ord succeeded in winning the esteem of the Mexicans, one of whose leaders became his son-in-law.

After supporting the presidential candidacy of Winfield S. Hancock (q.v.), in December 1880 Ord requested retirement. He spent his remaining years as an agent for American railroads and corporations in Mexico as well as an engineer for Jay Gould's (q.v.) Mexican Southern Railroad. He died of yellow fever at Havana in 1883.

*See also* Arkansas; *McCardle, ex parte*; Mississippi; Reconstruction Acts.

Bernarr Cresap, *Appomattox Commander: The Story of General E.O.C. Ord* (San Diego, 1981); James E. Sefton, *The United States Army and Reconstruction, 1865–1877* (Baton Rouge, 1867).

# P

PACKARD, STEPHEN B. (1839–1923), carpetbag leader and gubernatorial claimant in Louisiana (q.v.), was born in Auburn, Maine. He was a lawyer, and after joining the Twelfth Maine in 1861, he reached New Orleans, where, in 1864, he became Judge Advocate of the city. When the war was over, he established a law practice there. Appointed U.S. marshal for Louisiana in 1869, he was a leading member of the so-called Custom House ring, headed by collector James Casey, President Grant's brother-in-law, the Republican faction opposed to Governor Henry Clay Warmoth (q.v.). In 1872, temporarily combining with the powerful black leader Pinckney B. S. Pinchback (q.v.), Packard's faction nominated William Pitt Kellogg (q.v.) for Governor. After a disputed election and the emergence of rival legislatures, Packard succeeded in inducing federal Judge Edward H. Durell to issue orders for the seizure of the statehouse. Supported by the President, the Kellogg legislature was organized and impeached Warmoth, an outcome Packard had sought for some time. He remained influential in the Republican party (q.v.), particularly in 1874, when he served as permanent chairman of the state convention. A member of the committee notifying Rutherford B. Hayes (q.v.) of his nomination for President, Packard was himself nominated for Governor in 1876.

As a result of the disputed election, in which he gained one thousand more votes than Hayes, Packard laid claim to victory, but his opponent, Francis T. Nicholls (q.v.), disputed it. Consequently, at the beginning of the new year two rival administrations were installed in New Orleans. The Packard forces held the statehouse under the protection of federal troops, while the Democrats, meeting in St. Patrick's and Odd Fellows' Hall, were able to extend their sway to the rest of the state. Wounded in an assassination attempt, Packard, like his colleague in South Carolina (q.v.), was forced to capitulate when, as a result of the Compromise of 1877 (q.v.), following the inauguration of Hayes, the federal troops were withdrawn. From 1878 to 1885 he served as U.S. consul in Liverpool.

*See also* Compromise of 1877; Kellogg, William Pitt; Louisiana; Nicholls, Francis Tillou; Pinchback, Pinckney Benton Stewart; Warmoth, Henry Clay.

Joe Gray Taylor, *Louisiana Reconstructed, 1863–1877* (Baton Rouge, 1974); Fanny Z. Lovell Bone, "Louisiana in the Disputed Election of 1876," *Louisiana Historical Quarterly*, 14, 15 (1931–1932): 408–40, 549–66, 92–116, 234–65; *Herringshaw's National Library of American Biography* (5 vols., Chicago, 1909–1914).


**PENDLETON PLAN.** *See* OHIO IDEA.


**PHILLIPS, WENDELL** (1811–1884), abolitionist orator and reformer, was born in Boston, the son of John and Sarah Walley Phillips, well-to-do members of the city's Brahmin elite. Educated at the Boston Latin School and at Harvard College and Law School, Phillips was admitted to the bar in 1834. Converted to abolitionism by Ann Terry Greene, whom he married, he was shocked by the 1837 murder of Elijah Lovejoy and thereafter devoted himself wholly to the cause. He was a delegate of the Massachusetts Anti-Slavery Society to the World Anti-Slavery Congress in London, contributed frequently to William Lloyd Garrison's *Liberator*, and became one of the most effective speakers of the movement. Espousing disunion, he denounced the Constitution and refused to vote.

Notwithstanding his former condemnation of a union with slaveholders, at the outbreak of the Civil War Phillips supported the war effort. Constantly urging more thoroughgoing antislavery measures, he advocated not only emancipation (q.v.) but full civil rights for blacks (q.v.), including their enfranchisement. To accomplish these aims, he endorsed the 1864 candidacy of John C. Frémont. Only Frémont's withdrawal brought the orator grudgingly to the support of the Republican ticket.

In the meantime, a split was developing between Garrison and Phillips. Garrison, rejoicing in the imminent realization of the Anti-Slavery Society's goals, urged its disbandment. Phillips, insisting that its work was not complete until there was absolute racial equality in America, disagreed. He prevailed. Garrison dropped out, and the orator carried on the struggle. He also embraced the demand for an eight-hour day, temperance, and women's suffrage.

Deeply disappointed by the Reconstruction policies of Andrew Johnson (q.v.), Phillips early demanded the impeachment of the President. In 1866 he was nominated for Congress by the Workingmen's party but declined. He opposed the Fourteenth Amendment (q.v.) as an unworthy compromise on black rights and, despite his advocacy of women's suffrage, refused to allow the Anti-Slavery Society to endorse it. His policy was one of black rights first, and, though distrusting Ulysses S. Grant (q.v.), he wholeheartedly embraced the Fifteenth Amendment (q.v.). Its adoption led to the dissolution of the American Anti-Slavery Society in 1870, when Phillips accepted a nomination for Governor from the Labor Reform and Temperance parties. Badly defeated, he was not discouraged but continued his advocacy of labor reform and other progressive causes, including an endorsement of the Paris Commune. Locally, he favored the candidacy of Benjamin F. Butler (q.v.) and in 1872 finally endorsed the reelection of Grant. His strong support of Charles Sumner's Civil Rights Bill (Civil Rights Acts, q.v.) led him to denounce the compromise of omitting desegration of schools and cemeteries leading to its final passage. He died in Boston in 1884.

One of the America's foremost orators, Phillips' influence upon antislavery sentiment was profound. So well known was he that Andrew Johnson in his Washington's Birthday speech in 1866 included him among those of his opponents whom he compared to traitors. Phillips' advocacy of labor reforms stamps him as one of the more foreword looking radicals of the Reconstruction era.

*See also* Butler, Benjamin Franklin; Civil Rights Act of 1875; Johnson, Andrew.

James Brewer Stewart, *Wendell Phillips: Liberty's Hero* (Baton Rouge, 1986); Irving Bartlett, *Wendell Phillips: Brahmin Radical* (Boston, 1961); Oscar Sherwin, *Prophet of Liberty: The Life and Times of Wendell Phillips* (New York, 1958).


**PIERPONT, FRANCIS HARRISON** (1814–1899), Union Governor of Virginia and Father of West Virginia (q.v.), was born in Monongalia County, (West) Virginia, the son of Francis and Catherine Weaver Peirpont, the spelling of whose name he changed in 1881. He was educated at Allegheny College in Meadville, Pennsylvania, read law, and in 1842 was admitted to the bar. Settling in Fairmont, he established a flourishing practice, represented the Baltimore and Ohio Railroad, and engaged in various business ventures. He was an ardent Whig and Unionist, who criticized the slaveholders of the Tidewater and in 1860 supported the Bell-Everett ticket.

When Virginia (q.v.) seceded, Pierpont became active in the organization of the Second Wheeling Convention of Unionists and in June 1861 was elected Governor of the Restored Government of Virginia. He presided over the breakup of the state and after the establishment of West Virginia transferred his administration to Alexandria, where he exercised authority over the remaining portions of the old commonwealth under federal control. Reelected in December 1863, he advocated the summoning of a constitutional convention to abolish slavery. The convention met, provided for emancipation (q.v.), mandated free public education, and disenfranchised former Confederates. The Pierpont government was recognized and sustained by Abraham Lincoln (q.v.) who considered it as a first step in the reconstruction of Virginia.

After the fall of Richmond, in 1865 Pierpont moved his administration to the old capital. He extended its authority over the whole state and on May 9 was fully recognized by Andrew Johnson (q.v.). Seeking to win over former Confederates by a policy of leniency including the repeal of the disqualifying clauses of the Constitution, the Governor was soon faced with a conservative legislature that repealed its consent to the division of the state and, contrary to his advice, passed a black code (q.v.). Pierpont was not an advocate of black suffrage (q.v.), but he vainly pleaded for the equal treatment of both races before the law and the ratification of the Fourteenth Amendment (q.v.). The conservatives' hostility to these recommendations did not shield him from the opposition of the radicals, whom he could not even satisfy with his advocacy of the Reconstruction Acts (q.v.), and in 1868, after his term had expired, he was removed from office by General John M. Schofield (q.v.). When his protests to President U. S. Grant (q.v.) proved unavailing, he returned to Fairmont to resume his business and legal career. In 1869 he was elected to the state legislature, three years later supported Horace Greeley (q.v.), but afterward rejoined the Republicans. Appointed a collector of internal revenue by President James A. Garfield (q.v.), he served but a short time and died in Pittsburgh in 1899.

*See also* Johnson, Andrew; Virginia; West Virginia.

Charles H. Ambler, *Francis H. Pierpont: Union War Governor of Virginia and Father of West Virginia* (Chapel Hill, N.C., 1937).


**PIKE, JAMES SHEPHERD** (1811–1882), journalist and author, was born in Calais, Maine, the son of William and Hannah Shepherd Pike, who after the father's early death supported the family by running a boarding house. Pike engaged in journalism and business at an early age, acquired a good competence, and as Washington correspondent of the Boston *Courier* wrote incisive letters about men and affairs in the capital. In 1848 and 1850 he ran unsuccessfully for Congress as a Whig and in the latter year began his long-lasting association with the New York *Tribune*. His abolitionist predilections led him to advocate extreme measures, even disunion, although his employer, Horace Greeley (q.v.), immediately condemned so unpopular a measure. In 1861 Pike was appointed minister to the Netherlands, a post that he used to further the Union cause by strong antislavery positions in Europe.

In spite of his abolitionism, Pike had always been convinced of the inferiority of the black race. Nevertheless, upon his return in 1866 he favored the extension of the suffrage to the freedmen. Again writing for the *Tribune*, he championed radical Reconstruction as well as hard money and protection. In 1872, largely because of the nomination of Greeley and his brother's candidacy for Congress on the Liberal ticket, he reluctantly supported the Liberal Republicans (Liberal Republican Movement, q.v.). Disappointed in the outcome of the election, in 1873 he traveled to South Carolina (q.v.) to prepare a series of articles for the *Tribune*. Designed to vindicate the Liberals' unfavorable view of Reconstruction, these reports were edited and expanded to produce his famous book, *The Prostrate State*, a one-sided castigation of the radical government of South Carolina, in which he betrayed his ingrained racism by blaming the widespread corruption on the blacks (q.v.). Because of his abolitionist background, his testimony was considered unbiased and long used by historians to illustrate the alleged horrors of Congressional Reconstruction (q.v.).

After his return, Pike continued his journalistic and literary activities. Among other works, he published *The Finances, 1867–1878*, a book in which he sought to advocate his conservative monetary views, as well as *The New Puritan* and *The First Blows of the Civil War*. One was the story of one of his ancestors and the other a collection of his articles and correspondence before 1860. He died in Calais in 1882.

*See also* Congressional Reconstruction; Greeley, Horace; Liberal Republican Movement.

Robert Franklin Durden, *James Shepherd Pike: Republicanism and the American Negro, 1850–1882* (Durham, N.C., 1957).


**PINCHBACK, PINCKNEY BENTON STEWART** (1837–1921), leader of the freedmen and Governor of Louisiana (q.v.), was born in Macon, Georgia, the son of a planter, William Pinchback, and his freed mulatto slave, Eliza Stewart. Taken by his parents to Mississippi at an early age, he was later sent to school in Cincinnati. Upon his father's death, his mother, fearful of reenslavement, also moved to Cincinnati. In straitened circumstances, young Pinchback went to work as a cabin boy on canal and later riverboats. He became a servant of a gambler and finally rose to the position of steward. In 1860 he married Emily Hawthorne in Memphis.

Reaching New Orleans after the capture of the city, Pinchback raised a company for the Corps d'Afrique, but although he qualified for his captaincy, because of slights on racial grounds, he resigned in 1862. In the next year, he received permission to organize a cavalry troop but once again resigned when his commission was not recognized because of his race.

An early advocate of black suffrage, Pinchback moved back to Ohio, only to return to the South, this time to Alabama, in 1865 to resume his struggle for black enfranchisement. Settling in New Orleans, he became the leader of the Fourth Ward Republican Club and with the aid of Henry Clay Warmoth (q.v.) was elected a delegate to the 1867–1868 constitutional convention in which he played a prominent part. He was the author of the civil rights provisions of the new constitution and in 1868 was elected to the state Senate as well as to the Republican National Convention in Chicago. In addition, he was a member of the party's state executive committee, went into business and founded the *Louisianan*, a newspaper advocating radical causes.

In the corrupt 1871 legislative session, Pinchback profited by various lucrative deals, particularly from buying and then selling a piece of land as park commissioner. His influence among the blacks was undiminished, however, and in December 1871, having been elected president pro tem of the senate, he became lieutenant governor. It was a ploy arranged by Governor Warmoth who wanted to protect himself against impeachment by the rival Custom House ring, which was hostile to Pinchback.

But Pinchback and Warmoth were also drifting apart, partially because the Governor sought to gain support among conservatives. In 1872, when he endorsed the Liberal Republicans (Liberal Republican Movement, q.v.), Pinchback refused to follow suit. Campaigning for President U. S. Grant (q.v.) in the North, he visited the Republican National Committee in New York, only to find that Warmoth was also in the city. A number of bills designed to improve Republican chances in Louisiana had remained unsigned, and upon the committee's advice, Pinchback took a fast train to New Orleans to reach Louisiana in the Governor's absence in order to sign the bills. In the ensuing railroad race, however, Warmoth intercepted him, and the state was carried by Horace Greeley (q.v.).

Pinchback soon had his revenge. Following a disputed election, on December 9 the House, captured by the Custom House faction, impeached Warmoth, and Pinchback succeeded him. Now reconciled with the Governor's enemies, Pinchback accused Warmoth of having offered him a bribe to organize the legislature. Although his claim to office was challenged by a rival legislature, he was recognized by President Grant. The nation's first and only black Governor until 1991, he served out the remaining weeks of Warmoth's term until January 13, 1873.

The outgoing Acting Governor had no intention of retiring from politics. Elected to the House in the disputed contest of November 1872, in January 1873 he was also the choice of the Republican legislature for U.S. Senator. But that body's authority was equally challenged by its Democratic rival. Moreover, questions about his conduct had arisen, so neither the Senate nor the House seated the claimant. Nevertheless, in 1876, after years of investigation, the Senate agreed to pay his salary up to that time. Greatly disappointed, in the subsequent election he reluctantly supported his rival Stephen B. Packard (q.v.) for Governor; when the election again resulted in the organization of two rival administrations and the Packard legislature refused to send him to the Senate, Pinchback went over to the rival body recognizing Governor Francis T. Nicholls (q.v.), who triumphed after the election of Rutherford B. Hayes (q.v.) brought about the withdrawal of federal troops from the statehouse.

The end of Republican government in Louisiana diminished Pinchback's influence. In 1879 he was commissioned an internal revenue agent and elected to the constitutional convention, which met that year. In that body, however, he was unable to achieve anything other than to provide for the establishment of a black university. In 1882 President Chester A. Arthur appointed him surveyor of customs for New Orleans. He attended Republican National Conventions until 1892, studied law, and in 1886 was admitted to the bar. In 1890 he was one of the founders of the American Citizens' Equal Rights Association for the protection of the blacks' (q.v.) political and social gains but in the early 1890s left Louisiana to move north, first to New York, where he was employed as a federal marshal, and then to Washington. Always remaining active in black affairs, he stayed in the capital until he died in 1921.

An eloquent spokesman for his race, Pinchback, almost white but never denying his origins, was a highly intelligent, effective speaker, whose impact was lessened by the rumors of corruption that trailed him during much of his career.

*See also* Kellogg, William Pitt; Louisiana; McEnery, John; Nicholls, Francis Tillou; Packard, Stephen B.; Warmoth, Henry Clay.

James Haskins, *Pinckney Benton Stewart Pinchback* (New York, 1973); Agnes Smith Grosz, "The Political Career of Pinckney Benton Stewart Pinchback," *Louisiana Historical Quarterly*, 27 (1946): 400–715.

**PLESSY v. FERGUSON,** an 1896 Supreme Court case upholding segregation in railroad cars. Outraged by an 1890 Louisiana law mandating separate but equal railroad accommodations, the New Orleans black community, led by members of the Citizens Equal Rights Association, founded a committee to test the constitutionality of the measure. Louis A. Martinet, a prominent black physician, lawyer, and journalist and a member of the committee, retained the local attorney James Walker and the famous carpetbagger Albion W. Tourgée (q.v.) as counsel. The law was then challenged by Homer A. Plessy, a nearly white octaroon, who was arrested when refusing to move from a seat in the car of his choice. Counsel then argued the unconstitutionality of the law by relying on the Thirteenth and Fourteenth Amendments (q.v.), but Criminal District Judge John H. Ferguson overruled the plea. After a similar result in the state supreme court, the case was appealed to the Supreme Court of the United States. It was argued late in 1895 by Tourgée and Walker assisted by the North Carolina scalawags (q.v.) Samuel Phillips and F. D. McKenney and decided in a majority opinion written by Justice Henry Billings Brown. Declaring separate but equal facilities fully consonant with the provisions of the Fourteenth Amendment, the justice asserted that social prejudices could not be overcome by legislation. The minority opinion of one was written by Justice John Marshall Harlan, who not only arrived at the opposite conclusion but declared that "our Constitution is color blind."

Little noted at the time and in line with contemporary trends of legal reasoning and racial discrimination, the decision was the culmination of the process of whittling down the Fourteenth Amendment's usefulness in providing protection for blacks (q.v.) and provided a legal excuse for the ever more widespread applicability of Jim Crow legislation in the South. It was to be reversed only in 1954, when in *Brown* v. *Board of Education of Topeka* the Supreme Court in substance adopted Justice Harlan's arguments without formally reversing *Plessy*.

*See also* Fourteenth Amendment; Tourgée, Albion Winegar.

Charles A. Lofgren, *The Plessy Case: A Legal-Historical Interpretation* (New York, 1987); Otto H. Olsen, *Carpetbagger's Crusade: The Life of Albion Winegar Tourgée* (Baltimore, 1965).

**POPE, JOHN** (1823–1892), Union general and commander of the Third Military District, was born in Louisville, Kentucky, the son of an Illinois judge, and brought up in Kaskaskia, Illinois. An 1842 graduate of West Point, he was a topographical engineer who saw service in Mexico, led an expedition exploring the Red River of the North, and surveyed a railroad route to the Pacific in New Mexico. Appointed a brigadier general in 1861, he was promoted to major general after capturing New Madrid and Island No. 10 in 1862. Later that year, he was given command of the Army of Virginia but was badly defeated at the Second Bull Run. Transferred to the Department of the Northwest, he was active in suppressing the Sioux uprising in Minnesota.

After the war, Pope was put in charge of the Department of Missouri and in April 1867 appointed to command the Third Military District, embracing Georgia (q.v.), Alabama (q.v.), and Florida (q.v.). Known as a radical, he favored education for the freedmen and exasperated both the conservatives and President Johnson (q.v.) by so districting Georgia as to favor black constituencies. He also ordered that only registered voters could serve on juries and denied patronage to newspapers unfriendly to Congressional Reconstruction (q.v.). The result was that the President removed him in December 1867.

Following his service in the South, Pope was in command of various western districts, including the Department of Missouri and, after 1883, the Department of the Pacific. Retiring in 1886, he died in Sandusky, Ohio, in 1892.

*See also* Congressional Reconstruction; Johnson, Andrew.

Wallace Schutz and Walter Trennery, *Abandoned by Lincoln: A Military Biography of General John Pope* (Urbana, Ill., 1990); *New York Times*, September 24, 1892; James E. Sefton, *The United States Army and Reconstruction, 1865–1877* (Baton Rouge, 1967).

**PRESIDENTIAL RECONSTRUCTION,** the period of reorganization dominated by the President rather than by Congress, more particularly the era marked by Andrew Johnson's (q.v.) efforts to restore the Southern states, 1865–1867.

During the administration of Abraham Lincoln (q.v.), the process of reintegrating the South was largely in the hands of the White House. The President appointed Military Governors for various states, urged them to speed up the restoration of the Union, and in December 1863 formulated the Ten Percent Plan (q.v.), offering amnesty to all but leading insurgents. As soon as 10 percent of the electorate of 1860 had taken the proffered oath of allegiance to the Constitution (including the Emancipation Proclamation [q.v.] ), they were entitled to restore a loyal state government. Congress, dissatisfied with this proposal, countered with its own more stringent scheme, the Wade-Davis Bill (q.v.), but Lincoln pocket-vetoed it. In the meantime, the presidential plan had been set in motion in Louisiana (q.v.) and Arkansas (q.v.), although Congress refused to admit the Louisiana congressmen-elect.

When Andrew Johnson became President, he sought to continue carrying out what he believed to have been Lincoln's plans. He promised amnesty to all but fourteen exempted classes, appointed Provisional Governors for the seceded states, and instructed them to make an effort to bring back their commonwealths as quickly as possible. Suggesting that they abolish slavery and ratify the Thirteenth Amendment (q.v.), he also asked them to repudiate the Confederate debt and nullify the secession ordinances but did not insist on these conditions.

Quickly availing themselves of these mild terms, the states prepared constitutions abolishing slavery, ratified the amendment, and generally, but not always, complied with his conditions. Not one of them saw fit to enfranchise a single black; on the contrary, they passed back codes (q.v.) of varying severity, most of which tended to remand the freedmen to a status little removed from slavery. The delegates they sent to Congress included many Confederate officers of high rank, even Alexander H. Stephens, the Vice President of the defunct government.

Congress was appalled by these developments. Seeking to safeguard Southern blacks (q.v.) and Unionists, it passed the Freedmen's Bureau and Civil Rights Bills (Civil Rights Acts, q.v.), only to find that Johnson vetoed both of them. Thereupon the Republicans overrode the Civil Rights Bill veto, passed the Fourteenth Amendment (q.v.), and in the midterm elections of 1866 defeated the President's supporters. In early 1867 the congressional majority enacted the Reconstruction Acts (q.v.), which, remanding the states to military rule, initiated Congressional and ended Presidential Reconstruction.

*See also* Johnson, Andrew; Lincoln, Abraham; Ten Percent Plan.

W. R. Brock, *An American Crisis: Congress and Reconstruction, 1865–1867* (London, 1963); LaWanda and John H. Cox, *Politics, Principle, and Prejudice, 1865–1866: Dilemma of Reconstruction America* (New York, 1963): Herman Belz, *Reconstructing the Union: Theory and Practice During the Civil War* (Ithaca, N.Y., 1969).

# R

**RADICAL REPUBLICANS,** the most advanced group of the Republican party (q.v.). Opposed to compromise with the South before the Civil War and favoring emancipation after Fort Sumter, the radicals were the principal advocates of equal rights for the freedmen during Reconstruction. They never constituted an organized faction, their leaders agreeing on little except their commitment to black progress.

Long active in party ranks, during Reconstruction the radicals insisted upon a thorough reorganization of the South in order to realize their goals of black equality. Although their goals were similar, in 1864 they clashed with Abraham Lincoln (q.v.) because of his opposition to the Wade-Davis Bill (q.v.); after first hoping that Andrew Johnson (q.v.) would cooperate with them, they quickly became disillusioned with his policies and emerged as his most determined opponents. In December 1865 they were instrumental in refusing to seat Southern congressmen and in establishing the Joint Committee on Reconstruction (q.v.); thereafter, they continued to take the lead in the resistance to Johnson.

After they succeeded in inducing Congress to override the President's veto of the Civil Rights Bill (q.v.), although dissatisfied with its scope, they lent support to the passage of the Fourteenth Amendment (q.v.) and campaigned against Johnson during the midterm elections of 1866. Their efforts to impeach the President failed, but they continued to exert considerable influence, particularly in the newly installed governments in the reconstructed states.

During the administration of U. S. Grant (q.v.), the radicals' influence slowly began to wane. They were still able for a time to retain power in the South and successfully to advocate the passage of the Fifteenth Amendment (q.v.) as well as the Enforcement Acts (q.v.), but they were hard hit by deaths and retirements. Further weakened by the emergence of the Liberal Republican party (Liberal

Republican Movement, q.v.), they were also adversely affected by the Panic of 1873 and the diminishing interest in reform in the North. Terror did the rest, until the election of Rutherford B. Hayes (q.v.) and the Compromise of 1877 (q.v.) ended their importance.

Long regarded as vindictive and mainly interested in economic and political advantages for themselves, more recently the radicals have been credited with representing an ideologically committed faction of the Republican party. Keeping in mind the extent of the "rebellion," they did not even insist upon dealing very harshly with their Southern opponents. Not one of the Confederate leaders was executed, and only the most notorious war criminals suffered capital punishment. Nor are the radicals still considered to have been in control during the period formerly referred to as "radical Reconstruction"; always in a minority, at most they were able to exert pressure upon the moderates to enact a minimum of reforms. Radical leaders such as Charles Sumner (q.v.), Thaddeus Stevens (q.v.), and Benjamin F. Wade (q.v.) do not seem to have been animated by selfish motives, and while party interests cannot be denied, the radicals' contribution to racial justice is certain.

*See also* Civil Rights Acts; Fifteenth Amendment; Fourteenth Amendment; Johnson, Andrew; Liberal Republican Movement; Reconstruction Acts; Stevens, Thaddeus; Sumner, Charles; Wade, Benjamin Franklin.

Hans L. Trefousse, *The Radical Republicans: Lincoln's Vanguard for Racial Justice* (New York, 1968); Harold M. Hyman, *The Radical Republicans and Reconstruction, 1861–1870* (Indianapolis, 1967); T. Harry Williams, *Lincoln and the Radicals* (Madison, Wis., 1941).

**RAINEY, JOSEPH HAYNE** (1832–1887), South Carolina Republican leader, was born in Georgetown, South Carolina, the son of a barber who purchased the family's freedom when Rainey was still a child. The Raineys then moved to Charleston, where Joseph, after spending some time in Philadelphia, took up his father's trade. Drafted to work for the Confederacy, he escaped to Bermuda, not to return until the end of the war, when he became active in Republican politics. He was a member of the Central Committee of the state Republican party (q.v.) in 1867, participated in the South Carolina (q.v.) constitutional convention in 1868, and that year was elected to the state Senate. In 1870 he resigned and ran successfully for Congress to fill the vacancy created by the refusal of the House to seat B. Frank Whittemore, accused of selling West Point cadetships.

Rainey thus became the first black to enter the House of Representatives. Reelected three times, he served until 1879 and distinguished himself by favoring amnesty (q.v.) for former Confederates and persistently arguing for a strong Ku Klux and Civil Rights Bill (Civil Rights Acts, q.v.). Following constant challenges to the validity of his electoral victories, he was finally defeated in 1878.

After his retirement from Congress, Rainey was appointed an internal revenue agent for South Carolina, a position he held from 1879 to 1881, when he resigned to engage in banking and the brokerage business in Washington. He died in Georgetown, South Carolina, in 1887.

*See also* Amnesty; Civil Rights Act of 1875; South Carolina.

Maurine Christopher, *Black Americans in Congress* (New York, 1976); *Biographical Directory of the United States Congress, 1774–1989* (Washington, D.C., 1989).

**RANSIER, ALONZO JACOB** (1834–1882), Republican leader and Lieutenant Governor of South Carolina (q.v.), was born in Charleston, a free black who at the age of sixteen started working for a merchant as a shipping clerk. After the Civil War, he took a prominent part in the 1865 Friends of Equal Rights Convention at Charleston and was one of the delegates who went to Washington to present the gathering's memorial to Congress. Becoming active in the Republican party (q.v.), he served as chairman of its state central committee, as presidential elector, and as a member of the South Carolina constitutional convention of 1868–1869. A state legislator from 1868 to 1869, in 1870 he was nominated and elected Lieutenant Governor, defeating Confederate General Matthew C. Butler. In the graft-ridden Robert K. Scott administration that followed, he stood out because of his uncompromising honesty. After serving as president of the 1871 Southern Convention in Columbus and as a delegate to the Republican National Convention the next year—he was a firm supporter of U. S. Grant (q.v.)—he was elected to the Forty-third Congress (1873–1875).

In the House of Representatives, Ransier was a forceful advocate of civil rights legislation, but when the Civil Rights Bill of 1875 (Civil Rights Act of 1875, q.v.) was amended to delete the school clause, he vigorously opposed the change and, when the measure finally passed in its weakened version, refused to vote. He failed to be renominated partially because of factionalism in the party and partially because of his fearless attack upon the corruption of the Franklin J. Moses regime.

After the end of his term in Congress, Ransier was appointed collector of internal revenue for the Second District of South Carolina, a position he held until 1876. Losing his wife after the birth of his eleventh child, he began to suffer financial reverses and finally worked as a street cleaner in Charleston, where he died in 1882.

*See also* Civil Rights Act of 1875; South Carolina.

*Biographical Directory of the United States Congress, 1774–1989* (Washington, D.C., 1989); Maurine Christopher, *Black Americans in Congress* (New York, 1976).

**RAPIER, JAMES THOMAS** (1837–1883), black Alabama (q.v.) Republican leader and congressman, was born in Florence, Alabama, the son of a barber, John H. Rapier, and his wife, Susan, both free blacks. Educated at a black school in Nashville and at Buxton and Toronto in Canada, where the family owned property, he returned to the United States in 1864 to work as a journalist and to plant cotton in Maury Country, Tennessee. In 1865 he delivered the keynote address at the Tennessee Negro Suffrage Convention in Nashville, moved back to Florence the next year, and in 1867 served as a delegate to the first Alabama Republican convention. He was also elected to the state constitutional convention, in which he contended for moderate disfranchisement of ex-Confederates and provisions for equal accommodations for all races. After campaigning for U. S. Grant (q.v.) in 1868, he was forced to flee to Montgomery because of threats against his life but in 1870 was able to return and ran unsuccessfully for Secretary of State on the Republican ticket. Appointed an assessor of internal revenue in 1871, he found that he was unable to carry on his duties at Selma and moved his office to Montgomery, where the next year he founded the *Republican Sentinel* in preparation for a campaign for Congress. Elected in November 1872, he was sent as a commissioner to the Vienna International Exposition before taking his seat in the House.

In his one term in Congress, Rapier supported a measure of federal aid for Southern schools and a bill to make Montgomery a port of delivery, as well as legislation for the improvement of Alabama's waterways. He also spoke forcefully in favor of a civil rights bill (Civil Rights Acts, q.v.) but in 1874 was defeated for reelection. Trying to return to the House in 1876, after having rented a plantation in Lowndes County, he became a candidate from a district including his new home, but because the Republican vote was split between him and Jeremiah Haralson, another black contender, he was again unsuccessful. In 1878 he was appointed collector of revenue for the Second District of Alabama and in later years became interested in furthering black immigration to Kansas. In 1880 he attended his party's national convention in Chicago but was disappointed in the failure of his favorite, John Sherman (q.v.), to secure the nomination.

A highly educated and successful planter and businessman as well as an influential politician, in 1869 Rapier became the director of the Montgomery branch of the Freedman's Savings Bank (q.v.). He was also interested in the cause of black labor and played a prominent role in the organization of the National Negro Labor Convention in 1869. Three years later, he presided over the first meeting of the American Negro Labor Union. Although viciously attacked throughout his public career, particularly as collector, Rapier, a bachelor, was always able to prove his probity. He died in Montgomery in 1883.

*See also* Alabama; Freedman's Saving Bank.

Loren Schweninger, *James T. Rapier and Reconstruction* (Chicago, 1973).


**RAYMOND, HENRY JARVIS** (1820–1869), editor of the *New York Times*, was born near Lima, New York, the son of a farmer. Educated at the Genessee Wesleyan Seminary and the University of Vermont, he moved to New York City in 1840 to work for Horace Greeley (q.v.) at the *New-Yorker* and later the New York *Tribune*. In 1843 he joined James Watson Webb at the New York *Courier & Enquirer* but in 1851 broke with him because of differences about slavery, which Raymond opposed. That year, with the aid of George Jones and Edward B. Wesley, he founded the *New York Times*, with which he became permanently identified.

Closely cooperating with William H. Seward (q.v.) and Thurlow Weed, Raymond attended the 1848 Whig convention in Baltimore and in 1849 and 1850 was elected to the New York assembly, where in 1851 he served as speaker. Joining the anti-Nebraska coalition and becoming one of the organizers of the New York Republican party (q.v.), in 1854 he was elected Lieutenant Governor, thus alienating Greeley, who had ambitions for office himself. He wrote an address for the 1856 Republican convention in Pittsburgh, but he always remained a conservative, deploring the raid on Harper's Ferry and stressing the need for the maintenance of the Union. In 1860 he was disappointed at his friend Seward's failure to obtain the presidential nomination and gave only lukewarm backing to Abraham Lincoln (q.v.), although later he enthusiastically supported the Civil War President. In 1862 he was reelected to the Assembly and in 1863 again served as Speaker. A firm proponent of the renomination of Lincoln, he was chosen chairman of the National Union Executive Committee at the Baltimore Convention and directed the campaign leading to the President's reelection.

Raymond sympathized with many of Andrew Johnson's (q.v.) Reconstruction policies but maintained his independence on others. Like the President, he held that the seceded states were still members of the Union, but unlike Johnson, he favored the bill to enfranchise qualified blacks (q.v.) in the District of Columbia. He voted for the Freedmen's Bureau Bill (q.v.) but opposed the Civil Rights Act (q.v.) on constitutional grounds; nevertheless, despite Johnson's opposition, he supported the Fourteenth Amendment (q.v.).

In the summer of 1866, Raymond's equivocal position placed him in a difficult situation. Reluctantly backing the National Union Convention (q.v.) in Philadelphia, he took part in framing its resolutions but sought to prevent the Democrats from exerting undue influence upon it. It was partially upon his insistence that notorious Copperheads like Clement L. Vallandigham (q.v.) and Fernando Wood were kept out of the convention; yet after its adjournment he was unable to prevent the Unionist coalition from nominating the Democrat John T. Hoffman for governor of New York. Thereupon he broke with the movement and supported the Republican candidate, Reuben Fenton. Nevertheless, in September 1866 the majority of the Republican National Executive Committee had already voted for his deposition, and when Congress reassembled, he had great difficulty in being admitted to the Republican caucus. Still persevering in his conservatism, he opposed early efforts to impeach Johnson as well as the original House version of the first Reconstruction Act (q.v.) but finally supported the measure as amended in the Senate. Andrew Johnson's nomination of Raymond for minister to Austria was tabled.

Retiring from Congress in 1867, Raymond continued to edit the *Times*. He backed U. S. Grant (q.v.) in 1868 but opposed the impeachment of his predecessor. He died in New York in 1869.

*See also* Johnson, Andrew; National Union Convention; Seward, William Henry.

Francis Brown, *Raymond of the Times* (New York, 1951); Dorothy Dodd, *Henry J. Raymond and the New York "Times" During Reconstruction* (Chicago, 1936).

**READJUSTERS,** a group of independents in Virginia (q.v.) favoring the scaling down of the state's indebtedness by transferring some of it to West Virginia and refunding the rest in order to enable the state to meet its social and cultural obligations. Headed by General William Mahone (q.v.), the Readjusters relied on the support of western farmers and Tidewater and Southside blacks (q.v.). They succeeded in capturing the 1879 legislature and, with the aid of black votes, sent Mahone to the U.S. Senate.

During the next year's presidential election, the coalition of poor whites and blacks suffered a setback as the blacks refused to abandon the Republican party. When in 1881 Mahone's vote enabled the Republicans to organize the Senate, however, the coalition was restored so that it won the election that fall.

The result of the Readjuster victories was a reduction of the debt, the abolition of the whipping post and the poll tax, and the establishment of new schools for both races, including a black college. The Readjusters also increased patronage to the freedmen, authorized a black insane asylum, and admitted blacks to juries. Mahone even urged the nomination of a black congressman in the Southside, although in the end a white Republican was nominated.

The national Republican party's (q.v.) attitude toward the Readjusters was equivocal. After some hesitation, James A. Garfield (q.v.) supported them half-heartedly. Chester A. Arthur, on the other hand, tended to rely on them, at least until 1883. In fact, they offered the best chance of breaking the solid South, and the President was aware of this fact.

The effort to placate the blacks eventually spelled the doom of the movement. In 1883 the Funders, as the conservatives were known, launched an all-out attack of race-baiting that successfully defeated the Refunders. Racism thus triumphed over political and economic reform, and Virginia remained solidly Democratic.

*See also* Mahone, William; Virginia.

James T. Moore, "Black Militancy in Readjuster Virginia, 1879–1883," *Journal of Southern History*, 41 (1975), 167–86; Carl N. Degler, *The Other South: Southern Dissenters in the Nineteenth Century* (New York, 1974); Justus D. Doeneke, *The Presidencies of James A. Garfield and Chester A. Arthur* (Lawrence, Kans., 1981); Charles C. Pearson, *The Readjuster Movement in Virginia* (New Haven, 1917).

**RECONSTRUCTION, JOINT COMMITTEE ON,** established in December 1865 to inquire into the condition of the former Confederate States and to report whether any of them were entitled to representation. Although Thaddeus Stevens (q.v.) was partially responsible for the creation of the committee and continued to exert considerable influence on it, it consisted of moderates as well as conservatives, nine representatives and six Senators, and was chaired by the moderate William P. Fessenden (q.v.). In the beginning of 1866 it held extensive hearings about conditions in the South; interviewed 144 witnesses, including former Confederates, Unionists, and blacks (q.v.); and assembled a vast array of testimony concerning the plight of the latter. In the end, it wrote a strong report incorporating its findings and concluding that Andrew Johnson's policies (q.v.) were not sufficient to ensure Southern loyalty.

In addition to holding its hearings, the committee also reported the Fourteenth Amendment (q.v.) and the first Reconstruction Act (q.v.) Often depicted as an agency designed to deprive the South of its rights and to checkmate the President, its hearings constitute sufficient justification for its existence and form a good source for conditions in the South.

*See also* Johnson, Andrew; Stevens, Thaddeus.

Benjamin B. Kendrick, *The Journal of the Joint Committee of Fifteen on Reconstruction, 39th Congress, 1865–1867* (New York, 1914); Avery Craven, *Reconstruction: The Ending of the Civil War* (New York, 1969); J. G. Randall and David Donald, *The Civil War and Reconstruction* (Lexington, Mass., 1969); John Hope Franklin, *Reconstruction after the Civil War* (Chicago, 1961).

**RECONSTRUCTION ACTS,** a series of four measures providing the framework for Congressional Reconstruction (q.v.). After the refusal of the Southern states reorganized by Andrew Johnson (q.v.) to ratify the Fourteenth Amendment (q.v.), Congress proceeded to impose further conditions upon the South. The result, as reported by a committee headed by John Sherman (q.v.), was a compromise between radical demands, especially those put forward by Thaddeus Stevens (q.v.), and moderate counterproposals advocated by John A. Bingham (q.v.) and others. The first Reconstruction Act, passed March 2, 1867, over Johnson's veto, placed the ten unreconstructed states under military rule by dividing them into five military districts, each to be commanded by a general appointed by the President. In addition, elections based on universal suffrage modified by the exclusion of persons disfranchised for disloyalty or common crimes and those disqualified from office by the Fourteenth Amendment were to be held for constitutional conventions charged with the framing of basic laws including universal suffrage. After the adoption of these constitutions and the ratification of the amendment, the states were to be entitled to readmission. In the meantime, the Johnson governments were declared to be merely provisional.

Because of Southerners' refusal to initiate the constitutional processes outlined by this law, a supplementary measure became necessary. Enacted on March 23, 1867, it made the commanding generals of the five districts responsible for the administration of the registration process, spelled out the time frame for the elections as well as the voters' oath, required an ironclad oath (q.v.) of all registrars, and provided for the ratification of the constitutions by a majority of registered voters. This bill was again vetoed by the President, but Attorney General Henry S. Stanbery (q.v.) wrote an opinion that so restricted the legal powers of the military commanders and the registrars that on July 19, 1867, Congress passed a third Reconstruction Act in effect nullifying the Attorney General's interpretation. Stating that the Johnson governments were not legal and subject to the generals commanding, it conferred upon the latter the power to remove state officials and authorized registrars to determine the eligibility of voters by evidence in addition to the registrants' oath. Finally, it asserted succinctly that "all the provisions of this act and the acts to which this is supplementary shall be construed liberally, to the end that all the intents thereof may be fully and perfectly carried out." The President's veto of this bill was as unavailing as that of its predecessors.

Taking advantage of these arrangements, the conservatives in Alabama, eager to defeat Congressional Reconstruction, registered to vote but refused to cast ballots for the ratification of the new constitution, thus denying it the necessary majority. Thereupon Congress, on March 11, 1868, passed a fourth measure that became law without the President's signature and merely required a majority of the actual voters instead of a majority of those registered to ratify. Alabama's constitution was then declared to have been adopted.

Formerly considered the principal measures identified with so-called radical Reconstruction, the Reconstruction Acts have more recently been shown to have been framed in their final version largely as a result of moderate influences. They did, however, inaugurate Congressional Reconstruction (q.v.) within the states and thus marked the beginning of an entirely new phase of the Reconstruction process.

*See also* Bingham, John Armor; Congressional Reconstruction; Fourteenth Amendment; Johnson, Andrew; Sherman, John; Stanbery, Henry; Stevens, Thaddeus.

Michael Les Benedict, *A Compromise of Principle: Congressional Republicans and Reconstruction, 1863–1869* (New York, 1974); Eric Foner, *Reconstruction: America's Unfinished Revolution, 1863–1877* (New York, 1989); Rembert W. Patrick, *The Reconstruction of the Nation* (New York, 1967).

**"REDEMPTION,"** a term commonly used to describe the period following Congressional Reconstruction (q.v.). Allegedly "redeemed" from radical misrule, the Southern states considered themselves liberated and instituted new forms of government and race relations involving renewed subordination of the blacks (q.v.). Dominated by old-fashioned planters, the so-called Bourbons, who, like their French namesakes, supposedly never learned or forgot anything, the "Redeemer" governments instituted policies of extreme retrenchment, penury, and firm control of plantation labor. Although the freedmen were not yet denied all civil rights or the suffrage, they were kept under strict supervision. Hemmed in by legislation making any escape from virtual peonage almost impossible, they were confronted with difficult suffrage and registration procedures designed to reduce black participation in elections.

Because of the extravagance of many radical regimes, the "Redeemers" cut social services to such a degree that education, welfare institutions, and the penal system suffered considerably. In Florida (q.v.), the penitentiary system was abolished altogether, and there, as elsewhere, the custom of leasing out convicts extended. In Texas (q.v.), free public education was ended; in Alabama (q.v.) and Mississippi (q.v.), the entire burden of sustaining education shifted to local governments, and in most states, educational expenditures were greatly limited. As a result, in Louisiana (q.v.) the illiteracy rate actually increased. Various laws to enforce the obligations of tenants and sharecroppers were put upon the statute books, theft of live stock severely punished, and sales of seed at night prohibited. In some states, the firm alliance between governments and railroads was strengthened; in others, the old planter element remained dominant. Republican strength in the South precipitously declined, and the conservative Democratic party became the only viable political organization. The few pockets of Republican strength that remained (Eastern Tennessee, for example) were the exception. Black officeholding decreased sharply, although the last black congressman did not leave Washington until 1901.

The ''Redeemer'' regimes lasted until the 1890s, when combinations of Populists and Democrats completely disfranchised the blacks and instituted policies of total legal segregation.

*See also* Compromise of 1877; Congressional Reconstruction.

C. Vann Woodward, *Origins of the New South, 1877–1913* (Baton Rouge, 1951); Michael Perman, *The Road to Redemption: Southern Politics, 1869–1879* (Chapel Hill, N.C., 1984); Eric Foner, *Reconstruction: America's Unfinished Revolution, 1863–1877* (New York, 1989).

**REED, HARRISON** (1813–1899), Republican Governor of Florida (q.v.), was born near Lowell, Massachusetts, and after several moves taken by his parents to Castleton, Vermont, where his father kept a hotel. Educated at the Castleton Academy and apprenticed to a printer, he clerked in a store in Troy before immigrating to Wisconsin in 1836. He worked in a store in Milwaukee, did some farming, and became the editor of the Milwaukee *Sentinel.* He was also active in journalism in Madison and was one of the founders of the town of Neenah. An active Whig and later Republican, he was appointed to a position in the Treasury Department during the Lincoln administration. Saddened by the death of his daughter and wife, in 1863 he went to Fernandina, Florida, as a tax commissioner and sold confiscated property to freedmen at prices they could afford. But he fell out with one of his fellow commissioners, became estranged from Secretary Salmon P. Chase (q.v), and lost his position. In 1865, however, Andrew Johnson (q.v.) appointed him a special agent of the Post Office Department in Florida.

Settling in Jacksonville, Reed became a strong supporter of the President's Reconstruction policies. He edited the Jacksonville *Florida Times,* one of the state's leading Republican newspapers, but opposed the party's radical faction, the so-called Mule Team of Liberty Billings, Daniel Richards, and William O. Saunders, while enjoying friendly relations with former Confederates. Although he did not favor the Reconstruction Acts (q.v.), he succeeded in finally dominating the 1868 constitutional convention elected following their passage. Delegates beholden to him drew up a separate constitution agreeable to conservatives, which was eventually recognized in Washington in preference to the Mule Team's more radical document. It was under this constitution that Reed was then elected governor.

Reed's term of office was a stormy one. Although he tended to favor the conservatives, he was beset by Ku Klux Klan (q.v.) riots as well as by attacks of rival Republicans. An attempt in 1868 to impeach him was successful in the house, but no trial was held because he insisted that the Senate, before which the trumped-up charges were brought, did not have a quorum. Three more attempts at impeachment embittered his tenure; all but one failed, and on that occasion in 1872 the Senate eventually dismissed the spurious charges.

Reed's difficulties were due not only to the factionalism of Reconstruction Florida but also to the machinations of the railroads seeking state favors. Although he was honest, he was accused of taking bribes; a forged letter from the promoter George W. Swepson (q.v.) was used against him, and it was only with difficulty that he was able to give the state an administration that established schools, a university, and a penitentiary at reasonable cost.

After the end of his term, Reed, who had married Chloe Merrick, an instructor in freedmen's schools, retired to his farm and orange grove on the St. John's River. He edited *The Semi-Tropical* and in 1889 was appointed Postmaster by President Benjamin Harrison. Serving until 1893, he retired again and died in Florida in 1899.

*See also* Carpetbaggers; Florida; Johnson, Andrew.

Richard Nelson Current, *Those Terrible Carpetbaggers: A Reinterpretation* (New York, 1988); Jerrill H. Shofner, *Nor Is It Over Yet: Florida in the Era of Reconstruction, 1863–1877* (Gainesville, Fla., 1974); Richard N. Current, *Three Carpetbag Governors* (Baton Rouge, 1967).

**REPUBLICAN PARTY,** the political organization that originated in the 1850s in protest against the expansion of slavery and particularly the Kansas-Nebraska Act. Consisting of former Whigs, Know-Nothings, Free Soilers, and dissident Democrats, it emerged as the second major party in 1856 and in 1860 elected its presidential candidate, Abraham Lincoln (q.v.). In 1864 it briefly changed its name to National Union party and, to emphasize the change, nominated the War Democrat Andrew Johnson (q.v.) for Vice President.

In the meantime, the party, led by Lincoln and urged on by the radicals, had taken important steps toward emancipation (q.v.) and in 1865 succeeded in passing the Thirteenth Amendment (q.v.) abolishing the peculiar institution. Continuing to uphold the rights of freedmen after the war, it enacted the Fourteenth Amendment (q.v.) to safeguard their civil rights, the Fifteenth Amendment (q.v.) to give them the franchise, the Reconstruction Acts (q.v.) to help them secure power in the South, and civil rights and enforcement legislation to protect their gains. Although the reasons for the passage of these measures were mixed, often reflecting party needs as well as concern for the blacks (q.v.), the Republicans nevertheless deserve credit for persisting to press for them despite serious opposition, both from within their own ranks and from the Democrats.

The Republican party was always divided into factions. The radicals (Radical Republicans, q.v.) were at first devoted to an end of compromise with the South, then to emancipation, and finally to full civil rights for the freedmen, to be secured by thoroughgoing Reconstruction legislation; the conservatives, favoring speedy restoration of the South, believed the abolition of slavery was sufficient, and the moderates were somewhere in between. None of these was a permanent, strong grouping. Individuals moved easily from one position to the other, so these factions' strengths varied. The radicals, however, were generally in a minority. But all of them were devoted to the Republican ideal of free labor and individual enterprise, and although most favored some government aid to industry, their views on specific economic measures differed.

The party's factionalism continued during the Grant administration. Stalwarts loyal to the President fought Half-Breeds opposing some of his supporters, especially Roscoe Conkling (q.v.), and after 1871, dissatisfied Liberals broke away to form a Liberal Republican party (Liberal Republican Movement, q.v.) alienated from the President by his policies in the South, his diplomacy, and his attitude toward civil service reform (q.v.). Some of these later rejoined the party, only to reemerge as Mugwumps in the 1884 campaign.

To create a strong Republican base in the South proved to be difficult. Hampered by conservative opposition appealing to former Confederates, the party was further weakened by its appeal to the "bloody shirt" (q.v.) in the North, by racial animosities, and by the rivalry between native "scalawags" (q.v.) and Northern-born "carpetbaggers" (q.v.). In spite of some early signs of growing Republican strength in the border states and the Upper South, particularly among Unionist whites, in the long run white support failed to develop, except in Tennessee (q.v.). Party needs in the North caused the organization to funnel funds there; terror and loss of interest did the rest, until by the end of Reconstruction only a corporal's guard of faithful remained. Repeated efforts by Gilded Age Presidents to appeal either to conservatives or to dissidents in the South proved unavailing.

In the North, the Republicans appealed mainly to persons of Yankee origin, to Congregationalists, Presbyterians, Baptists, and Methodists disliking slavery but often prejudiced against blacks. The latter, too, voted Republican, and the party was strengthened by an addition of immigrants from Scandinavia and some groups of Germans. The large veterans' vote, particularly when marshaled by the Grand Army of the Republic (q.v.), was also a reliable source of support. The effort to encourage Republicans in the South by the organization of the Union League (q.v.) was only partially successful.

In spite of its difficulties, the Republican party, holding on to power in the House of Representatives until 1875, in the Senate until 1879, and in the White House until 1885, established a remarkable record in winning the Civil War and passing the three postwar amendments.

*See also* Congressional Reconstruction; Grand Army of the Republic; Presidential Reconstruction; Radical Republicans; Union League.

Arthur M. Schlesinger, Jr., ed., *History of U.S. Political Parties* (4 vols., New York, 1973), particularly the essay by David Herbert Donald, "The Republican Party, 1864–1876"; Richard B. Abbott, *The Republican Party and the South, 1855–1877* (Chapel Hill, N.C., 1986); William Starr Myers, *The Republican Party: A History* (New York,

1931); Hans L. Trefousse, *The Radical Republicans: Lincoln's Vanguard for Racial Justice* (New York, 1969).

**REVELS, HIRAM RHODES** (1827–1901), Senator from Mississippi (q.v.), was born a free black in Fayetteville, North Carolina. Educated in seminaries in Indiana, in Ohio, and at Knox College in Illinois, he became a minister of the African Methodist Episcopal Church and carried on religious work in the Midwest. In Baltimore, he was credited with raising two black regiments and in 1864 went to Vicksburg, Mississippi, to serve as a chaplain. In 1866 he was elected alderman in Natchez, where he was active as a minister, and in 1870 was sent to the state senate. That same year, he was elected to complete a term in the U.S. Senate, which expired on March 4, 1871, thus becoming the first black to enter Congress.

Revels' appearance in the Capitol created a sensation. After having been sworn in, he proved to be a man of moderate opinions who generally supported the administration of General U. S. Grant (q.v.). He favored the readmission of Georgia (q.v.), including the extension of the term of its legislature, to which the excluded black members had been readmitted. He introduced a measure for federal aid to construct and repair levees in Mississippi, spoke in support of the desegregation of schools in the District of Columbia, and, in spite of his admiration for Senator Charles Sumner (q.v.), voted for Grant's scheme to annex the Dominican Republic.

After his retirement from Congress, Revels, who settled in Hollis Springs, was appointed president of Alcorn University for Negroes and in 1873 served as Mississippi Secretary of State pro tem. Never a radical, he supported James Lusk Alcorn (q.v.) against Adelbert Ames (q.v.), who removed him from his post in 1874. He was seemingly unaffected by the violence in the Mississippi elections of 1875 and in November wrote a letter to the President accusing the Republican party of having become corrupt while suggesting that hate had been obliterated in the state. Consequently, it was not surprising that the resurgent Democrats reappointed him to the presidency of the university in 1876, a post he occupied until 1882. For the remainder of his life, he was active in church work and died in Aberdeen, Mississippi, in 1901.

*See also* Alcorn, James Lusk; Ames, Adelbert; Mississippi.

Elizabeth Lawson, *The Gentleman from Mississippi: Our First Negro Congressman, Hiram R. Revels* (New York, 1960); *Biographical Directory of the United States Congress, 1774–1989* (Washington, D.C., 1989).

**ROSS, EDMUND GIBSON** (1826–1907), Senator from Kansas, was born in Ashland, Ohio, the son of Sylvester Flint Ross and of Cynthia Rice. When he was eleven, he was apprenticed as a printer to the Huron *Advertiser*, thus starting a lifelong career in journalism. In 1841 he joined his father's printing firm in Sandusky and in the 1850s worked in Wisconsin, where, as an employee of Sherman Booth of the Milwaukee *Free Democrat*, he was present at the rescue of the fugitive slave Joshua Glover. Moving to Kansas in 1856, he continued his career in journalism. In 1862 he became a captain in the Eleventh Kansas Regiment, distinguished himself at Prairie Grove, and, promoted to major, took part in the later fighting along the Kansas-Missouri line.

Mustered out of the service in September 1865, Ross returned to Lawrence and engaged in Republican politics. He attacked Senator James H. Lane for supporting Andrew Johnson (q.v.), and after Lane's suicide in June 1866, Governor Samuel J. Crawford, impressed with Ross' war record, appointed him to the vacant seat. When the legislature met in January 1867, it elected Ross, aided by elements interested in Indian contracts, Senator in his own right.

Considered a reliable radical, Ross supported most measures in support of Congressional Reconstruction (q.v.). Thus he astonished his colleagues when during the impeachment trial of Andrew Johnson he deserted his party to vote "not guilty." He did so because he was afraid of loss of patronage if Benjamin F. Wade (q.v.), next in line to the presidency, should succeed Johnson and, after receiving assurances that the White House would not oppose the admission of South Carolina (q.v.) and Arkansas (q.v.), decided to sustain the President despite enormous pressure. The clamor for party regularity increased after the first vote on May 16, 1868, but the Senator remained steadfast and on May 26, during the final effort to convict Johnson, again voted for acquittal.

Because his name started with the letter "R", Ross' vote has often been described as crucial, and John F. Kennedy included him in his book *Profiles of Courage*. Ross' importance, however, has been exaggerated; other Senators further down the alphabet stood ready to opt for acquittal had their ballots been needed.

Immediately after the vote, Ross asked Johnson for positions for supporters, a request that was granted. Not reelected in 1871, he resumed his journalistic career in Coffeyville and, when a tornado destroyed his plant, in Lawrence. A Liberal Republican (Liberal Republican Movement, q.v.) in 1872, he was an unsuccessful Tilden elector in 1876 and a Democratic candidate for governor in 1880. Four years later he moved to Albuquerque, New Mexico, and in 1885 Grover Cleveland appointed him governor of the territory. At the conclusion of his term in 1889, he returned to his newspaper work and in 1896 published his *History of the Impeachment of Andrew Johnson* in which he tried to emphasize his service in saving the presidential form of government. He died in Albuquerque in 1907.

*See also* Impeachment of Andrew Johnson; Johnson, Andrew; Wade, Benjamin Franklin.

Edward Bumgardner, *Life of Edmund G. Ross: The Man Whose Vote Saved a President* (Kansas City, Mo., 1949); Mark A. Plummer, "Profiles in Courage? Edmund G. Ross and the Impeachment Trial," *Midwestern Quarterly*, 27 (Autumn 1985): 30–48; Hans L. Trefousse, *Impeachment of a President: Andrew Johnson, the Blacks, and Reconstruction* (Knoxville, 1975).

# S

SCALAWAGS, Southerners who collaborated with the Republicans during Reconstruction. Commonly vilified as traitors to their section, they do not deserve the opprobrious terms applied to them. Many, especially those in the hill country, were Unionists of long standing; others, former Whigs who detested the Democrats; and still others, small farmers in economic trouble. Some were even ex-Democrats eager for the social and economic development of the South. Nor were they, as their critics have charged, persons of no consequence. Many scalawags had long played important political roles in their states, and several belonged to the wealthy planter class. James L. Alcorn (q.v.) is a good example.

The scalawags' motives were often mixed. Anxious to avoid black rule, they attempted to control the Republican party (q.v.) while keeping the freedmen, whom they considered inferior, loyal to the organization without giving them lucrative positions. Realizing that the Republicans were going to be in power for some time, they decided to stake their careers on the success of the party of the future and joined with the carpetbaggers (q.v.) to govern their states. Although they often complained that the carpetbaggers obtained all the well-paying offices, in reality, it was generally the scalawags (especially in Alabama [q.v.]) who held the majority of elective and appointive positions. Although some scalawags, like Franklin J. Moses and George W. Swepson (q.v.), were corrupt, others, like James L. Orr and James L. Alcorn (q.v.), were undoubtedly honest.

The scalawags, who were generally moderates on the race and Reconstruction issues, were ill equipped to deal with the rampant racist campaigns waged by the conservatives. When this and other factors resulted in "Redemption" (q.v.), some scalawags rejoined the Democratic party (q.v.) while others remained Republicans in order to benefit from federal patronage. If their attempt to create a native Republican party (q.v.) of substance was unsuccessful in the end, they nevertheless made a valiant effort under difficult circumstances.

*See also* Alcorn, James Lusk; Carpetbaggers.

Sarah Woolfolk Wiggins, *The Scalawag in Alabama Politics, 1865–1881* (University, Ala., 1971); David Herbert Donald, "The Scalawags in Mississippi Reconstruction," *Journal of Southern History*, 10 (November 1944): 447–60; Otto Olsen, "Reconsidering the Scalawags," *Civil War History*, 22 (December 1966): 304–327; Allen Trelease, "Who Were the Scalawags," *Journal of Southern History*, 24 (November 1963): 445–68; Warren A. Ellen, "Who Were the Mississippi Scalawags," *Journal of Southern History*, 38 (May 1972): 217–40.

**SCHOFIELD, JOHN McALLISTER** (1831–1906), Union general, Secretary of War, and commander of the First Military District, was born in Gerry, Chautauqua County, New York, the son of a Baptist minister and his wife, Caroline McAllister. He was taken by his parents to Illinois in 1843, lived in Freeport, and entered West Point in 1849. Upon graduation in 1853, he served in several Southern posts until 1855, when he was appointed a professor of philosophy at West Point. Taking a leave of absence from the army in 1860, he accepted a professorship of physics at Washington University in St. Louis but when war broke out became a major and General Nathaniel Lyon's Adjutant General. He distinguished himself at Wilson's Creek, was promoted to the rank of brigadier general, and assumed command of the Missouri militia. In 1862 he held the positions of commanding general of the Military District of Missouri and then of the "Army of the Frontier"; in 1863, of the XIV Corps of the Army of the Cumberland and of the Department of the Missouri. Ordered the next year to take command of the Army of the Ohio, his troops generally constituted the left flank of William T. Sherman's (q.v.) forces in the campaigns leading to the capture of Atlanta. He again distinguished himself at Franklin, for which he received a brevet as major general; took part in the rout of his old West Point classmate John B. Hood in Nashville; and, as commanding general of the XXIII Corps, ended the war with Sherman in North Carolina.

When the fighting was over, Schofield, already in command of North Carolina (q.v.), suggested a scheme of Reconstruction similar to Andrew Johnson's (q.v.), except that it was to be carried out by the military. Transferred to the command of the Department of the Potomac, including Virginia (q.v.), in June 1865, in November he undertook a diplomatic mission to France to persuade Napoleon III to evacuate Mexico. Although opposing the Fourteenth Amendment (q.v.), he urged Virginians to ratify it to avoid worse terms. After the passage in spring 1867 of the Reconstruction Acts (q.v.), he was appointed commanding general of the First Military District, where he had already been well known because of his previous service in command of Virginia and enjoyed the confidence of even some of the conservatives.

As commandant of the First Military District, Schofield pursued moderate policies. Although he removed Governor Francis H. Pierpont (q.v.), whose mandate had expired, he interfered but little with the civilian government, initiated and directed the registration and voting process, and attempted to modify the severe disfranchisement clauses of the constitution. Failing to persuade the convention, he suspended the ratification elections, for which Congress had not appropriated any money, but was recalled to Washington when appointed Secretary of War following Johnson's acquittal. The readmission of Virginia had to await another session of Congress.

Schofield's choice as Secretary of War was the result of one of the concessions Johnson made to the moderates to secure the failure of the impeachment by guaranteeing his willingness to abide by the Reconstruction Acts. The general's tenure as Secretary of War enabled him to carry out the policies of Congress without coming into conflict with the President. He retired when U. S. Grant (q.v.) was inaugurated Johnson's successor.

After his resignation as Secretary of War, Schofield held several important commands: the Department of the Missouri from 1869 to 1870, the Department of the Pacific from 1870 to 1876, the Superintendency of West Point from 1876 to 1878, the Division of the Pacific in 1882, the Division of the Missouri from 1883 to 1886, and the Division of the Atlantic from 1886 to 1888. He served as President of the Fitzjohn Porter Board of Review and surveyed the site of Pearl Harbor. In 1888 he was appointed commanding general of the army and, in 1895, shortly before his retirement, lieutenant general. He died in St. Augustine, Florida, in 1906.

*See also* Impeachment of Andrew Johnson; Johnson, Andrew; Reconstruction Acts; Virginia.

James L. McDonough, *Schofield: Union General in the Civil War and Reconstruction* (Tallahassee, 1972); James Sefton, *The United States Army and Reconstruction, 1865–1877* (Baton Rouge, 1967); *New York Times*, March 5, 1906; John M. Schofield, *Forty-Six Years in the Army* (New York, 1897).

**SCHURZ, CARL** (1829–1906), immigrant leader, major general, Senator from Missouri, and Secretary of the Interior, was born in Liblar near Cologne, the son of a schoolteacher and the daughter of the local tenant-in-chief. Educated at a gymnasium in Cologne and the University of Bonn, Schurz, a radical democrat, took part in the Revolution of 1848 and barely avoided capture by fleeing through a sewer from the besieged fortress of Rastatt to reach the Rhine and safety in France. He returned to Germany in disguise to rescue his professor, Gottfried Kinkel, from a penitentiary in Spandau and escaped with him to Great Britain. Arriving in the United States in 1852, Schurz, now married to Margarethe Meyer, a rich merchant's daughter, settled in Watertown, Wisconsin, where he dabbled in journalism, real estate, and Republican politics. In 1857 he was nominated Lieutenant Governor, but although he lost while his running mates were successful and failed to obtain a gubernatorial nomination in 1859, he remained faithful to the party, which rewarded him with the chairmanship of the Wisconsin delegation to the 1860 national convention. He campaigned strenuously for Lincoln (q.v.), was appointed minister to Spain, but returned to join the army as a brigadier general in 1862. Taking part in the second Battle of Bull Run, he was promoted to major general and saw further action at Chancellorsville, Gettysburg, and in Tennessee.

After the war, Schurz, recognized as a leader of German-Americans, undertook a trip to the South for Andrew Johnson (q.v.). Considering the President's policies a failure, he freely voiced his opinion, so Johnson gave him a very cool reception upon his return. Nevertheless, the radicals used the report he wrote as a campaign document that castigated the results of Presidential Reconstruction (q.v.).

In 1867 Schurz moved to St. Louis to assume the editorship of the *Westliche Post*, a leading German newspaper in the Midwest. He delivered the keynote address at the Chicago convention, which nominated U. S. Grant (q.v.), and in early 1869 was elected Senator from Missouri (q.v.). But differences with the administration concerning civil service reform (q.v.); foreign policy, especially in the Dominican Republic; and Reconstruction, caused Schurz to break with Grant and to take a leading part in the Liberal Republican Movement (q.v.), first in Missouri and then in the country at large. His interest in conciliating the South carried him as far as to oppose the Ku Klux Act (Ku Klux Klan, q.v.), although he never abandoned his interest in equal rights for blacks (q.v.). He presided over the 1872 Liberal Republican convention in Cincinnati, only to be greatly disappointed at the nomination of Horace Greeley (q.v.), whom he supported only reluctantly. Failing of reelection to the Senate, he was appointed Secretary of the Interior by Rutherford B. Hayes (q.v.), a position in which he furthered civil service reform, the conservation of natural resources, and a more honest Indian policy.

At the expiration of his term of office, Schurz moved to New York to become, at least for a few years, one of the editors of the New York *Evening Post*. In 1884, disgusted with the nomination of James G. Blaine (q.v.), he was one of the Mugwumps supporting Grover Cleveland. In his later years, he devoted more and more time to the National Civil Service Reform League, represented the Hamburg-America steamship line in New York, and wrote editorials for *Harper's Weekly*. At the turn of the century, he became one of the country's foremost anti-imperialists. He died in New York in 1906.

Schurz's greatest achievement was to serve as a role model for his fellow German-Americans. Preaching assimilation as well as the retention of ethnic heritage, he was the most influential German-American of his time. If his devotion to black rights was temporarily eclipsed by his leadership in the Liberal Republican party, he recurred to it later and tirelessly advocated the freedmen's full integration into American society.

*See also* Civil Service Reform; Johnson, Andrew; Grant, Ulysses Simpson; Liberal Republican Movement.

Hans L. Trefousse, *Carl Schurz: A Biography* (Knoxville, Tenn., 1982); Claude M. Fuess, *Carl Schurz, Reformer* (New York, 1932).

**SEA ISLANDS,** isolated area off the coast of South Carolina (q.v.) seized by Union troops in November 1861, which became a laboratory for Reconstruction. Characterized by large plantations and a population consisting of a great number of slaves with few white owners, the Sea Islands were abandoned by the planters upon the approach of the Union fleet. The slaves, a Gullah-speaking group that had had little contact with the outside world, were left behind and became the object of solicitude for Northern benevolent societies. Secretary of the Treasury Salmon P. Chase (q.v.) commissioned Edward L. Pierce to take charge of them; a dedicated number of abolitionists, "the Gideonites," came to Port Royal and Beaufort to spread out on the neighboring islands and tried to accustom the blacks (q.v.) to the ways of freedom. They taught school, set up plantations employing free labor, and, attempting to transfer some land to the freedmen, inaugurated the process of Reconstruction. Land became available because of the owners' failure to pay taxes. Some of it was sold to blacks who, by planting crops on their own, had accumulated a little property, while other parcels passed into the hands of white newcomers, Treasury officials, as well as philantropist businessmen, who had a hard time overcoming their black laborers' resistance to planting cotton instead of crops less linked to slavery.

In April 1862 the Secretary of War placed General Rufus Saxton in charge of the experiment. Favorably inclined toward the aspirations of the blacks, Saxton sought to further their development. Nevertheless, friction developed between the army and the freedmen, who resented forced efforts at conscription and some of the soldiers' racist attitudes.

When in January 1865 General William T. Sherman (q.v.) set aside the Sea Islands and a strip thirty miles wide inland for the sole occupancy of freedmen, more blacks acquired titles to abandoned lands. The newly established Freedmen's Bureau (q.v.) rendered some help, but soon reaction set in. Determined to carry out his plans of "restoration," President Andrew Johnson (q.v.) in September issued orders for the return of land to former owners who had taken an oath of allegiance, and some of the blacks had to surrender their hard-won parcels of soil.

In the meantime, Northern ideas of political activity had spread among the freedmen. As early as 1864, a set of delegates was elected from Beaufort to attend the Union party National Convention in Baltimore and to press for black suffrage (q.v.). During the administration of U. S. Grant (q.v.), the Beaufort district habitually sent black legislators to Columbia and Washington, and because some of the freedmen still retained their farms, a comparatively strong black community continued to exist on the islands. With the coming of "Redemption," however, the freedmen gradually lost their political rights.

The Sea Island experiment, while not necessarily a model for Reconstruction everywhere, nevertheless was widely reported and could furnish a precedent for the integration of the freedmen into society.

*See also* Johnson, Andrew; Land Policies; Presidential Reconstruction; Sherman, William Tecumseh.

Willie Lee Rose, *Rehearsal for Reconstruction: The Port Royal Experiment* (Indianapolis, 1964).

**SENTER, DEWITT CLINTON** (1830–1898), Governor of Tennessee (q.v.), was born in McMinn County, the son of William T. Senter, a Methodist minister and later Whig congressman. Educated at an academy in Strawberry Plains, he studied law and was admitted to the bar in 1861. From 1857 to 1865 he served in the state House of Representatives as a delegate from the district including Grainger County, opposed secession, and was reelected in 1861. Continuing his opposition to the breakup of the Union, he was arrested by the Confederates but eventually released on parole and fled to safety in Union-held territory.

In 1865 Senter was a member of the constitutional convention and was elected to the state Senate. A conservative Republican, he took a strong stand against black enfranchisement and jury service. Reelected two years later, he became Speaker, an office placing him next in line to the Governor, and when Governor William G. Brownlow (q.v.) resigned to accept his election to the U.S. Senate, in February 1869 Senter succeeded him.

In the election that August, Senter sought a term in his own right. But his claims were challenged by congressman William B. Stokes, and in the ensuing contest, the Nashville Republican convention split. One faction nominated Senter, the other, Stokes, whereupon the Governor made common cause with disfranchised ex-Confederates, whose disabilities he sought to lift by various strategems. As the Democrats did not put up a candidate, Senter won overwhelmingly. A Democratic legislature was also elected, thus ushering in "Redemption" (q.v.) in Tennessee.

The new administration now reversed the course taken by Brownlow. The legislature removed the Franchise Law barring former Confederates from the ballot box and repealed legislation to control the Ku Klux Klan (q.v.), whereupon the Imperial Wizard declared the organization dissolved. Nevertheless, terrorism continued, and Senter had to ask for federal troops to quell disorders, a request with which the Grant administration failed to comply. The state militia was also disbanded. In addition, a new constitutional convention was called, which, while providing for universal male suffrage, nevertheless made the right to vote contingent on the payment of poll taxes.

Senter did not run again in the 1870 election under the new constitution. Ex-Confederate General John C. Brown, who had presided over the constitutional convention, was elected Governor. Senter left office in 1871 to retire to Morristown in Hamblin County, where he died in 1898.

*See also* "Redemption"; Tennessee.

Philip M. Hamer, *Tennessee: A History* (2 vols., New York, 1933); Alrutheus A. Taylor, *The Negro in Tennessee, 1865–1910* (Washington, D.C., 1941); Oliver Perry Temple, *Notable Men of Tennessee* (New York, 1912); John Trotwood Moore, ed., and Austin B. Foster, *Tennessee, the Volunteer State, 1709–1923* (4 vols., Chicago, 1923); Thomas B. Alexander, *Political Reconstruction in Tennessee* (Nashville, 1950).

**SEWARD, WILLIAM HENRY** (1801–1872), New York Governor, Senator, and Secretary of State, was born in Florida, Orange County, New York, the son of a county judge and local entrepreneur. He was educated at Union College, read law in Goshen and in New York City, and was admitted to the bar in 1822. Settling in Auburn, he married Frances Miller, a judge's daughter. He entered politics as a National Republican and Anti-Mason, and in 1830, with the help of his lifelong collaborator, Thurlow Weed, was elected to the state Senate. After an unsuccessful try for Governor in 1834, Seward, now a Whig, in 1838 and 1840 was elected the state's chief executive. He distinguished himself by refusing to extradite blacks to the South and by favoring education for immigrants and Catholics. In 1849 he entered the U.S. Senate, where he opposed the Compromise of 1850 by declaring that there was a higher law than the Constitution. Reelected in 1855, he rapidly rose to leadership in the new Republican party (q.v.), expressed his conviction that there was an ''irrepressible conflict'' between slavery and freedom, and confidently expected to be nominated for President in 1860. However, his close association with Weed, the hostility of the Know-Nothings, and the enmity of Horace Greeley (q.v.), with whom he had formerly collaborated, frustrated his hopes, and Abraham Lincoln (q.v.) obtained the nomination.

Although sorely disappointed, Seward remained one of the most influential of Republican statesmen. Lincoln appointed him Secretary of State, and after first attempting to impose his leadership upon the President, to whom he suggested a foreign war to stop secession, he loyally cooperated with his chief. In spite of his reputation for hostility to Great Britain, he successfully terminated the *Trent* affair caused by Captain Charles Wilkes' seizure of two Confederate envoys traveling on a British ship by surrendering them. He conducted foreign affairs in such a way that no other nation recognized the Confederacy or succeeded in interfering by mediating the Civil War. Yet because of his moderate attitude he was thoroughly distrusted by the radicals, so an effort was made to displace him during the cabinet crisis of December 1862. Only the adroit handling of the situation by Lincoln, who secured not only Seward's but also his rival Salmon P. Chase's (q.v.) resignation and then rejected both, enabled the Secretary to remain in the cabinet.

On April 14, 1865, while in bed because of injuries sustained in a carriage accident, Seward was attacked by Lewis Paine, one of John Wilkes Booth's coconspirators. The assassination attempt failed; Seward recovered to continue as Secretary of State in the cabinet of Andrew Johnson (q.v.). Conciliatory by nature, he sympathized with the President's Reconstruction policy, although at times he attempted to tone down the harsh language of Johnson's messages and vetoes. Although he sought to bridge the rift between the administration and Congress, his increased identification with the policies of his chief rendered him more and more unpopular with congressional Republicans, particularly the radicals, while Johnson's Democratic supporters also distrusted the former Whig. Yet in spite of frequent rumors of his resignation, he held on to his position until the end of Johnson's term.

Seward achieved his greatest diplomatic successes during the postwar period. Skillfully exerting pressure upon the French, he managed to effect their withdrawal from Mexico without recourse to war. His most significant triumph was the purchase of Alaska, then called Russian America, which he completed in 1867. His adroit handling of the transaction involving the payment of $7.2 million to the Russians overcame serious opposition in the Senate, which ratified the treaty, and finally even in the House, which, despite its hostility to the administration in general and to Seward in particular, voted the necessary funds. The Secretary's other expansionist schemes, such as his efforts to acquire the Danish West Indies and a naval base in the Dominican Republic, came to naught, although he was able to acquire Midway Island.

After the conclusion of his term of office, Seward retired to Auburn. Traveling widely, he undertook a trip around the world and devoted time to writing. He died in Auburn in 1872.

*See also* Foreign Affairs; Greeley, Horace; Johnson, Andrew.

Glyndon G. Van Deusen, *William Henry Seward* (New York, 1967).

**SEYMOUR, HORATIO** (1810–1886), Governor of New York and Democratic presidential candidate, was born in Pompey, New York, the son of a well-to-do merchant and canal commissioner. The family moved to Utica when he was barely ten, and he was educated in the local schools, at Geneva Academy, and at Partridge's Military Academy in Middletown, Connecticut. After reading law in Utica, he was admitted to the bar in 1832. Between 1833 and 1839 he served as military secretary to Governor William L. Marcy, in 1841 and 1843 was elected to the Assembly, and between 1842 and 1843 was Mayor of Utica. After marrying Mary Bleeker, the daughter of a wealthy Albany landowner, he devoted much of his time to managing his properties.

Seymour's consuming interest in the Erie Canal and his association with Marcy marked him as a Hunker, but in 1849, collaborating with John Van Buren, he sought to patch up the party rift by becoming a Softshell Democrat. Nominated for Governor in 1850, he lost to Washington Hunt, only to win two years later. During his term of office, he furthered the construction of canals but vetoed a prohibition law, an action that contributed to his defeat in 1854. He returned to Utica and took an interest in canals in Wisconsin.

The outbreak of the Civil War found Seymour in opposition to the Lincoln administration. A strong opponent of emancipation (q.v.), in 1862 he was again elected Governor of New York. His administration was marked by clashes with the federal government; he attempted to quell the New York draft riots of 1863 by addressing the crowd as "my friends" and vetoed a soldiers' franchise bill. In 1864 he presided over the Democratic convention, which nominated George B. McClellan on a peace platform, but he himself was defeated for reelection.

Seymour had announced his views on Reconstruction even before the end of the war. Long hostile to the Emancipation Proclamation (q.v.), which he considered unconstitutional, in his 1864 annual message as Governor he had called for a speedy restoration of the Southern states on the basis of local self-government. Never changing his mind, during the administration of Andrew

Johnson (q.v.) he continued to insist upon the right of the states to regulate their own affairs, including the suffrage, and vigorously opposed the Fourteenth Amendment (q.v.) as well as Congressional Reconstruction (q.v.).

In 1868 Seymour was the presiding officer of the New York Democratic national convention. Resisting the inflationary ideas of George H. Pendleton, he had favored the candidacy of Thomas A. Hendricks and then of Chief Justice Salmon P. Chase (q.v.). As the balloting proceeded, however, despite his repeated assertions that he was not a candidate, he was nominated after the Ohio delegation switched to him on the twenty-second ballot. His reluctant acceptance included a virtual repudiation of the party's soft-money platform. The subsequent campaign against the Republicans and U. S. Grant (q.v.) centered largely on the question of Congressional Reconstruction, which Seymour's running mate, Francis P. Blair, Jr. (q.v.), wanted to be immediately jettisoned by the next President. This attitude, Republican reminders of Seymour's actions during the draft riots, and the financial problem lost the Democrats enough votes to make victory unlikely, and the New Yorker was defeated in November.

After his unsuccessful bid for the presidency, Seymour remained active in politics in his city, state, and nation. In 1871 he collaborated with Samuel J. Tilden (q.v.) to contribute to the victory over William M. Tweed (q.v.) and Tammany Hall; in 1874 he refused an election to the Senate and in 1876 a nomination for Governor, and as late as 1880 he still campaigned vigorously for the Democratic ticket. He died in Utica in 1886.

*See also* Democratic Party; Grant, Ulysses Simpson; Ohio Idea; Tilden, Samuel Jones.

Stewart Mitchell, *Horatio Seymour of New York* (Cambridge, Mass., 1938); Adrian Cook, *Armies of the Streets: The New York City Draft Riots of 1863* (Lexington, Ky., 1974); Joel Silbey, *A Respectable Minority: The Democratic Party in the Civil War Era* (New York, 1977).

**SHARKEY, WILLIAM LEWIS** (1798–1873), Chief Justice and Provisional Governor of Mississippi (q.v.), was born near Mussel (or Muscle) Shoals in the Holston Valley of Tennessee, the son of Patrick Sharkey, a farmer from Ireland and his American wife. Taken by his parents to Warren County, Mississippi, as a child, he was educated in Greeneville, Tennessee, read law in Lebanon and Natchez, and was admitted to the bar in 1822. In 1825 he moved to Natchez to practice his profession. Elected to the legislature in 1828 and 1829, he became a circuit judge in 1832 and then was elected Chief Justice of the Mississippi High Court of Errors and Appeal, a position he held for the next eighteen years. A conservative Whig slaveholder, he presided over the 1850 Southern Nashville Convention, opposed radical measures, and was offered the post of Secretary of War, which he declined. He was a convinced Unionist who favored the Bell-Everett ticket in 1860 and continued to resist secession until he was able to take the oath of allegiance to the Union in 1863.

After the war, Andrew Johnson (q.v.) appointed Sharkey Provisional Governor of Mississippi. He failed to take seriously the President's suggestion that, for strategic reasons, the suffrage be extended to a few freedmen, although he directed that black testimony be admitted in the courts. At the expiration of his term, he was elected to the U.S. Senate but was never seated. A passionate advocate of the Presidential Plan of Reconstruction (q.v.), he favored the 1866 Philadelphia National Union Convention (q.v.), opposed the Fourteenth Amendment (q.v.), and reluctantly endorsed a compromise plan worked out by North Carolina. When the Reconstruction Acts (q.v.) were passed instead, he joined in the effort to block them by filing the injunction suit of *Mississippi* v. *Johnson* (q.v.) which he lost. Nothing daunted, he became one of counsel in the *McCardle* case (*McCardle, ex parte,* q.v.) and was greatly disappointed at its failure. Although a convinced Whig, to fight against Reconstruction he finally joined the Democratic party. Toward the end of his life, he practiced law in Jackson and in Washington, where he died in 1873.

*See also McCardle, Ex Parte*; Mississippi; *Mississippi* v. *Johnson*; Presidential Reconstruction.

L. Marshall Hall, "William L. Sharkey and Reconstruction, 1866–1873," *Journal of Mississippi History*, 27 (February 1965): 1–17; James D. Lynch, *The Bench and Bar of Mississippi* (New York, 1881); William C. Harris, *Presidential Reconstruction in Mississippi* (Baton Rouge, 1967); Dan T. Carter, *When the War Was Over: The Failure of Self-Reconstruction in the South, 1865–1867* (Baton Rouge, 1985); *Dictionary of American Biography*, ed. Allan Johnson (17 vols., New York, 1927–1988), 19.

**SHERIDAN, PHILIP HENRY** (1831–1888), Union cavalry leader and commanding general of the Fifth Military District, was probably born in Albany, New York, the son of Irish immigrants who settled in Somerset, Ohio, where he grew up. Only five feet, five inches tall, wiry, and aggressive, Sheridan graduated from West Point in 1853 and then saw service in Texas, California, and the Northwest. As captain of the Thirteenth Infantry, in 1861 he was assigned to Henry W. Halleck's staff in Missouri and then acted as quartermaster for General Samuel R. Curtis as well as for Halleck. Promoted to colonel of the Second Michigan Cavalry in 1862, he distinguished himself at Boonville, was rewarded with a brigadier general's star, and took part in the battles of Perryville and Stone's River. Now a major general, he commanded a division at Chickamauga and Missionary Ridge. In 1864 he was transferred to command the cavalry of the Army of the Potomac; defeated J.E.B. Stuart, who was killed at Yellow Tavern; and in September took over all forces in the Shenandoah Valley. Winning the battles of Winchester and Fisher's Hill, he achieved national renown at Cedar Creek by his famous ride to rally the fleeing troops and turning defeat into victory. After thoroughly devastating the valley, he finished the war in operations around Petersburg, at Five Forks, and Appomattox.

With the return of peace, Sheridan, who sympathized with the radicals, was sent to the Texan frontier to put pressure on the French to evacuate Mexico. In command of Louisiana (q.v.) and Texas (q.v.) during the New Orleans riot (q.v.), in his report he characterized the affair as an outrage instigated by the police and blamed the mayor, a passage deleted by Andrew Johnson (q.v.). Under the Reconstruction Acts (q.v.), Sheridan was put in charge of the Fifth Military District, in which he sought to carry out fully the aims of Congress. He removed various refractary state and local officials, including the Governors of Texas and Louisiana, and saw to it that the voting registration provisions were strictly enforced. These measures brought him into conflict with the President, who removed him in August and transferred him to the Department of the Missouri.

In his new post, Sheridan was engaged mainly in Indian fighting. He defeated the Cheyenne at the Washita and continued his operations after succeeding William T. Sherman (q.v.) as lieutenant general and commander of the Division of the Missouri when his friend U. S. Grant (q.v.) assumed the presidency. With headquarters at Chicago, the division comprised much of the Mississippi Valley as well as the entire region between the river and the Rockies. Sheridan thus presided over the "pacification" of numerous Indian nations, including the Cheyenne, Apaches, Sioux, and others. In 1870 he went to Europe to observe the Prussian army in action during the Franco-Prussian War. In 1874 he returned to Louisiana at the behest of President Grant to straighten out that state's tangled political affairs. Greeted with hostility by the white population, he determined to crush terrorism. Troops under his command entered the state legislature to remove several Democratic members who had been seated under questionable circumstances. Proposing to the Secretary of War that Congress declare the White Leagues (q.v.) "banditti," he asserted that he would then have little trouble controlling the state. His actions caused a great outcry throughout the country, and his military interference in legislative affairs was widely criticized.

Returning to Chicago, he married Irene Rucker, the daughter of his quartermaster general, who was twenty years younger than he. He resumed his warfare with "refractory" Indian nations and in 1883 became general-in-chief of the army. Promoted to full general in 1888, he died soon afterward in Nonquitt, Massachusetts.

*See also* Grant, Ulysses Simpson; Kellogg, William Pitt; Louisiana; New Orleans Riot.

Richard O'Connor, *Sheridan the Inevitable* (Indianapolis, 1953); Paul Andrew Hutton, *Philip Sheridan and His Army* (Lincoln, Neb., 1985).


**SHERMAN, JOHN** (1823–1900), moderate Republican Senator, Secretary of the Treasury, and Secretary of State, was born in Lancaster, Ohio, the son of Charles and Mary Hoyt Sherman and the brother of William Tecumseh Sherman (q.v.). After his father, a lawyer and judge, died when John was a child, he was brought up by a paternal cousin in Mt. Vernon. Educated at the public schools in Mt. Vernon and Lancaster, he read law with his brother Charles in Mansfield and was admitted to the bar in 1844. He was elected to Congress as an antislavery Whig in 1854, rendered a report on the Kansas troubles in 1856, was twice reelected as a Republican, and was a candidate for Speaker of the

House in 1859. Deprived of this honor because of his endorsement of Hinton Rowan Helper's book *The Impending Crisis of the South*, in 1861 he was elected to the Senate, where Salmon P. Chase (q.v.) relied on him to pass the Legal Tender and National Banking Acts.

During Reconstruction, as a moderate Republican, he sought to bridge the gap between Congress and President Andrew Johnson (q.v.) but was alienated by the President's veto of the Civil Rights Bill (Civil Rights Acts, q.v.). During the debates on the Fourteenth Amendment (q.v.), he attempted to change it in such a way that the suffrage would be based on the number of actual voters, and his final version of the Reconstruction Bill in the Senate secured provisions for the eventual readmission of the affected states. He opposed the Tenure of Office Act's (q.v.) applicability to members of the cabinet and was the author of the compromise formula that could be understood as either covering or excluding the Secretary of War. Consequently, while he agreed to the conviction of the President on the articles of impeachment actually submitted to a vote, the Senate never took up Article I concerning the dismissal of Stanton, which Sherman could not have supported. During the negotiations leading to the Compromise of 1877 (q.v.), he was one of the Senators arranging the final terms.

Sherman was particularly interested in financial affairs. Opposed to Secretary Hugh McCulloch's efforts to retire the greenbacks (q.v.) immediately after the war, he was the author of the law of 1874 calling for the resumption of specie payments by 1879 as well as the Silver Purchase Act of 1890, which was a compromise to satisfy the silver elements. In 1877 Rutherford B. Hayes (q.v.) appointed him Secretary of the Treasury; in 1880, 1886, and 1892 he was reelected to the Senate, over which he presided from 1885 to 1887, and in 1890 he gave his name to the Sherman Anti-Trust Act, the first measure seeking to control the formation of combinations in business. A candidate for the presidential nomination in 1880, 1884, and 1888, he failed to secure the prize. In 1897 William McKinley appointed him Secretary of State, but he was too feeble to carry out his duties efficiently and resigned in 1898. He died in Washington in 1900.

*See also* Greenbacks; Johnson, Andrew; Sherman, William Tecumseh; Tenure of Office Act.

Theodore E. Burton, *John Sherman* (Boston, 1906); Hans L. Trefousse, *The Radical Republicans: Lincoln's Vanguard for Racial Justice* (New York, 1969); Patrick Riddleberger, *1866: The Critical Year Revisited* (Carbondale, Ill., 1979); *New York Times*, October 23, 1900.

**SHERMAN, WILLIAM TECUMSEH** (1820–1891), Union general, was born in Lancaster, Ohio, the son of Charles Sherman, a lawyer and later judge. Upon his father's death, young Sherman was raised by Thomas Ewing, his father's protégé and future Whig Senator and member of the cabinet, whose daughter Ellen he eventually married. Educated at West Point (class of 1840), he served in various western and especially southern posts but resigned from the army in

1853 to engage in the law, business, and banking. In 1859 he was appointed superintendent of the Military Academy of Louisiana.

Sherman's long stay in the South had made him sympathetic to Southern notions of race relations. Yet he was a loyal Unionist, and when Louisiana seceded, he resigned to assume the presidency of a traction company in St. Louis. Rejoining the army in May 1861 as a colonel of the Thirteenth Infantry, he participated in the first Battle of Bull Run and was promoted to brigadier general. After a troublesome tour of duty in the Department of the Cumberland, where he was even accused of insanity, he was transferred to Henry W. Halleck's command, and in April 1862 he distinguished himself at Shiloh. Promoted to major general, in May 1862 he was placed in command of Memphis and served under U. S. Grant (q.v.), who became a close friend. Repulsed at Chickasaw Bluffs, he took part in the capture of Arkansas Post and the Vicksburg campaign. In November 1863 he commanded the left wing in the battles around Chattanooga, and after Grant became general-in-chief, Sherman took over all the armies in the West, a position that enabled him to undertake the successful campaign leading to the capture of Atlanta in September 1864. This was followed by the unprecedented march to the sea, in which the troops, living off the country, inflicted great damage upon Georgia's economy. Turning north into South Carolina, Sherman's army wreaked vengeance upon that hated state, pursued Joseph E. Johnston into North Carolina, and finally accepted his surrender.

While merciless in waging war, Sherman believed in a mild peace. He had no sympathy with the aspirations of the blacks and opposed the Emancipation Proclamation (q.v.), although in January 1865 he issued Special Field Order No. 15 setting aside the Sea Islands (q.v.) and a strip of land extending thirty miles inland for the occupancy of the freedmen who were to receive forty acres each. Convinced that the war was being fought merely for the maintenance of the Union, in April 1865 he negotiated an armistice with Johnston and Confederate Secretary of War John C. Breckinridge that would have permitted the Southern legislatures to reassemble and called for the surrender of all remaining Southern armies. It contained no reference to slavery, but Sherman was convinced that he was merely carrying out the wishes of Abraham Lincoln (q.v.), whom he had met shortly before aboard the *River Queen* at City Point and who had apparently told him to end the war as quickly as possible. As the President himself had offered to allow the Virginia legislature to take the state out of the Confederacy, Sherman was under the impression that he could offer similar terms to Johnston. But by the time of Sherman's armistice, Lee had already surrendered at Appomattox; the Confederacy was clearly lost, and Lincoln, who had long made all negotiations dependent upon emancipation, had withdrawn the offer to the Virginia legislature. Then the President was assassinated, and his successor, Andrew Johnson (q.v.), countermanded the armistice. Secretary of War Edwin M. Stanton (q.v.) even intimated that Sherman was acting from improper motives. When General Grant in person informed Sherman of the government's disapproval, a new armistice with purely military terms was negotiated. Sherman, however, was so furious about Stanton's insults that during the grand review of the army in Washington he refused to shake the Secretary's hand.

The general was fully in sympathy with the Reconstruction policies of the President and bitterly opposed to the radicals' demands for black suffrage (q.v.). Enjoying Johnson's goodwill, in July 1865 he assumed command of the Department of the Mississippi. Promoted to lieutenant general one year later, in November 1866 he accompanied the American minister to Mexico. In January 1868 he came to Washington to recodify army regulations and collaborated with Grant in the controversy with Johnson about the surrender of the War Department to Stanton. Sherman suggested that the President appoint Jacob D. Cox Secretary of War; Johnson, however, wanted to elevate Sherman himself. Upon the latter's refusal, the President attempted to establish a Division of the Atlantic to keep Sherman in Washington, but the general insisted upon returning to St. Louis.

When Grant assumed the presidency, Sherman succeeded him as general in chief, a position he occupied until his retirement in 1883. Stationed in Washington and St. Louis, he was extremely popular and in 1875 refused an offer of the presidency. That year he published his *Memoirs*, which caused considerable controversy, Jefferson Davis (q.v.) and Pierre Gustave Toutant Beauregard especially taking offense. In 1884 Sherman once again refused to be considered for the presidency, this time declaring that he would not accept if nominated nor serve if elected. In 1886 he moved to New York, where he died in 1891.

*See also* Grant, Ulysses Simpson; Johnson, Andrew; Land Policies; Stanton, Edwin M.

James M. Merrill, *William Tecumseh Sherman* (Chicago, 1971); Lloyd Lewis, *Sherman: Fighting Prophet* (New York, 1932); Basil H. Liddell Hart, *Sherman: Soldier, Realist, American* (New York, 1929); LaWanda Cox, "The Promise of Land for the Freedmen," *Mississippi Valley Historical Review*, 45 (1958): 413–40.

**SICKLES, DANIEL EDGAR** (1819–1914), Union general and commander of the Second Military District, was born in New York, the son of George G. Sickles, a successful lawyer, and of Susan Marsh Sickles. Educated at an academy at Glens Falls and the University of New York, he worked intermittently as a typesetter, studied law with Attorney General Benjamin F. Butler, and was admitted to the bar in 1846. He was a Hunker Democrat, active in Tammany Hall, and in 1847 was elected to the state Assembly. While serving as James Buchanan's secretary of the legation in London from 1853 to 1855, he took part in the drafting of the Ostend Manifesto for the acquisition of Cuba. In 1857 and 1859 he was elected to Congress, but his career seemed to be cut short when he shot to death his wife's lover, Philip Barton Key, the district attorney of Washington. Indicted for murder, Sickles was defended by Edwin M. Stanton (q.v.), who procured an acquittal on a then novel plea of temporary insanity, and to the horror of society, the couple were later reunited.

In 1861 Sickles raised the Excelsior Brigade in New York. Appointed brigadier general of U.S. Volunteers, his commission was not confirmed until 1862, but after taking part in the Peninsular Campaign, he was promoted to major general and given command of the Third Corps, which he led at Chancellorsville, Antietam, and Gettysburg. On the second day of that battle, without authority from the commanding general, he chose an advance line and lost a leg in the ensuing Confederate attack. His active military career was over, but he continued in the army, sought vindication from the Joint Committee on the Conduct of the War, and established close relations with the White House. In 1864 Abraham Lincoln (q.v.) sent him on a fact-finding tour to Tennessee, Louisiana, and Arkansas, and the general, a War Democrat, endorsed the President's reelection. Early in 1865 he was entrusted with a diplomatic mission to Colombia.

After the war, Sickles secured command of the Department of South Carolina, and in 1867, after the passage of the Reconstruction Acts (q.v.), was placed in charge of the Second Military District consisting of North and South Carolina (q.v.). Combining a policy of rigor with one of compassion, he forbade the possession of firearms and acts of discrimination, and he cooperated with Governor James L. Orr of South Carolina by issuing General Order No. 10 ending imprisonment for debt and delaying foreclosures. After he refused to obey a writ of habeas corpus issued by a federal judge, he incurred the displeasure of President Andrew Johnson (q.v.), who removed him in August 1867. Now a wholly committed radical, he fully supported the impeachment of the President and later maintained that, by remaining in the home of the sculptress Vinnie Ream almost all night before the vote, he had vainly tried to convince Senator Edmund G. Ross (q.v.) not to desert the party, an occurrence not borne out by contemporary evidence.

After campaigning for U. S. Grant (q.v.) and the latter's election, Sickles was appointed minister to Spain. He attempted to bring about the sale of Cuba and intrigued against the government to which he was accredited, but he resigned in 1874 following the transfer of negotiations to Washington after the *Virginius* incident. Moving briefly to Paris, he returned to New York in 1879, and in the Republican convention of 1880 was active in the unsuccessful movement for a third term for Grant.

During the remainder of his long life, Sickles was busy as head of the New York Monuments Commission, as the chairman of the New York Civil Service Commission (1887), and as sheriff of New York (1890). Rejoining the Democrats, in 1892 he was once more elected to the House of Representatives, where he was instrumental in the passage of a bill for the purchase of the Gettysburg battlefield by the federal government. He was defeated for reelection, broke with the Democrats, and in 1896 supported William McKinley.

Sickles had married a second time in Spain but lived apart from his wife. Still active in the task of erecting monuments at Gettysburg, during the last years of his life he narrowly escaped prison because of his failure to account for discrepancies in the records of the New York Monuments Commission. The amount in question was raised by friends, and he died in New York in 1914 at the age of ninety-five.

*See also* Impeachment of Andrew Johnson; Johnson, Andrew; Reconstruction Acts.

W. A. Swanberg, *Sickles the Incredible* (New York, 1956); Edgcumb Pinchon, *Dan Sickles: The Yankee King of Spain* (Garden City, N.Y., 1945); James Sefton, *The United States Army and Reconstruction, 1867–1877* (Baton Rouge, 1967); Joel Williamson, *After Slavery: The Negro in South Carolina During Reconstruction, 1861–1867* (New York, 1965).

**SLAUGHTERHOUSE CASES,** 1873 Supreme Court decision curtailing the application of the Fourteenth Amendment. In 1869 the legislature of Louisiana passed a law mandating that all landing and butchering of livestock take place on the premises of the Crescent City Stock Landing and Slaughterhouse Company, thus conferring a monopoly upon that corporation. The butchers of the city, resenting this interference with their trade, then filed a suit challenging the monopoly's constitutionality. Their counsel, former Associate Justice John A. Campbell, argued that the law violated the Thirteenth Amendment (q.v.) as well as the due process clause of the Fourteenth (q.v.). When the suit reached the Supreme Court in 1873, a five to four majority decided that the butchers had no case because the Thirteenth Amendment applied only to personal servitude and the Fourteenth protected only federal- but not state-derived rights. In fact, wrote Justice Samuel Miller, speaking for the majority, the amendments had been designed merely to protect the rights of the newly freed blacks (q.v.). The minority, and particularly Justice Stephen Field, disagreed and held that the amendment did indeed affect the states' police powers.

The result of this decision, the first important case testing the Fourteenth Amendment, was to limit severely the powers of the federal government to make use of the due process and equal protection clauses in upholding the rights of the blacks. Although in later years the minority opinion was generally accepted in decisions favoring laissez faire, the blacks did not benefit from this interpretation.

*See also* Fourteenth Amendment; Supreme Court; Thirteenth Amendment.

Harold M. Hyman and William M. Wiecek, *Equal Justice Under Law: Constitutional Development, 1835–1875* (New York, 1982); Charles Fairman, *Reconstruction and Reunion, 1864–88*, Vol. 6 of the Oliver Wendell Holmes Devise, *History of the Supreme Court of the United States, 1864–88* (New York, 1971); Stanley Kutler, *Judicial Power and Reconstruction Politics* (Chicago, 1968).

**SMALLS, ROBERT** (1839–1915), black congressman from South Carolina (q.v.), was born a slave in Beaufort. Employed as a house servant, he was taken to Charleston in his youth, worked as a lamplighter, rigger, stevedore, and pilot and was permitted to hire himself out. He made enough money to effect a deal for the purchase of his wife and child to set them free.

The Civil War brought Smalls national fame. Spiriting away the steamer *Planter* with its black crew, his family, and its cargo of artillery and sailing it past the fortifications of Charleston for delivery to the Union, he was commissioned a second lieutenant in the army and employed in piloting the ship along the Atlantic coast. He also went North to enlist support for the Port Royal experiment on the Sea Islands (q.v.).

After the war, Smalls acquired real estate and founded a black school in Beaufort. Having attended the Union National Convention in Baltimore in 1864, he became one of the organizers of the Beaufort Republican club and was a delegate to the state constitutional convention in 1868. A moderate on disfranchisement, he stood out for his interest in measures favoring compulsory universal education as well as the exemption of homesteads from court action. After the adjournment of the convention, he was elected to the Assembly and in 1870 and 1872, in the latter year against determined opposition, to the state Senate. A committed advocate of the enforcement of civil rights legislation, as a legislator he also sought to curb the prevalent financial extravagance.

In 1874 and 1876 Smalls was elected to the national House of Representatives. Defeated in 1878, he ran again two years later, when he successfully challenged the victory claimed by his opponent, George Tillman, and served another term in Congress. After losing his bid for renomination in a three-way contest in 1882, he threw his support to Edward M. Mackey, who was elected. Upon the winner's death, Smalls won the congressional seat for the unexpired term as well as for the new one in 1884. He was finally ousted in 1886 and did not run for Congress again.

While in Washington, Smalls distinguished himself by fearlessly speaking out against the injustices committed against his race, particularly the excesses of "Redemption" (q.v.). He strongly supported a bill facilitating the purchase of federally owned land with the result that by 1890 three-fourths of the land in Beaufort was owned by blacks (q.v.). Able to speak Gullah, he enjoyed the trust of the black majority in his district but was hated by the "Redeemers." They even indicted him on charges of bribery. Although probably innocent, he was found guilty upon dubious evidence, only to be pardoned as a result of a deal with the Democrats.

During his later years, Smalls remained active in the Republican party (q.v.). From 1889 to 1894, and again from 1898 to 1913, he served as collector of Beaufort. He was a delegate to many Republican national conventions between 1868 and 1900 and in 1884 the Republican candidate for the U.S. Senate. In the constitutional convention of 1895, he sought to avert the virtual disfranchisement of his race but was unable to prevail against the Democratic majority. Never abandoning his faith in the "party of Lincoln," he died in Beaufort in 1915.

*See also* "Redemption"; Sea Islands; South Carolina.

Okon Edet Uya, *From Slavery to Public Service: Robert Smalls, 1939–1915* (New York, 1971).

**SOUTH CAROLINA,** one of the states subject to Reconstruction. Badly devastated during the Civil War, South Carolina did not have any kind of civil government until Andrew Johnson (q.v.) on June 30, 1865, appointed Benjamin

F. Perry Provisional Governor in accordance with the Presidential Plan of Reconstruction (q.v.). Perry then called for an election of a convention by those having the suffrage in 1860; the convention met, instituted some democratic electoral reforms, abolished slavery, and nullified the secession ordinance. But it refused to extend the franchise to any blacks (q.v.) or to repudiate the Confederate debt.

The legislature elected under the new dispensation showed little more political wisdom. Although it ratified the Thirteenth Amendment (q.v.), it passed a black code (q.v.) of great severity, which relegated the black majority to a status little better than slavery. The election of the ex-Confederate James L. Orr to succeed Perry ushered in a renewed period of conservatism.

When in 1867 Congress passed the Reconstruction Acts (q.v.), South Carolina underwent a complete change in government. A new constitutional convention with a black majority not only enfranchised the freedmen and sought to protect their economic rights but also set up a universal free public school system. The constitution it wrote was so well framed that it was retained for many years after the end of radical rule.

In the elections that followed the Republicans won the governorship with the Ohio carpetbagger Robert A. Scott. They also carried both houses of the legislature as well as the state's congressional districts. A majority of the Assembly consisted of blacks, who, together with their scalawag (q.v.) and carpetbagger (q.v.) allies, dominated South Carolina for the next nine years.

Faced with grave difficulties in rebuilding the state in the midst of the unrelenting hostility of the whites, the new government attempted to set up schools; to contribute to economic development, particularly by aiding various railroads; and to establish welfare institutions. But the process soon became enmeshed in corruption, especially in connection with the railroads, and by 1871 the Governor, who despite the emergence of a Union Reform party had been reelected in 1870, was threatened with impeachment. Although the effort failed, extensive Ku Klux Klan (q.v.) activity could only be stayed by federal intervention. In 1872 the corrupt Adjutant General, Franklin J. Moses, Jr., was nominated for Governor and defeated a bolting faction led by Reuben Tomlinson; however, during the next two years the orgy of spending and corruption was such that reform forces headed by the Republican carpetbagger Daniel H. Chamberlain (q.v.) took over in 1874, when he beat the independent John T. Greene.

In the meantime, the state had sent some able blacks to Congress. In 1871 Joseph H. Rainey (q.v.), Richard H. Cain, and Robert Brown Elliott (q.v.) entered the House, followed in 1873 by Alonzo J. Ransier (q.v.) who had previously been lieutenant governor (1871–1873). Some of these congressmen, particularly Elliott, distinguished themselves by able speeches in favor of Charles Sumner's Civil Rights Bill (Civil Rights Acts, q.v.).

Although Governor Chamberlain sought to reform the administration, corrupt practices continued. When the legislature elected two dubious candidates to judgeships, Chamberlain refused to commission them, and his approaches to the conservatives estranged him from other Republicans. The party became so faction-ridden that it enabled the conservatives to try for a comeback. At first some of the latter tried to cooperate with Chamberlain, but after the Hamburg Massacre (q.v.) in July 1876, which the Governor denounced in no uncertain terms, and other terrorist activities, they endorsed the candidacy of Wade Hampton (q.v.), a Confederate general who ran against Chamberlain in the ensuing election. The outcome was in doubt; widespread fraud and intimidation resulted in the emergence of two governments, one Democratic and one Republican, which for a few days jointly occupied the house. The Electoral Commission (q.v.) in Washington awarded the state's electoral vote to Rutherford B. Hayes (q.v.), the Republican presidential candidate, but the latter's subsequent withdrawal of federal troops caused the fall of Chamberlain's government, so that the "Redeemers" ("Redemption," q.v.) were able to take over. Enacting various measures to impede black voting, they gradually reduced the black majority to impotence, until in 1895 a new constitution finally signalized the end of all vestiges of Reconstruction by giving sanction to a strict policy of racial segregation.

*See also* Chamberlain, Daniel Henry; Congressional Reconstruction; Elliott, Robert Brown; Presidential Reconstruction; Rainey, Joseph Hayne; Ransier, Alonzo Jacob.

Francis Butler Simkins and Robert Hillard Woody, *South Carolina During Reconstruction* (Chapel Hill, N.C., 1932); Joel Williamson, *After Slavery: The Negro in South Carolina During Reconstruction, 1861–1877* (New York, 1965); Thomas Holt, *Black Over White: Negro Political Leadership in South Carolina During Reconstruction* (Urbana, Ill., 1979); Peggy Lamson, *The Glorious Failure: Black Congressman Robert Brown Elliott and the Reconstruction in South Carolina* (New York, 1973).

**SOUTHERN LOYALIST CONVENTION,** held in Philadelphia in September 1866, was the reply to the National Union Convention (q.v.) convened there shortly before. Delegates from every Southern state attended, including well-known figures such as Thomas J. Durant (q.v.) and Henry C. Warmoth (q.v.) of Louisiana, Andrew J. Hamilton (q.v.) of Texas, John Minor Botts of Virginia, and Albion W. Tourgée (q.v.) of North Carolina. Among the able border-state representatives were Robert J. Breckinridge and James Speed (q.v.) of Kentucky and William G. Brownlow (q.v.) and Joseph S. Fowler of Tennessee. Northern supporters were also invited, and a number of Governors, Senators, and other active Republicans made an appearance. Following a joint meeting in Independence Square, the Northern delegates separated to hold their own sessions.

After appointing Thomas J. Durant temporary presiding officer, the convention chose James Speed as permanent chairman. The former Attorney General, who had only recently resigned from Johnson's cabinet, delivered a slashing address attacking his former chief, whom he called the "tyrant at the White House," an appellation he later retracted by maintaining he had said "tenant," not "tyrant." But the issue of black suffrage (q.v.) caused great difficulty. Delegates from the North and the border states, afraid of alienating the voters, refused to endorse a plank calling for the enfranchisement of the freedmen, and only after they had withdrawn did their Southern colleagues adopt the controversial program. The appearance of Frederick Douglass (q.v.) and other black leaders caused additional embarrassment. Largely ignored, Douglass was finally made a member of a committee to tour the North during the subsequent campaign, although some delegates vigorously objected.

In the end, the Convention adopted an address calling for radical Reconstruction and attacking the President. The subsequent victory of the party seemed to justify its proceedings.

*See also* Philadelphia National Union Convention; Speed, James.

Patrick W. Riddleberger, *1866: The Critical Year Revisited* (Carbondale, Ill., 1979); Michael Les Benedict, *A Compromise of Principle: Congressional Republicans and Reconstruction, 1863–1869* (New York, 1974); George Fort Milton, *The Age of Hate: Andrew Johnson and the Radicals* (New York, 1930).


**SPECIE RESUMPTION ACT** (1875), a measure providing for the resumption of specie payments within four years. Because of the financial needs of the Civil War, the free convertibility of paper notes into specie had been suspended in 1862. The subsequent issue of more than $400 million in greenbacks (q.v.) led to a premium upon gold that made the resumption of specie payments difficult. In addition, questions of monetary policy divided both parties, each having inflationist and conservative (contractionist) wings. When in 1874 the Democrats recaptured the House of Representatives, the Republicans, worried about the next election, under the leadership of John Sherman (q.v.) perfected and in early 1875 passed a measure designed to unify the party. Providing for the resumption of specie payments in January 1879 and fixing the total amount of greenbacks at $300 million, as desired by the conservatives, the legislation also restored free banking as a sop to the inflationists. It was passed with very little debate. Later efforts to repeal it failed, and after the amount of greenbacks permitted had been raised to $346 million, it fell to Sherman, now Secretary of the Treasury, to preside over the implementation of the measure on January 2, 1879.

The Specie Resumption Act fulfilled its purpose of unifying the Republican party, at least temporarily. Although it did not end the controversy over financial matters, on the day it went into effect the greenbacks had risen to par so that very little monetary disruption occurred.

*See also* Greenbacks; Sherman, John.

Irwin Unger, *The Greenback Era: A Social and Political History of American Finance, 1865–1879* (Princeton, N.J., 1964).


**SPEED, JAMES** (1812–1887), Attorney General of the United States, was born in Jefferson County, Kentucky (q.v.), the son of John Speed, a local salt manufacturer. Educated at St. Joseph's College, he studied law at Lexington and in 1833 opened a practice in Louisville. Elected to the legislature in 1847, he stood out for his opposition to slavery and in 1849 was the unsuccessful emancipation candidate for the state constitutional convention. Between 1855 and 1858 he taught law at Louisville University.

At the outbreak of the Civil War, Speed was one of the most outspoken supporters of the Union. Elected to the state Senate in 1861, he served until 1863. In the next year, Abraham Lincoln (q.v.), who was a close friend of Speed's brother Joshua Frye, appointed him Attorney General.

The succession of Andrew Johnson (q.v.) soon brought Speed into conflict with the President. Having already protested against Lincoln's efforts to reassemble the Confederate legislature of Virginia, he became a strong believer in black suffrage (q.v.), a stand that differed markedly from Johnson's. His opposition to the President's veto of the Freedmen's Bureau Bill (q.v.), his support of the Fourteenth Amendment (q.v.), and his refusal to participate in the Philadelphia National Union Convention (q.v.) led to his resignation in July 1866.

As Attorney General, Speed advised Johnson to try the assassins of Abraham Lincoln (q.v.) by a military tribunal. Approving the death sentences handed out by the court, he subsequently became involved in the controversy concerning the recommendation of mercy for Mary Surratt (q.v.). Although strongly urged to corroborate Joseph Holt's (q.v.) claim that the President had seen the document, he always refused to do so on the grounds of cabinet confidentiality.

In September 1866 Speed presided over the Southern Loyalist Convention (q.v.) at Philadelphia, where he referred to Johnson as "the tyrant at the White House," although he later maintained that he had merely called the President the "tenant at the White House." In 1867 he wrote the platform of the Kentucky Republican state convention and was an unsuccessful candidate for the U.S. Senate. A delegate to the Chicago Republican National Convention in 1868, he was his state's choice for Vice President. His work for the Republican party continued when he ran for the House in 1870 and attended the 1876 national convention.

After his retirement from office, Speed resumed the practice of law in Louisville, taught again at the university in 1872, and died at his home in 1887.

*See also* Black Suffrage; Holt, Joseph; Johnson, Andrew; Southern Loyalist Convention; Surratt, Mary Eugenia Jenkins.

James Speed, *James Speed: A Personality* (Louisville, 1905); Helen L. Springer, "James Speed, The Attorney General, 1864–1866," *Filson Club Historical Quarterly*, 11 (July 1937): 169–88; *The Biographical Encyclopedia of Kentucky of the Dead and Living Men of the Nineteenth Century* (Cincinnati, 1878).

**STANBERY, HENRY** (1803–1881), Attorney General of the United States, was born in New York, the son of a physician. The family moved to Zanesville, Ohio, in 1814, and Stanbery went to Washington College. Graduating at the age of sixteen, he became a lawyer at twenty-one and was admitted to the bar in Gallipolis three years later. He then joined Thomas Ewing in his law practice at Lancaster and in 1846 was elected Attorney General of Ohio. A member of the constitutional convention of 1851, in 1852 he settled in Cincinnati, which he made his permanent home.

Stanbery was an active Whig and joined the Republicans only after the demise of the old party and its successors. In 1864 Abraham Lincoln (q.v.) called upon him to investigate the military division bordering upon and west of the Mississippi, and after Andrew Johnson (q.v.) became President, Stanbery earned the esteem of the administration. His conservative tendencies—he had opposed black suffrage (q.v.) in Ohio—naturally won the President's favor. Early in 1866 Johnson sought to elevate the Ohioan to the Supreme Court, but Congress reduced the number of justices, and the appointment was not confirmed.

In July 1866 the President appointed Stanbery Attorney General of the United States. He sustained Johnson throughout, helped write the veto of the Reconstruction Act (q.v.), and later so interpreted it and its successor as to lessen materially its impact on the former Confederates. The result was the passage of still another Reconstruction measure specifically negativating Stanbery's interpretation.

In March 1868 Stanbery resigned to be able to serve as one of Johnson's defense counsel in the impeachment trial. After telling the President not to grant any more interviews, he prepared a powerful defense, and, though falling sick in the middle of the trial, returned to finish his assignment.

After the President's acquittal, Johnson attempted to reappoint Stanbery to his former cabinet position, but the Senate failed to confirm him. He retired to Cincinnati to resume his practice and, in keeping with his conservative tendencies, successfully argued the case of *U.S.* v. *Reese et al.* (q.v.) against the rights of the blacks. He died in New York in 1881.

*See also* Impeachment of Andrew Johnson; Johnson, Andrew; Reconstruction Acts; *U.S.* v. *Reese et al.*

George Irving Reed, ed., *Bench and Bar of Ohio* (Chicago, 1897); LaWanda and John H. Cox, *Politics, Principle, and Prejudice, 1865–66: Dilemma of Reconstruction America* (New York, 1963).

**STANTON, EDWIN McMASTERS** (1814–1869), Attorney General and Secretary of War of the United States, was born in Steubenville, Ohio, the son of Lucy Norman and Dr. David Stanton. Educated at Kenyon College, he was admitted to the bar in 1835. After practicing in Cadiz and Steubenville, he moved to Pittsburgh and, after his second marriage (his first wife had died), to Washington. A prominent attorney, he defended Daniel Sickles (q.v.) in the trial for the murder of Philip Barton Key and won an acquittal on a plea of temporary insanity.

Always a Jacksonian Democrat, in December 1860 Stanton was appointed Attorney General in James Buchanan's cabinet. He counseled firmness toward the seceding states and secretly collaborated with William H. Seward (q.v.), the spokesman for the incoming Republican administration. Although at first he had a low opinion of Abraham Lincoln (q.v.), in January 1862 he joined the cabinet as Secretary of War and collaborated closely with his chief, with whom he established a firm friendship. He rendered such efficient service in the War

Department that he came to be known as the "American Carnot," the organizer of victory.

Because of the army's role in occupying the South, Stanton soon found himself involved in questions of Reconstruction. He worked closely with Lincoln in formulating the latter's Reconstruction policies and in January 1865 met with William T. Sherman (q.v.) in Atlanta to plan for the settlement of freedmen on the Sea Islands (q.v.).

During the night of the assassination of Lincoln, Stanton quickly assumed temporary control. He directed the capture of the assassins and the secret burial of John Wilkes Booth and favored a trial by a military commission. Although he was later accused of deliberately withholding the recommendation of mercy for Mrs. Mary Surratt (q.v.), his responsibility has never been proven.

At the very beginning of the new administration, Stanton became involved in a severe altercation with William T. Sherman (q.v.), whose armistice negotiations with Joseph E. Johnston he criticized in such severe terms that the general was deeply insulted and publicly refused to shake the Secretary's hand on the day of the national review of the victorious armies.

In the meantime, Stanton had been playing an important role in the Reconstruction of the South. Asked by Lincoln to draw up a plan for the conquered states, he presented it at the cabinet meeting on the day of the assassination. It provided for the appointment of a Military Governor for Virginia (q.v.) and North Carolina (q.v.) but did not touch on the question of black suffrage (q.v.). Upon Gideon Welles' (q.v.) protest that the two states should be separated because Virginia (q.v.) already had a loyal government, Lincoln directed Stanton to change his scheme accordingly. He did so and then presented it to Andrew Johnson (q.v.).

The new President, however, had different plans, and as time went on, the Secretary of War found himself more and more in opposition to the President. Anxious to safeguard the gains of the war, he attempted to bridge the gap between Johnson and Congress. Remaining at his post even when other secretaries in disagreement with Presidential Reconstruction (q.v.) resigned, he eventually became the representative of the radicals in cabinet. He resisted the President's veto of the Freedmen's Bureau and Civil Rights Bills (Civil Rights Acts, q.v.), sympathized with portions of the Fourteenth Amendment, and approved of parts of the Reconstruction Acts (q.v.). Yet he favored the veto of the Tenure of Office Act (q.v.), although in part it was designed to protect him. At the same time, in collaboration with U. S. Grant (q.v.), he attempted to maintain the army's function in reconstructing the South, even in opposition to the President's wishes.

While increasingly critical of these activities, Johnson hesitated to rid himself of his popular subordinate. Not until the summer of 1867 did he decide to appoint Grant to Stanton's office. Acting in compliance with the Tenure of Office Law, he suspended Stanton in August. The Secretary yielded under protest, but in January 1868 the Senate failed to uphold the President and ordered that Stanton be reinstated. After quarreling with Grant about the general's refusal to cooperate, Johnson decided to dismiss his unwanted adviser once and for all; after a search for a replacement, on February 21 he finally discharged Stanton and appointed Adjutant General Lorenzo Thomas in his stead.

This action in defiance of the Tenure of Office Act led to the President's impeachment. Stanton, insistent upon his rights, refused to leave the war office and had Thomas arrested. When Thomas, released on bail, sought to take over the department, Stanton ordered him back to his own office and maintained his vigil in the building. Only the acquittal of Johnson caused him to resign.

After campaigning for the election of Grant, Stanton resumed his practice in Washington. Appointed to the Supreme Court in December 1869, he died before he could enter upon his new duties.

A powerful, often overbearing administrator devoted to the maintenance of the Union, Stanton not only organized the victorious Union armies during the Civil War but did his best to safeguard the gains of the conflict afterward. His unprecedented refusal to resign from office when no longer wanted was due to his conviction that the army must be safeguarded to achieve this purpose.

*See also* Grant, Ulysses Simpson; Impeachment of Andrew Johnson; Johnson, Andrew; Lincoln, Abraham; Lincoln, Abraham, Assassination of; Sherman, William Tecumseh; Sickles, Daniel Edgar; Surratt, Mary Eugenia Jenkins; Tenure of Office Act.

Benjamin P. Thomas and Harold M. Hyman, *Stanton: The Life and Times of Lincoln's Secretary of War* (New York, 1962).


**STEVENS, THADDEUS** (1792–1868), radical leader in the House, was born in Danville, Vermont, the son of the farmer and surveyor Joshua Stevens and his wife, Sarah Merrill Stevens. Brought up by his mother after the father abandoned the family, Stevens was educated at Peacham Academy and Dartmouth College. In 1815 he moved to York, Pennsylvania, where he taught school while studying law. After admission to the bar in Bel Air, Maryland, in 1816 he opened an office in Gettysburg and soon acquired a large practice, real estate, and ironworks.

Stevens' political career began with his commitment to anti-Masonry. Prominent at the first presidential nominating convention of the new party at Baltimore, he was elected to the state legislature in 1833, 1834, and 1835 and made a name for himself as a tireless proponent of free public education who was influential in preventing the repeal of the state's free school law. In 1836 he was appointed to the canal commission but was defeated for reelection to the Assembly only to reappear in the legislature in 1837, 1838, and 1841. He took a prominent part in the so-called Buckshot War, an affray concerning disputed election returns, and served in the 1837–1838 constitutional convention, in which he vainly fought for rights for blacks (q.v.) and unsuccessfully sought to prevent their disfranchisement.

In 1842 Stevens moved to Lancaster, where he again established a flourishing law practice. Elected to Congress as a Whig in 1848 and 1850, he took a strong antislavery stand. After the collapse of the Whig party he briefly joined the Know-Nothings and then the Republicans, who in 1858 sent him back to Congress and consistently reelected him afterward.

When in 1861 the Republicans gained full control of the House, Stevens became chairman of the powerful Ways and Means Committee and stood out as one of the most active advocates of emancipation (q.v.). In addition, he was partially responsible for the financial measures passed during the war, particularly the Legal Tender Act of 1862.

Stevens took an early interest in Reconstruction. Holding that Lincoln's establishment of a blockade of the Southern coast constituted a recognition of the belligerency of the Confederacy, he considered recaptured portions of the South "conquered provinces" under the law of nations. Consequently, he argued that in dealing with the South, the federal government need not be bound by constitutional restraints and pleaded for the confiscation of insurgent property.

After the inauguration of Andrew Johnson (q.v.), Stevens, now called the "Commoner," became one of the leaders of the radical opposition. Appalled by Johnson's scheme of Presidential Reconstruction (q.v.), he was instrumental in blocking admission to Congress of Southern representatives, when in December 1865 his friend, Edward McPherson (q.v.), the clerk of the House, omitted their names from the roll call. At the same time, he successfully moved for the establishment of a joint committee on Reconstruction (q.v.) to which all questions concerning restoration were to be referred. As chairman of the House contingent of the committee, he vigorously strove for the implementation of black rights. In addition, he still favored the confiscation of rebel property and the distribution of land to the freedmen.

In the developing struggle with the President, Stevens assumed ever more radical positions. He piloted the Fourteenth Amendment (q.v.) through Congress and, when finding that his original desire for a stronger measure could not be realized, supported the final version. After the election of 1866, he introduced the Tenure of Office (Tenure of Office Act, q.v.) and Reconstruction bills (Reconstruction Acts, q.v.), again deploring the moderate modifications of the latter.

As time went on, Stevens became one of the principal advocates of the impeachment of Johnson (q.v.). Disappointed in the failure of the first effort, as chairman of the Reconstruction committee he vainly tried to obtain a vote for impeachment after the President's quarrel with U. S. Grant (q.v.) about the surrender of the War Department. Then, when Johnson dismissed Edwin M. Stanton (q.v.) and an impeachment resolution finally passed, Stevens was one of the two representatives chosen to notify the Senate. He also was the author of the eleventh article of impeachment and served on the board of managers prosecuting the case. Only his physical disabilities prevented him from taking a leading part in the proceedings; in fact, he was too weak to finish his final plea, which had to be continued by a colleague. Infuriated by the failure of the trial, he actively sought to revive it but was unsuccessful, even though he introduced the bills for the admission of most of the reconstructed states. He died in Washington in August 1868.

Thaddeus Stevens, who had a club foot and never married, was one of the most influential representatives ever to serve in Congress. Dominating the House with his wit, knowledge of parliamentary law, and sheer willpower, even though he was often unable to prevail, he was widely considered the incarnation of the radical spirit and the driving force behind Congressional Reconstruction (q.v.). He was buried in an interracial cemetery, his epitaph a tribute to his principles, "equality of man before his creator."

*See also* Congressional Reconstruction; Fourteenth Amendment; Impeachment of Andrew Johnson; Johnson, Andrew; Presidential Reconstruction; Radical Republicans; Reconstruction Acts.

Fawn Brodie, *Thaddeus Stevens: Scourge of the South* (New York, 1959); Ralph Korngold, *Thaddeus Stevens: A Being Darkly Wise and Rudely Great* (New York, 1955); Richard N. Current, *Old Thad Stevens: A Story of Ambition* (Madison, Wis., 1942).

**SUMNER, CHARLES** (1811–1874), antislavery Senator from Massachusetts, was born in Boston, the son of sheriff Charles Pinckney and Mrs. Relief Jacobs Sumner. Educated at the Boston Latin School and at Harvard College and Law School, he was admitted to the bar in 1834 and from 1835 to 1837 taught law at Harvard. After a three-year trip to Europe, he resumed his law practice in Boston. Becoming vitally interested in the antislavery struggle, in 1848 and 1850 he was an unsuccessful Free Soil candidate for Congress and in 1849, in the *Roberts* case, argued against the legality of segregated schools by citing the harmful sociological effects of segregation.

In 1851 a Free Soil-Democratic coalition elected Sumner to the Senate. One of the most outspoken members of the small antislavery contingent in the upper house, he attacked the peculiar institution in lengthy and carefully prepared orations. He was a determined opponent of the Kansas-Nebraska Act and became one of the founders of the Republican party (q.v.) in Massachusetts. In 1856 he delivered his Crime Against Kansas speech, in which he not only castigated the proslavery forces in the territory but made personal aspersions upon Senator Andrew P. Butler of South Carolina, whereupon the latter's infuriated kinsman Representative Preston Brooks attacked Sumner with a gutta percha cane. The assault disabled the Senator for several years, made him a martyr to the antislavery cause, and led to his reelection in 1857.

During the Civil War, Sumner, now chairman of the Senate Committee on Foreign Relations, exercised a powerful influence on diplomacy as well as upon emancipation. Collaborating with the administration in settling the *Trent* affair, he facilitated its peaceful conclusion. He was on friendly terms with the President and Mrs. Lincoln, a relationship he used to further his emancipation (q.v.) policies. At the same time, he advocated the admission of black testimony in the federal courts, the desegregation of street cars in Washington, and equal pay for black soldiers.

Seeking to reconstruct Southern society, as early as February 1862 he introduced resolutions declaring that the seceded states had committed suicide and therefore were liable to be governed as territories. He was dissatisfied with Lincoln's slow progress on Reconstruction and in 1864 supported the Wade-Davis Bill (q.v.). When the Louisiana (q.v.) government elected under the President's plan of Reconstruction sought admission, the Senator strenuously opposed it because the state had not granted suffrage to the blacks (q.v.). Subsequently, he insisted on impartial suffrage for every territory and state seeking organization or admission, even though his dogmatism often prevented the adoption of measures otherwise favorable to radical Reconstruction.

When Andrew Johnson (q.v.) assumed the presidency, Sumner at first thought the President was in agreement with his ideas. Upon the unfolding of the Presidential Plan of Reconstruction, however, the Senator became one of Johnson's principal antagonists. Favoring congressional measures to undo the President's actions, he reluctantly supported the Fourteenth Amendment (q.v.) even though he deplored its failure to provide for universal suffrage and voted for the Reconstruction Acts (q.v.) despite the fact that he considered them too moderate. He believed Johnson to be the chief obstacle to Reconstruction, avidly sought his impeachment, and was greatly disappointed at the Senate's failure to convict. Nevertheless, a convinced expansionist, the Senator collaborated with Secretary of State William H. Seward (q.v.) in the purchase of Russian America, to which he himself gave the name of Alaska. He not only opposed the Johnson-Clarenden Convention for the settlement of the Alabama claims but in 1869 delivered a determined address in which he saddled Great Britain with the responsibility for prolonging the war by two years, for which he asked not only for direct but also indirect damages, together amounting to some $2 billion, a sum that could be satisfied only by the cession of Canada, which he favored.

During the administration of U. S. Grant (q.v.), Sumner at first sought to dominate the conduct of foreign relations. He virtually dictated instructions to his favorite, John Lothrop Motley, the minister to the Court of St. James. When the President, however, attempted to annex the Dominican Republic, the Senator took the lead in opposing the scheme. Although the President had visited him and believed he had obtained his approval, Sumner not only spoke strongly against the treaty but eventually broke off relations with Secretary of State Hamilton Fish (q.v.). Even after the defeat of the treaty in July 1870 he continued his opposition by thundering against a proposed committee of inquiry in his Naboth's Vineyard Speech (December 1870) and in personal attacks upon the President. The resulting breach with the administration led to Sumner's removal from the Foreign Relations Committee in March 1871. He refused an alternative assignment as chairman of the Committee on Privileges and Elections and carried on his feud with the President with such venom that in 1872, after some hesitation, he actually came out in support of the Liberal Republican (Liberal Republican Movement, q.v.) ticket, although it was endorsed by the Democrats.

Sumner's last great effort was his attempt to pass a Civil Rights Bill granting equal access to public facilities for all races. Failing in an effort to attach it to the Amnesty Bill of 1872, he tried to revive it in subsequent sessions but was unsuccessful. Among his last words as he lay dying in Washington in 1874 was a plea for its passage, and it fell to his opponent, Benjamin F. Butler (q.v.), finally to carry it as a tribute to the departed Senator in the lame-duck session of 1875.

Often overbearing and tactless, Sumner, a bachelor except for a short period of marriage in 1866, nevertheless stood out as one of the most determined foes of slavery and racial discrimination. His tireless fight for human rights and his utter incorruptibility guaranteed his place as one of the leading congressional radicals.

*See also* Black Suffrage; Civil Rights Act of 1875; Fish, Hamilton; Foreign Affairs; Grant, Ulysses Simpson; Johnson, Andrew; Radical Republicans.

David Donald, *Charles Sumner and the Coming of the Civil War* (New York, 1960); David Donald, *Charles Sumner and the Rights of Man* (New York, 1970).

**SUPREME COURT.** During the Reconstruction period, the nation's highest judicial tribunal, headed by Chief Justice Salmon P. Chase (q.v.) and dominated by a Republican majority, rendered a series of far-reaching decisions. Formerly seen as an endangered branch of the government afraid to interfere with Congressional Reconstruction (q.v.), while in 1866 its membership was reduced to seven and in 1868 an attempt was made to require a two-thirds majority to overturn laws of Congress, in reality it appears to have acted freely according to constitutional precedent.

In matters directly affecting Reconstruction, the Court played an important role. Starting with *ex parte Milligan* (q.v.), in 1866 it held that in loyal areas where the civil courts were open, military commissions were illegal. That same year, it nullified test oaths for lawyers in *ex parte Garland* (q.v.) and for clergymen in *Cummings* v. *Missouri* (q.v.). Declining to grant injunctions against the President and Secretary of War in *Mississippi* v. *Johnson* (q.v.) and *Georgia* v. *Stanton* (q.v.), it refused to become involved in the struggle between Andrew Johnson (q.v.) and Congress. Although it also acquiesced in the withdrawal of jurisdiction in certain habeas corpus cases while *ex parte McCardle* (q.v.) was pending, it granted the writ in *ex parte Yerger* (q.v.), a case involving a Southerner who had murdered a federal officer on Reconstruction duty. Finally, in 1869 in *Texas* v. *White* (q.v.), it decided that the seceded states had never been out of the Union but that Congress had the right to restore them to their proper function within it.

Starting with the *Slaughterhouse* cases (q.v.) in 1873, the justices began to dilute the application of the Reconstruction amendments and contributed to the failure of Reconstruction. The process continued under Chief Justice Morrison R. Waite (q.v.), when the court failed to interpret the Fourteenth and Fifteenth Amendments (q.v.) so as to protect the blacks (q.v.) (*U.S.* v. *Reese et al.*, 1876, and *U.S.* v. *Cruikshank*, 1876, q.v.). In 1883 it declared the Civil Rights Act of 1875 (q.v.) unconstitutional and, finally, in 1896 sanctioned separate but equal accommodations in railroads.

In fields other than those directly associated with Reconstruction the court also asserted itself. Declaring unconstitutional more laws of Congress than any of its predecessors, it firmly established its role as final arbiter of the Constitution. In the *Legal Tender* cases (q.v.) in 1870 and 1871, after first failing to uphold the Legal Tender Act of 1862 as applied to prior debts, following the appointment of two new justices, it reversed itself. Likewise, in the matter of state regulation of railroads, in the 1877 *Granger* cases, it looked with favor on the practice, only to change its mind in the *Wabash* case in 1886. It increasingly became an exponent of laissez faire and interpreted the Fourteenth Amendment in such a way as to protect corporations rather than the freedmen.

*See also* Chase, Salmon Portland; *Georgia* v. *Stanton*; Legal Tender Cases; *McCardle, Ex Parte; Milligan, Ex Parte; Mississippi* v. *Johnson; Plessy* v. *Ferguson*; Slaughterhouse Cases; *Texas* v. *White*; U.S. v. *Cruikshank; U.S.* v. *Reese et al.*; Waite, Morrison Remick; *Yerger, Ex Parte*.

Charles Fairman, *Reconstruction and Reunion, 1864–88*, Vols. 6 and 7 of the Oliver Wendell Holmes Devise, *History of the Supreme Court of the United States, 1864–88* (New York, 1971, 1987); Stanley I. Kutler, *Judicial Power and Reconstruction Politics* (Chicago, 1968).

**SURRATT, MARY EUGENIA JENKINS** (1817–1865), alleged accomplice in the assassination of Abraham Lincoln (q.v.), was born near Waterloo, Maryland, and educated at a Catholic seminary in Alexandria. In 1835 she married John H. Surratt, for a time a contractor on the Orange and Alexandria Railroad, and later a farmer and tavern keeper at Surrattsville, Maryland, where he also served as postmaster. A man of Southern sympathies and a slave owner, he died in 1862, leaving her with three children, of whom one joined the Confederate army, another became a Southern dispatch runner, and a third, a daughter, remained with her mother. Eventually, she rented out the tavern to John M. Lloyd and kept a boardinghouse in Washington.

The establishment served as a rendezvous for the conspirators against the President. John Wilkes Booth, David E. Herold, Lewis Paine, and George A. Atzerodt all met there with John H. Surratt, Jr. On April 11 Surratt's boarder, Louis J. Weichmann, in a buggy hired with Booth's money, drove her to Surrattsville and, according to Lloyd, whom she met on the road, told him that the shooting irons would be needed soon. On the day of the assassination, she again went to Surrattsville, and shortly before she left, Booth gave her a package to be delivered. When a few days later detectives came to arrest her, Paine arrived, but she denied knowing him.

At the conspiracy trial, she was ably defended; however, largely on the testimony of Lloyd and Weichmann, she was convicted and condemned to death. Although the military commission attached a plea for clemency to the verdict, she was executed on July 7.

Her guilt and the recommendation for mercy became the subject of intense controversy. Judge Advocate Joseph Holt (q.v.) brought the papers to President Andrew Johnson (q.v.) on July 5, when the President confirmed the sentences. However, whether he had actually seen the plea for clemency is not clear. The question of Mrs. Surratt's guilt was raised again in March 1867, when in the House Benjamin F. Butler (q.v.) accused John A. Bingham (q.v.), who had been assistant judge advocate, of responsibility for the hanging of an innocent woman and the spoliation of Booth's diary, which might have exonerated her. A few months afterward, Johnson, about to dismiss Secretary of War Edwin M. Stanton (q.v.), intimated that Holt and the Secretary had withheld the recommendation from him and asserted he had never seen it. In addition, during the contemporary civilian trial of John H. Surratt, Jr., the veracity of the witnesses against his mother was seriously questioned. Lloyd was shown to have been drunk, and Weichmann was accused of having testified as part of a bargain with the government not to prosecute him. When in 1873 Johnson was about to seek reelection to the Senate the controversy heated up once more. Holt published a *Vindication*, which contained seeming corroboration from cabinet members; Johnson countered with accusations against Holt, and the dispute dragged on even after Johnson's death. Holt repeatedly called on Attorney General James Speed (q.v.) to substantiate his account, but Speed refused to divulge cabinet secrets. As for Weichmann, he insisted on his deathbed that his testimony had been accurate.

Whether Mrs. Surratt actually knew of the plot to kill is questionable, although it is likely that she had some connection with the conspiracy to kidnap. The controversy between Holt and Johnson may possibly be explained by the fact that on the day he was shown the record, the President was ill, and he may not have remembered seeing the plea for clemency. At any rate, he clearly stated at the time that he thought Mrs. Surratt guilty and probably would have disregarded the plea whether or not he had seen it.

*See also* Bingham, John Armor; Holt, Joseph; Johnson, Andrew; Lincoln, Abraham, Assassination of.

Guy W. Moore, *The Case of Mrs. Surratt: Her Controversial Trial and Execution for Conspiracy in the Lincoln Assassination* (Norman, Okla., 1954); Lloyd Lewis, *Myths after Lincoln* (New York, 1929); David Miller DeWitt, *The Assassination of Abraham Lincoln and Its Expiation* (New York, 1909).

**SWAYNE, WAGER** (1834–1902), Union general and assistant commissioner of the Freedmen's Bureau in Alabama, was born in Columbus, Ohio, the son of Chief Justice Noah Swayne, later an Associate Justice of the Supreme Court of the United States. Educated at Yale and the Cincinnati Law School, from which he graduated in 1859, he practiced law in Columbus and then joined the Forty-first Ohio Volunteers. He took part in the Battles of New Madrid, Island No. 10, Shiloh, Corinth, and Iuka and in 1863 was appointed provost marshal of Memphis. In 1864 he marched with Sherman to the sea and in 1865 was so severely wounded in South Carolina that he lost his right leg. A brigadier general at the end of the war, in June 1865 he was promoted to major general.

In the summer of 1865 Swayne was appointed assistant commissioner of the Freedmen's Bureau (q.v.) and served in Alabama (q.v.) until 1868. Seeking to find a practical way of integrating the blacks (q.v.) into society, he was hampered by local prejudices that sometimes coincided with his own. By attempting to cooperate with state officials, he sought to temper the black code (q.v.) and ordered state courts to accept black testimony. To protect black youth, he finally stopped the indiscriminate apprenticing of freed youngsters, often to their former owners, and he was active in the inauguration of the Republican party in the state. As a strong believer in education for blacks, he took a special interest in the establishment of schools for freedmen, including high schools at Selma, Montgomery, and Mobile and the black college at Talladega. Removed by Andrew Johnson (q.v.) in 1868, he retired from the army in 1870. Thereafter he practiced law in Toledo and after 1880 in New York, where he acquired a large corporate practice and died in 1902.

A controversial commissioner, Swayne seems to have tried to find a middle way between the radicals and conservatives but was unable to please either.

*See also* Alabama; Freedmen's Bureau; Howard, Oliver Otis.

Kenneth B. White, "Wager Swayne, Racist or Realist?" *Alabama Review,* 31 (April 1978): 92–109; J. Fletcher Brennan, ed., *Biographical Cyclopaedia . . . of the State of Ohio* (2 vols., Cincinnati, 1880); Donald Nieman, *To Set the Law in Motion: The Freedmen's Bureau and the Legal Rights of Blacks, 1865–1868* (Millwood, N.Y., 1979); Peter Kolchin, *First Freedom: The Responses of Alabama's Blacks to Emancipation and Reconstruction* (Westport, Conn., 1972).

**SWEPSON, GEORGE** (1811–1883), North Carolina speculator and railroad promoter, was born in Mecklenburg County, Virginia, and moved to North Carolina (q.v.) in 1840. He married Virginia Yancey, the daughter of Bartlett Yancey, a wealthy political leader, and settled at Haw River in Alamance County. Involved in cotton mills before the war, during Reconstruction he became the manipulator of North Carolina railroads, serving as banker, President of the Western Division of the Western North Carolina Railroad, and director of various other enterprises. Together with General Milton S. Littlefield (q.v.), he controlled a powerful railroad ring that bribed state legislators and others to gain its purposes. Working closely with Governor William W. Holden (q.v.), he sought to create a great railroad empire linking the seaboard South.

Cleverly manipulating the Reconstruction legislature, but also collaborating with conservatives, Swepson received millions of dollars to build or maintain railroads and often diverted funds into other companies. In December 1868 the legislature passed the Universal Railroad Act as a result of which Swepson received some $6.3 million in bonds for the Western Division of the Western North Carolina Railroad. Instead of putting this money to use in finishing construction, Swepson diverted some $843,633 for use in his railroad schemes in Florida (q.v.), where he bought three roads, manipulated state railroad bonds, and received some $4 million to construct the Jacksonville, Pensacola and Mobile Railroad. These bonds he sold for a considerable profit in the North and in Europe, while devoting but $300,000 to the completion of the line.

Swepson's methods usually involved forcing railroads into bankruptcy and then picking them up at bargain prices, but in 1869 his schemes went awry when the Gold Corner broke in New York. Suffering severe financial losses, he was faced with charges by the North Carolina legislature but was never convicted, although his friend Holden was impeached and removed in part for his collusion with Swepson.

Swepson was a robber baron much like many Northern counterparts, but his schemes failed and he suffered shipwreck instead of becoming a great builder.

*See also* Holden, William Woods; Littlefield, Milton Smith.

Charles L. Price, "The Railroad Schemes of George W. Swepson," *East Carolina College Publications in History*, 1 (1964): 32–50; Paul E. Fenlon, "The Notorious Swepson-Littlefield Fraud: Railroad Financing in Florida, 1868–71," *Florida Historical Quarterly*, 32 (1954): 231–61; C. K. Brown, "The Florida Investments of George W. Swepson," *North Carolina Historical Review*, 5 (1928): 275–88.


**SWING AROUND THE CIRCLE,** President Andrew Johnson's (q.v.) campaign trip to the Midwest in August and September 1866. Ostensibly undertaken to assist in the laying of a cornerstone for a monument to Stephen A. Douglas, the tour was in reality a canvass for votes, unusual as such presidential efforts were in the nineteenth century. Accompanied, among others, by members of his cabinet as well as by General U. S. Grant (q.v.) and Admiral David Farragut, Johnson left Washington on August 28. After a great reception in New York, he went on to Albany, Buffalo, Cleveland, and Chicago, everywhere delivering substantially the same speech full of allusions to his rise from alderman to President and attacks upon his enemies. In addition, stung by hecklers who became more and more insistent, he allowed himself to make undignified replies tending to demean his high office.

The trip was marked by a series of unpleasant incidents. In Albany, Governor Reuben E. Fenton snubbed William H. Seward (q.v.); in Cleveland, General Grant was under the influence of alcohol; and Johnson encountered a hostile crowd that shouted its approval of Congress; and in Chicago local authorities refused to welcome him. After leaving the Windy City, he visited Lincoln's tomb and then proceeded to St. Louis, where his encounter with the crowd was particularly disturbing. In reply to cries of "New Orleans," he blamed Congress for the riot. He had been called a Judas, he said, but if he had been a Judas, who had been the Christ that he had played the Judas with? Thad Stevens (q.v.)? Charles Sumner (q.v.)?

On his return, in Louisville William H. Seward (q.v.) fell ill and could not go on; the party continued to Indianapolis, Cincinnati, Columbus, and Pittsburgh, causing tumults in the places the President visited and inducing local dignitaries to shun him. When he came back to Washington on September 15, he had suffered a serious loss of prestige and support, and the fall elections resulted in an overwhelming victory for his opponents.

*See also* Johnson, Andrew.

Hans L. Trefousse, *Andrew Johnson: A Biography* (New York, 1989); Albert Castel, *The Presidency of Andrew Johnson* (Lawrence, Kans., 1979); Patrick W. Riddleberger, *1866: The Critical Year* (Carbondale, Ill., 1979).

# T

TEN PERCENT PLAN, popular designation for Lincoln's (q.v.) plan of Reconstruction as detailed in his Proclamation of Amnesty (q.v.) of December 8, 1863. Promulgated as a measure to help the war effort, it offered amnesty to former Confederates willing to take an oath of allegiance to the Constitution of the United States and to declare their intention of supporting all measures taken by Congress or the President "in reference to slaves." Exempted from this offer were only high officers of the insurgent government such as diplomats, colonels and generals, former U.S. members of Congress or judicial officers, and those who had mistreated black soldiers or their commanders. As soon as 10 percent of the legal voters of the seceded states in 1860 had taken this oath, they were to be empowered to reconstitute a state government loyal to the United States.

It was in accordance with the provisions of this proclamation that Reconstruction governments were set up in Louisiana (q.v.) and Arkansas (q.v.). In July 1864, however, Congress, disturbed by the undemocratic features of the 10 percent provision and the assumption of presidential control of Reconstruction, passed the Wade-Davis Bill (q.v.) with more stringent conditions, which Lincoln pocket-vetoed.

The Ten Percent Plan has been compared with Andrew Johnson's (q.v.) plan of Reconstruction outlined in his North Carolina Proclamation (q.v.), and it has been asserted that the new President was merely following his predecessor's example. Lincoln, however, promulgated his plan in time of war, as a measure to weaken the enemy, while Johnson launched his scheme in time of peace, when there was no such necessity. What Lincoln would have done had he survived is unknown, and the comparison would seem to be invalid.

*See also* Amnesty; Arkansas; Johnson, Andrew; Lincoln, Abraham; Louisiana; Presidential Reconstruction; Wade-Davis Bill.

Herman Belz, *Reconstructing the Union: Theory and Practice During the Civil War* (Ithaca, N.Y. 1969); William B. Hesseltine, *Lincoln's Plan of Reconstruction* (Tuscaloosa, Ala., 1960).

**TENNESSEE,** one of the seceded states subject to Reconstruction. The restoration of Tennessee, starting with the appointment of Andrew Johnson (q.v.) as Military Governor in March 1862, was a long and difficult process, complicated by the fact that East Tennessee, the Unionist portion of the state, remained under Confederate occupation during much of the war. Calling for a judicial election in Nashville as early as in May 1862, Johnson arrested the winner, a rank secessionist, and appointed his opponent in his place. He ruled the state with an iron hand, arrested Southern sympathizers, and sought to reanimate Unionist feelings. Limited elections in West Tennessee early in 1863 were frustrated by General Bedford Forrest's raids; the Emancipation Proclamation (q.v.) created further difficulties by splitting the Unionists, and the restoration of civilian government was delayed. Johnson himself finally endorsed emancipation (q.v.), while his conservative opponents resisted it. But when they sought to displace him with William B. Campbell in elections in August 1863, they failed. Another effort to hold county elections in March 1864 was also ineffectual, hampered by the fact that Johnson's test oath was harsher than Lincoln's in his Proclamation of Amnesty (q.v.).

In 1864 Johnson became Abraham Lincoln's (q.v.) running mate, and a Unionist convention in Nashville endorsed the ticket while prescribing a test oath so vigorous as effectively to exclude even Unionist supporters of George B. McClellan. Lincoln carried the state, and following the election, the time seemed ripe for a constitutional convention. Icy conditions and the battle of Nashville intervened, so that it was not until January 1865 that the convention met. Dominated by the radical followers of Parson William Gannaway Brownlow (q.v.) and encouraged by Johnson, the delegates called for a plebiscite to abolish slavery, nominated Brownlow for Governor in a subsequent general election, and nullified the actions of the Confederate state government.

The election on March 4 resulted in a radical sweep of offices. Brownlow became Governor, and the radical regime that was inaugurated was kept in power largely by a Franchise Law enacted by the legislature. Disqualifying former Confederates for five years, the measure assured East Tennessee Unionist control of the state, but Brownlow's ever-increasing radicalism alienated so many that by 1866 a new Franchise Law, even more stringent than the first and permanently disfranchising Southern sympathizers, was necessary to insure his continued dominance. In July 1866 the Governor, who had broken with Johnson, brought about the ratification of the Fourteenth Amendment (q.v.) by forcefully preventing conservatives from averting a quorum in the legislature, and Tennessee was readmitted to the Union. Its two Senators, both moderates, and its congressmen were seated.

By the fall of 1866, Brownlow realized that if he wanted to sustain himself, in spite of the unpopularity of the change, blacks (q.v.) would have to be given the vote. Accordingly, upon his recommendation, in the beginning of 1867 the legislature enfranchised the freedmen without giving them the right to hold office. Because of its ratification of the Fourteenth Amendment, Tennessee was not subject to Congressional Reconstruction (q.v.); nevertheless, it gave birth to the Ku Klux Klan (q.v.), which terrorized potential voters.

In 1869 Brownlow was elected U.S. Senator, and DeWitt C. Senter (q.v.), the president of the state Senate, succeeded him. When Senter sought the governorship in his own right, however, he was opposed by congressman William B. Stokes. This split in the Union party led Senter to seek the support of the conservatives, whose disfranchisement he effectively nullified by appointing new registrars. He was successful, and the conservative legislature elected with him repealed the Franchise Law.

Reconstruction was thus effectively at an end in Tennessee. In 1870 the conservatives called a new constitutional convention, which enacted a poll tax and provided for strict spending limits. The conservatives received a strong boost by the debates on the Civil Rights Act of 1875 (q.v.), a measure that lost even East Tennessee for the Republicans in 1874, but unlike in other Southern states, a strong Republican faction survived there until the twentieth century.

*See also* Brownlow, William Gannaway; Johnson, Andrew; Senter, Dewitt C.

Thomas B. Alexander, *Political Reconstruction in Tennessee* (Nashville, 1950); Alreutheus Taylor, *The Negro in Tennessee, 1865–1880* (Washington, D.C., 1941).

**TENURE OF OFFICE ACT** (1867), a measure to restrict the President's patronage powers by requiring the consent of the Senate to dismissals of officers appointed by and with its consent. Passed on March 2, 1867, over Andrew Johnson's (q.v.) veto, it was one of the devices to assert congressional control over Reconstruction and to rein in the President. Its provisions exempted members of the cabinet who were to hold office during the term of the President by whom they were appointed and for one month thereafter, a clause accepted as a compromise after several Senators objected to the inclusion of the secretaries. Whether members of the cabinet appointed by Abraham Lincoln (q.v.), such as Secretary of War Edwin M. Stanton (q.v.), whom the radicals wanted to protect, were included was left in question.

Under the law, the President had the right to suspend appointees when the Senate was not in session but had to give his reasons in writing when Congress met again, so that the Senate could either uphold or reject the action.

It was in accordance with this law that on August 12, 1867, Johnson suspended Stanton and appointed General U. S. Grant (q.v.) Secretary of War ad interim. When in January 1868 the Senate failed to uphold this change, the President broke with Grant and on February 21 appointed Lorenzo Thomas in his place, thus openly challenging the law. On February 24 the House reacted by impeaching him for this violation of the Tenure of Office Act and other matters. The

Senate failed to sustain the charges, but the law remained on the books only to be modified in 1869 to allow the removal of officers during the recess of the Senate without requiring explanations and finally to be totally repealed in 1887. In the case of *Myers* v. *United States* in 1926 it was held to have been unconstitutional.

*See also* Impeachment of Andrew Johnson; Stanton, Edwin McMasters.

Hans L. Trefousse, *Impeachment of a President: Andrew Johnson, the Blacks, and Reconstruction* (Knoxville, Tenn., 1975); Michael Les Benedict, *The Impeachment and Trial of Andrew Johnson* (New York, 1973); David Miller DeWitt, *The Impeachment and Trial of Andrew Johnson* (New York, 1903).

**TEST OATH CASES.** *See* CUMMINGS V. MISSOURI; GARLAND, EX PARTE.

**TEXAS,** one of the states subject to Reconstruction. Largely spared from active warfare, Texas contained an intransigent majority loath to accept the results of the conflict. Abraham Lincoln (q.v.) appointed a Military Governor, Andrew Jackson Hamilton (q.v.), who, however, never succeeded in establishing his government fully. Hamilton was also appointed Provisional Governor by Andrew Johnson (q.v.) in June 1865 in accordance with the Presidential Plan of Reconstruction (q.v.), but the disordered affairs and the large distances involved delayed the electoral process until January 1866 so the constitutional convention met only in February of that year. Consisting of arch-conservatives, many of them former secessionists, that body framed a constitution ending slavery but limiting the suffrage to whites and holding ex-Confederates immune from damage suits. The conservative Unionist James W. Throckmorton was elected Governor, while the new legislature emphasized its conservatism by refusing to ratify the Fourteenth Amendment (q.v.), passing the usual black codes (q.v.), and electing Confederate officers to Congress.

Congressional Reconstruction (q.v.) ended the Throckmorton regime. In July 1867 General Philip H. Sheridan (q.v.) removed the Governor from office and appointed his defeated rival, Elisha M. Pease, instead. A radical convention based on black suffrage (q.v.) met in June 1868; although the radicals met opposition from former allies such as Hamilton and Pease, they succeeded in framing a constitution conferring large powers on the Governor, enfranchising the blacks (q.v.), and disfranchising those insurgents excluded by the Fourteenth Amendment. They also proposed dividing the state in two and actually wrote a constitution for West Texas. Their candidate for Governor, Edmund J. Davis, defeated Pease in the subsequent elections.

The Davis administration was marked by the Governor's efforts to overcome serious and often violent conservative opposition. Introducing free public education for both blacks and whites alike, the legislature ratified the Fourteenth and Fifteenth Amendments (q.v.), furthered railroad construction amid the usual charges of corruption, passed homestead acts, and sought to protect the frontier.

The state was readmitted in March 1870, but the Governor earned great unpopularity by attempting to postpone elections from 1870 to 1872.

In fact, the radical regime could not last. With the passage of the Amnesty Act of 1872, the Democrats, who had already made gains in 1871, were assured of victory in the following year. In spite of a last-minute attempt by Governor Davis to postpone the inevitable by relying on a dubious court decision to annul the 1872 elections leading to a Democratic triumph and the Republicans' refusal to vacate the statehouse, the Democrats prevailed. Stealthily climbing into the second story of the Republican-occupied capitol, they seized control. President U. S. Grant (q.v.) refused to intervene, and "Redemption" began. In 1875 a new constitution was adopted that diminished the appointive prerogatives of the Governor, decentralized power, and ended mandatory education. As in other states, the blacks were gradually reduced to political impotence, and Reconstruction was over.

*See also* Congressional Reconstruction; Hamilton, Andrew Jackson; Presidential Reconstruction.

Ernest Wallace, *Texas in Turmoil* (Austin, 1965); W. C. Nunn, *Texas Under the Carpetbaggers* (Austin, 1962); Charles W. Ramsdell, *Reconstruction in Texas* (New York, 1910).

**TEXAS v. WHITE** (1869), a Supreme Court case concerning the constitutional position of the states during Reconstruction. Involving the recovery of U.S. bonds sold during the Civil War by the Confederate state government of Texas (q.v.), the case was brought to the Supreme Court by Texas on the assumption that it had always been a state, even when not represented in Congress. Because their jurisdiction hinged on this proposition, the justices first had to decide this issue, and Chief Justice Salmon P. Chase (q.v.), speaking for the majority, rendered an opinion that constituted the tribunal's judgment on Reconstruction. Stating that the Constitution, in all its provisions, looked "to an indestructible Union, composed of indestructible States," he reasoned that Texas (q.v.) had never lost its character as a state. Nevertheless, relying on Article IV, Section 4, of the Constitution, obligating the United States to guarantee to each state a republican government, he also concluded that the federal government had the right, largely by legislative action, to enable Texas to resume its proper relations to the Union once secession had obliterated normal government.

In this case, Chase, on the one hand, upheld the concept endorsed by Abraham Lincoln (q.v.) and Andrew Johnson (q.v.) that the states had never been out of the Union while, on the other hand, underpinning constitutional theories under which Congress assumed the power to pass its Reconstruction legislation. The court thus upheld, even if only indirectly, the Reconstruction Acts (q.v.).

*See also* Chase, Salmon Portland; Congressional Reconstruction; Reconstruction Acts.

Charles Fairman, *Reconstruction and Reunion, 1864–88*, Vol. 6 of the Oliver Wendell Holmes Devise, *History of the Supreme Court of the United States* (New York, 1971); Stanley Kutler, *Judicial Power and Reconstruction Politics* (Chicago, 1968).

**THIRTEENTH AMENDMENT** (1865), the constitutional amendment abolishing slavery in the United States. The extinction of human bondage had long been the goal of the radical Republicans (q.v.), while Abraham Lincoln (q.v.) himself desired it. Constrained by the necessity of rallying the proslavery Democrats and the loyal border states to the national cause, however, he declared that the maintenance of the Union, and not the abolition of slavery, was the issue of the Civil War. Yet, as time went on, he signed two Confiscation Bills as well as laws for freedom in the District of Columbia and in the territories. In September 1862, spurred on by the radicals and anxious to frustrate foreign recognition of the Confederacy, he issued the Preliminary Emancipation Proclamation and on January 1, 1863, followed it with the final document that freed all slaves in areas still in rebellion.

Because the Emancipation Proclamation (q.v.), promulgated under Lincoln's authority as commander-in-chief of the army, might easily be overturned by adverse court decisions, the President began to champion an amendment to effect emancipation throughout the United States. Upon his urging, the Union platform of 1864 contained a plank calling for such a measure. In fact, on April 8, 1864, by a vote of thirty-eight to six, the Senate had already passed an amendment providing for the prohibition of slavery in the language of the Northwest Ordinance while giving Congress the right to enforce it. In the House, however, it ran into difficulty. It failed on June 15 by a vote of ninety-three to sixty-five, less than the necessary two-thirds majority, whereupon Representative James M. Ashley (q.v.) switched his vote in order to be able to move for a reconsideration.

The amendment was one of the issues in the election of 1864. Lincoln's victory would guarantee Reconstruction with emancipation (q.v.), whereas his defeat would signify the opposite. After he was reelected in the fall, the President in his annual message urged speedy passage of the reform. Standing ready to call for a special session of the new Congress should the old one fail to act and using his powers of patronage and persuasion upon wavering Democratic congressmen, he cooperated with Ashley, who on January 3, 1865, called up the measure. Enough Democrats either absented themselves or changed their vote so that on January 31 the amendment passed by a vote of 119 to 56.

When Andrew Johnson (q.v.) assumed the presidency, ratification by the states had not yet been completed. Making a strong plea for ratification part of his plan of Presidential Reconstruction (q.v.), he induced eight Southern states to give their assent, and on December 18, 1865, Secretary of State William H. Seward (q.v.) certified that the amendment had received the endorsement of the necessary three-fourths of the states to make it part of the Constitution. The fact that the eight Southern states among them had not yet completed their Reconstruction process and that their delegations had not been admitted to Congress was not considered important enough to vitiate their ratifications.

The passage of the Thirteenth Amendment marked the triumph of the antislavery struggle in the United States. Its enforcement clauses enabled Congress to pass the Civil Rights Act of 1866 (q.v.), and it remained as a permanent legacy of Reconstruction.

*See also* Ashley, James Mitchell; Johnson, Andrew; Lincoln, Abraham; Presidential Reconstruction.

Charles Fairman, *Reconstruction and Reunion, 1864–88*, Vol. 6 of the Oliver Wendell Holmes Devise, *History of the Supreme Court of the United States* (New York, 1971); J. G. Randall and Richard N. Current, *Lincoln the President: Last Full Measure* (New York, 1955); Harold M. Hyman and William M. Wiecek, *Equal Justice Under Law: Constitutional Development, 1835–1875* (New York, 1982).

**TILDEN, SAMUEL JONES** (1814–1884), Democratic politician and presidential candidate, was born in New Lebanon, New York, the son of Elam Tilden, a farmer and shopkeeper, and his wife, Polly Y. Jones Tilden. Educated briefly at Yale and intermittently at New York University and its new law school, Tilden was admitted to the bar in 1841 and eventually became one of New York's most successful lawyers who tried some of the chief railroad cases of the time. A Jacksonian Democrat, he was a member of the Assembly from 1845 to 1847 and of the 1846 New York constitutional convention. With other Barnburners, he followed his friend Martin Van Buren into the Free Soil party of 1848 but during the 1850s returned to the Democratic fold.

During the Civil War Tilden was a lukewarm War Democrat. His states rights and racial convictions led him to support the Reconstruction policies of Andrew Johnson (q.v.), and he was an enthusiastic delegate to the 1866 National Union Convention (q.v.) in Philadelphia. From 1866 to 1874 he served as chairman of the New York State Democratic Committee and was a member of the constitutional convention of 1867.

Tilden's rise to national prominence was due to his successful exposure of the corruption of William M. Tweed (q.v.). Although at first on good terms with the boss, in 1870 and 1871 he took the lead in bringing down the infamous Tweed Ring. He was returned to the Assembly in 1871 and his achievements in bringing the malefactors to justice made possible his election as Governor in 1874.

Governor Tilden's administration established a good record, particularly in breaking up the Canal Ring, which had been defrauding the state for years. The result was his nomination for the presidency in 1876.

In the disputed election of 1876, Tilden gained a majority of the popular vote over the Republican candidate, Rutherford B. Hayes (q.v.), but contested returns from three Southern states still in Republican hands enabled the Republicans to claim an electoral college victory for his opponent. On the face of it, Tilden had 184 electoral votes to Hayes' 165; if the disputed 20 in South Carolina (q.v.), Louisiana (q.v.), and Florida (q.v.), as well as 1 in Oregon, were all conceded to Hayes, he would win; if, however, Tilden could retain but one of them he would be the victor.

In this quandary, Congress, much against Tilden's wishes, established an Electoral Commission (q.v.), which awarded the disputed votes to Hayes. As a result of this verdict as well as economic and political bargains, involving the withdrawal of federal troops from Southern statehouses in return for the seating of Hayes (Compromise of 1877, q.v.), Tilden lost the presidency. Although he himself always insisted that he had been rightfully elected, his desire to maintain peace and his respect for the forms of law made him unwilling to resist. Because of widespread frauds on both sides and the terrorization of the black vote, the real facts are hard to determine. It is likely, however, that had there been a really free vote in all the Southern states, the freedmen's support would have enabled Hayes to win.

After the election Tilden retired to his law practice in New York. Involved in a long suit concerning allegations of irregularities in his income tax returns, he was also embarrassed by revelations concerning the cipher dispatches, telegrams in code sent in 1877 by Democrats to the South offering bribes for votes, of which he maintained he knew nothing. He declined renomination in 1880 and 1884 and died at his estate, Greystone, in Yonkers. Part of his legacy, in spite of lengthy and largely successful lawsuits contesting his will, contributed to the establishment of the New York Public Library.

*See also* Compromise of 1877; Electoral Commission; Hayes, Rutherford B.

Alexander Clarence Flick, *Samuel Jones Tilden: A Study in Political Sagacity* (New York, 1939).

**TOURGÉE, ALBION WINEGAR** (1838–1905), radical North Carolina judge and author, was born in Williamsfield, Ohio, the son of Albion and Emma Winegar Tourgée. Losing his mother at the age of five, he lived for a while with maternal relatives in Lee, Massachusetts, before returning to his father at Kingsville, Ohio. He was educated at Kingsville Academy and the University of Rochester, taught school at Wilson Collegiate Institute in upstate New York, and, despite the loss of one eye at fourteen, in 1861 enlisted in a New York regiment. A severe injury suffered in the aftermath of the Battle of Bull Run invalided him for months. He studied law in Ashtabula, Ohio, and returned to the army, only to be wounded again at Perryville and captured at Murfreesboro. After his exchange, he married Emma L. Kilbourne, rejoined the army, but resigned following a renewed injury to his back and resentment about his failure to be promoted.

After the war, Tourgée practiced journalism in Erie, Pennsylvania, and then moved to North Carolina (q.v.), where he started a nursery and law practice in Greensboro. Entering politics as a Republican of the most extreme sect and a friend of the freedmen, he was an active member of the Southern Loyalist Convention (q.v.) in Philadelphia, advocated black suffrage (q.v.), and campaigned strenuously in the election of 1866. As a member of the constitutional convention of 1868, he was instrumental in securing the election of judges, local self-government, and retroactive homestead protection for farmers. His reward was an appointment to the Code Commission, which prepared a Code of the Civil Procedure of North Carolina, and his election as a judge of the Superior Court.

Tourgée's tenure as a judge was a stormy one. Constantly harassed by the Ku Klux Klan (q.v.) and attacked as a carpetbagger (q.v.), he nevertheless succeeded in administering justice evenhandedly and eventually completed *A Digest of the Cited Cases of North Carolina Reports*. In 1871 he invested in a handle business, which he lost following the Panic of 1873, and in 1874, his political future uncertain because of the conservatives' control of the legislature, he resigned his judgeship. Accused of accepting money from Milton S. Littlefield (q.v.) and George W. Swepson (q.v.), he did not allow his relations with these speculators to influence his decisions, although he never seems to have repaid their loans for his house.

After the loss of his business and office, Tourgée briefly served as a pension agent in Raleigh. Returning to Greensboro, in 1878 he ran unsuccessfully for Congress and then left the South for good.

Tourgée's fame rests largely on his writings. His first novel, *Toinette*, a tale of slavery, appeared in 1874. *Figs and Thistles* followed, and in 1879 he published his best-selling account of Reconstruction, *A Fool's Errand*, which clearly reflected his disappointment with the results of the war and Reconstruction. He removed to Denver, Colorado, and to other Northern cities and in 1881 bought a house, Thorheim, at Maysville, New York. Other books, principally attacks upon prejudice like his *Bricks Without Straw*, followed, while he continued to support himself by lecturing and writing for newspapers and magazines. In 1880 he influenced the Republican convention to include an education plank in its platform, and he never ceased to advocate federal aid to schools in the South. In 1882 he founded a weekly called *Our Continent* but lost money in the venture. An untiring advocate of the rights of blacks (q.v.), in the 1890s he became the unpaid attorney for the plaintiffs in *Plessy* v. *Ferguson* (q.v.) and wrote the main brief in the case, the unsuccessful outcome of which did not deter him from continuing his campaign for racial justice. He also sought to protect the poor and differed from his conservative employers at the Chicago *Inter-Ocean* by sympathizing with the Pullman strikers. In 1897 he was appointed U.S. consul at Bordeaux, where he died in 1905.

*See also* Carpetbaggers; North Carolina; *Plessy* v. *Ferguson*.

Otto H. Olsen, *Carpetbagger's Crusade: The Life of Albion Winegar Tourgée* (Baltimore, 1965); Richard Nelson Current, *Those Terrible Carpetbaggers: A Reinterpretation* (New York, 1988).

**TRUMBULL, LYMAN** (1813–1896), Republican Senator from Illinois, was born in Colchester, Connecticut, the son of the attorney Benjamin Trumbull and his wife, Elizabeth Mather. Although descended from illustrious Puritan ancestors, the Trumbulls were not wealthy, and their son, after attending Bacon Academy, taught school. At age nineteen he accepted the post of principal of Greenville Academy in Georgia, read law, and in 1837 was admitted to the bar. Moving to Belleville, Illinois, he started a law practice. In 1840 he was elected a Democratic member of the legislature and the next year appointed Secretary of State. Removed from office in 1843, he made a name for himself by waging legal struggles against the remnant of slavery in Illinois.

After marrying Julia Jayne of Springfield, in 1848 Trumbull ran unsuccessfully for Congress. Two years later, having moved to Alton, he was elected to the Illinois Supreme Court, on which he served until 1853. In 1854 he succeeded in his bid for Congress, but before he could take his seat, he became the anti-Nebraska choice for U.S. Senator and, with the help of Abraham Lincoln (q.v.), who had been a rival candidate, was elected in 1855. He joined the emerging Republican party (q.v.) and was returned to his seat in 1861.

During the Civil War, Trumbull, who had been a moderate, gradually became more and more radical. In collaboration with Zachariah Chandler (q.v.) and Benjamin F. Wade (q.v.), he put pressure on Lincoln for a more determined prosecution of the war and, as chairman of the Senate Judiciary Committee, prepared the Habeas Corpus and Second Confiscation Acts. After moving to Chicago, in 1864 he supplied the wording of the Thirteenth Amendment (q.v.), which he successfully piloted through the Senate.

Trumbull's Reconstruction career was marked by a generally moderate course. After first opposing the admission of Senators from Arkansas (q.v.), he nevertheless favored Lincoln's scheme of restoration in Louisiana (q.v.) and unsuccessfully supported the seating of that state's delegation. He concurred with Andrew Johnson (q.v.) in the belief that suffrage was a state concern and therefore at first did not endorse votes for freedmen. Yet he was the author of the Freedmen's Bureau Bill (q.v.) of 1866, which would have confirmed land titles for the blacks (q.v.), as well as of the Civil Rights Act (q.v.), which conferred citizenship upon them and guaranteed their civil rights.

Johnson's veto of these two measures brought about a complete break between the President and Trumbull, who had been led to believe that Johnson would sign them. Accordingly the Senator, who was reelected in 1867, wrote the preamble to the bill readmitting Tennessee (q.v.), which asserted the right of Congress to reconstruct a state, and later favored the Reconstruction Acts (q.v.). He also appeared as counsel for the government in *ex parte McCardle* (q.v.).

Nevertheless, Trumbull did not rejoin his wartime radical associates. Taking an unfavorable view of the impeachment of Johnson (q.v.), he considered the trial a judicial proceeding, carefully weighed the evidence, and found it wanting. Consequently, he became one of the seven ''recusant'' Republicans who voted for the President's acquittal.

Although Trumbull supported U. S. Grant (q.v.) for the presidency, he soon drifted into the Liberal Republican (Liberal Republican Movement, q.v.) camp. He favored civil service reform (q.v.), authored the 1871 amendment to an appropriations bill setting up a civil service commission, and in the next year was an active contender for the Liberal Republican presidential nomination. Defeated for reelection in 1873, he retired to Chicago to resume his law practice. In 1876 he rejoined the Democratic party (q.v.), argued its case before the 1877 Electoral Commission (q.v.) and in 1880 was its unsuccessful candidate for

Governor. In 1886 he appealed to the Governor of Illinois for a commutation of the Hay Market anarchists' death sentences and, sympathizing with the Populists in the 1890s, appeared for Eugene V. Debs in his habeas corpus case. He died in Chicago in 1906.

Called a "conservative radical" by one of his biographers, Trumbull was a fair-minded jurist whose independence contributed to his considerable influence during Reconstruction.

*See also* Civil Rights Act of 1866; Freedmen's Bureau Bill; Johnson, Andrew; Liberal Republican Movement; Thirteenth Amendment.

Ralph J. Roske, *His Own Counsel: The Life and Times of Lyman Trumbull* (Reno, 1979); Mark M. Krug, *Lyman Trumbull: Conservative Radical* (New York, 1965); Horace White, *The Life of Lyman Trumbull* (Boston, 1913).

**TWEED, WILLIAM MAGEAR** (1823–1878), New York political leader and Democratic boss, was born in New York, the son of Richard Tweed, a chairmaker, and his wife, Eliza Magear. After attending the public schools until he was eleven, Tweed learned his father's trade, spent a year at a boarding school in Elizabeth, and later married Jane C. Skaden, the daughter of the elder Tweed's partner in the brush-making business. Gregarious and politically astute, he joined a fire company and fraternal organizations and in 1850 ran unsuccessfully for assistant alderman. Elected alderman the next year, in 1852 he won a seat in Congress, where he served one term. In 1856 he became a member of the Board of Education and in 1858 a member of the Board of Supervisors. Joining Tammany in 1859, in 1861 he ran unsuccessfully for sheriff, suffered bankruptcy, and began the practice of law. Reelected a supervisor in 1862, he became president of the board and deputy street commissioner.

His rise to notoriety came after the Civil War. Closely associated with James Fisk of the Erie Railroad and retained by Jay Gould (q.v.), he was able to sell political influence. In 1867 he was elected to the state Senate, and together with Richard B. Connolly, who became comptroller, and Peter B. Sweeney, who was elected chamberlain, Tweed and his associates, including after 1869 Mayor A. Oakey Hall, occupied important positions in the city government. Tweed became Grand Sachem of Tammany, superintendent of public works, county supervisor, and supervisor of the new county courthouse. He and his collaborators, commonly called the "Tweed Ring," influenced elections and apparently received kickbacks from contractors as well as bribes from the Erie Railroad. Yet at the same time, Tweed took an interest in beautifying the city, widening its streets, and laying the foundations for the Metropolitan Museum of Art and the public library.

In 1870 Tweed was instrumental in procuring a new charter for the city of New York that centralized municipal government, but he was unable to reap its benefits for long. After Thomas Nast (q.v.) of *Harper's Weekly* had begun to pillory the Boss in a series of savage cartoons, the *New York Times* launched an editorial attack against him. A clerk in the auditor's office supplied the paper with documents, and in 1871 a Committee of Seventy to investigate the frauds was set up. Although there was little direct evidence of wrongdoing, the chairman of the Democratic State Committee, Samuel J. Tilden (q.v.), leading the fight against the ring in the state, produced seemingly sufficient proof to bring about Tweed's indictment. A sensational trial before a prejudiced judge ended in a hung jury; but Tweed, who was reelected Senator in 1871, was tried again, convicted, and sentenced to some twelve years imprisonment and a fine. Although an appeals court overturned the sentence, Tweed was imprisoned once more for failure to raise bail in a civil suit. Escaping from jail in 1875, he fled to Cuba and Spain but was extradited, having been tried and found liable on pending charges, so he remained in prison. In 1877 he wrote a confession of his peculations; the document was unsubstantiated, however, and may merely have been his bid for freedom, since he was the only member of the ring who had been imprisoned for any length of time. He died in his cell in 1878.

Long considered the embodiment of the perpetrators of urban corruption during Reconstruction and accused of looting millions from the city, more recently Tweed has been pictured more as a victim than a villain. While he was probably corrupt, his political enemies did seek him out for special punishment and made him a scapegoat for widespread malpractices.

*See also* Nast, Thomas; Tilden, Samuel Jones.

Leo Hershkowitz, *Tweed's New York: Another Look* (Garden City, N.Y., 1977); Seymour J. Mandelbaum, *Boss Tweed's New York* (New York, 1965); Dennis Tilden Lynch, *"Boss" Tweed: The Story of a Grim Generation* (New York, 1927).

# U

UNDERWOOD, JOHN CURTISS (1809–1873), radical Virginia (q.v.) jurist, was born in Litchfield, New York, the son of John and Mary Curtiss Underwood. After graduating from Hamilton College in 1832, Underwood settled in Clarke County, Virginia. He was an ardent Free Soiler and Republican, who attended the 1856 and 1860 Republican National Conventions. Forced to leave Virginia because of his antislavery opinions, he moved to New York to work in a land company.

The triumph of the Republican party (q.v.) advanced Underwood's career. Offered a consulship in Callao, Peru in 1861, he accepted a position as Fifth Auditor of the Treasury instead. In 1864 President Lincoln (q.v.) appointed him to the United States District Court in Alexandria, Virginia, where he soon became nationally known because of the trial of Jefferson Davis (q.v.). It was in Underwood's court that the Confederate President was indicted for treason in May 1866 after the judge delivered a spirited charge. In May 1867 he held Davis bailable, and the defendant was released on bail. In the final proceedings in November 1868, Underwood disagreed with Chief Justice Salmon P. Chase (q.v.), in whose circuit the court was located, about dropping the case, but Chase succeeded in ending the proceedings.

Underwood was also active in Virginia Reconstruction politics. Friendly to black aspirations, in 1867 he presided over the radical constitutional convention, which drew up a charter named after him. The Underwood Constitution contained provisions for free schools for both races, equal rights provisions, and reforms of local government. Except for its disfranchising clauses, it was ratified by the electorate, and although the conservatives took over the state in 1869, with some changes it remained in effect until 1902. Underwood died in Washington in 1873.

*See also* Davis, Jefferson; Virginia.

Lyon Gardiner Tyler, ed., *Encyclopedia of Virginia Biography* (5 vols., New York, 1915); Jack P. Maddex, Jr., *The Virginia Conservatives, 1867–1879* (Chapel Hill, N.C., 1970).

**UNION LEAGUE,** secret Republican political organization, first appeared in the border states during the Civil War. By 1862 a National Council was established in the North, and the organization gradually spread to the South as well. Initially appealing to loyal mountaineers in East Tennessee, northern Alabama, and elsewhere in Appalachia, as time went on it became more and more identified with the freedmen. It was financed by the National Union Republican Executive Committee, and the organization, also called the Loyal League, attracted blacks (q.v.) particularly after the passage of the Reconstruction Acts (q.v.).

The Union League was modeled after other fraternal organizations, such as the Free Masons. Standing in front of a podium decorated with a Bible, the Declaration of Independence, a flag, a censer, a sword, a gavel, and a ballot box, as well as emblems of industry, the initiates had to take an oath to elect only true and reliable men for public office. Passwords and hand signals stressed the four "L's": liberty, Lincoln, loyal, and league, and new members swore to protect their fellows and never to divulge the order's secrets.

The league played an important part in initiating Congressional Reconstruction (q.v.) in the South. It marshaled the black vote, called attention to the duties of citizenship, and helped elect Republican candidates. It also mobilized black labor against exploitation, thus becoming a veritable thorn in the side of the conservatives. When threats against league members proved unavailing, conservatives had recourse to terror, particularly through the Ku Klux Klan (q.v.), and by 1870, most of the leagues in the South had been effectively neutralized. The organization continued to exist in the North, lent aid to the freedmen's migration to Kansas in 1879, and agitated for black rights, but eventually disappeared in the 1890s.

Long held responsible for many of the alleged ills of Reconstruction, in reality the Union League, plagued though it was by factionalism, played an important role in politicizing the blacks, spreading Republican ideals among them, and contributing greatly to the change in Southern agriculture from the old plantation to the new tenant farming and sharecropping system.

*See also* Congressional Reconstruction; Ku Klux Klan.

Michael F. Fitzgerald, *The Union League Movement in the Deep South: Politics and Agricultural Change During Reconstruction* (Baton Rouge, 1989); Richard H. Abbott, *The Republican Party and the South, 1855–1877* (Chapel Hill, N.C., 1986).

**U.S. v. CRUIKSHANK** (1876), a Supreme Court decision weakening particularly the equal protection of the laws provision of the Fourteenth Amendment (q.v.).

As a result of the Colfax Riot (q.v.), several white offenders accused of massacring blacks were indicted for violation of Section 6 of the Enforcement

Act (q.v.) of 1870, forbidding conspiracies against the free enjoyment of constitutional rights. A number of defendants were convicted, but a division among the judges concerning the nature of the indictment brought the case to the Supreme Court, where the majority held for the defendants. Asserting that the postwar amendments protected individuals only from state and not from private action and that the Fourteenth Amendment did not add anything to the rights of one citizen against another under the Constitution, Chief Justice Morrison R. Waite (q.v.) made clear his limited interpretation of the appropriate clauses of the Fourteenth Amendment. He stated that they covered only those rights specifically within the power of the federal as distinct from the state governments. Since the indictment neither charged that the victims' privileges had been violated as a result of a state law nor labeled as such the racially motivated criminal actions in question, the federal government did not have the constitutional power to afford protection. Not even the Fifteenth Amendment (q.v.) was applicable, because the indictment did not specify that the victims' right to vote had been abridged on the grounds of race. Thus by reasoning that the indictment had been too vague, the court in effect rendered the relevant provisions of the amendments unenforceable.

*See also* Enforcement Acts; Fourteenth Amendment; Supreme Court; Waite, Morrison Remick.

Robert J. Kaczorowski, *The Politics of Judicial Interpretation: The Federal Courts, Department of Justice, and Civil Rights, 1866–1876* (New York, 1985); Charles Fairman, *Reconstruction and Reunion, 1864–88*, Vol. 7 of the Oliver Wendell Holmes Devise, *History of the Supreme Court of the United States, 1864–88* (New York, 1987).

**U.S. v. REESE ET AL.** (1876), Supreme Court decision declaring Sections 3 and 4 of the Enforcement Act (q.v.) of 1870 unconstitutional and limiting the scope of the Fifteenth Amendment (q.v.).

The *Reese* case reached the Supreme Court from Kentucky, where Lexington registration officials had refused to allow a black citizen to vote in a municipal election on the grounds that he did not have the receipt for a capitation tax required by the state's suffrage laws. Declaring that the Fifteenth Amendment did not confer the right to vote upon anyone, Chief Justice Morrison R. Waite (q.v.) held that the amendment's enforcement clauses applied only to the explicit denial of the right to vote for reasons of race, color, and previous condition of servitude. Thus they did not empower the federal government to set punishments for state registrars who refused to accept voters on other grounds, so Sections 3 and 4 of the Enforcement Act of 1870 providing for such penalties were unconstitutional. This decision in favor of the defendants was rendered in spite of the fact that collectors had refused the offered payment of the tax in order to prevent blacks (q.v.) from voting, and despite the presentation of an affidavit concerning the attempt to pay to the registrars.

The result of the decision was the practical weakening of the Fifteenth Amendment. Together with its companion case, *U.S* v. *Cruikshank* (q.v.), *Reese* is a good example of the Court's retreat from Reconstruction.

*See also* Enforcement Acts; Fifteenth Amendment; Supreme Court; *U.S.* v. *Cruikshank*; Waite, Morrison Remick.

Robert J. Kaczorowski, *The Politics of Judicial Interpretation: The Federal Court, Department of Justice, and Civil Rights, 1866–1876* (New York, 1985); Charles Fairman, *Reconstruction and Reunion, 1864–88*, Vol. 7 of the Oliver Wendell Holmes Devise, *History of the Supreme Court of the United States* (New York, 1987).

# V

VALLANDIGHAM, CLEMENT LAIRD (1820–1871), leader of the Peace Democrats, was born in New Lisbon, Ohio, the son of a Presbyterian minister. Educated at Jefferson College, he was admitted to the bar in 1842 and entered upon the practice of law. He served in the Assembly from 1845 to 1847, when he moved to Dayton to edit the Dayton *Empire* and establish his permanent home. A member of Congress from 1856 to 1862, he was a strong advocate of states rights and a supporter of Stephen A. Douglas.

During the Civil War, Vallandigham became notorious as the leading Copperhead and opponent of the administration. In May 1863, after delivering an antiwar speech at Mt. Vernon, he was arrested by General Ambrose E. Burnside for violation of General Order No. 38, prohibiting declarations of sympathy for the enemy. Tried by a military commission, he was sentenced to imprisonment for the duration of the war, but Abraham Lincoln (q.v.) commuted the sentence to banishment to the Confederacy. Vallandigham, however, who had been nominated by the Democrats for Governor of Ohio, left the South for Canada, where he waged a strenuous campaign. After he was defeated by John Brough, in 1864 he returned to the United States, appeared at the Democratic National Convention in Chicago, and insisted upon a peace plank, which was adopted.

During Reconstruction, Vallandigham, who opposed all the postwar amendments, was a strong supporter of the policies of Andrew Johnson (q.v.). Elected a delegate to the National Union Convention (q.v.) in Philadelphia in 1866, he was prevailed upon to withdraw. In 1867 he was an unsuccessful candidate for his party's choice for Senator, and at the 1868 Democratic Convention in New York, Vallandigham, who had unsuccessfully sought his party's endorsement for Senator in 1867, favored the candidacy of Salmon P. Chase but then reluctantly campaigned for Horatio Seymour (q.v.), the Democratic nominee. He lost another bid for Congress and afterward preached the "new departure" policy to enable the Democrats to end the controversy about the amendments by reluctantly accepting them. He accidentally shot himself during a trial in New Lebanon and died as a result.

*See also* Democratic Party; Johnson, Andrew; National Union Convention.

Frank L. Klement, *The Limits of Dissent: Clement L. Vallandigham and the Civil War* (Lexington, Ky., 1970).

**VANCE, ZEBULON BAIRD** (1830–1894), North Carolina (q.v.) Governor and Senator, was born in Buncombe County, the son of the farmer David Vance and his wife Mira Margaret Baird. Educated at Washington College and the University of North Carolina, he entered upon the practice of law in Asheville in 1852. Two years later, he was elected as a Whig to the state legislature, was defeated for the next term, but was sent to Congress in 1858 and 1859. He was an avid Unionist, who gave his allegiance to secession only after Abraham Lincoln's (q.v.) call for troops. Then he served in the Confederate army, saw action at New Bern and Malvern Hill, and attained the rank of colonel. In 1862, supported by William W. Holden (q.v.), he was elected Governor. A determined chief executive, he sought to maintain civil liberties in spite of the war, an attitude that often brought him into conflict with the Confederate authorities at Richmond. In 1864, opposed to a separate peace, he defeated Holden, who had broken with him, and was reelected Governor.

At the end of the war, Vance was briefly held at the Old Capitol Prison in Washington. Returning to North Carolina to practice law in Charlotte, he counseled peaceful reunification. But, vigorously insisting that his old Whig party had been completely different from the Republicans, he joined the Conservative Democrats, who in 1870 elected him to the Senate. Although he was denied his seat, he was reelected Governor in 1876 and proved to be an outstanding "Redeemer" ("Redemption," q.v.). Furthering the education of both races, he was instrumental in the establishment of a normal school for blacks (q.v.). In 1879 he was sent to the Senate and won reelection in 1884 and 1890. Although a Democrat, he feuded with Grover Cleveland concerning patronage, but in 1890 firmly opposed the Force Bill as well as the McKinley tariff. He died in Washington in 1894.

*See also* Holden, William Woods; North Carolina; "Redemption".

Glenn Tucker, *Zeb Vance: Champion of Personal Freedom* (Indianapolis, 1965).

**VIRGINIA,** one of the states subject to Reconstruction, was partially restored as early as 1861 because of the revolt of the northwestern counties against the secessionists. A "restored government of Virginia" was established in Wheeling; Francis H. Pierpont (q.v.) became Governor, and the state's loyal congressional delegation was seated in both Houses.

In May 1862, after a convention had framed a constitution for a separate state of West Virginia (q.v.), the Wheeling legislature gave its consent, and Governor

Pierpont transferred his government to Alexandria, where he continued to administer the Union-occupied portions of the commonwealth. Although the House of Representatives refused to seat Virginia's loyal claimants, the Pierpont regime maintained itself. In 1864 a convention disfranchised Confederates and abolished slavery; it did not, however, confer the suffrage upon the freedmen.

At the end of the war, Andrew Johnson (q.v.) recognized the Pierpont government, which had already ratified the Thirteenth Amendment (q.v.) and in May moved to Richmond. While the legislature passed laws recognizing the legality of black marriages, it also eased the disfranchisement clauses of the constitution, and after an election in October, a conservative victory resulted in the passage of strict vagrancy laws as well as the practical repeal of Confederate disabilities. Despite Pierpont's advice to the contrary, the legislators, like those of other Johnson states, refused its consent to the Fourteenth Amendment (q.v.), and accordingly, in 1867 Virginia was remanded to military rule under the Reconstruction Acts. It became the first military district.

In the meantime, Pierpont's term of office had expired, whereupon, in April 1867 the military commander, General John M. Schofield (q.v.), removed him and appointed Henry H. Wells Governor. After an election based on universal manhood suffrage, a constitutional convention met in December. Dominated by Republicans, it framed a basic law named after its presiding officer, Judge John C. Underwood (q.v.) and containing provisions for black suffrage (q.v.), the establishment of free public schools for both races, and the liberalization of local government. The new constitution also included stringent citizens clauses for former Confederates, provisions so unpopular that General Schofield postponed elections for the document's ratification.

This delay gave rise to a coalition of moderate Republicans and conservatives who delegated a Committee of Nine to go to Washington to induce the federal government to authorize separate votes on the disqualification clauses. The committee was successful. Congress gave its consent, although it also required Virginia to ratify the Fifteenth as well as the Fourteenth Amendment before applying for readmission. Elections were held in July 1869; the constitution was accepted but the disfranchising clauses rejected. At the same time, the coalition candidate, Gilbert C. Walker, defeated Governor Wells, and a conservative legislature was elected. After this body ratified the amendments, in January 1870 the state was readmitted to the Union.

The triumph of the conservative coalition enabled Virginia to avoid radical rule. In an administration dominated by conservatives the blacks (q.v.) continued to hold office and vote, but power rested in the hands of the white establishment. In compliance with the Underwood constitution, the new rulers established free schools for both races; like "redeemers" ("Redemption," q.v.) everywhere, however, they sought to save money, enacted poll taxes and other devices to reduce black voting, and in general benefited the business interests of the state.

In 1871 the conservative legislature enacted a funding bill for the payment of the state's debt. This measure later became a subject of bitter controversy, with the so-called Readjusters (q.v.), led by General William Mahone (q.v.) attacking the concept of diverting funds from social services to pay prewar debts. In 1879 the Readjusters captured the legislature, ending the rule of the conservative party and later electing Mahone to the Senate. This victory was made possible because of the support of the blacks, for whom the Readjusters enacted a number of vital measures. They repealed the poll tax, established a black normal school, and abolished the whipping post. But Mahone's collaboration with the Republicans and his limited favors to the freedmen alienated enough whites to allow the Democrats in 1883 to recapture the state. The Underwood constitution, however, remained in force until 1902.

*See also* Congressional Reconstruction; Pierpont, Francis Harrison; Presidential Reconstruction; Underwood, John Curtiss; West Virginia.

Richard Lowe, *Republicans and Reconstruction in Virginia, 1856–1870* (Charlottesville, Va., 1990); Jack P. Maddex, Jr., *The Virginia Conservatives, 1867–1879* (Chapel Hill, N.C., 1970); Alrutheus Ambush Taylor, *The Negro in the Reconstruction of Virginia* (Washington, D.C., 1926); H. J. Eckenrode, *The Political History of Virginia During Reconstruction* (Baltimore, 1904).

# W

WADE, BENJAMIN FRANKLIN (1800–1878), radical Senator from Ohio, was born in Feeding Hills, Massachusetts, the descendant of an old impoverished Puritan family. Educated in the local schools and by his mother, Mary Upham Wade, the daughter of a minister, he joined an older brother in Andover, Ohio, at the age of twenty-one. He taught school, was engaged as a drover, and was a laborer on the Erie Canal. But he also read law with Elisha Whittlesey and in 1828 was admitted to the bar. After settling in Jefferson, where he established his practice, he was elected prosecuting attorney (1835). In 1837 and 1841 the Whigs elected him to the state Senate, where he made a name for himself because of his opposition to slavery and the state's black codes. In 1847 the legislature elected him presiding judge of the Third Judicial District of Ohio.

Wade's antislavery convictions were soon rewarded. The passage of the 1850 Fugitive Slave Law was so distasteful to him that he declared he would never enforce it, and in 1851 he was elected to the U.S. Senate by a coalition of Whigs and Free Soilers. In Washington, he was one of a small band of radicals, fought against the Kansas-Nebraska Act, and advocated a homestead law. One of the founders of the Republican party (q.v.) in Ohio, he was reelected in 1856 and was one of the candidates for the presidential nomination four years later. During the secession crisis, he stood staunchly against compromise and supported Abraham Lincoln (q.v.).

When Civil War broke out, Wade became one of the leading radicals agitating for firm military measures and the abolition of slavery. He served as chairman of the Joint Committee on the Conduct of the War, which he used to further radical aims and often clashed with the administration about its deliberate policies.

The Senator was also the head of the Committee on Territories, a position of special importance because he believed that secession reduced the disloyal states to a territorial condition. Consequently, he held that Congress, and not the President, possessed the sole right to set terms for Reconstruction. He opposed Lincoln's Proclamation of Amnesty (q.v.) and in the summer of 1864 became the cosponsor of the Wade-Davis Bill (q.v.). Providing for a majority rather than a 10 percent vote before a state could qualify for readmission and stringent disabilities for ex-Confederates, the measure mandated emancipation (q.v.) but not black suffrage (q.v.). Because it superseded his own scheme, Lincoln pocket-vetoed it.

Wade was furious at this action. Although his party was in the midst of an election campaign, he joined Henry Winter Davis (q.v.) in publishing the Wade-Davis Manifesto (q.v.), accusing the President of seeking to manufacture votes for himself. Badly received by the public, the Manifesto accomplished little except to discredit its authors. But although Wade finally lent his support to the Republican ticket, he continued to maintain his views on Reconstruction and in early 1865 opposed the admission of Louisiana (q.v.).

The Senator welcomed the accession of Andrew Johnson (q.v.) to the presidency. Believing him to be in sympathy with radical ideas because of his cooperation with the Committee on the Conduct of the War, Wade was in hopes of intimate collaboration with the White House. Johnson's inauguration of his plan of Reconstruction, however, totally alienated the Senator, who became one of the President's most determined opponents. Supporting the main measures of Reconstruction, such as the Civil Rights Act (q.v.), the Fourteenth Amendment (q.v.), and the Reconstruction Acts (q.v.), he was instrumental in securing the admission of Nebraska. He became so prominent that in March 1867 he was elected President pro tem of the Senate, a position that put him next in line for the presidency.

But Wade's fortunes soon took a turn for the worse. Campaigning strenuously for black suffrage in Ohio in 1867, he lost his own bid for reelection when the Democrats captured the state legislature. In addition, the Senator, who was as radical about the rights of women and labor as he was about those of the blacks (q.v.), alienated many of his more conservative colleagues, some of whom believed him more dangerous than Johnson.

When in February 1868 the President was impeached, Wade's elevation to the White House seemed probable. Holding that Ohio was entitled to two votes, he took the oath as one of the members of the court despite a challenge. He did not participate actively in most of the subsequent proceedings of the trial, but on May 16, when the President was acquitted, cast his vote for conviction, although, called too late because his name began with a ''W,'' he was no longer able to influence the outcome. To some degree, fear of his radicalism had contributed to the failure of the impeachment.

Frequently mentioned for Vice President on the ticket with U. S. Grant (q.v.), in the aftermath of the acquittal of Johnson he was set aside at the Philadelphia National Convention, which nominated Schuyler Colfax instead. Another impeachment vote on May 26, 1868, again resulted in failure to convict, and on March 4, 1869, Wade retired from the Senate.

The old radicals' public career was practically over. Although General Grant appointed him one of the government directors of the Union Pacific Railroad and a member of the Santo Domingo Commission, he never again ran for office. An elector for Rutherford B. Hayes (q.v.) in 1876, he was deeply disappointed at the President's withdrawal of troops from Southern statehouses and the end of radical rule in the South. He died in Jefferson in 1878.

A true radical, Wade contributed materially to the racial reforms of the nineteenth century. In spite of his bluff ways, he was not vindictive and entertained pleasant personal relations with many of his opponents.

*See also* Davis, Henry Winter; Impeachment of Andrew Johnson; Radical Republicans; Wade-Davis Bill; Wade-Davis Manifesto.

Hans L. Trefousse, *Benjamin Franklin Wade: Radical Republican from Ohio* (New York, 1963).

**WADE-DAVIS BILL** (1864), the congressional Reconstruction measure passed on July 2, 1864, but pocket-vetoed by President Abraham Lincoln (q.v.) and cosponsored by Senator Benjamin F. Wade (q.v.), it required the President to appoint, by and with the consent of the Senate, a Provisional Governor for each seceded state. But unlike Lincoln's Proclamation of Amnesty (q.v.), it stipulated that the process of Reconstruction could begin only after resistance to the United States had ceased and a majority, rather than 10 percent, of the citizens had taken an oath of loyalty. Then those not disfranchised by the ironclad oath (q.v.) would elect a convention to amend state constitutions by outlawing slavery, disfranchising ranking Confederates, and repudiating the Confederate debt. Although the bill abolished slavery and extended the privilege of the writ of habeas corpus to the freedmen, its final version did not require black suffrage (q.v.).

The President, however, refused to sign the bill. Issuing a proclamation declaring the measure to be "one very proper plan for the loyal people of any State choosing the adopt it," he nevertheless declined to approve of it because Arkansas (q.v.) and Louisiana (q.v.) had already accepted his own scheme of Reconstruction. Although he favored a constitutional amendment to end slavery, he doubted the competence of Congress to emancipate by ordinary legislation.

Lincoln's pocket veto infuriated the sponsors of the bill. On August 5 Representative Davis and Senator Wade issued the Wade-Davis Manifesto (q.v.) accusing the President of seeking to manufacture votes for himself. The manifesto, however, designed to displace Lincoln with another candidate, had little effect, and because the bill was more demanding than the President's scheme, no state availed itself of its provisions.

Often criticized as a radical measure directed against the President, the Wade-Davis Bill, while framed to assert the power of Congress to guarantee to each state a republican government, contained conservative features such as white suffrage and limited disfranchisement, provisions enabling moderates to vote for it. It was passed by an overwhelming majority, and Lincoln's veto was totally unexpected.

*See also* Amnesty; Davis, Henry Winter; Wade, Benjamin Franklin; Wade-Davis Manifesto.

Michael Les Benedict, *A Compromise of Principle: Congressional Republicans and Reconstruction, 1863–1869* (New York, 1974); Gerald S. Henig, *Henry Winter Davis, Antebellum and Civil War Congressman from Maryland* (New York, 1973); Herman Belz, *Reconstructing the Union: Theory and Practice During the Civil War* (Ithaca, N.Y., 1969); H. L. Trefousse *Benjamin Franklin Wade: Radical Republican from Ohio* (New York, 1963).

**WADE-DAVIS MANIFESTO** (1864), the indictment of President Abraham Lincoln (q.v.) for pocket-vetoing the Wade-Davis Bill (q.v.). Outraged by Lincoln's refusal to sign the Reconstruction measure and infuriated by his subsequent explanatory proclamation, Representative Henry Winter Davis (q.v.), the author, and Senator Benjamin Franklin Wade (q.v.), the cosponsor of the bill, on August 5 published in the New York *Tribune* a stinging attack upon the President. Accusing him of manufacturing votes for himself and of "holding for naught the will of Congress" in matters of Reconstruction, which they believed to be exclusively a legislative responsibility, they declared that the authority of Congress was paramount, and if the President wished their support, "he must confine himself to his executive duties—to obey and execute, not make the laws."

Published in the midst of a presidential campaign and designed to further the movement to displace Lincoln with some other candidate, the Manifesto was badly received by the press and public. Far from damaging the President, it caused people to rally behind him. The effort to displace him failed, and his position was greatly strengthened by Union victories in Georgia and the Valley of Virginia. Davis was not even renominated, and Wade's reputation severely damaged. Nevertheless, the Manifesto expressed the radical view of congressional authority over Reconstruction.

*See also* Davis, Henry Winter; Wade, Benjamin Franklin; Wade-Davis Bill.

Gerald S. Henig, *Henry Winter Davis: Antebellum and Civil War Congressman from Maryland* (New York, 1973); Herman Belz, *Reconstructing the Union: Theory and Policy During the Civil War* (Ithaca, N.Y., 1969); H. L. Trefousse, *Benjamin Franklin Wade: Radical Senator from Ohio* (New York, 1963).

**WAITE, MORRISON REMICK** (1816–1888), Chief Justice of the United States, was born in Old Lyme, Connecticut, the son of Marie Selden and Henry Matson Waite, a lawyer who later became Chief Justice of Connecticut. After graduating from Yale and reading law with his father, in 1838 he moved to Maumee, Ohio, to establish a practice. In 1850 he settled in Toledo, where he became a leading member of the bar. An active Whig, he made an unsuccessful race for Congress in 1848 but was elected to the state legislature in 1849. Defeated for the state constitutional convention in 1850, after 1855 he joined the Republicans.

Waite was always a conservative. In 1862, in a three-way contest, he challenged James M. Ashley (q.v.) for his congressional seat and lost, but he loyally supported the party in 1863 and 1864.

In 1871 Waite was appointed as one of the three U.S. attorneys before the Geneva Tribunal. Upon his return, in 1873 he presided over the state constitutional convention, and in that same year President U. S. Grant (q.v.) appointed him Chief Justice of the United States.

On the Supreme Court Waite proved to be a steady but not innovating Chief Justice. In *U.S.* v. *Reese* (q.v.) and *U.S.* v. *Cruikshank* (q.v.), as well as in the *Civil Rights* cases (q.v.), he interpreted the postwar amendments so narrowly as to render them practically useless for the protection of the freedmen, although, like his friend Rutherford B. Hayes (q.v.), he was a strong supporter of black education and the Peabody and Slater Funds. In dealing with the economy, his decisions, particularly *Munn* v. *Illinois*, upheld the right of the states to regulate railroads, and he refused to be guided by the extreme laissez-faire notions of Justice Stephen J. Field and others. He died in Washington in 1888.

*See also* Ashley, James Mitchell; Civil Rights Cases; *U.S.* v. *Cruikshank*; *U.S.* v. *Reese*.

C. Peter Magrath, *Morrison R. Waite: The Triumph of Character* (New York, 1963).

**WALLS, JOSIAH THOMAS** (1842–1905), black Republican leader in Florida (q.v.), was born a slave in Winchester, Virginia, probably the son of his master, Dr. John Walls, a physician. After joining the Third Infantry Regiment, U.S. Colored Troops, in 1863 he saw service in South Carolina and Florida and, upon his discharge in Florida, eventually settled in Gainesville. Elected to the constitutional convention in 1868, he carefully maneuvered between the various Republican factions and campaigned for the constitution drawn up by the moderates. In 1868 he was sent to the state legislature, where he worked for bills guaranteeing blacks (q.v.) equal access to public facilities and more successfully for a measure securing black county clerks the right to practice law. He also pleaded in vain for funds to fight the Ku Klux Klan (q.v.).

In the meantime, Walls acquired great wealth. He owned vast landholdings, including an estate formerly the property of Confederate General James H. Harrison; he had an interest in a corporation to build a cross-state canal, and he apparently benefited from the corrupt scheme of constructing the Great Southern Railway from St. Mary's River to Key West. In addition, he practiced law, directed sawmills, and served as mayor of Gainesville.

In 1870 Walls won election to Congress, although his victory was challenged by his Democratic opponent, Silas Niblack, whose claims were finally sustained by the House in 1873. In the meantime, however, Walls, who had a powerful base among the blacks in Alachua County, had secured reelection.

In Congress, Walls was a firm advocate of black rights, although he sought to couple amnesty (q.v.) with Charles Sumner's Civil Rights Bill. In addition, he voted for the establishment of a national education fund as well as for various measures of economic benefit to his state. When he ran for Congress once more, he was successful, but was again challenged by his opponent, Jesse J. Finlay, who was seated by the House in 1876. Denied renomination by his party that year, Walls was elected to the state Senate. He tried again to run for Congress in 1884 but then witnessed the decline of his political and personal fortunes in the wake of "Redemption" (q.v.). He died in Tallahassee in 1905.

*See also* Florida; "Redemption."

Peter D. Klingman, *Josiah Walls: Florida's Black Congressman of Reconstruction* (Gainesville, Fla., 1976); Eric Foner, *Reconstruction: America's Unfinished Revolution, 1863–1877* (New York, 1989).

**WARMOTH, HENRY CLAY** (1842–1931), Reconstruction Governor of Louisiana, was born in McLeansboro, Illinois, the son of the saddler Isaac Sanders Warmoth and his wife, Eleanor Lane. After an education in the local schools and the study of some law books belonging to his father, a Justice of the Peace, in 1860 he removed to Lebanon, Missouri, was admitted to the bar, and appointed county attorney. When war broke out, he raised troops for the Union and became a lieutenant colonel in the Thirty-second Missouri. Wounded in the Vicksburg campaign, he was dishonorably discharged by General U. S. Grant (q.v.) for allegedly spreading unfavorable reports about the army but was reinstated after the personal intervention of President Abraham Lincoln (q.v.). He participated in the battles around Chattanooga and ended the war as a provost judge in New Orleans.

Louisiana (q.v.) became Warmoth's permanent home. Active in the organization of the Republican party (q.v.) in the state, he held that Louisiana was merely a territory and was elected "territorial delegate" but was not seated. In 1866 he took part in the Southern Loyalist Convention (q.v.) in Philadelphia and campaigned for the Republican ticket in the North. In 1868, despite his youth, he was elected Governor by the moderate Republicans.

Warmoth's administration was marked by widespread corruption, the worst excesses of which he tried to prevent. Although his Lieutenant Governor, Oscar J. Dunn, was black and he was an advocate of black suffrage (q.v.), Warmoth alienated many freedmen by his failure to press for school integration and his veto of an equal accommodations bill. At the same time, the conservatives despised him as a carpetbagger (q.v.), and although he sought to strengthen his position by the organization of the metropolitan police, in 1868 their use of intimidation and terror enabled the Democrats to carry the state for Horatio Seymour (q.v.). By 1870, however, the legislature had passed several measures giving the Governor control over the election machinery, so the Republicans were able to win the elections that year.

Yet the Republican party was plagued by factionalism. Warmoth, who had earlier collaborated with collector James F. Casey, the President's brother-in-law, now failed to support him and earned the enmity of the Custom House ring. Warmoth also had differences with his Lieutenant Governor, and when Dunn died, the Governor saw to it that his then ally, Pinckney B. S. Pinchback (q.v.), was elected president of the Senate and his putative successor. In 1872, however, he also broke with Pinchback, who refused to follow him into the Liberal Republican party (Liberal Republican Movement, q.v.). In alliance with the Democrat John McEnery (q.v.), he attempted to bring about McEnery's success while hoping that the Democrats would elect him to the Senate. After meeting Pinchback in New York, he engaged in a railroad race with the Lieutenant Governor who had sought to hurry back to New Orleans to sign a series of bills favorable to the Republicans and overtook him. The result was that Horace Greeley (q.v.) carried Louisiana, but the state results were in dispute. McEnery and his legislature's claim to victory were challenged by the Republican William Pitt Kellogg (q.v.), who assembled his own legislature, and two state governments attempted to function until federal Judge E. H. Durell issued an order favoring the Republicans. Warmoth was then accused of having solicited a bribe from Pinchback; he was impeached, removed from office, and superseded by the Lieutenant Governor, although the charges against him were never proven.

Now distrusted by Republicans and Democrats alike, Warmoth retired to buy a plantation on the Mississippi, where he raised sugar and established a sugar refinery. In addition, he was active as a railroad promoter.

But he did not eschew politics. Continuing actively to oppose the disfranchisement of blacks (q.v.), he was challenged to a duel by a journalist. Before he could meet his opponent, however, he was waylaid in the street in an affray that ended in the death of his attacker. Elected in 1876 as a Republican to the state legislature, two years later he was a member of the state constitutional convention and in 1888 ran unsuccessfully for Governor. From 1890 to 1893 he served as collector of the Port of New Orleans; in 1896, 1900, and 1908 he was a delegate to the Republican National Convention and finally took up residence in New Orleans. When he was over eighty years of age, he wrote his memoirs, *War, Politics, and Reconstruction*, an effort at self-justification. He died in New Orleans in 1931.

*See also* Carpetbaggers; Kellogg, William Pitt; Louisiana; McEnery, John; Pinchback, Pinckney Benton Stewart.

Richard Nelson Current, *Those Terrible Carpetbaggers: A Reinterpretation* (New York, 1988); Henry Clay Warmoth, *War, Politics, and Reconstruction: Stormy Days in Louisiana* (New York, 1930).

**WASHINGTON, TREATY OF** (1871), treaty between the United States and Great Britain settling claims arising from the Civil War. Great Britain's failure to prevent the escape of ships built for the Confederacy, particularly the *Alabama*, caused great damages to American shipping and resulted in popular indignation against the British. In addition, a festering boundary dispute with Canada about the San Juan Islands and the expiration of inshore fishing rights of Americans in Canadian waters contributed to the prevalent Anglophobia.

In 1868 and 1869 Secretary of State William H. Seward (q.v.) sought to solve these difficulties. The American minister in London, Senator Reverdy Johnson (q.v.), negotiated a settlement with Foreign Secretary Lord Clarendon that provided for the adjustment of certain claims against Great Britain but failed to mention the *Alabama* question or contain any expressions of regret for the damages inflicted. Accordingly, in 1869 the Senate refused to ratify the Johnson-Clarendon Convention, and tensions were increased when in April 1869 Senator Charles Sumner (q.v.) in a forceful speech held Great Britain responsible not merely for the direct damages inflicted by the cruisers but also for the indirect costs of the prolongation of the Civil War for two years. The total of these indirect claims amounted to some $2 billion, a sum so vast that it was understood only the cession of Canada could satisfy it. Eventual war between the two countries seemed likely.

The new administration of General U. S. Grant (q.v.) at first seemed to agree with Sumner's views. But the Secretary of State, Hamilton Fish (q.v.), was not anxious for conflict. Gradually drifting apart from Sumner, he allowed passions to cool and eventually undertook new negotiations, making use of a Canadian intermediary, Sir John Rose. Because of the outbreak of the Franco-Prussian War and Russia's denunciation of the Black Sea neutralization clauses of the Treaty of Paris, Great Britain was anxious for a settlement, while the Grant administration, needing a foreign policy success, was concerned about the uninterrupted flow of British capital into the American market. A joint high commission met in Washington in 1871, and in May the two countries were able to sign the Treaty of Washington. Providing for the submission of the *Alabama* and related claims to an international tribunal to meet at Geneva, it referred the San Juan dispute to the German emperor. In addition, it expressed Great Britain's regret for the escape of the cruisers, contained a new formulation of international law concerning the obligation of neutrals, and settled the controversies with Canada. Americans were to regain their inshore fishery rights for a period of years and obtain free navigation of a number of Canadian rivers; in return Canadians were to be allowed to fish in American coastal waters up to the 39th parallel and to sail in certain American rivers. Other mutual trade concessions were included as well.

The Geneva Tribunal, consisting of representatives of the United States, the United Kingdom, Brazil, Italy, and Switzerland, met late in 1871, but its deliberations were almost ended at the very beginning by the reemergence of the indirect claims. Only when the British and their representative, Sir Alexander Cockburn, agreed to an informal understanding that the tribunal would dismiss these claims was the arbitration able to proceed. In the end, despite Cockburn's objections, the tribunal awarded $15.5 million to the United States for the depredations of the Confederate cruisers; the British received $7,429,819 from commissions adjudicating counterclaims and setting an amount in compensation for the fisheries, and the German emperor awarded the San Juan Islands to the United States. The result was the preservation of peace between the United Kingdom and the United States and the establishment of a valuable precedent for international arbitration.

*See also* Fish, Hamilton; Foreign Affairs; Seward, William Henry; Sumner, Charles.

Adrian Cook, *The Alabama Claims: American Politics and Anglo-American Relations, 1865–1872* (Ithaca, N.Y., 1975); Allan Nevins, *Hamilton Fish: The Inner History of the Grant Administration* (New York, 1936).

**WELLES, GIDEON** (1802–1876), Secretary of the Navy, was born in Glastonbury, Connecticut, the son of the merchant and politician Samuel and his wife, Anne Hale Welles. Educated at the American Literary, Scientific, and Military Academy in Norwich, Vermont, Welles, after briefly studying law, in 1825 became associated with the Hartford *Times*, a Jacksonian newspaper he edited from 1826 to 1836. In 1825 he was elected to the General Assembly but was defeated for Congress in 1833. In 1835, after marrying his cousin Mary Jane Hale, he accepted the position of state comptroller.

One of the most influential Jacksonian Democrats in Connecticut, Welles was appointed postmaster of Hartford in 1836 and chief of the Bureau of Provisions and Clothing in the Navy Department in 1846. In 1850 he made an unsuccessful try for the U.S. Senate but in 1855 broke with the Democrats on the issue of slavery and became one of the founders of the Republican party (q.v.) in the state. He helped to establish the party newspaper, the Hartford *Evening Press*, made an unsuccessful run for Governor in 1856, and served on the Republican National Committee. The chairman of Connecticut's delegation to the 1860 Chicago Convention, he contributed to the defeat of William H. Seward (q.v.), and his services were rewarded when Abraham Lincoln (q.v.) appointed him Secretary of the Navy.

During the Civil War, Welles as responsible for the rapid expansion of the navy. He favored John Ericson's ironclads, endeavored to keep the department free of corruption, and contributed greatly to the success of the blockade of the Southern coast. But in the cabinet, he feuded frequently with Seward and Edwin M. Stanton (q.v.), and he was unable to stifle criticism of his handling of the department.

In matters of Reconstruction, Welles, a strict constructionist and Jacksonian advocate of states rights, took a conservative position. He held the creation of West Virginia (q.v.) unconstitutional but favored Lincoln's later efforts to restore the seceded states. Andrew Johnson (q.v.) retained Welles as Secretary of the Navy, and the New Englander became one of the President's firmest supporters. Like his chief, he believed the states were still in the Union, that the federal nature of the government must be preserved, and that the question of black suffrage (q.v.) was strictly a state, not a federal, matter. Frequently warning the President against Stanton, he advised Johnson to veto various congressional measures of Reconstruction, favored the 1866 National Union Convention (q.v.) in Philadelphia, and loyally supported his chief during the impeachment trial. In 1868 he rejoined the Democrats and after the conclusion of his term returned to Hartford, where he resumed his literary and journalistic activities.

Throughout much of his tenure as Secretary of the Navy, Welles kept a diary that became one of the main sources for the study of the period. Well written but highly prejudiced in favor of conservative policies, it influenced much of later historical writing. In addition, in reply to efforts to build up the reputation of Seward to the detriment of Lincoln, Welles, who early recognized Lincoln's genius, published a series of articles in *Galaxy* magazine and elsewhere, as well as a book, *Lincoln and Seward*, which contributed markedly to the rising reputation of the martyred President. Interested in the Liberal Republican movement in 1872, he favored the candidacy of B. Gratz Brown (q.v.) but withdrew from active participation after the nomination of Horace Greeley (q.v.). He died in Hartford in 1876.

*See also* Johnson, Andrew; Lincoln, Abraham; Seward, William Henry; Stanton, Edwin McMasters.

John Niven, *Gideon Welles, Lincoln's Secretary of the Navy* (New York, 1973); Richard S. West, *Gideon Welles: Lincoln's Navy Department* (Indianapolis, 1943).

**WELLS, JAMES MADISON** (1808–1899), Reconstruction Governor of Louisiana, was born in Rapides Parish, the son of the planter Samuel Levi Wells and his wife, Elizabeth Calvit. Orphaned at the age of eight, Wells was brought up by an aunt and educated in the local schools as well as at St. Joseph's College in Bardstown, Kentucky, a military academy in Middletown, Connecticut, and at the Cincinnati Law School. When he was thirty, he returned to Louisiana (q.v.), married Mary Ann Scott, and took over his plantations near Alexandria. A wealthy Whig and slaveholder, in 1839 he was appointed sheriff of Rapides Parish and then tax collector, a position that made him personally responsible for the amount of taxes in arrears, so he was later accused of having defaulted on more than $12,000. In 1860, as an ardent Unionist, he supported Stephen A. Douglas and defied the Confederacy even after secession. After escaping to a federal gunboat in 1863, he reached New Orleans, where he was nominated for Lieutenant Governor on both the radical ticket of Benjamin F. Flanders and the moderate slate headed by Michael Hahn (q.v.). He was elected in 1864, and when in the following February Governor Hahn was elected Senator, Wells succeeded as chief executive.

Once in office, Governor Wells sought to win over the returning Confederates by substantially making common cause with them. He appointed them to office, drew up new voter lists, and installed the conservative Hu Kennedy as Mayor of New Orleans. When General Nathaniel P. Banks (q.v.) countermanded some of these actions, Wells appealed to President Andrew Johnson (q.v.) who sustained him and removed the general. In the subsequent elections of 1865, Wells was nominated for Governor by both the National Democrats and Conservative Unionists and elected to office together with a solidly conservative and Democratic legislature.

But the Governor soon broke with his supporters. Vetoing bills granting tax relief to former Confederates and mandating new elections for New Orleans, he alienated them, and they turned completely against him when he agreed to the recall of the constitutional convention of 1864. After the resulting New Orleans riot (q.v.) of 1866 and his endorsement of the Fourteenth Amendment (q.v.), they attempted to impeach him, although the passage of the Reconstruction Acts (q.v.) ended this endeavor.

The Reconstruction Acts did not solve Wells' difficulties. He began feuding with General Philip H. Sheridan (q.v.), the commander of the Fifth Military District, and in June 1868, in a dispute about the appointment of levee commissioners, Sheridan dismissed him. Remaining active in politics, in 1872 Wells at first supported the Liberal Republicans (Liberal Republican Movement, q.v.), whose national convention at Cincinnati he attended, but, disappointed at the nomination of Horace Greeley (q.v.) and unable to back the conservative ticket of John McEnery (q.v.), in the end favored the reelection of President U. S. Grant (q.v.) and the Republican ticket of William Pitt Kellogg (q.v.). A Republican appointment to the state returning board followed, and in 1874 and 1876 he saw to it that the party's claims were sustained. From 1875 to 1880 he served as surveyor of the Port of New Orleans; an attempt to indict him on various charges stemming from his political actions failed, and he retired to Lecompte, where he died in 1899. Accusations of corruption against him could never be proved.

*See also* Banks, Nathaniel Prentiss; Hahn, Michael; Johnson, Andrew; Louisiana; Scalawags; Sheridan, Philip Henry.

Walter McGehee Lowrey, "The Political Career of James Madison Wells," *Louisiana Historical Quarterly*, 31 (1948): 995–1157; Joe Gray Taylor, *Louisiana Reconstructed, 1863–1877* (Baton Rouge, 1974); Peyton McCrary, *Abraham Lincoln and Reconstruction: The Louisiana Experiment* (Princeton, N.J., 1978).

**WEST VIRGINIA,** a border state separated from Virginia by its Unionist leaders following secession. Long resentful of the domination of the commonwealth by eastern slaveholders, Unionists in northwestern Virginia met in convention at Wheeling to call for action in the event of passage of the secession ordinance. Accordingly, a second Wheeling Convention met on May 23, 1861, and established a Restored Government of Virginia with Francis H. Pierpont (q.v.) as Governor. Abraham Lincoln (q.v.) recognized this government on July 4, but the advocates of separate statehood, in an adjourned convention at Wheeling in August, succeeded in passing a dismemberment ordinance. A constitution for the new state was drawn up in November; the Wheeling legislature gave its consent in May 1862, and in July the Senate, followed in December by the House of Representatives, agreed to the necessary legislation. After the addition of the so-called Willey Amendment calling for the gradual abolition of slavery, Lincoln signed the statehood bill on December 31. The amendment was ratified in March 1863 and the new state admitted in June.

From the very beginning the Unionists and later the Republicans in West Virginia were divided. Neither the conservatives nor the radicals favored black suffrage (q.v.), but the radicals tended to be less backward looking than their opponents. In February 1865 they succeeded in abolishing slavery, but because of the incorporation of twenty-five secessionist counties, the Unionist majority in the state was always in a precarious situation. Under the leadership of Governor Arthur I. Boreman, in the beginning of 1865 the Unionists found it necessary to pass stringent disfranchising laws to restrict the political power of returning Confederates, and in 1866 they added provisions for an ironclad oath (q.v.) for attorneys, suitors, juries, and teachers, but by 1869 many of the more conservative Republicans were urging greater leniency toward their former opponents. They were further alienated by the passage of the Fifteenth Amendment (q.v.), and because of lax enforcement of the disfranchising regulations, in 1870 the Democrats carried the legislature and elected the Governor. Their victory had been made possible by a combination of conservative Republicans and returned Confederates in the secessionist counties.

"Redemption" (q.v.) had thus begun in West Virginia. Making the most of their victory, the Democrats called a constitutional convention and in 1872 wrote a new conservative constitution, which was adopted by the electorate. It enabled them to dominate the state for the next generation.

*See also* Pierpont, Francis Harrison; Virginia.

Richard O. Curry, "Crisis Politics in West Virginia, 1861–1870," in Richard Curry, ed., *Radicalism, Racism, and Realignment: The Border States During Reconstruction* (Baltimore, 1969); Charles H. Ambler and Festus R. Summers, *West Virginia: The Mountain State* (2d ed., New York, 1965).

**WHISKEY RING,** a scandal involving the withholding of taxes on distilled liquor. The proceeds, more than $2 million, were used for campaign contributions to the Republican party as well as the personal enrichment of the participants.

The chief beneficiaries of the ring were a number of distillers in St. Louis and some other cities together with public officials, all with connections in Washington. In St. Louis, John A. McDonald, one of U. S. Grant's (q.v.) friends and the supervisor of internal revenue, was at the center of the conspiracy. He provided the President with expensive hotel accommodations and a team of splendid horses with a carriage, with which Grant did not scruple to drive around in Washington. Also involved was the President's intimate and private secretary, Orville E. Babcock (q.v.), who used his close relations with Grant to shield the conspirators.

When in 1874 Benjamin H. Bristow (q.v.) became Secretary of the Treasury, he unearthed damning evidence against the ring. But he was hampered in his investigations by the interference of the President, who, though stating "Let no guilty man escape," sought to protect Babcock. Eventually, the evidence became so damning that Babcock, afraid of a civilian trial, asked for a military court of inquiry, which acquitted him. In the meantime, however, a grand jury had found a true bill against him, and he was tried in St. Louis. Grant actually proposed that he go to the city to testify in his friend's behalf, but the cabinet dissuaded him, although he did make a written deposition in Babcock's favor. This helped the defendant, who, though most probably guilty, was acquitted, while McDonald was convicted and went to jail. Grant took Babcock back into his employ; however, he never forgave Bristow, whom in 1876 he replaced with Lot M. Morrill. The scandal contributed greatly to the unsavory reputation of the Grant administration.

*See also* Babcock, Orville E.; Bristow, Benjamin Helm; Corruption; Grant, Ulysses Simpson.

William S. McFeely, *Grant: A Biography* (New York, 1981); Ross A. Webb, *Benjamin Helm Bristow* (Lexington, Ky., 1969).

**WHITE LEAGUE,** a terrorist organization in Louisiana (q.v.) dedicated to the overthrow of Republican rule and the reestablishment of white supremacy. Following the disputed elections in 1872, the rival governments of William Pitt Kellogg (q.v.) and John McEnery (q.v.) struggled for possession of the statehouse, and even though the federal authorities recognized Kellogg and his regime, the conservatives remained restless. In March 1874 the Alexandria *Caucasian* called for a jettisoning of party differences in order to reassert white supremacy, and in April, disgruntled Democrats at Opelousas organized the White League for the purpose of overthrowing the alleged black rule of the state. Similar leagues soon spread to other parishes, intimidated Republican officeholders until they resigned, and terrorized the freedmen. The Coushatta Massacre (q.v.) followed, and when in September the McEnery forces were about to receive a shipment of arms in the port of New Orleans and the Metropolitan Police sought to interfere, the local White League organized armed resistance. A public meeting was held to force Kellogg to resign; the White League mustered some eight thousand armed followers and supporters who challenged the police in the "Battle of Liberty Place," and the result was an insurgent victory costing the lives of eleven policemen and twenty-one of their opponents, as well as the wounding of sixty of the former and nineteen of the latter. The successful rioters then sought to install the McEnery government, and it took federal troops to restore order.

In the elections of 1874 the White League again sought to defeat the Republicans and afterward continued to make it difficult for Kellogg to govern. In January 1877 Francis T. Nicholls (q.v.), the Democratic claimant for Governor, finally accepted the White League forces as the legal militia of the state, and with the end of Reconstruction, the organization ceased to function.

*See also* Coushatta Massacre; Kellogg, William Pitt; Louisiana; McEnery, John; Nicholls, Francis Tillou; "Redemption."

Joe Gray Taylor, *Louisiana Reconstructed, 1863–1877* (Baton Rouge, 1974); H. Oscar Lestrup, "The White League in Louisiana and Its Participation in Reconstruction Riots," *Louisiana Historical Quarterly*, 18 (July 1935): 615–99.

**WILSON, HENRY** (1812–1875), Senator from Massachusetts and Vice President of the United States, was born near Farmington, New Hampshire, the son of Winthrop Colbath, a laborer, and his wife, Abigail Witham. After finishing his apprenticeship to a farmer, he changed his name to Henry Wilson and at age twenty-one moved to Natick, Massachusetts, to become a shoemaker. He studied briefly at various New Hampshire academies but returned to Natick, where his cobbler's shop grew into a sizable manufacturing establishment and where he married Malvina Howe in 1840.

Wilson's life's work was politics. An unsuccessful temperance candidate for the state legislature in 1839, he was elected as a Whig the next year. In 1844 he was transferred to the state Senate, where he remained until 1852. Hating slavery, in 1848 he was one of the main organizers of the Free Soil party in the state and served as its chairman from 1849 to 1851. He was also one of the principal movers for the coalition of Free Soilers and Democrats that elected Charles Sumner (q.v.) to the U.S. Senate.

In 1854 Wilson took part in the founding of the Republican party (q.v.) in Massachusetts but then briefly joined the Know-Nothings who dominated the legislature that in 1855 elected him to the U.S. Senate. Never really intolerant, however, he revolted against the Know Nothing Council's failure to take a stand against slavery, and in 1859 the Republicans reelected him to his Senate seat.

During the Civil War, Wilson served as chairman of the powerful Senate Committee on Military Affairs. Responsible for the raising and maintenance of large numbers of troops, he saw to it that the necessary legislation was passed. In addition, he was the author of the bill emancipating the slaves in the District of Columbia and persistently struggled for the elevation of the blacks (q.v.). He even advocated black suffrage (q.v.) as early as 1865.

Wilson's solicitude for the freedmen—he was one of the sponsors of the Freedmen's Bureau (q.v.)—brought him into conflict with President Andrew Johnson (q.v.). Reelected in 1865, he was ever willing to compromise in order to achieve results, but the President's policy of Reconstruction was totally unacceptable to him. He favored radical legislation, supported the Freedmen's Bureau and Civil Rights Bills as well as the Fourteenth Amendment (q.v.), and was the sponsor of the Second Reconstruction Act (q.v.). In trips to the South in 1867 he sought to win Southern support and voted for the conviction of Johnson. A contender for second place on the ticket of U. S. Grant (q.v.), he enthusiastically supported the general's election.

During the first Grant administration, Wilson argued for a Fifteenth Amendment (q.v.) much more inclusive than the one that finally passed. He also took an interest in women's rights and the claims of labor, favored Sumner's Civil Rights Bill (Civil Rights Acts, q.v.), and was an advocate of amnesty (q.v.) for Southerners. Reelected in 1871, the next year he was nominated and elected Vice President on Grant's ticket. During the campaign, he was accused of buying some shares of Crédit Mobilier stock but successfully explained that he divested himself of them soon afterward.

During his Vice Presidency, Wilson, who had recently been widowed and lost his only son, was in declining health. Nevertheless, he continued his literary labors, which he had started some years earlier with the publication of the history of various congressional measures. His most important work was the three-volume *History of the Rise and Fall of the Slave Power in America*, finished by his friend Samuel Hunt after his death. Marked by a lack of vindictiveness, his account pictured his former opponents as engaged in a conspiracy to perpetuate slavery but expressed hope that the Reconstruction measures would work out for the best. He died in Washington in 1875.

*See also* Radical Republicans; Reconstruction Acts; Sumner, Charles.

Richard H. Abbott, *Cobbler in Congress: The Life of Henry Wilson, 1812–1875* (Lexington, Ky., 1972); Ernest A. McKay, *Henry Wilson: Practical Radical, A Portrait of a Politician* (Port Washington, N.Y., 1971).


**WIRZ, HENRY** (1823–1865), commander of the interior of Andersonville Prison, was born Heinrich Hartmann Wirz in Zurich, Switzerland, the son of a tailor. After obtaining some commercial training, he worked for his father but for some cause was sentenced to a term in prison and in 1849 left for the United States. His claims to medical degrees from European universities are spurious.

After working as a weaver in Lawrence, Massachusetts, he moved to Hopkinsville, Kentucky, where he became the medical assistant to two physicians and opened his own practice in Cadiz before moving on to Milliken's Bend, Louisiana. When the Civil War broke out, he joined the Fourth Louisiana Infantry, was severely wounded at Seven Pines, and then was appointed Acting Adjutant General to General John H. Winder. Following the command of two military prisons, he undertook a mission to Europe for the Confederacy.

Upon his return, in March 1864 Captain Wirz was given command of the interior of the notorious Andersonville prison in Georgia, where some twelve thousand Union soldiers died of maltreatment and neglect. In pain because of his wound, he was unduly rancorous and coarse, thus earning the hatred of the inmates. Apprehended at the end of the war despite protests that he was covered by Joseph Johnston's terms of surrender, he was indicted for murder and mistreatment of prisoners in a plot involving Jefferson Davis (q.v.) and other Confederate officials and tried by a military commission. He was found guilty, sentenced to death, and executed on November 10, 1865, after President Andrew Johnson (q.v.) refused to commute the sentence.

The justice of Wirz's conviction has been questioned ever since. Resting on dubious evidence, the testimony against him left room for doubt, and he was certainly innocent of plotting with Jefferson Davis (q.v.) and other Confederate officials. Nevertheless, he was a harsh martinet, and as commanding officer of the interior of the prison, he could hardly escape responsibility for the cruelties perpetrated upon Union prisoners at Andersonville.

*See also* Amnesty; Johnson, Andrew.

Ovid L. Futch, *History of Andersonville Prison* (Gainesville, Fla., 1968); Darrett B. Rutman, "The War Crimes and Trial of Henry Wirz," *Civil War History*, 6 (June 1960): 117–33; N. P. Chipman, *The Horrors of Andersonville Rebel Prison: Trial of Henry Wirz* (San Francisco, 1891).

**WOMEN'S RIGHTS MOVEMENT,** the campaign to procure equal rights, particularly the suffrage, for women. The proponents of feminism, who were active before the Civil War, often made common cause with the foes of slavery, and immediately after Abraham Lincoln (q.v.) promulgated the Emancipation Proclamation (q.v.), Susan B. Anthony and Elizabeth Cady Stanton organized the National Loyal Women's League to agitate for a constitutional amendment abolishing slavery.

The hopes of the advocates of women's rights were raised by the postwar tendency to broaden the suffrage in connection with Reconstruction, and in May 1866 the militant suffragists founded the American Equal Rights Association to work for both black and female suffrage. But the feminists soon encountered difficulties; many former abolitionists and radicals favored the attainment of one goal at a time and believed black rights and enfranchisement should take precedence over the claims of women. For this reason, they supported the Fourteenth Amendment (q.v.), which, for the first time adding the word *male* to the Constitution, provided for the possible reduction of representation for states disfranchising males over age twenty-one. Consequently, militants such as Anthony and Stanton opposed the amendment. The split between the former abolitionists and the feminists became even more pronounced during the 1867 campaign in Kansas, where a referendum to drop the words *white* and *male* from the voting requirements was on the ballot. Lucy Stone, Anthony, and Stanton crisscrossed the state in a search for votes, but the radical Eastern newspapers, especially the New York *Tribune*, gave them only lukewarm support. In desperation, Anthony went as far as to ally herself with Francis Train, a Democrat and racist, who in 1868 enabled her to launch her newspaper, *The Revolution*, but could not help her win.

Not all feminists followed the militants. Lucy Stone, for example, continued to work with the Republicans, even when the party failed to include a prohibition of restrictions on the right to vote on account of sex in the Fifteenth Amendment (q.v.) and when in 1869 Frederick Douglass (q.v.), an old ally, publicly declared that black rights were more pressing than those of women. The result was a complete split. The American Equal Rights Association and the newly founded New England Women Suffrage Association, which concentrated on winning the vote in the states, continued to cooperate with the Republicans, and in 1869 the dissidents organized the new National Women Suffrage Association, which barred men from membership and pursued an independent course.

While the Fifteenth Amendment was under consideration, some friends of the women's movement favored the passage of a sixteenth barring disfranchisement on account of sex. Senator Samuel C. Pomeroy of Kansas introduced such a measure in the Senate in December 1868 and George W. Julian (q.v.) offered a joint resolution in the House in 1869, but Congress was unwilling to pass it. Nevertheless, the suffrage movement achieved some success when the Territory of Wyoming enfranchised women in 1869 and Utah followed suit the next year. The constitutional amendment, however, had to await the coming of the next century.

*See also* Fifteenth Amendment; Fourteenth Amendment.

Ellen Carol DuBois, *Feminism and Suffrage: The Emergence of an Independent Women's Movement in America, 1848–1869* (Ithaca, N.Y., 1978); Eleanor Flexner, *Century of Struggle: The Women's Rights Movement in the United States* (Cambridge, Mass., 1959 and 1975).

**WORMLEY CONFERENCE** (1877), final bargain between the Democrats and the representatives of Rutherford B. Hayes (q.v.) to end the filibuster to prevent the completion of the count of the Electoral Commission (q.v.) in return for the removal of federal troops from Southern statehouses. The importance of the conference, which took place at Washington in Wormley's Hotel on February 26, 1877, following the disputed election of 1877 has been greatly exaggerated. The various economic and political bargains sealing the Compromise of 1877 (q.v.) preceded the conference by several weeks and days, so the meeting at Wormley's Hotel at best merely confirmed agreements reached earlier.

*See also* Compromise of 1877; Electoral Commission; Hayes, Rutherford B.

C. Vann Woodward, *Reunion and Reaction: The Compromise of 1877 and the End of Reconstruction* (Boston, 1951); Ari Hoogenboom, *The Presidency of Rutherford B. Hayes* (Lawrence, Kans., 1988).

# Y

**YERGER, EX PARTE** (1869), Supreme Court case reaffirming the right to petition for a writ of habeas corpus in the states under military rule during Reconstruction. Edward M. Yerger, a Mississippi newspaper editor, was tried by a military commission for the murder of Major Joseph C. Crane, who had been detailed to act as mayor of Jackson. Yerger, a fiery secessionist, had stabbed his victim in a dispute about the seizure of a piano in a tax case. After the denial of an application for a writ of habeas corpus by the circuit court, the case was taken to the Supreme Court in accordance with the court's jurisdiction under the Judiciary Act of 1789 rather than that under the Habeas Corpus Act of 1867, repealed in 1868 in the course of *ex parte McCardle* (q.v.). The Chase court accepted jurisdiction, and after the readmission of Mississippi (q.v.), despite vain efforts by Congress to interfere, the case was transferred to the local civilian courts.

Contrary to the popular opinion that the Supreme Court supinely yielded to Congress during Reconstruction, particularly in the *McCardle* case, *ex parte Yerger* has been cited as an example of its continued independence.

*See also McCardle, Ex Parte*; Supreme Court.

Stanley I. Kutler, *Judicial Power and Reconstruction Politics* (Chicago, 1968); Charles Fairman, *Reconstruction and Reunion, 1864–88*, Vol. 6 of the Oliver Wendell Holmes Devise, *History of the Supreme Court of the United States* (New York, 1971).

# SELECT BIBLIOGRAPHY

Abbott, Richard H. *Cobbler in Congress: The Life of Henry Wilson, 1812–1875*. Lexington, Ky., 1972
———. *The Republican Party in the South, 1855–1877: The First Southern Strategy*. Chapel Hill, N.C., 1986.
Alexander, Thomas B. *Political Reconstruction in Tennessee*. Nashville, 1950.
Beale, Howard K. *The Critical Year: A Study of Andrew Johnson and Reconstruction*. New York, 1930.
Beauregard, Erving E. *Bingham of the Hills: Politician and Diplomat Extraordinary*. New York, 1989.
Belz, Herman. *A New Birth of Freedom: The Republican Party and Freedmen's Rights, 1861–1866*. Westport, Conn., 1976.
———. *Reconstructing the Union: Theory and Practice During the Civil War*. Ithaca, N.Y., 1969.
Benedict, Michael L. *A Compromise of Principle: Congressional Republicans and Reconstruction, 1863–1869*. New York, 1974.
———. *The Impeachment and Trial of Andrew Johnson*. New York, 1973.
Bentley, George R. *A History of the Freedmen's Bureau*. Philadelphia, 1955.
Blue, Frederick J. *Salmon P. Chase: A Life in Politics*. Kent, Ohio, 1987.
Bowers, Claude G. *The Tragic Era*. Cambridge, Mass., 1929.
Brock, W. R. *An American Crisis: Congress and Reconstruction, 1865–1867*. New York, 1963.
Carpenter, John A. *Sword and Olive Branch: Oliver Otis Howard*. Pittsburgh, 1964.
Carter, Dan T. *When the War Was Over: The Failure of Self-Reconstruction in the South, 1865–1867*. Baton Rouge, 1985.
Conway, Alan. *The Reconstruction of Georgia*. Minneapolis, 1966.
Cook, Adrian. *The Alabama Claims: American Politics and Anglo-American Relations, 1865–1872*. Ithaca, N.Y., 1975.
Cox, LaWanda. *Lincoln and Black Freedom: A Study in Presidential Leadership*. Columbia, S.C., 1981.

Cox, LaWanda, and Cox, John H. *Politics, Principle, and Prejudice, 1865–1866: Dilemma of Reconstruction America*. New York, 1963.

Current, Richard Nelson. *Those Terrible Carpetbaggers*. New York, 1988.

Curry, Richard O., ed. *Radicalism, Racism, and Party Realignment: The Border States During Reconstruction*. Baltimore, 1969.

Donald, David. *Charles Sumner and the Coming of the Civil War*. New York, 1960.

——. *Charles Sumner and the Rights of Man*. New York, 1970.

——. *The Politics of Reconstruction, 1863–1867*. Baton Rouge, 1965.

Du Bois, Ellen C. *Feminism and Suffrage: The Emergence of an Independent Women's Movement in America, 1848–1869*. Ithaca, N.Y., 1978.

Du Bois, W.E.B. *Black Reconstruction in America*. New York, 1935.

Dunning, William A. *Reconstruction, Political and Economic, 1865–1877*. New York, 1907.

Fairman, Charles. *Reconstruction and Reunion, 1864–88*. Vols. 6 and 7 of the Oliver Wendell Holmes Devise *History of the Supreme Court*. New York, 1971 and 1987.

Fitzwater, Michael F. *The Union League Movement in the Deep South: Politics and Agricultural Change During Reconstruction*. Baton Rouge, 1989.

Foner, Eric. *Reconstruction: America's Unfinished Revolution, 1863–1877*. New York, 1988.

Franklin, John Hope. *Reconstruction after the Civil War*. Chicago, 1961.

Gerteis, Louis S. *From Contraband to Freedman: Federal Policy toward Southern Blacks, 1861–1865*. Westport, Conn., 1973.

Gillette, William. *Retreat from Reconstruction, 1869–1879*. Baton Rouge, 1979.

——. *The Right to Vote: Politics and the Passage of the Fifteenth Amendment*. Baltimore, 1965.

Hanchett, William. *The Lincoln Murder Conspiracies*. Urbana, Ill., 1983.

Harrington, Fred H. *Fighting Politician: Major General N. P. Banks*. Philadelphia, 1948.

Harris, William C. *The Day of the Carpetbagger: Republican Reconstruction in Mississippi*. Baton Rouge, 1979.

——. *Presidential Reconstruction in Mississippi*. Baton Rouge, 1967.

Henig, Gerald S. *Henry Winter Davis: Antebellum and Civil War Congressman from Maryland*. New York, 1973.

Hesseltine, William B. *Ulysses S. Grant, Politician*. New York, 1935.

Hoogenboom, Ari. *Outlawing the Spoils: A History of the Civil Service Reform Movement, 1865–1883*. Urbana, Ill., 1961.

——. *The Presidency of Rutherford B. Hayes*. Lawrence, Kans., 1988.

Horowitz, Robert. *The Great Impeacher: A Political Biography of James M. Ashley*. New York, 1979.

Howard, Victor B. *Black Liberation in Kentucky: Emancipation and Freedom, 1862–1884*. Lexington, Ky., 1983.

Hyman, Harold M. *A More Perfect Union: The Impact of the Civil War and Reconstruction on the Constitution*. New York, 1973.

Hyman, Harold M., and Wiecek, William M. *Equal Justice Under Law: Constitutional Development, 1835–1875*. New York, 1982.

James, Joseph B. *The Framing of the Fourteenth Amendment*. Urbana, Ill., 1956.

Jellison, Charles A. *Fessenden of Maine*. Syracuse, 1962.

King, Willard L. *Lincoln's Manager: David Davis*. Cambridge, Mass., 1960.

Krug, Mark. *Lyman Trumbull: Conservative Radical*. New York, 1965.

Kutler, Stanley I. *Judicial Power and Reconstruction Politics*. Chicago, 1968.

Litwak, Leon F. *Been in the Storm So Long: The Aftermath of Slavery*. New York, 1979.

Lowe, Richard. *Republicans and Reconstruction in Virginia, 1856–1870*. Charlottesville, Va., 1990.

Maddex, Jack P. *The Virginia Conservatives, 1867–1879*. Chapel Hill, N.C., 1970.

McCrary, Peyton. *Abraham Lincoln and Reconstruction: The Louisiana Experiment*. Princeton, N.J., 1978.

McFeely, William S. *Frederick Douglass*. New York, 1991.

———. *Grant: A Biography*. New York, 1981.

———. *Yankee Stepfather: General O. O. Howard and the Freedmen*. New Haven, 1968.

McKitrick, Eric L. *Andrew Johnson and Reconstruction*. Chicago, 1960.

McPherson, James M. *Ordeal by Fire: The Civil War and Reconstruction*. New York, 1982.

Milton, George F. *The Age of Hate: Andrew Johnson and the Radicals*. New York, 1930.

Montgomery, David. *Beyond Equality: Labor and the Radical Republicans, 1863–1872*. New York, 1967.

Nathans, Elizabeth S. *Losing the Peace: Georgia Republicans and Reconstruction, 1865–1871*. Baton Rouge, 1968.

Nevins, Allan. *Hamilton Fish: The Inner History of the Grant Administration*. New York, 1936.

Nieman, Donald G. *To Set the Law in Motion: The Freedmen's Bureau and the Legal Rights of Blacks, 1865–1868*. Milwood, N.Y., 1969.

Niven, John. *Gideon Welles: Lincoln's Secretary of the Navy*. New York, 1973.

Nunn, W. C. *Texas Under the Carpetbaggers*. Austin, 1962.

Olsen, Otto H. *Carpetbagger's Crusade: The Life of Albion Winegar Tourgée*. Baltimore, 1965.

Parrish, William E. *Missouri Under Radical Rule, 1865–1870*. Columbia, Mo., 1965.

Patrick, Rembert W. *The Reconstruction of the Nation*. New York, 1967.

Perman, Michael. *Reunion Without Compromise: The South and Reconstruction, 1865–1868*. New York, 1973.

———. *The Road to Redemption: Southern Politics, 1869–1879*. Chapel Hill, N.C., 1984.

Polakoff, Keith I. *The Politics of Inertia: The Election of 1876 and the End of Reconstruction*. Baton Rouge, 1973.

Rabinowitz, Howard N., ed. *Black Leaders of the Reconstruction Era*. Urbana, Ill., 1982.

Rable, George C. *But There Was No Peace: The Rule of Violence in the Politics of Reconstruction*. Athens, Ga., 1984.

Randall, J. G., and Donald, David. *The Civil War and Reconstruction*. Lexington, Mass., 1969.

Raper, Horace W. *William W. Holden: North Carolina's Political Enigma*. Chapel Hill, N.C., 1985.

Riddleberger, Patrick W. *1866: The Critical Year Revisited*. Carbondale, Ill., 1979.

———. *George W. Julian: Radical Republican*. Indianapolis, 1966.

Rose, Willie Lee. *Rehearsal for Reconstruction: The Port Royal Experiment*. Indianapolis, 1964.

Roske, Ralph J. *His Own Counsel: The Life and Times of Lyman Trumbull*. Reno, 1979.

Schutz, Wallace, and Trennery, Walter. *Abandoned by Lincoln: A Military Biography of General John Pope*. Urbana, Ill., 1990.

Sefton, James E. *Andrew Johnson and the Uses of Constitutional Power*. Boston, 1980.
———. *The United States Army and Reconstruction, 1865–1877*. Baton Rouge, 1967.
Shoffner, Jerrell H. *Nor Is It Over Yet: Florida in the Era of Reconstruction, 1863–1877*. Gainesville, Fla., 1974.
Silbey, Joel. *A Respectable Minority: The Democratic Party in the Civil War Era*. New York, 1977.
Simkins, Francis B., and Woody, Robert H. *South Carolina During Reconstruction*. Chapel Hill, N.C., 1932.
Stampp, Kenneth M. *The Era of Reconstruction, 1865–1877*. New York, 1965.
Summers, Mark W. *Railroads, Reconstruction, and the Gospel of Progress: Aid Under the Radical Republicans, 1865–1877*. Princeton, N.J., 1984.
Taylor, Joe G. *Louisiana Reconstructed, 1863–1877*. Baton Rouge, 1974.
Thomas, Benjamin P., and Hyman, Harold M. *Stanton: The Life and Times of Lincoln's Secretary of War*. New York, 1962.
Thompson, George H. *Arkansas and Reconstruction*. Port Washington, N.Y., 1976.
Trefousse, Hans L. *Andrew Johnson: A Biography*. New York, 1989.
———. *Ben Butler: The South Called Him Beast*. New York, 1956.
———. *Benjamin Franklin Wade: Radical Republican from Ohio*. New York, 1963.
———. *Impeachment of a President: Andrew Johnson, the Blacks, and Reconstruction*. Knoxville, Tenn., 1975.
———. *The Radical Republicans: Lincoln's Vanguard for Racial Justice*. New York, 1969.
Trelease, Allen W. *White Terror: The Ku Klux Klan Conspiracy and Southern Reconstruction*. New York, 1971.
Unger, Irwin. *The Greenback Era: A Social and Political History of American Finance, 1865–1879*. Princeton, N.J., 1964.
Van Deusen, Glyndon G. *Horace Greeley: Nineteenth Century Crusader*. Philadelphia, 1953.
———. *William H. Seward*. New York, 1967.
Vaughn, William P. *Schools for All: The Blacks and Public Education in the South, 1865–1877*. Lexington, Ky., 1974.
Wagandt, Charles L. *The Mighty Revolution: Negro Emancipation in Maryland, 1862–1864*. Baltimore, 1964.
Wallace, Ernest. *Texas in Turmoil: The Saga of Texas, 1849–1875*. Austin, 1965.
Webb, Ross A. *Kentucky in the Reconstruction Era*. Lexington, Ky., 1979.
Wharton, Vernon L. *The Negro in Mississippi, 1865–1890*. Chapel Hill, N.C., 1947.
Wiggins, Sarah W. *The Scalawag in Alabama Politics, 1865–1881*. University, Ala., 1977.
Williamson, Joel. *After Slavery: The Negro in South Carolina During Reconstruction, 1861–1877*. Chapel Hill, N.C., 1965.
Woodward, C. Vann. *Reunion and Reaction: The Compromise of 1877 and the End of Reconstruction*. Garden City, N.Y., 1956.

# INDEX

Pages in *italics* indicate main entries.

## About the Author

HANS L. TREFOUSSE is Distinguished Professor of History at Brooklyn College and Graduate Center at CUNY. He has written and published widely on Civil War issues for various periodicals. His previously published books include: *Germany and American Neutrality, 1939–1941* (1951); *Ben Butler: The South Called Him Beast* (1956); *Benjamin Franklin Wade* (1964); and *The Radical Republicans* (1969). He is currently writing a biography of Andrew Johnson.

00022 0453

REF E 668 .T66 1991
Trefousse, Hans Louis.
Historical dictionary of
  reconstruction

REF E 668 .T66 1991
Trefousse, Hans Louis.
Historical dictionary of
  reconstruction

025576

Discard

WITHDRAWN

DEMCO